Hal Leonard
GUITAR METHOD
Supplement to
Any Guitar Method

2nd EDITION

INCREDIBLE CHORD FINDER

Easy-to-Use Guide to Over 1100 Guitar Chords

ISBN 0-88188-140-6

HAL•LEONARD®
CORPORATION
7777 W. BLUEMOUND RD. P.O. BOX 13819 MILWAUKEE, WI 53213

Visit Hal Leonard Online at
www.halleonard.com

READING THE CHORD NAMES

Chord symbols used in this book:	Chord names:	Alternate symbols for the same chords:
C	C major	C pure
C6	C sixth	
C7	C seventh	Cdom7
C9	C ninth	
C11	C eleventh	
C11+	C eleventh sharp	C9(♯11)
C13	C thirteenth	
Cmaj7	C major seventh	CM7, C△7
Cmaj9	C major ninth	CM9, C△9
Cmaj11	C major eleventh	CM11, C△11
C7-5	C seventh, flat fifth	C7(♭5)
C7-9	C seventh, flat ninth	C7(♭9)
C7-10	C seventh, flat tenth	C7(♯9)
C7+5	C augmented seventh	C7(♯5)
C9+5	C augmented ninth	C9(♯5)
$C7^{-9}_{+5}$	C augmented seventh, flat ninth	$C7^{(\flat 9)}_{(\sharp 5)}$
C6•9	C sixth, ninth	C^{6}_{9}, C6/9
C dim.	C diminished	C°
C+5	C augmented	C aug., C(♯5), C+
Csus4	C suspended fourth	C sus.
C7sus4	C seventh, suspended fourth	C7 sus.
Cm	C minor	C-, Cmin
Cm6	C minor sixth	C-6
Cm7	C minor seventh	C-7, Cmin7
Cm9	C minor ninth	C-9
Cm7-5	C minor seventh, flat fifth	Cm7(♭5)
Cm7-9	C minor seventh, flat ninth	Cm7(♭9)
Cm+7	C minor, major seventh	Cm(maj. 7)
Cm9+7	C minor ninth, major seventh	Cm9(maj. 7)
Cm+5	C minor, sharp fifth	Cm(♯5)
Cm6•9	C minor sixth, ninth	Cm^{6}_{9}, Cm6/9

GUITAR CHORD DIAGRAMS

The *Incredible Chord Finder* gives you instant access to over 1100 chord voicings. The top diagram for each chord is the most common voicing, followed by two alternates.

STRINGS

The vertical lines in each diagram represent the six strings of the guitar, with the first string (high E) on the right.

FRETS

The frets are indicated by horizontal lines. If a chord voicing is to be played in an upper position, the fret number will appear in the upper left-hand corner of the diagram. For example, the diagram to the right shows the number 4 in the upper left-hand corner, indicating that the top fret in the diagram corresponds with the 4th fret on the fingerboard.

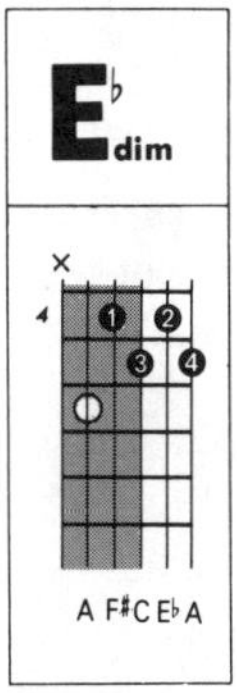

LEFT-HAND FINGERS

The fingers of your left hand are numbered from 1 through 4, starting with your index finger. The numbered black circles graphically show the correct fingering for that chord.

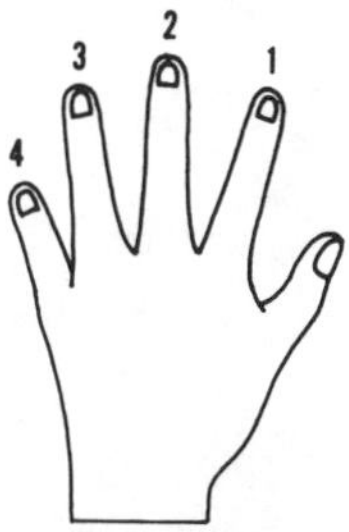

UNPLAYED STRINGS

Strings that are not played are marked with an "X" at the top of the diagram.

OPEN STRINGS

Strings with neither a black circle nor an "X" are played open. (For example: the 1st and 3rd strings of the C chord are played open).

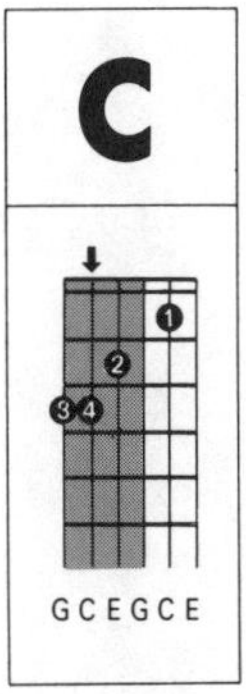

BARRING

The figure indicates that several strings are "barred," or held down simultaneously with the finger shown. The C7 diagram on the right shows the first finger barring all six strings behind the third fret.

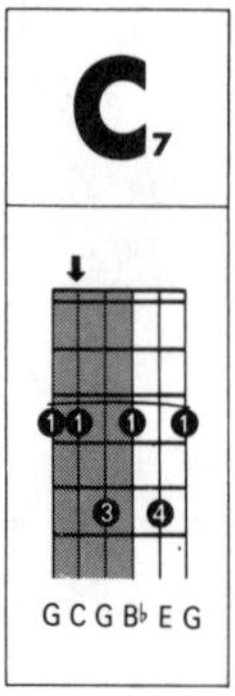

NOTE NAMES

The letter at the bottom of each string names the individual notes of that particular chord.

FINDING THE ROOT

The black circle on the string indicated by an arrow shows the root of the chord. In diagrams where there is no arrow, the root is shown by a white circle.

BASS CHORD DIAGRAMS

The *Incredible Chord Finder* can also be used by bass players. When using a diagram to find an electric bass note, refer to the four bottom strings in the shaded part of the diagram. These lower strings are the same on guitar and electric bass.

Generally the bass player does not play full chords but must know where the different members of the chord (for example, root, 3rd, or 5th) occur. Any of the notes shown with 6-string fingerings can be played as a bass note at your discretion.

The fingering numbers in the black circles apply basically to the 6-string guitar and can be changed for ease of playing the electric bass.

CONTENTS

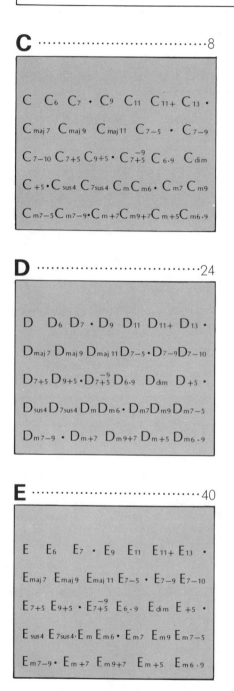

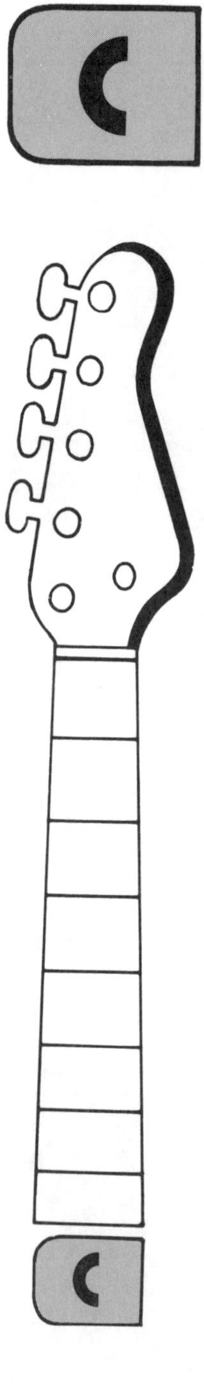
C
C

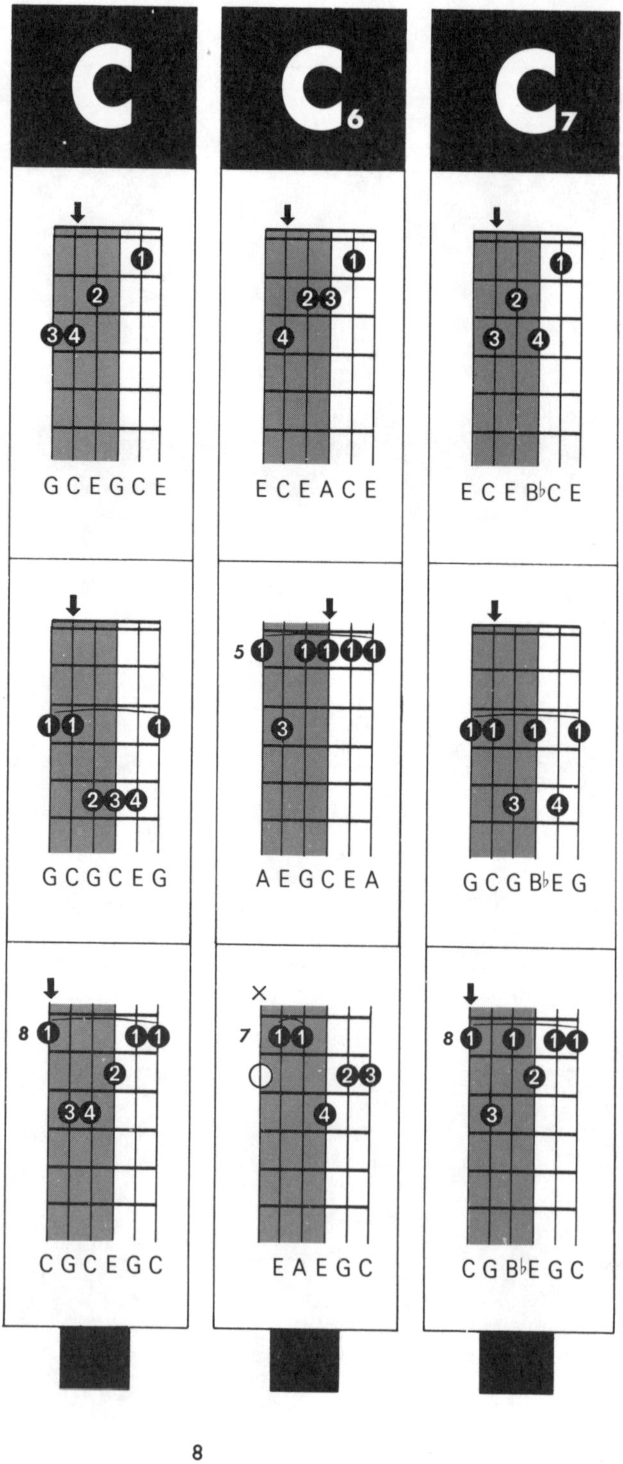
C
C6
C7
G C E G C E
E C E A C E
E C E B♭C E
G C G C E G
5
A E G C E A
G C G B♭E G
8
C G C E G C
7
E A E G C
8
C G B♭E G C

C

C_{9}

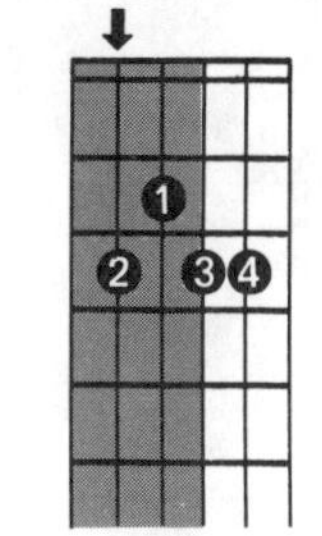

E C E B♭D E

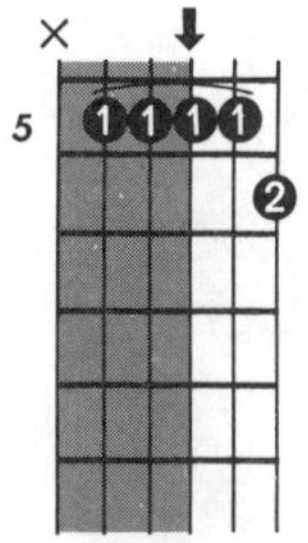

D G C E B♭

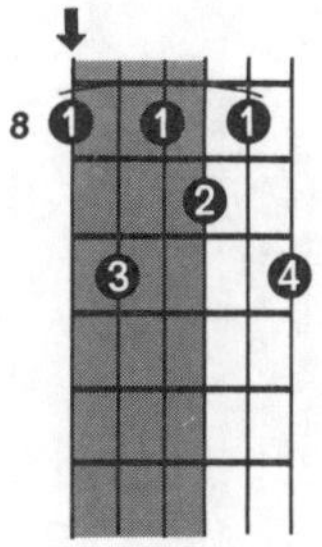

C G B♭E G D

C_{11}

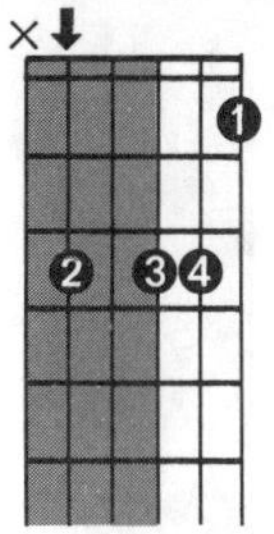

C D B♭D F

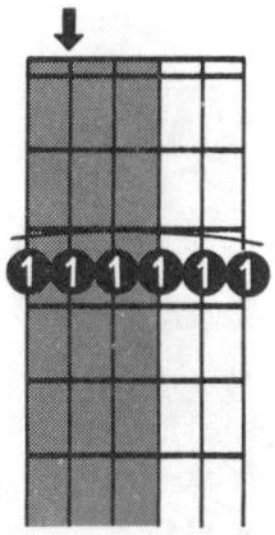

G C F B♭D G

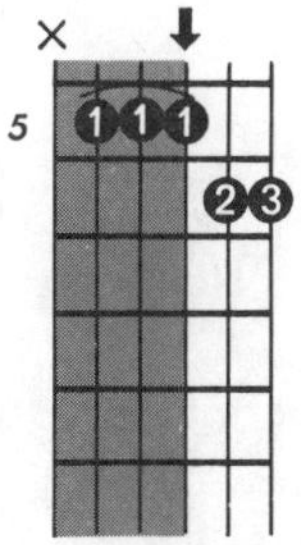

D G C F B♭

C_{11+}

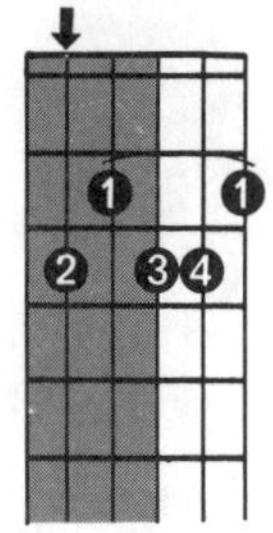

E C E B♭D F♯

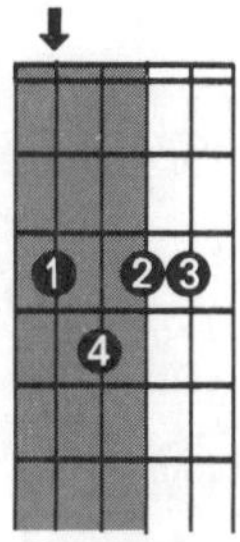

E C F♯B♭D E

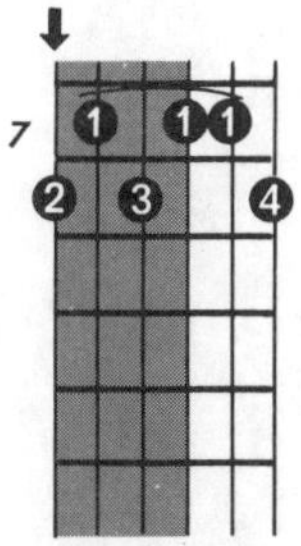

C E B♭D F♯C

C_{13}

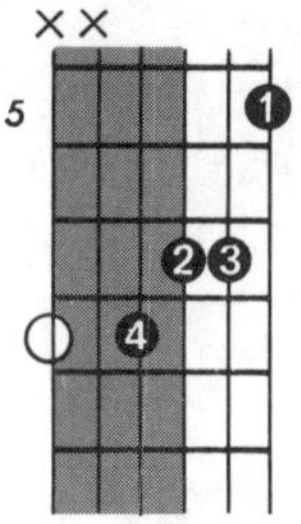

B♭D F♯A

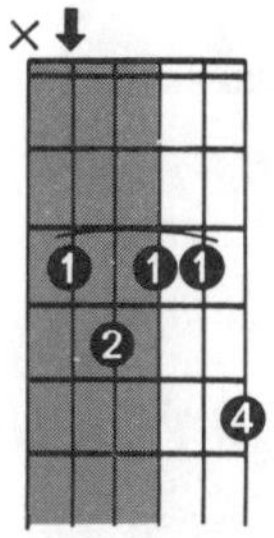

C F♯B♭D A

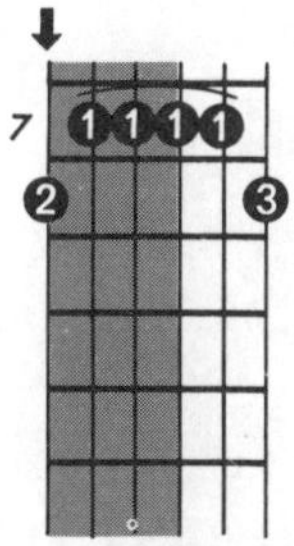

C E A D F♯C

C

Cmaj7

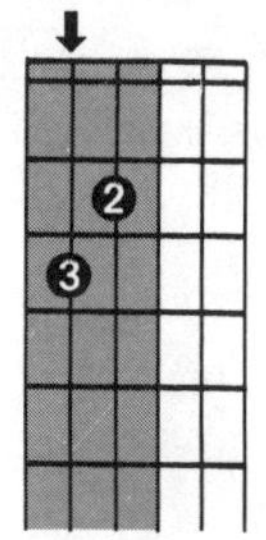

E C E G B E

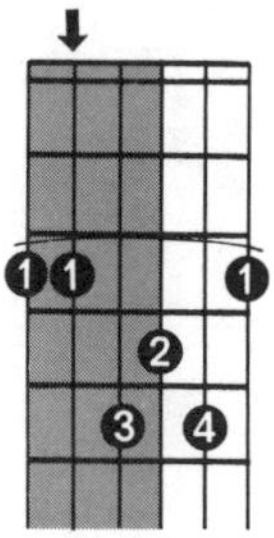

G C G B E G

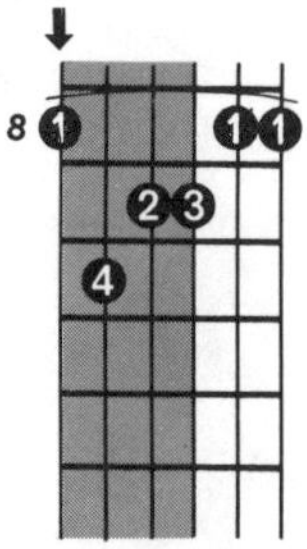

C G B E G C

Cmaj9

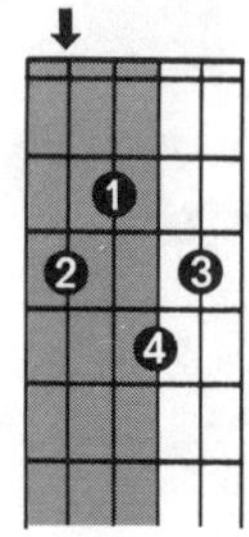

E C E B D E

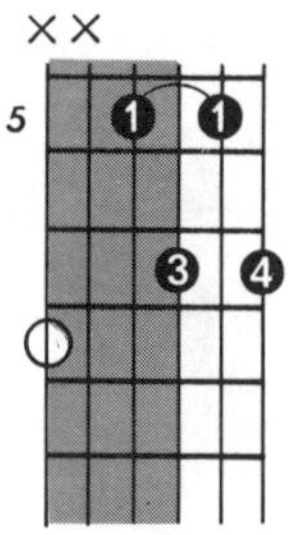

G D E B

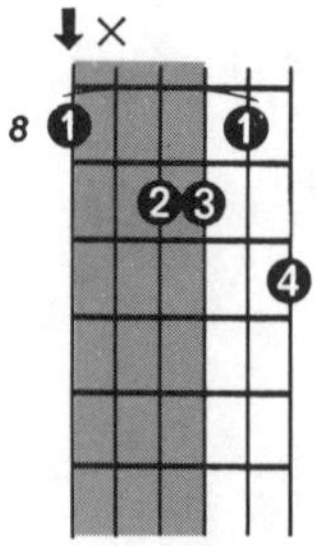

C B E G D

Cmaj11

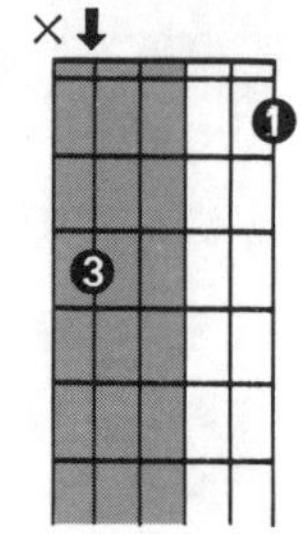

C D G B F

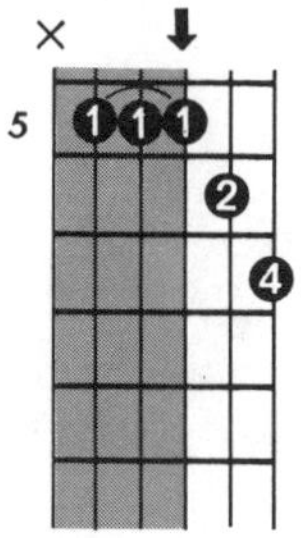

D G C F B

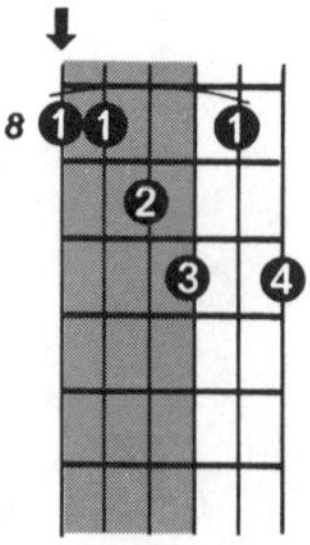

C F B F G D

C7−5

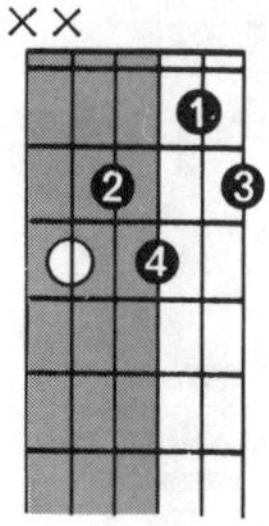

E B♭ C G♭

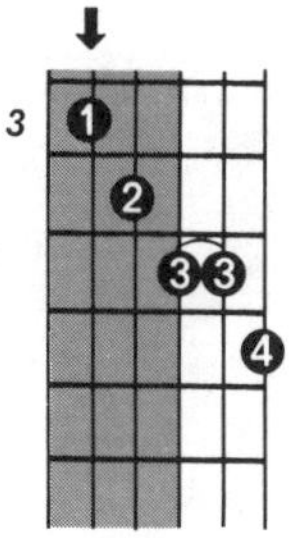

E C G♭ C E B♭

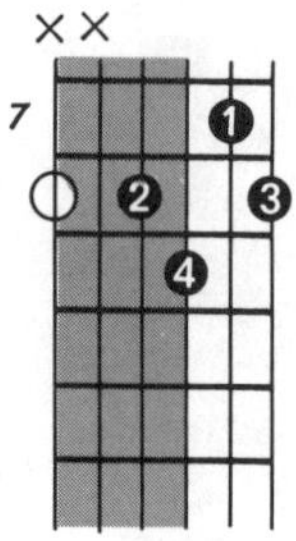

B♭ E G♭ C

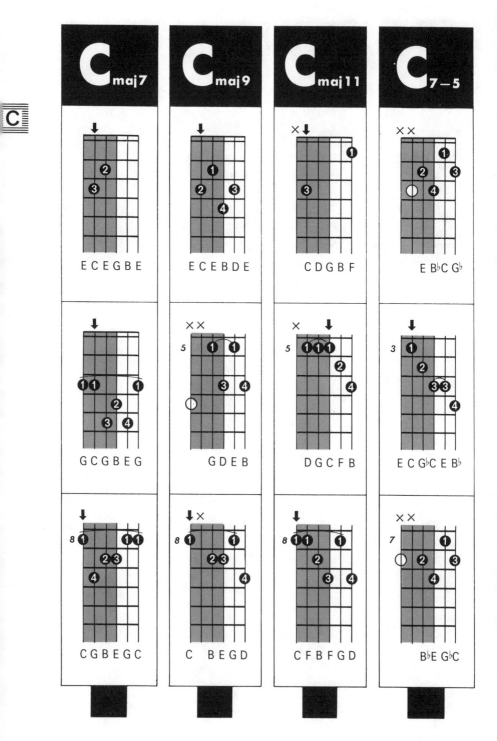

C_{7-9}

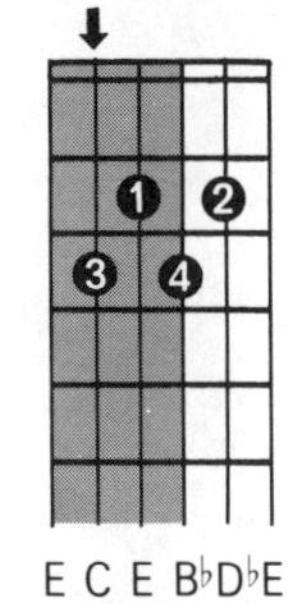

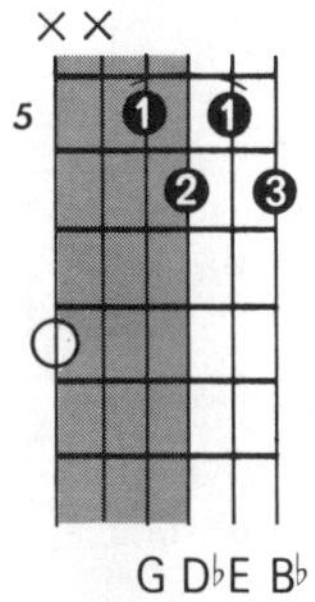

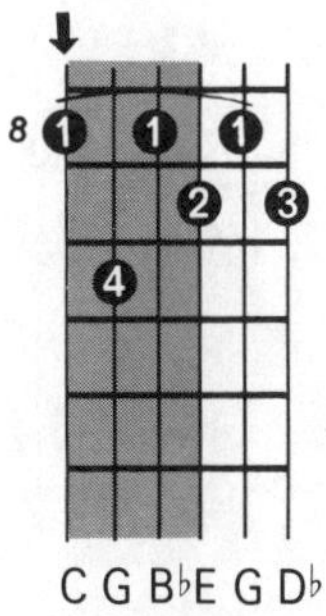

C_{7-10}

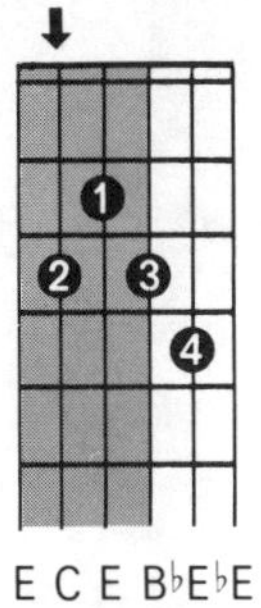

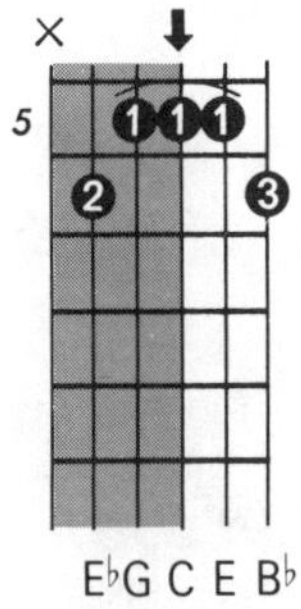

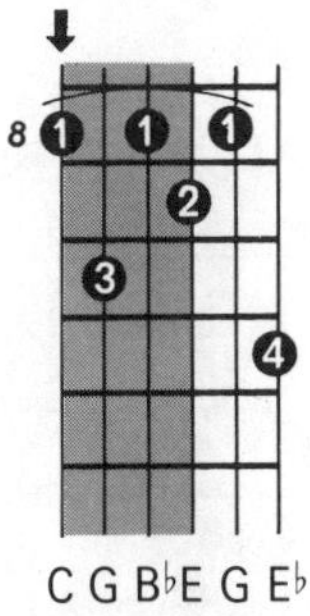

C_{7+5}

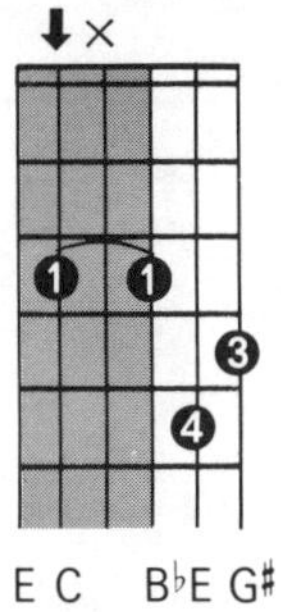

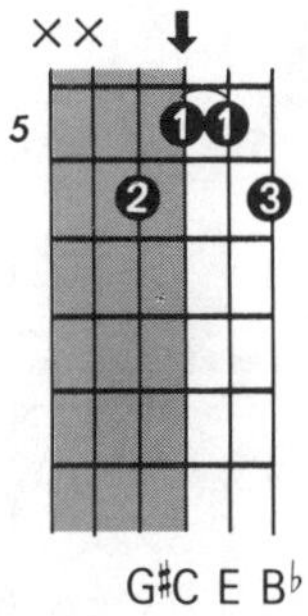

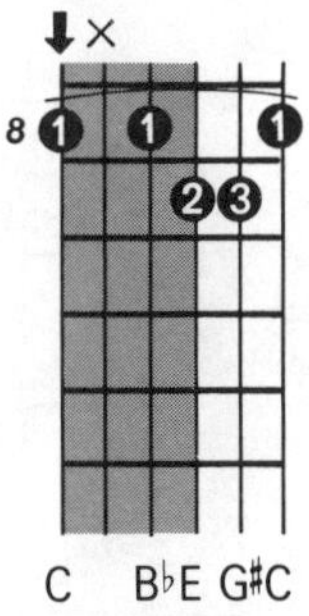

C_{9+5}

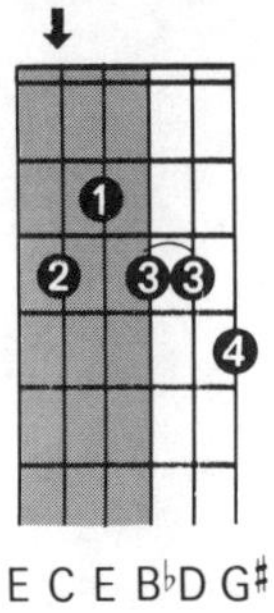

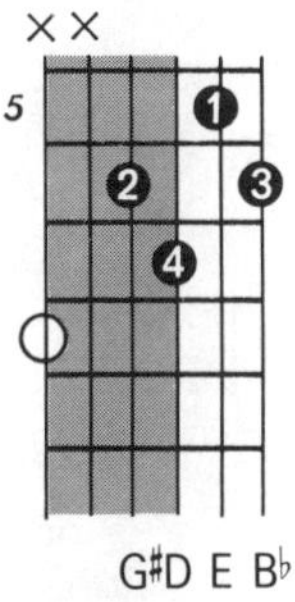

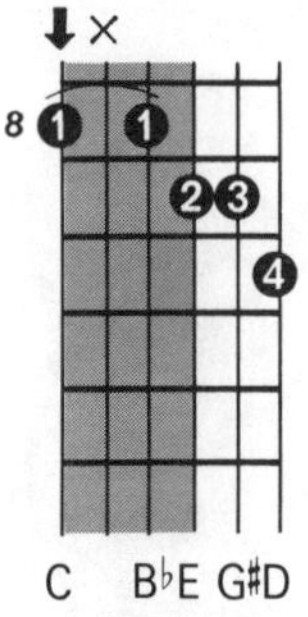

C

C_{7+5}^{-9}

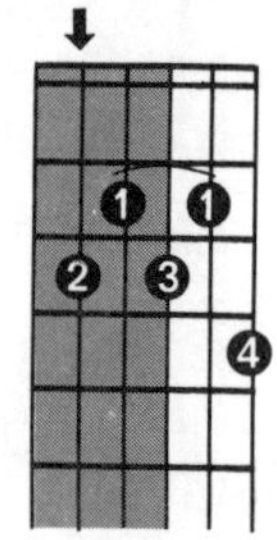

E C E B♭D♭G♯

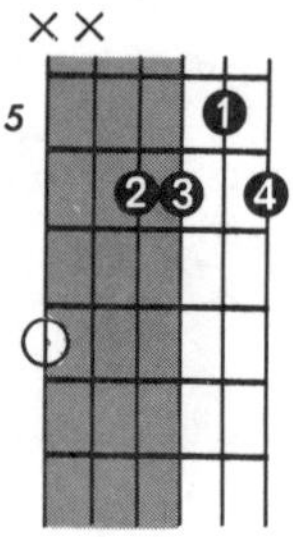

G♯D♭E B♭

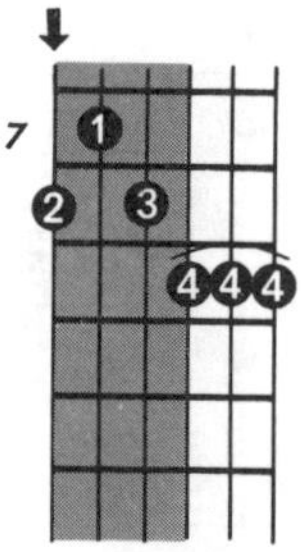

C E B♭E G♯D♭

$C_{6\cdot9}$

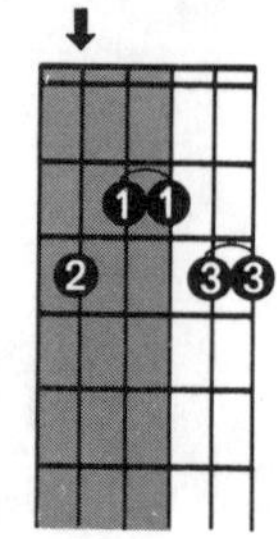

E C E A D G

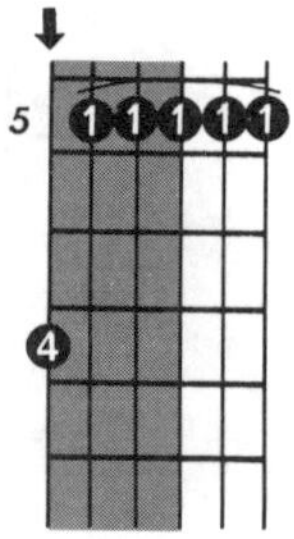

C D G C E A

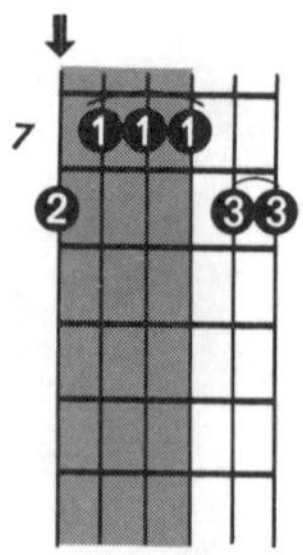

C E A D G C

C_{dim}

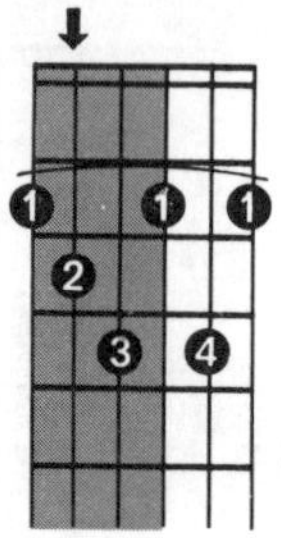

F♯C F♯A E♭F♯

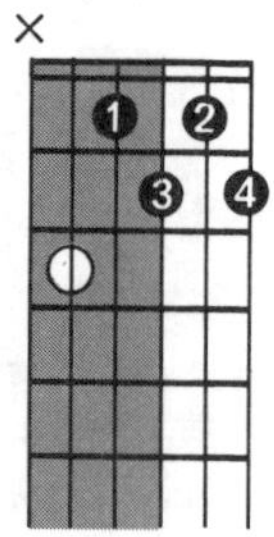

A E♭A C F♯

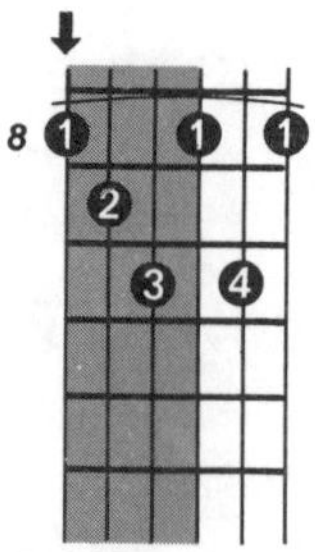

C F♯C E♭A C

C_{+5}

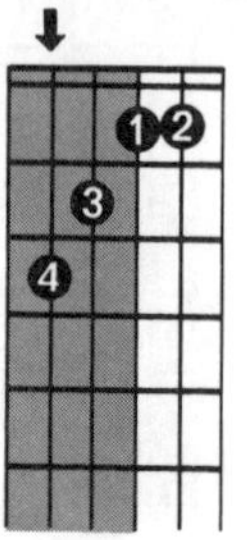

E C E G♯C E

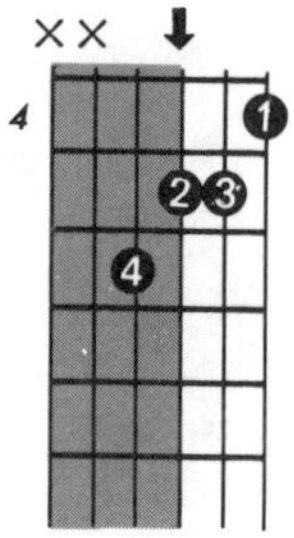

G♯C E G♯

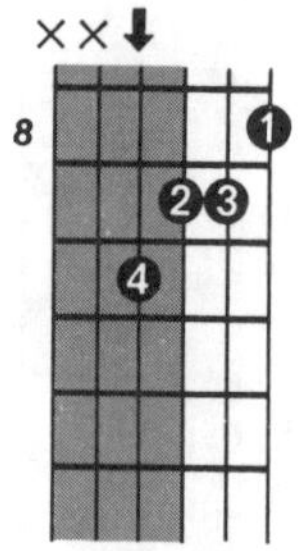

C E G♯C

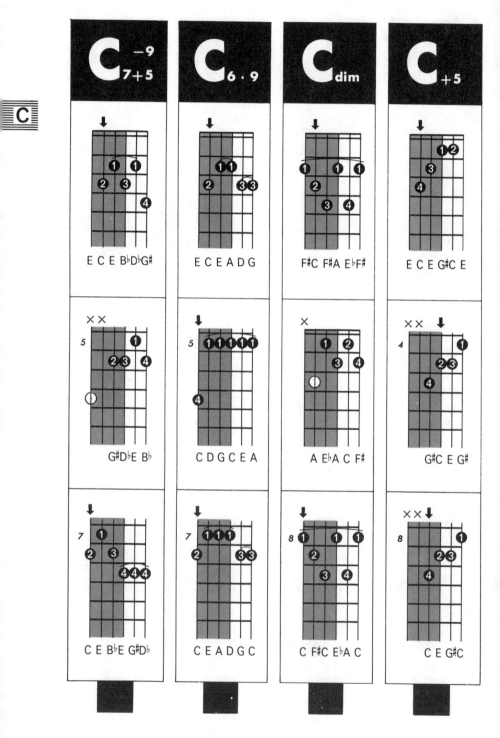

Csus4

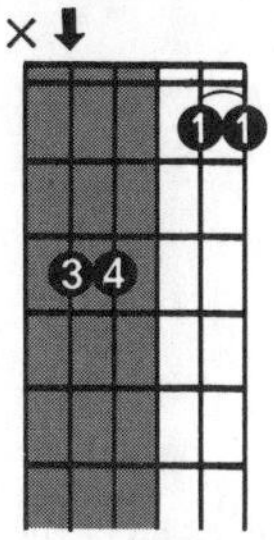

C F G C F

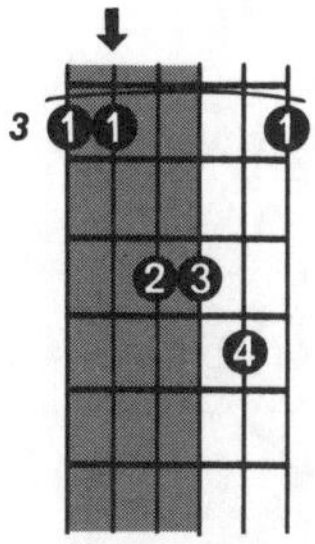

G C G C F G

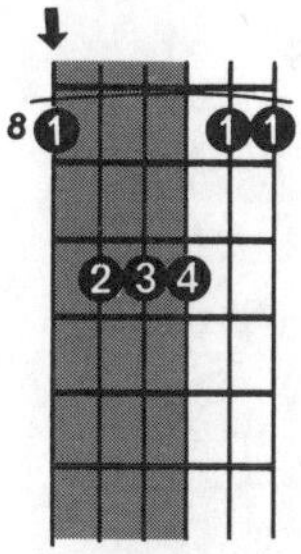

C G C F G C

C7sus4

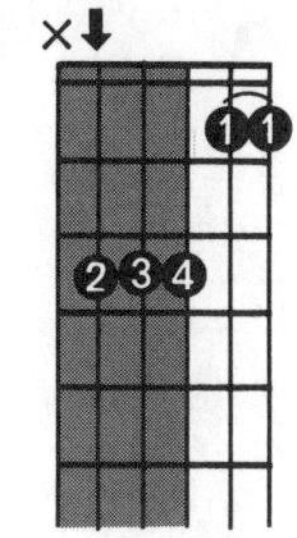

C F B♭C F

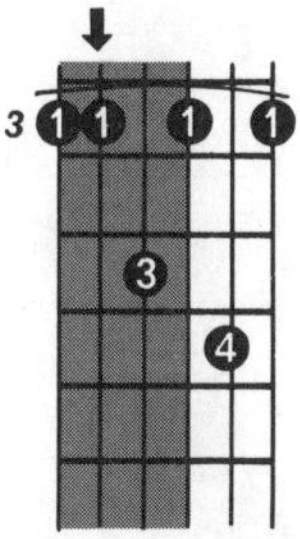

G C G B♭F G

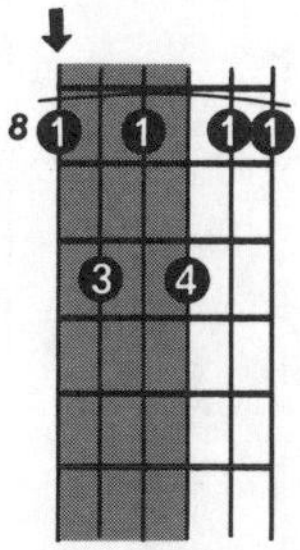

C G B♭F G C

Cm

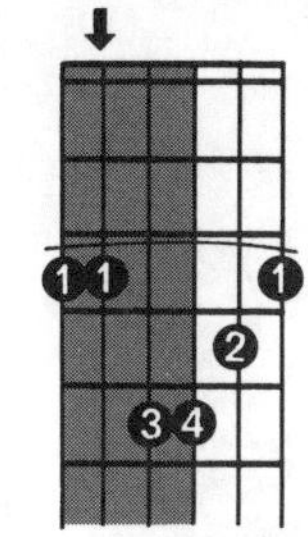

G C G C E♭G

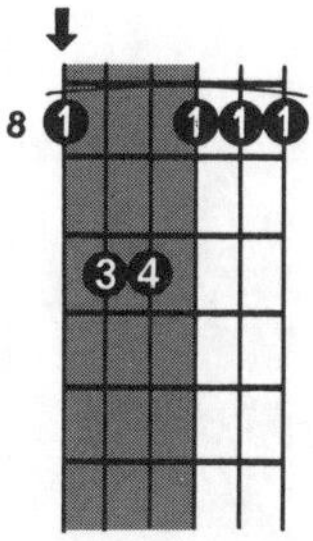

C G C E♭G C

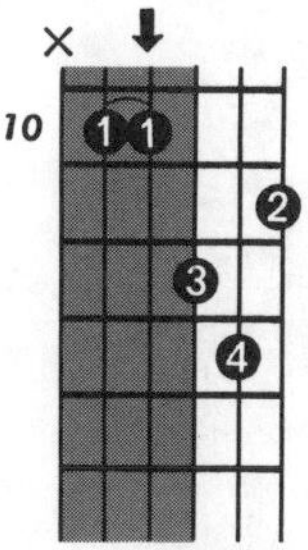

G C G C E♭

Cm6

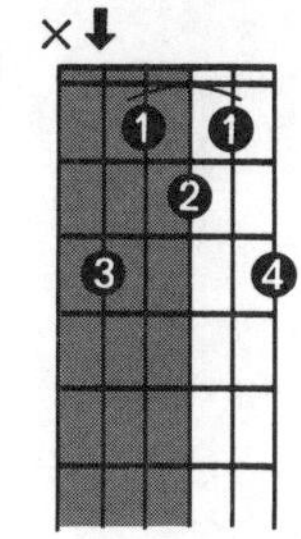

C E♭A C G

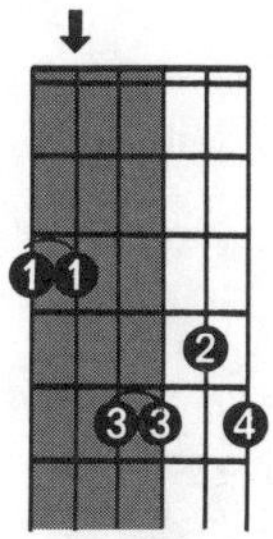

G C G C E♭A

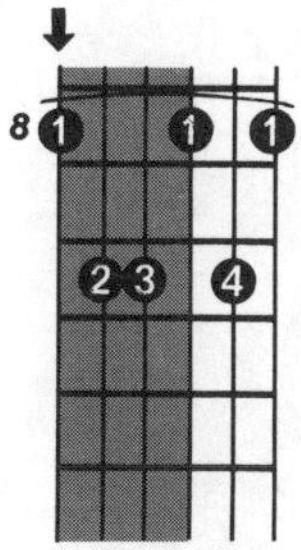

C G C E♭A C

Cm7

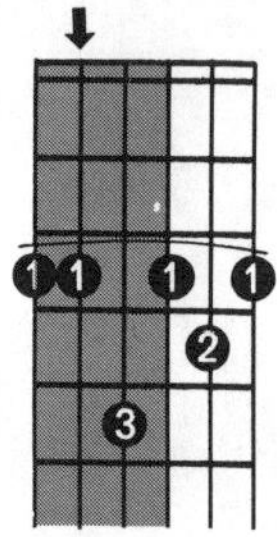

G C G B♭E♭G

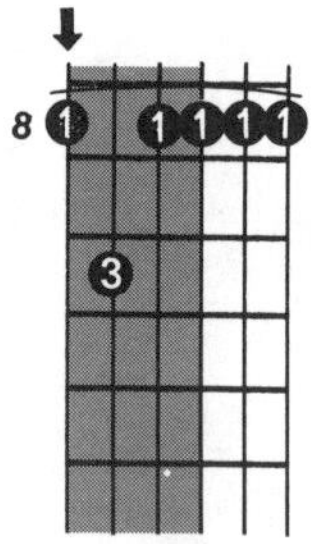

C G B♭E♭G C

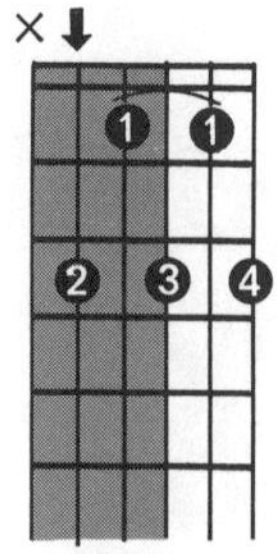

C E♭B♭C G

Cm9

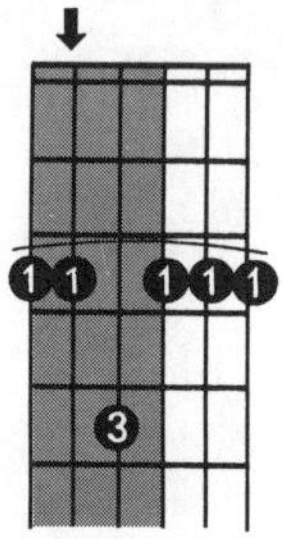

G C G B♭D G

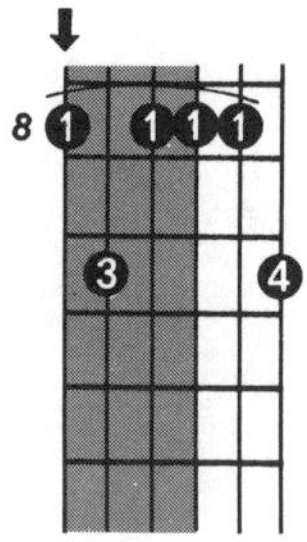

C G B♭E♭G D

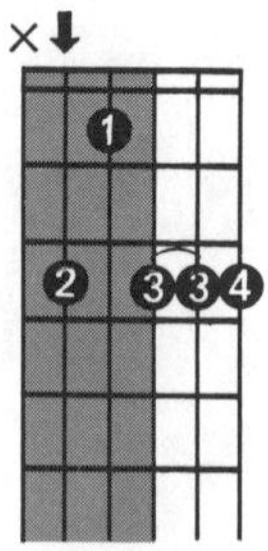

C E♭B♭D G

Cm7–5

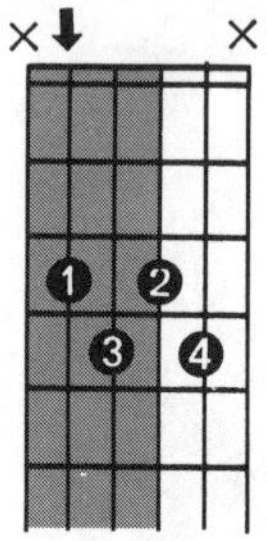

C G♭B♭E♭

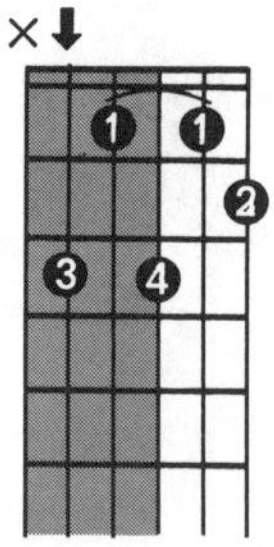

C E♭B♭C G♭

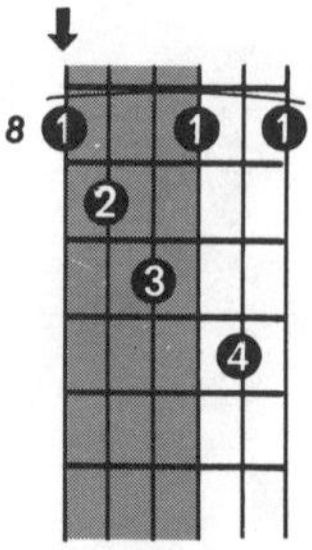

C G♭C E♭B♭C

Cm7–9

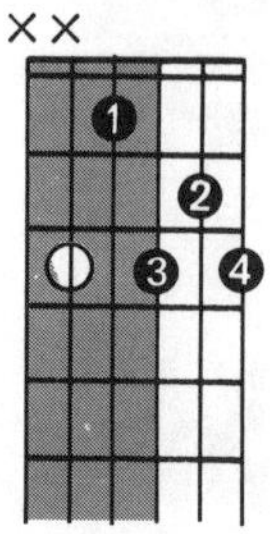

E♭B♭D♭G

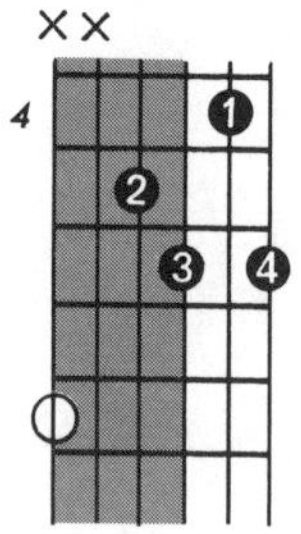

G D♭E♭B♭

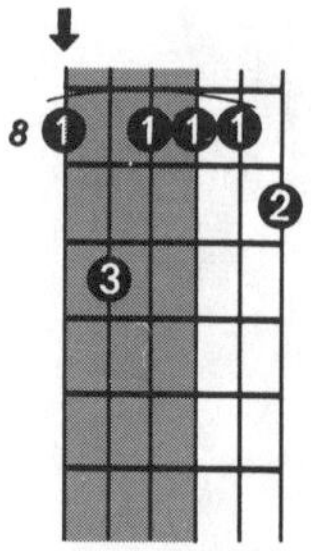

C G B♭E♭G D♭

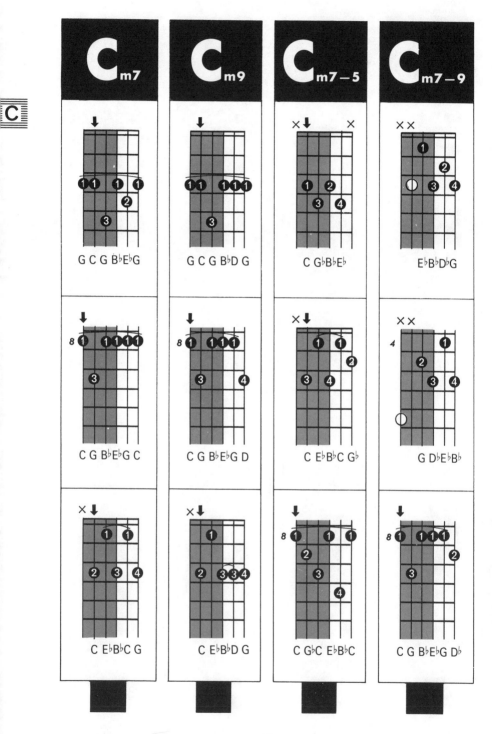

Cm+7

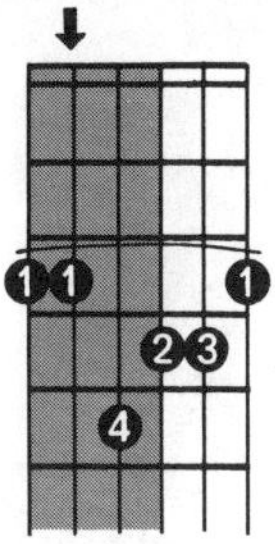

G C G B E♭G

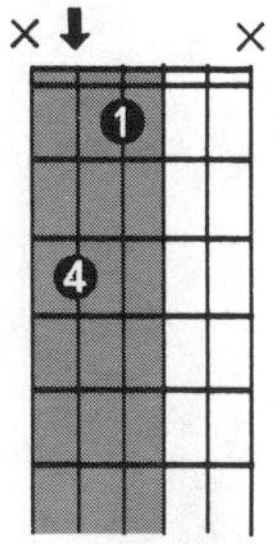

C E♭G B

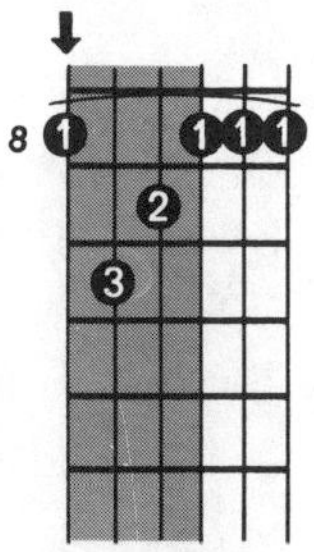

C G B E♭G C

Cm9+7

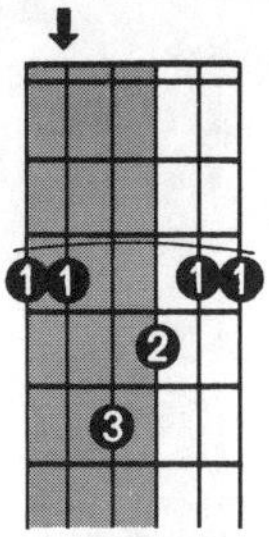

G C G B D G

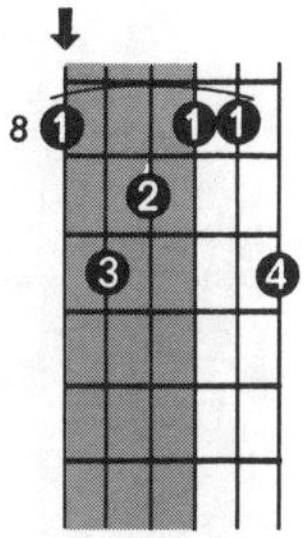

C G B E♭G D

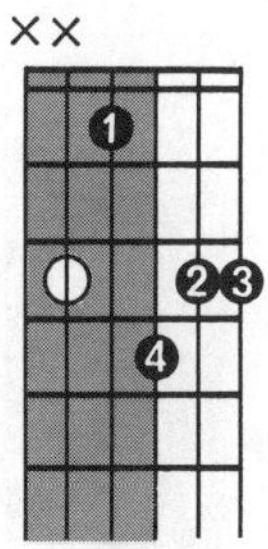

E♭B D G

Cm+5

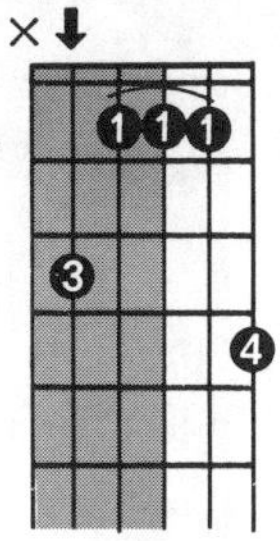

C E♭G♯C G♯

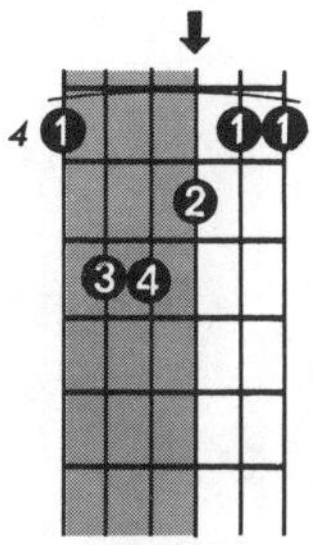

G♯E♭G♯C E♭G♯

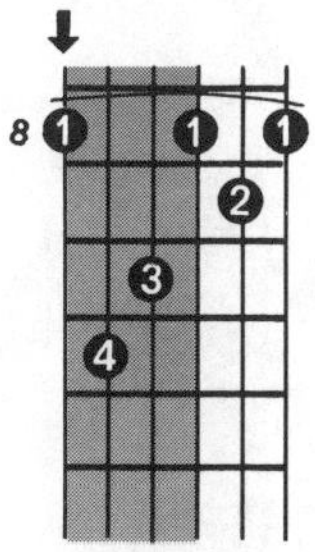

C G♯C E♭G♯C

Cm6 · 9

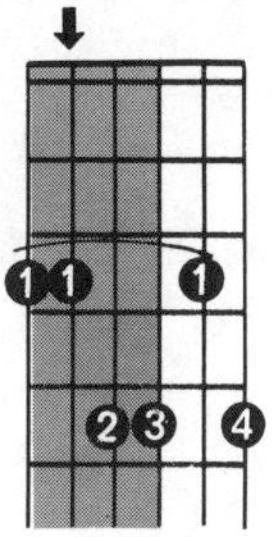

G C G C D A

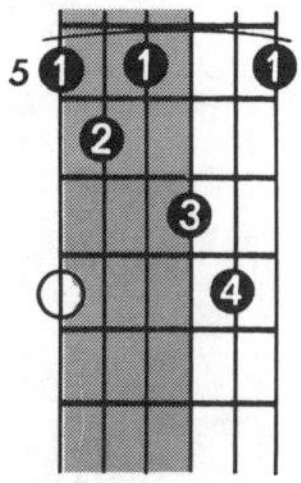

A E♭G D G A

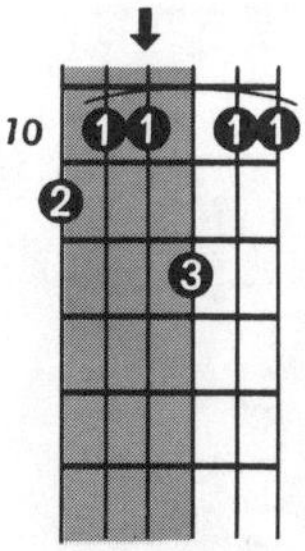

E♭G C G A D

C

D♭

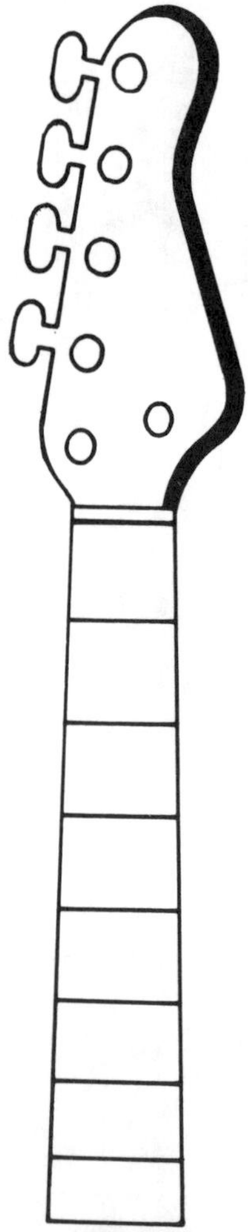

C♯

D♭

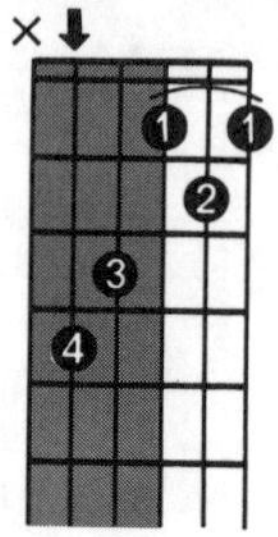

D♭F A♭D♭F

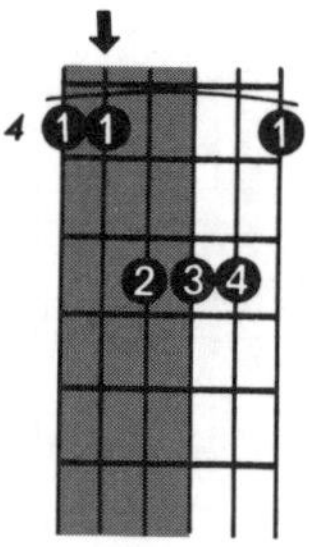

A♭D♭A♭D♭F A♭

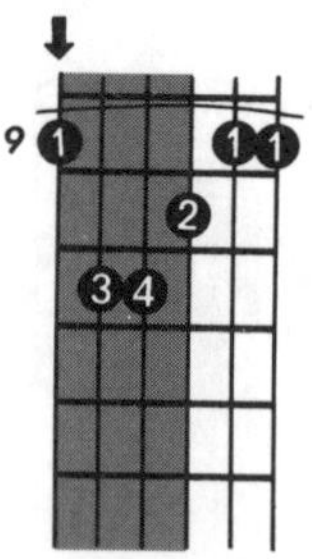

D♭A♭D♭F A♭D♭

C♯

D♭6

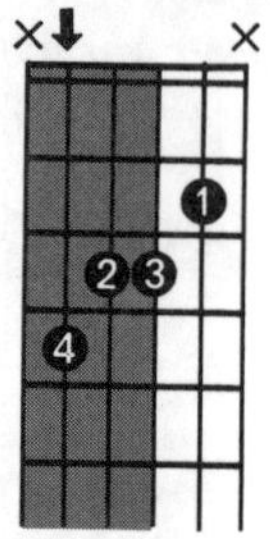

D♭F B♭D♭

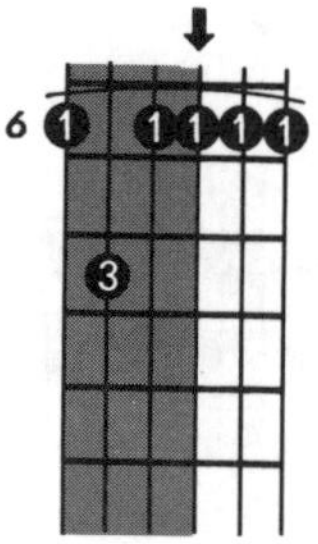

B♭F A♭D♭F B♭

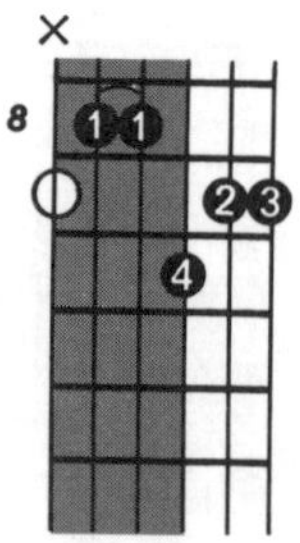

F B♭F A♭D♭

C♯6

D♭7

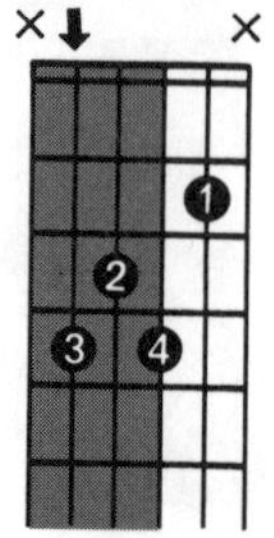

D♭F B D♭

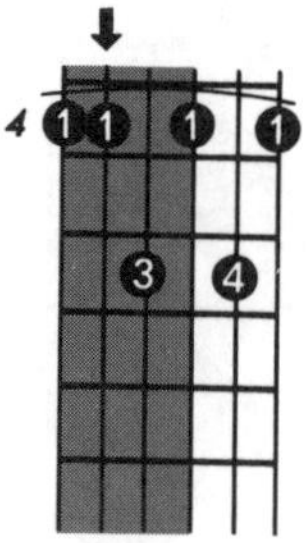

A♭D♭A♭B F A♭

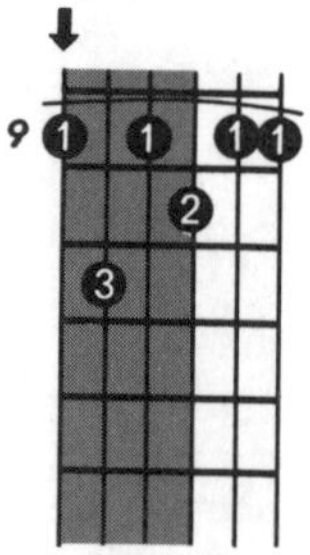

D♭A♭B F A♭D♭

C♯7

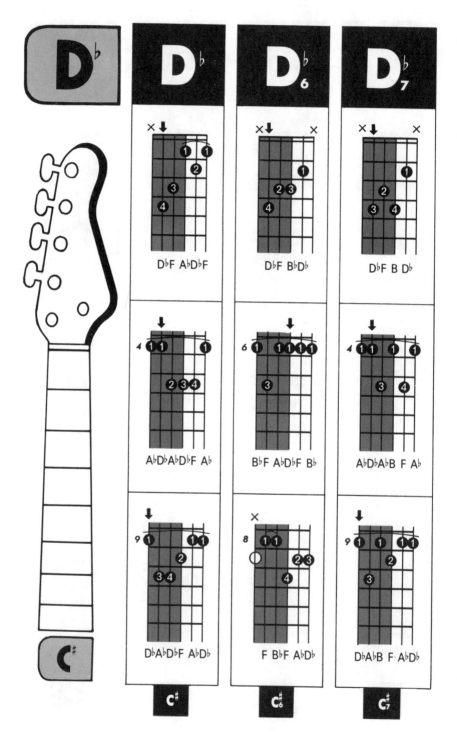

D♭9

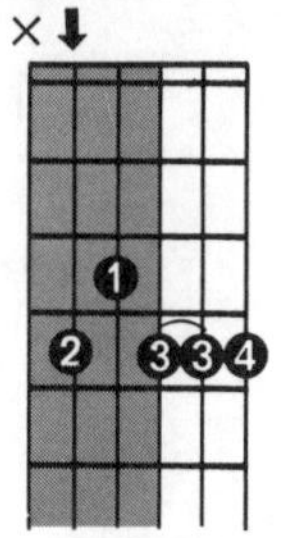

D♭F B E♭A♭

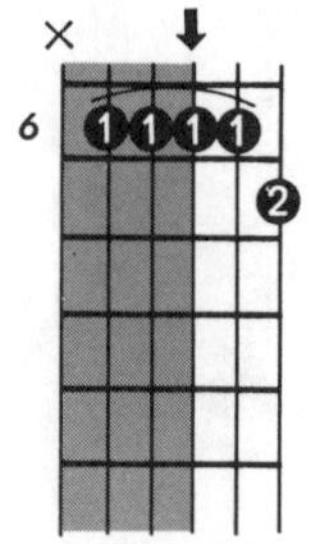

E♭A♭D♭F B

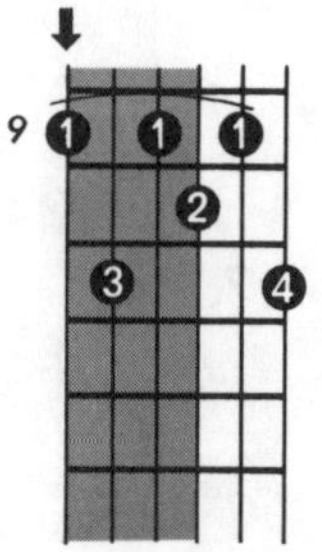

D♭A♭B F A♭E♭

C♯9

D♭11

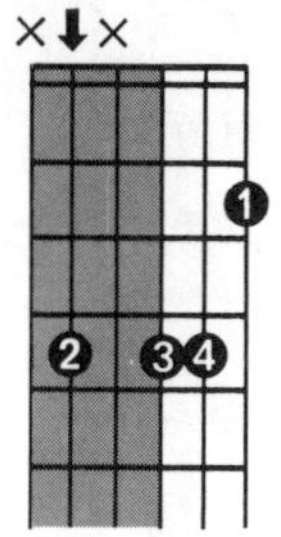

D♭ B E♭G♭

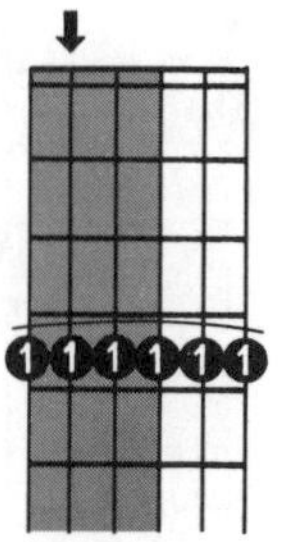

A♭D♭G♭B E♭A♭

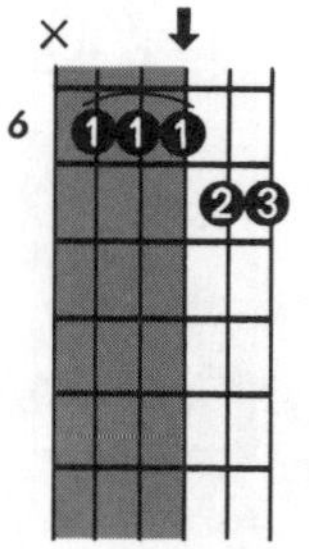

E♭A♭D♭G♭B

C♯11

D♭11+

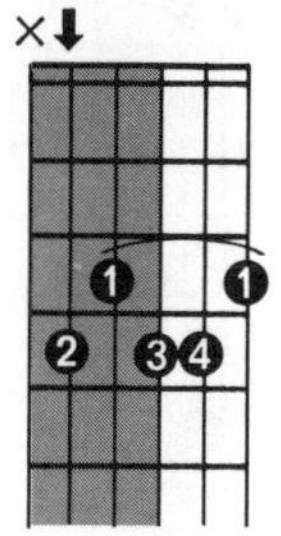

D♭F B E♭G

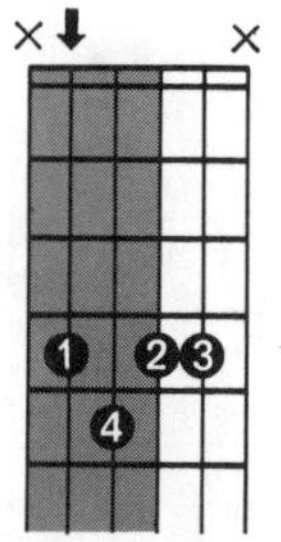

D♭G B E♭

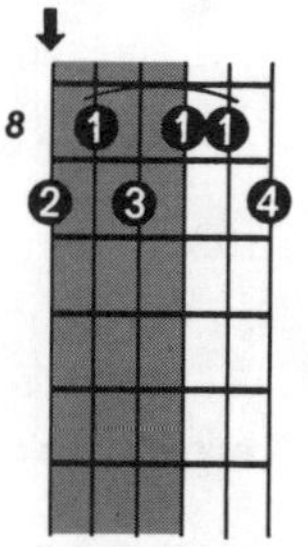

D♭F B E♭G D♭

C♯11+

D♭13

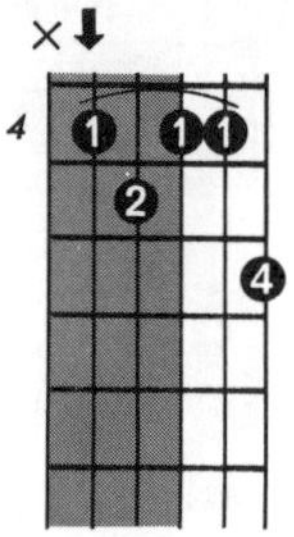

D♭G B E♭B♭

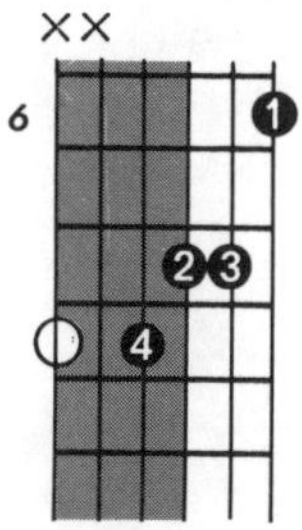

B E♭G B♭

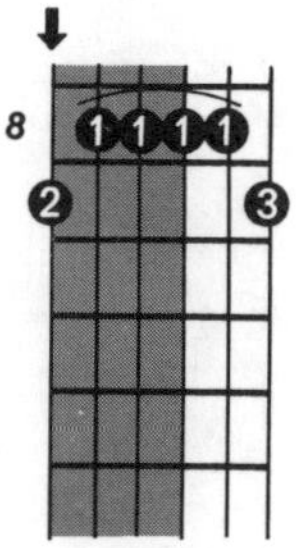

D♭F B♭E♭G D♭

C♯13

D♭

C♯

D♭maj7

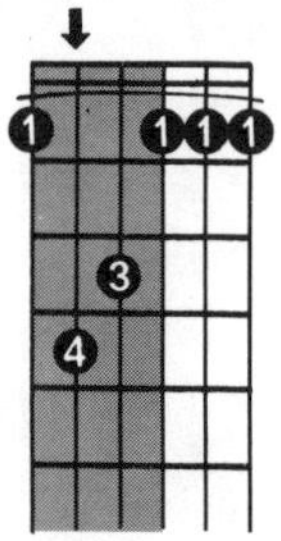

F D♭F A♭C F

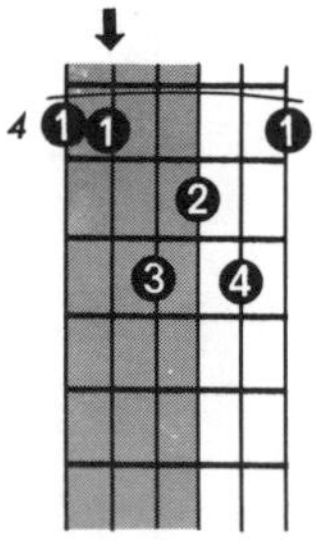

A♭D♭A♭C F A♭

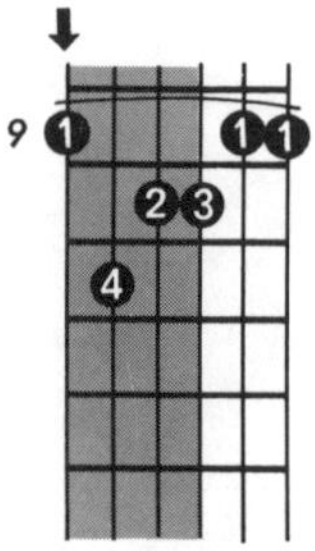

D♭A♭C F A♭D♭

C♯maj7

D♭maj9

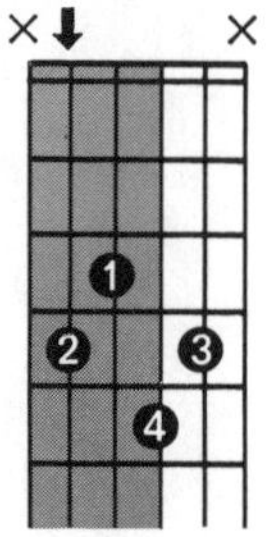

D♭F C E♭

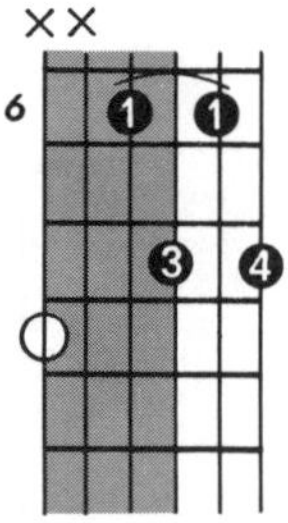

A♭E♭F C

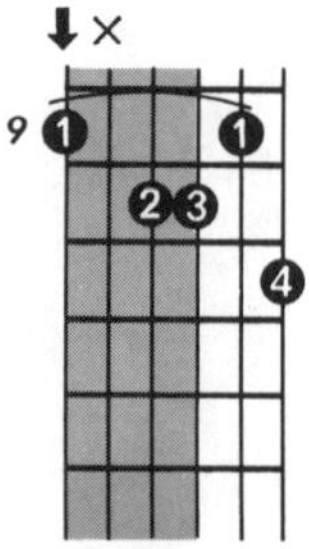

D♭ C F A♭E♭

C♯maj9

D♭maj11

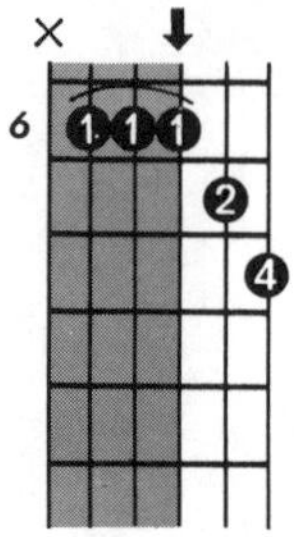

E♭A♭D♭G♭C

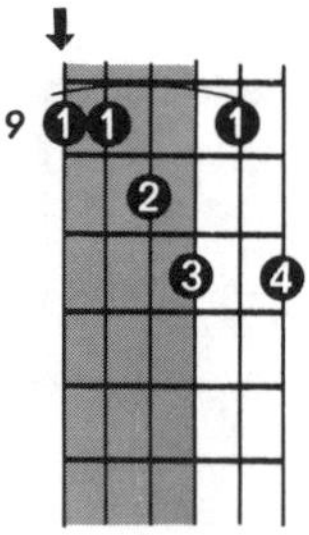

D♭G♭C G♭A♭E♭

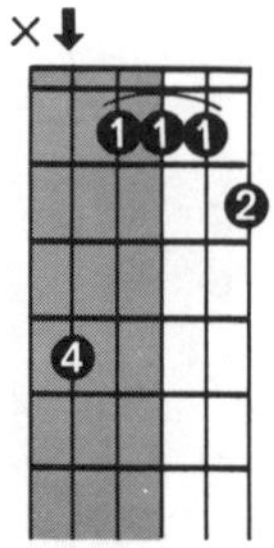

D♭E♭A♭C G♭

C♯maj11

D♭7−5

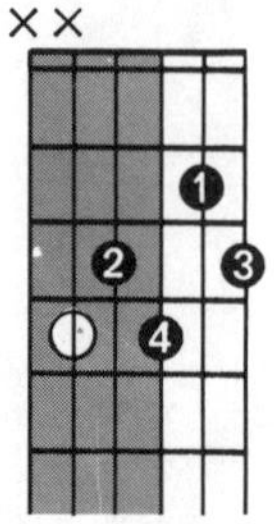

F B D♭G

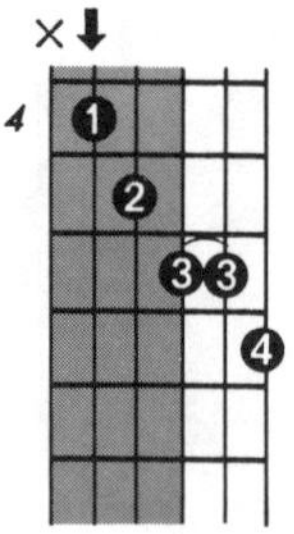

D♭G D♭F B

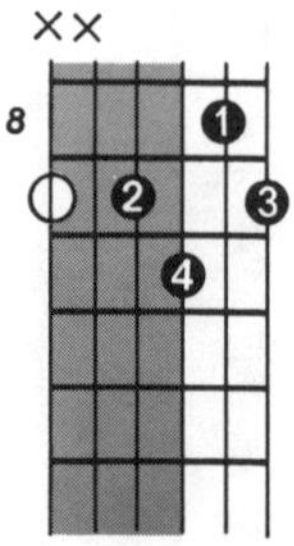

B F G D♭

C♯7−5

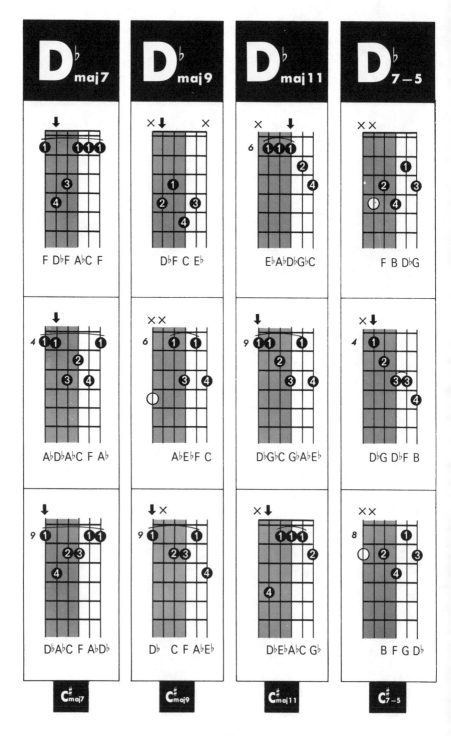

D♭7−9

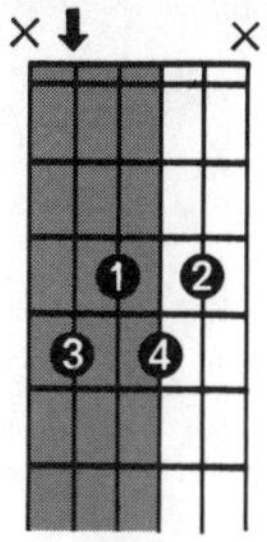

D♭F B D

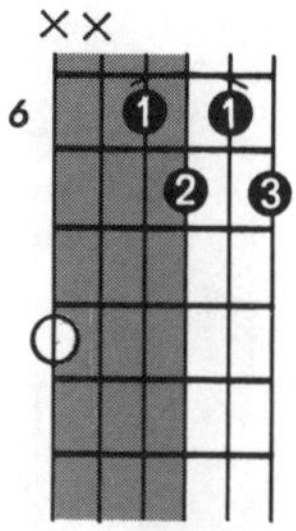

A♭D F B

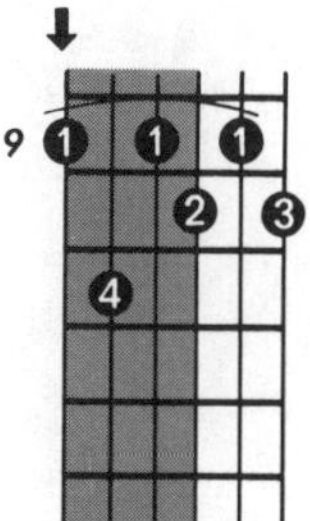

D♭A♭B F A♭D

C♯7−9

D♭7−10

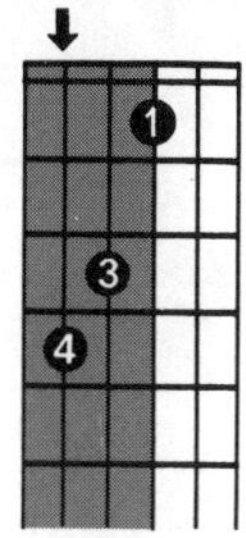

E D♭F A♭B E

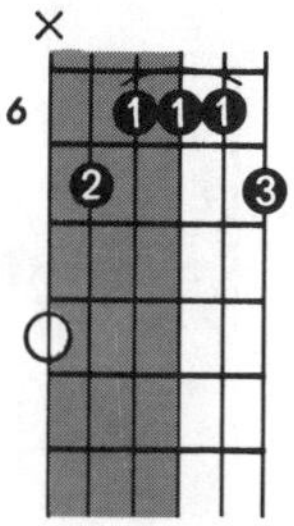

E A♭D♭F B

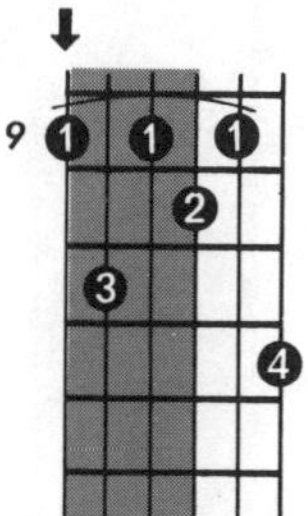

D♭A♭B F A♭E

C♯7−10

D♭7+5

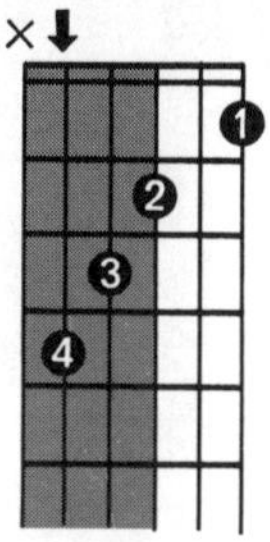

D♭F A B F

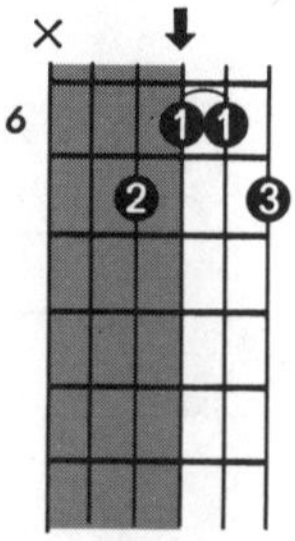

A A D♭F B

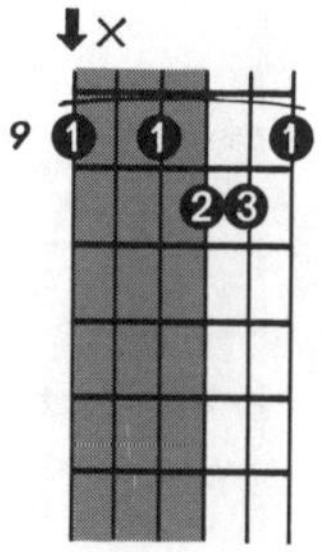

D♭ B F A D♭

C♯7+5

D♭9+5

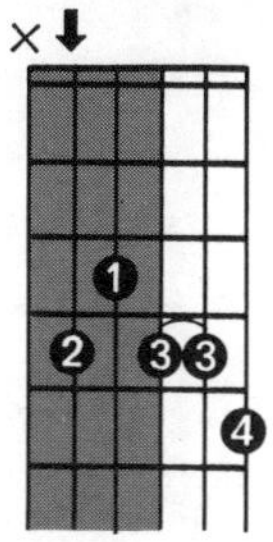

D♭F B E♭A

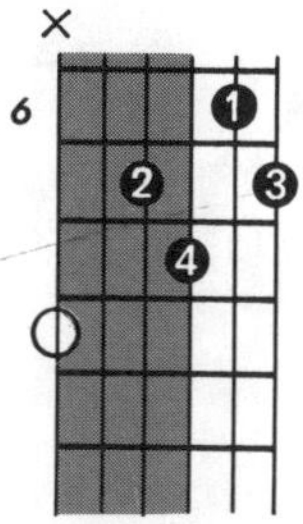

A A E♭F B

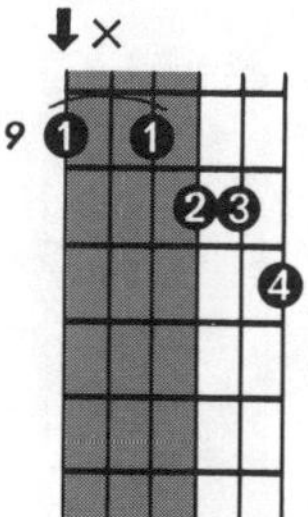

D♭ B F A E♭

C♯9+5

C♯

$D\flat^{-9}_{7+5}$

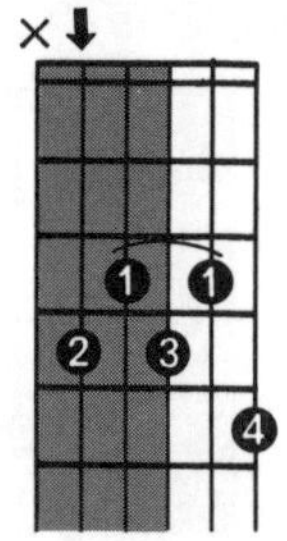

D♭F B D A

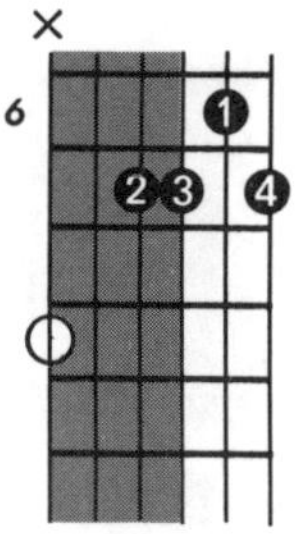

A A D F B

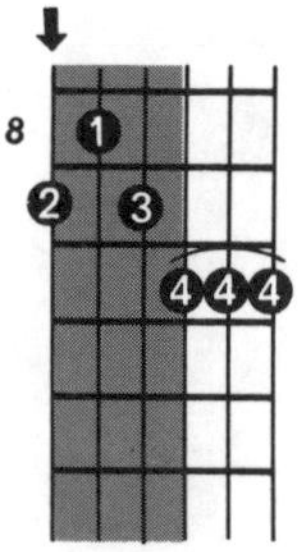

D♭F B F A D

$C\sharp^{-9}_{7+5}$

$D\flat_{6 \cdot 9}$

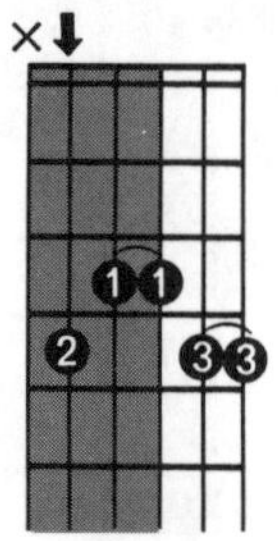

D♭F B♭E♭A♭

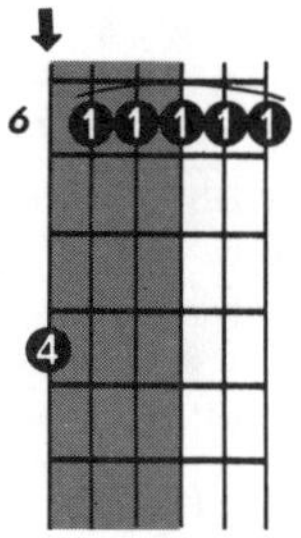

D♭E♭A♭D♭F B♭

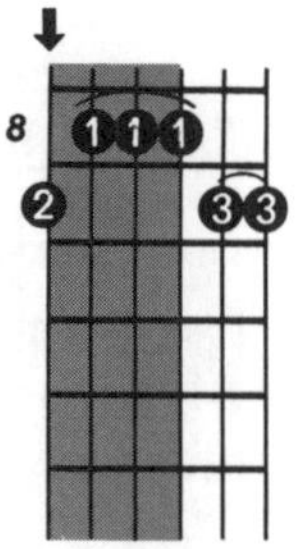

D♭F B♭E♭A♭D♭

$C\sharp_{6 \cdot 9}$

$D\flat_{dim}$

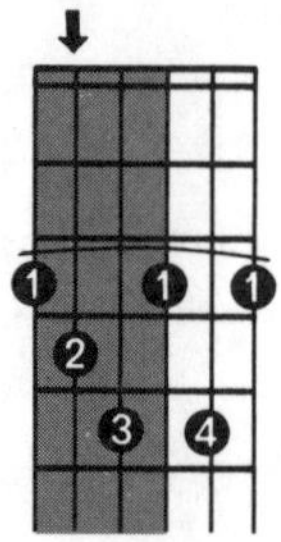

G D♭G B♭E G

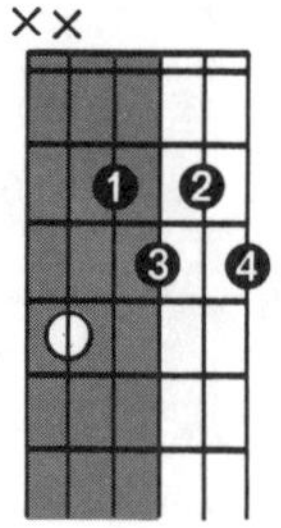

E B♭D♭G

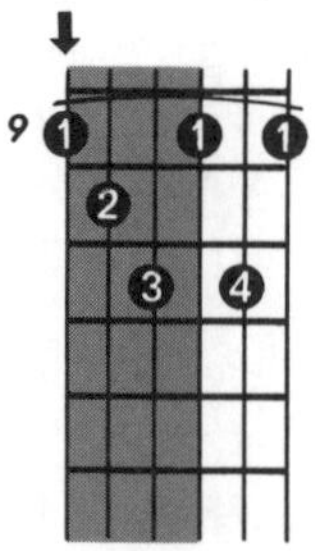

D♭G D♭E B♭D♭

$C\sharp_{dim}$

$D\flat_{+5}$

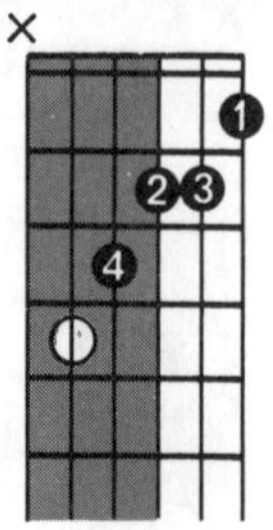

A F A D♭F

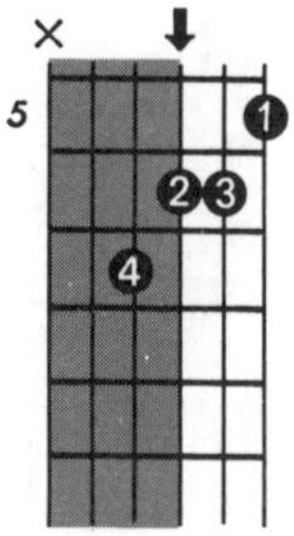

A A D♭F A

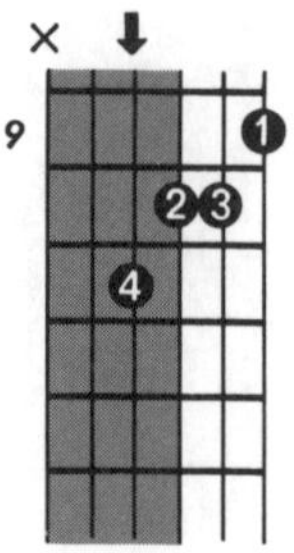

A D♭F A D♭

$C\sharp_{+5}$

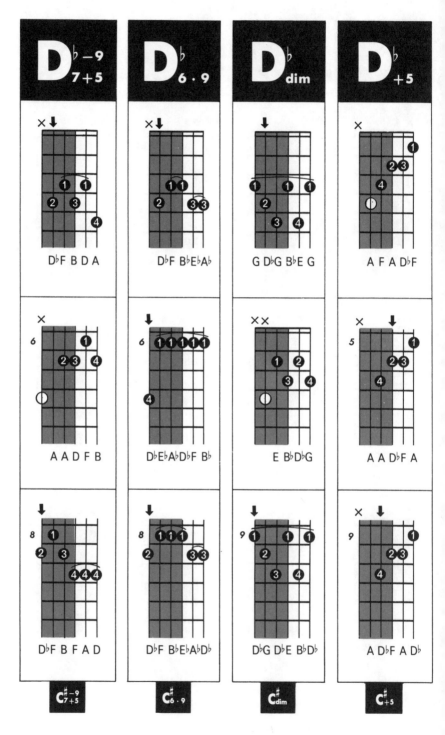

D♭

D♭sus4

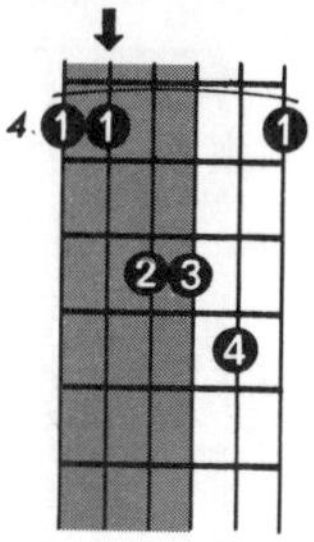

A♭D♭A♭D♭G♭A♭

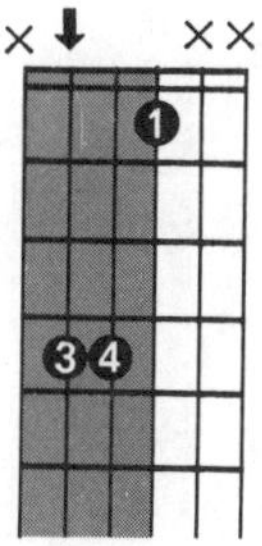

D♭G♭A♭

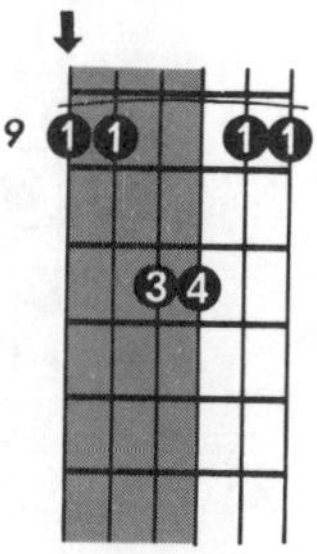

D♭G♭D♭G♭A♭D♭

C♯sus4

D♭7sus4

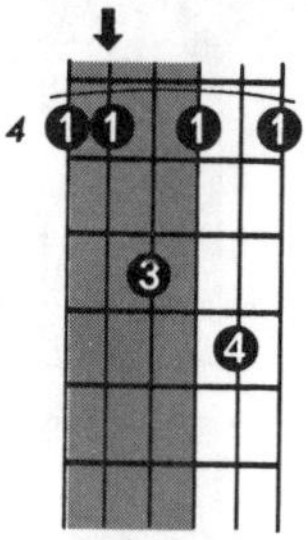

A♭D♭A♭B G♭A♭

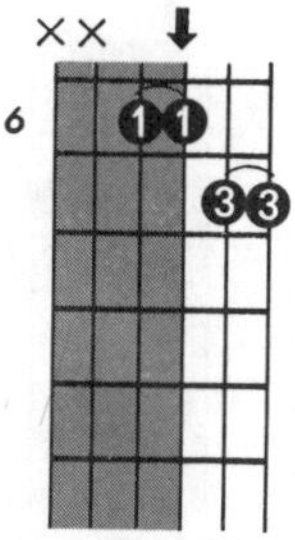

A♭D♭G♭B

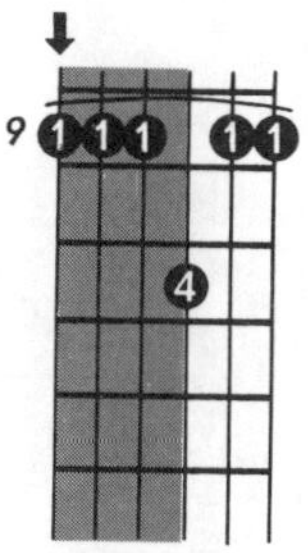

D♭G♭B G♭A♭D♭

C♯7sus4

D♭m

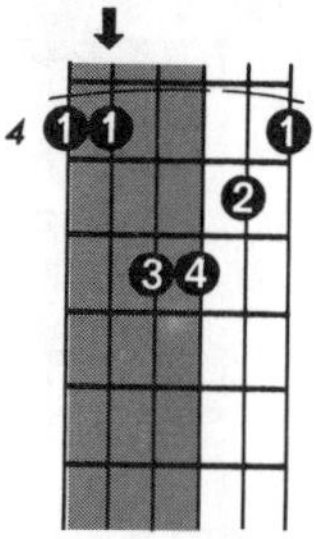

A♭D♭A♭D♭E A♭

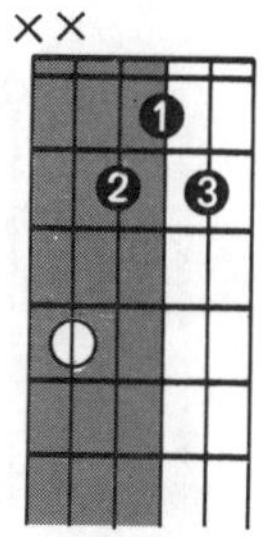

E A♭D♭E

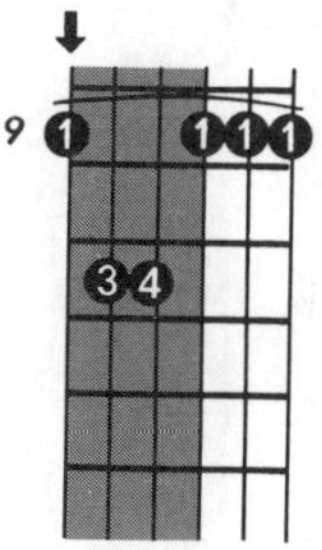

D♭A♭D♭E A♭D♭

C♯m

D♭m6

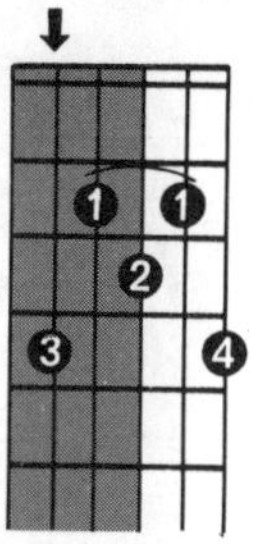

E D♭E B♭D♭A♭

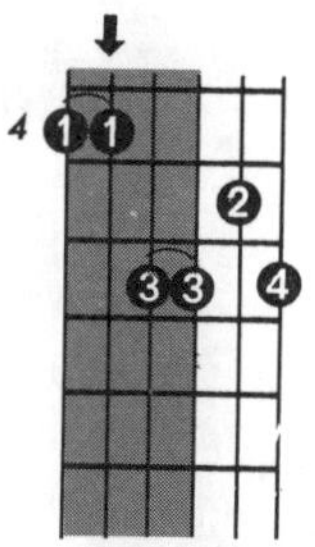

A♭D♭A♭D♭E B♭

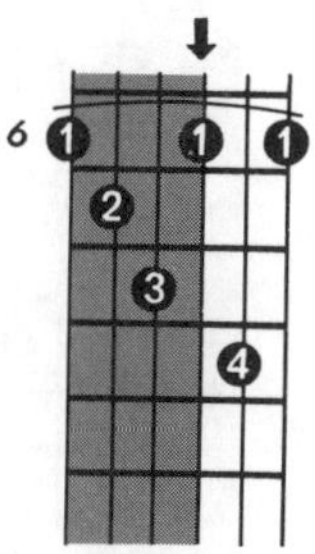

B♭E B♭D♭A♭B♭

C♯m6

C♯

D♭m7

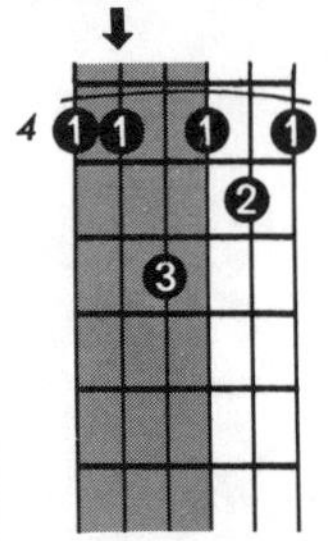

A♭D♭A♭B E A♭

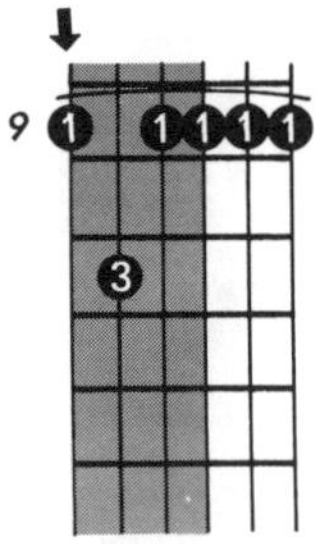

D♭A♭B E A♭D♭

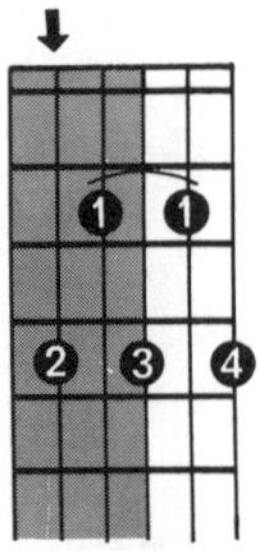

E D♭E B D♭A♭

C♯m7

D♭m9

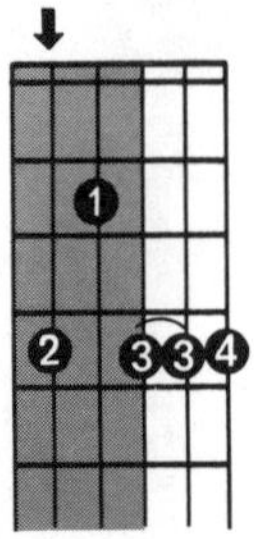

E D♭E B E♭A♭

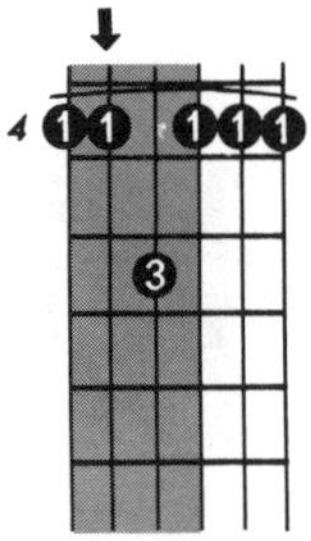

A♭D♭A♭B E♭A♭

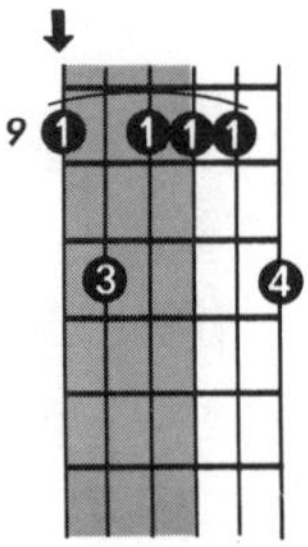

D♭A♭B E A♭E♭

C♯m9

D♭m7–5

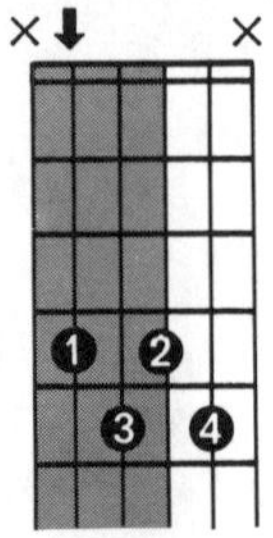

D♭G B E

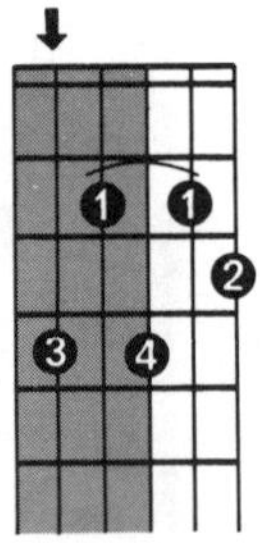

E D♭E B D♭G

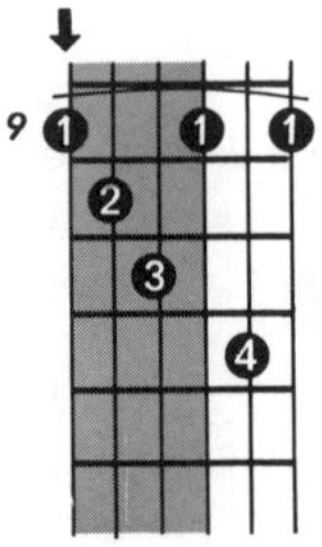

D♭G D♭E B D♭

C♯m7–5

D♭m7–9

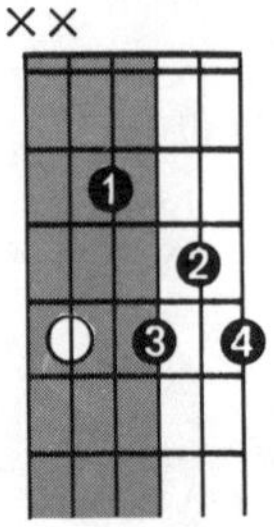

E B D A♭

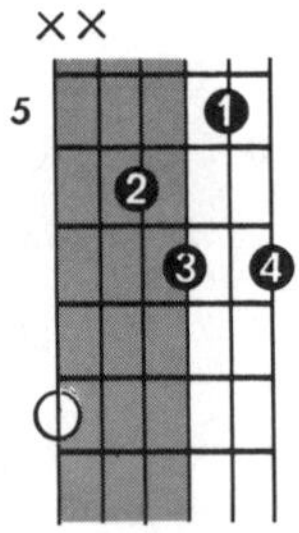

A♭D E B

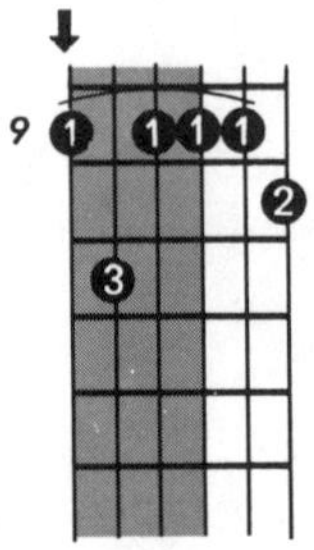

D♭A♭B E A♭D

C♯m7–9

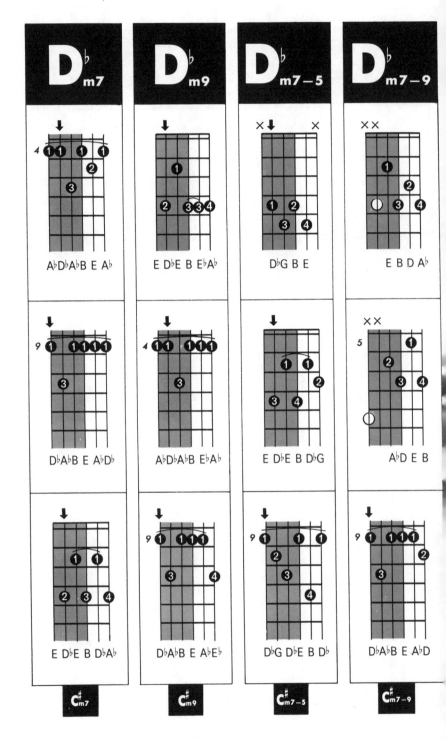

D♭m+7

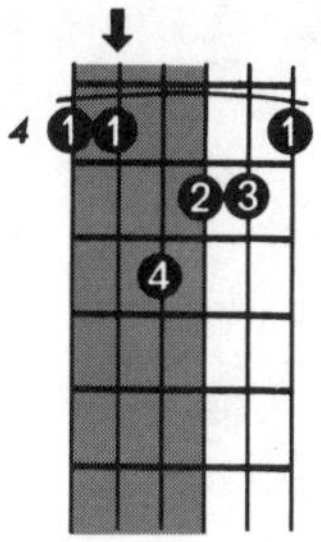

A♭D♭A♭C E A♭

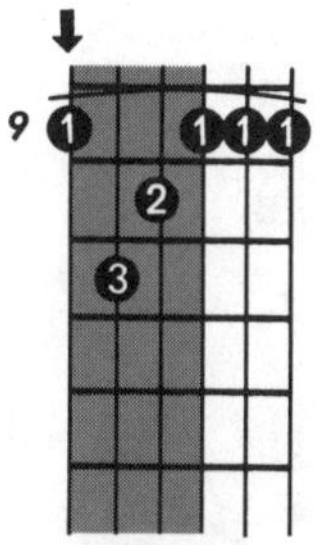

D♭A♭C E A♭D♭

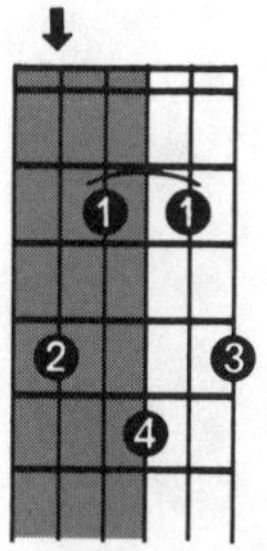

E D♭E C D♭A♭

C♯m+7

D♭m9+7

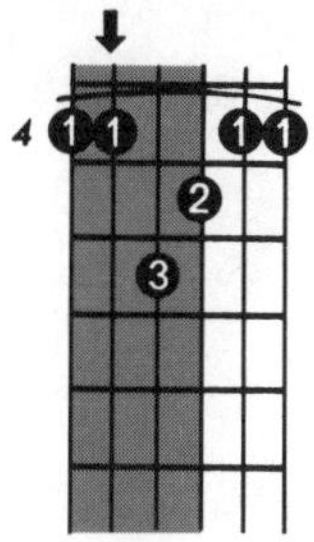

A♭D♭A♭C E♭A♭

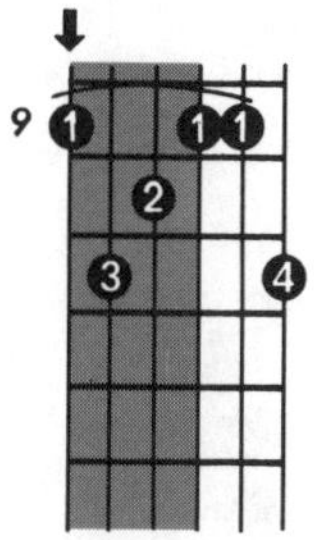

D♭A♭C E A♭E♭

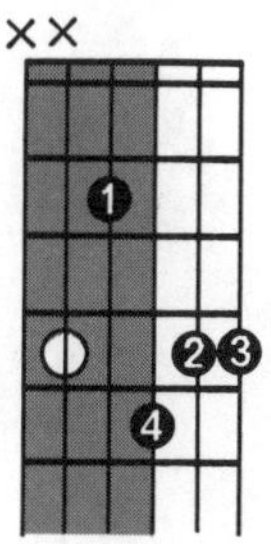

E C E♭A♭

C♯m9+7

D♭m+5

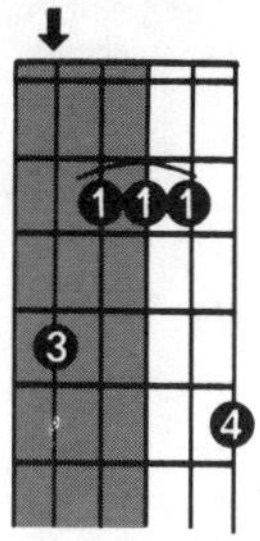

E D♭E A D♭A

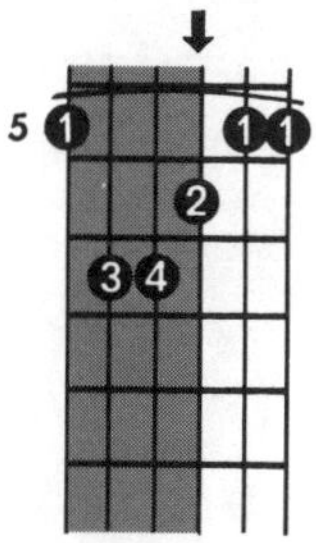

A E A D♭E A

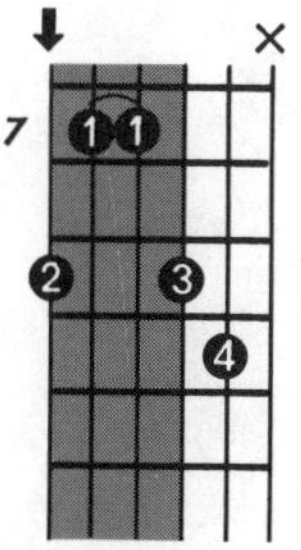

D♭E A E A

C♯m+5

D♭m6·9

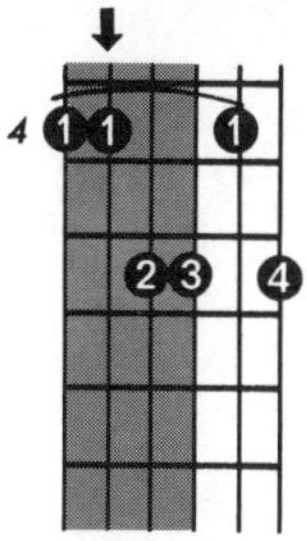

A♭D♭A♭D♭E♭B♭

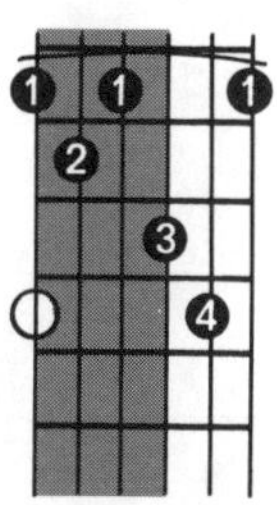

B♭E A♭E♭A♭B♭

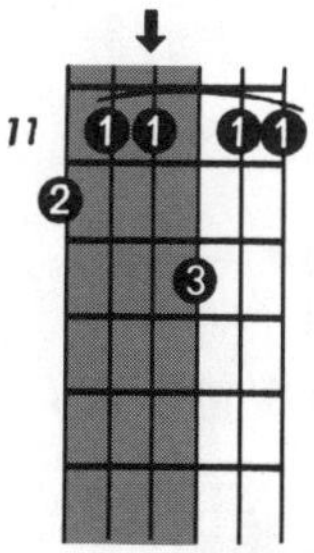

E A♭D♭A♭B♭E♭

C♯m6·9

D♭

D

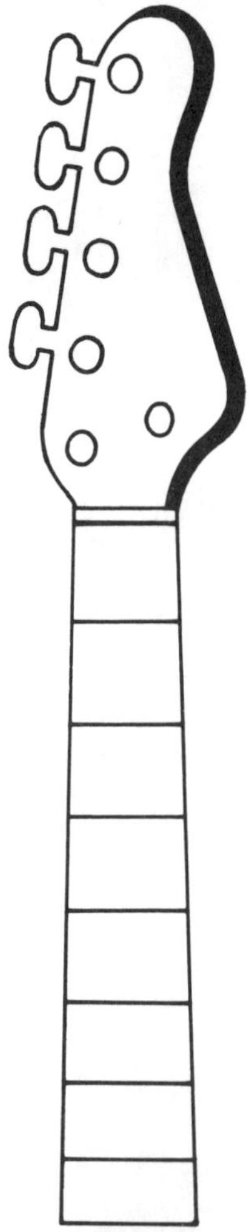

D

D

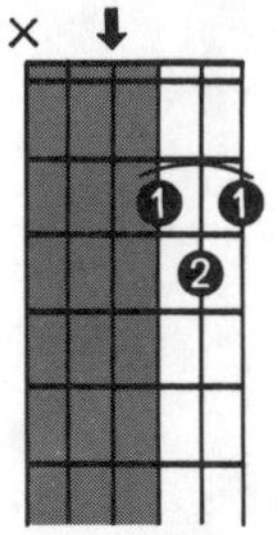

A D A D F#

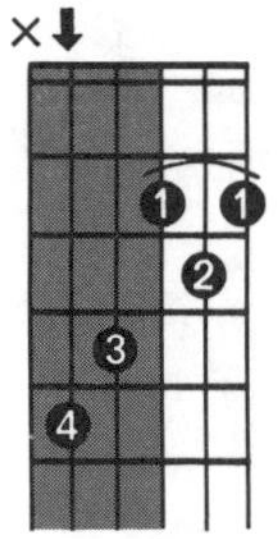

D F#A D F#

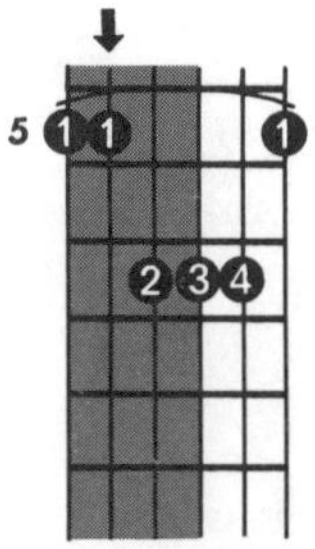

A D A D F#A

D_6

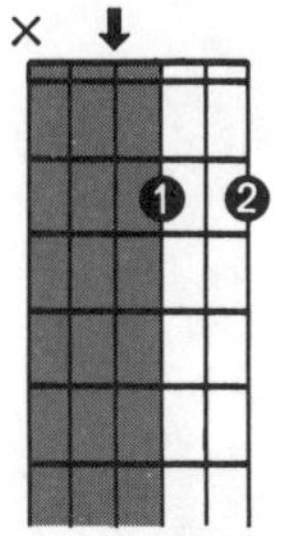

A D A B F#

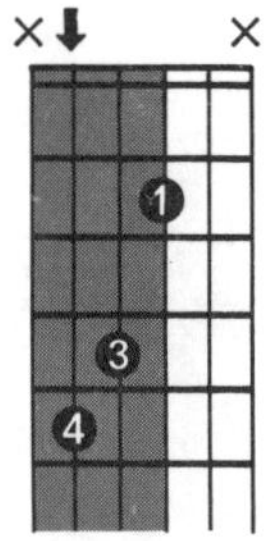

D F#A B

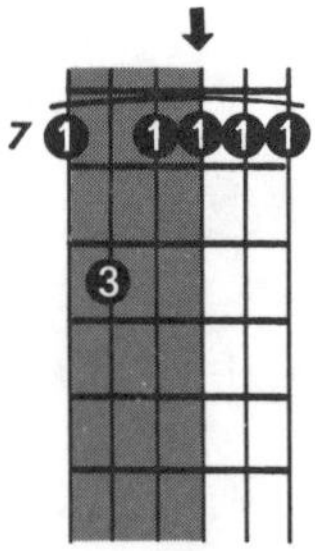

B F#A D F#B

D_7

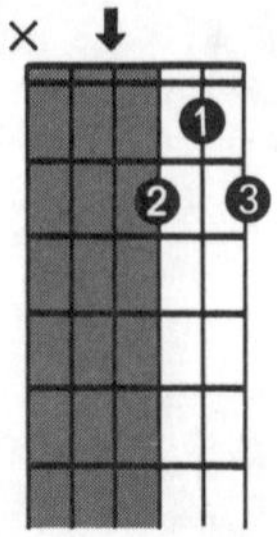

A D A C F#

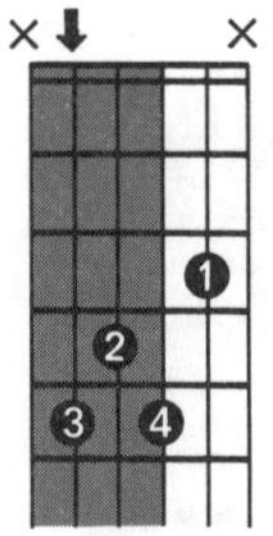

D F#C D

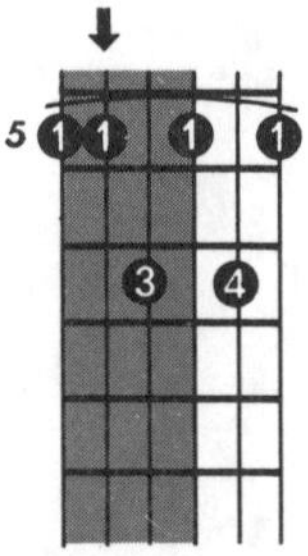

A D A C F#A

D9

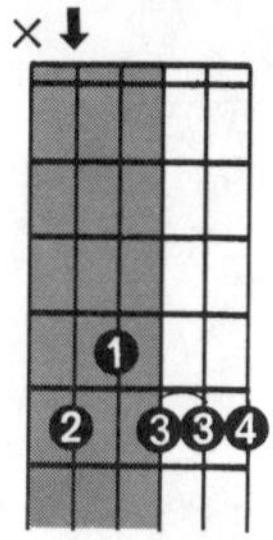

D F♯C E A

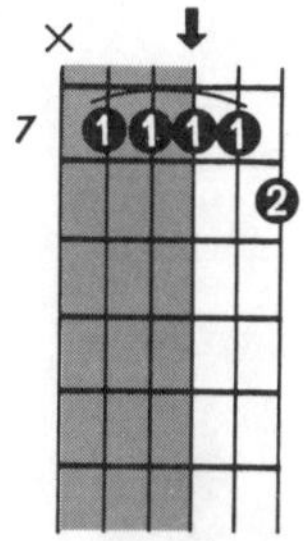

E A D F♯C

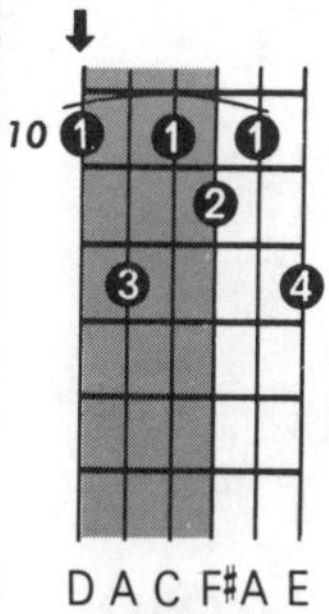

D A C F♯A E

D11

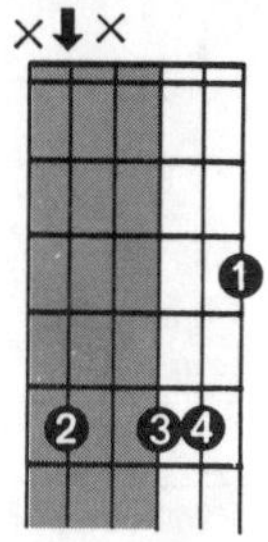

D C E G

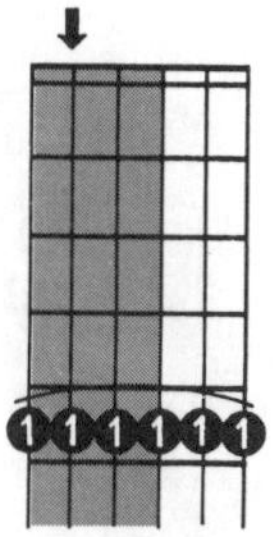

A D G C E A

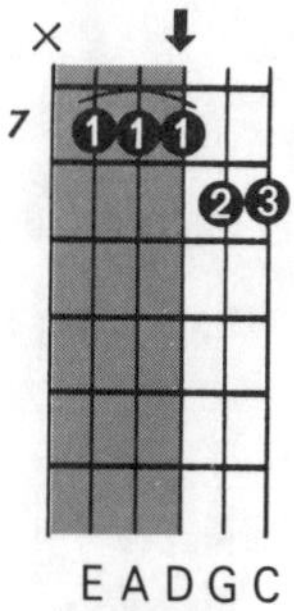

E A D G C

D11+

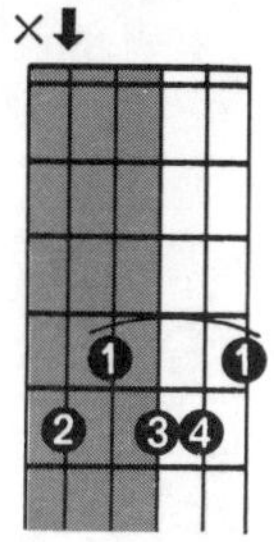

D F♯C E G♯

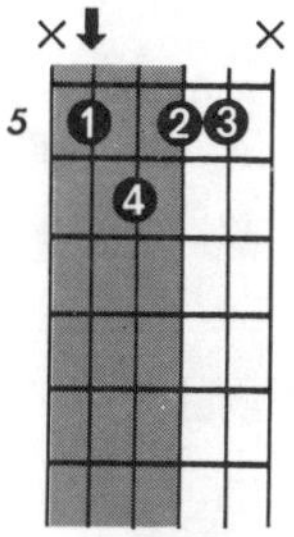

D G♯C E

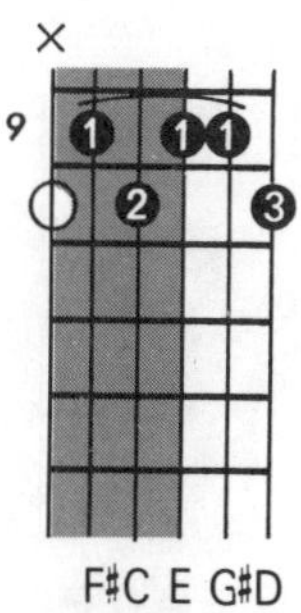

F♯C E G♯D

D13

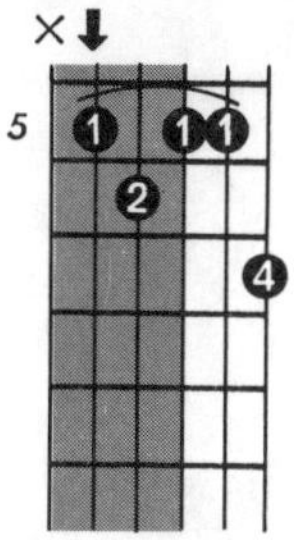

D G♯C E B

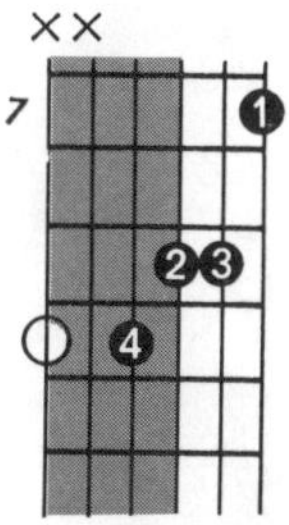

C E G♯B

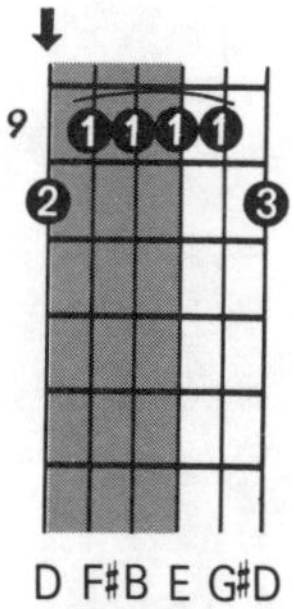

D F♯B E G♯D

D

Dmaj7

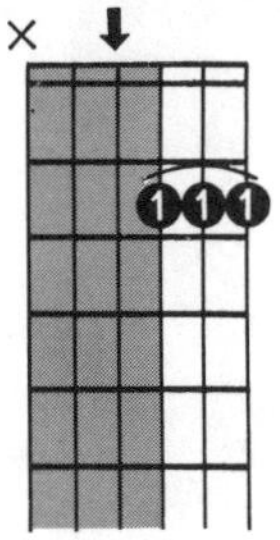

A D A C♯F♯

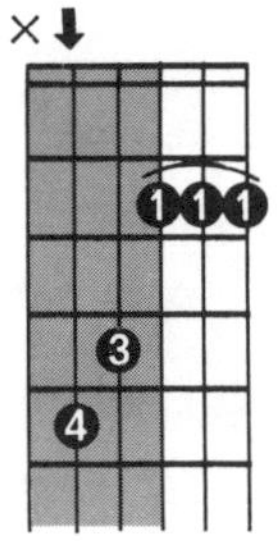

D F♯A C♯F♯

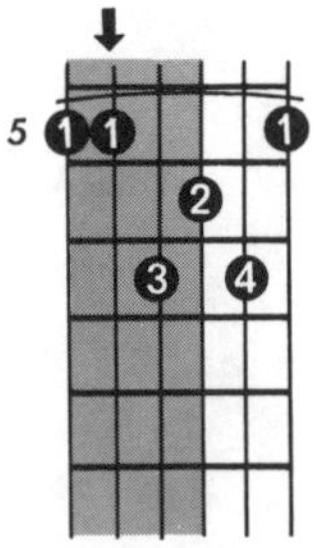

A D A C♯F♯A

Dmaj9

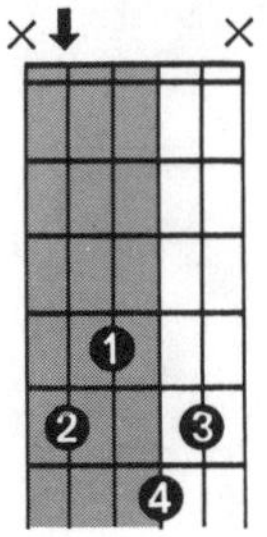

D F♯C♯E

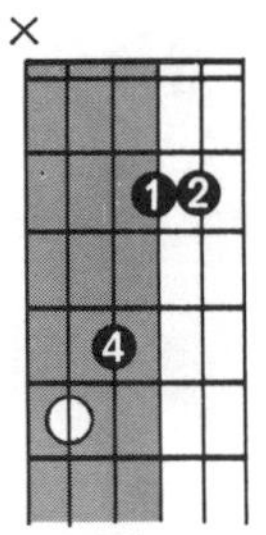

A F♯A C♯E

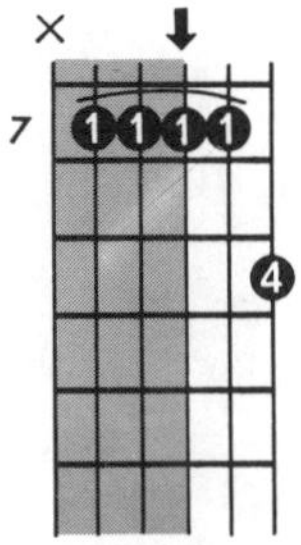

E A D F♯C♯

Dmaj11

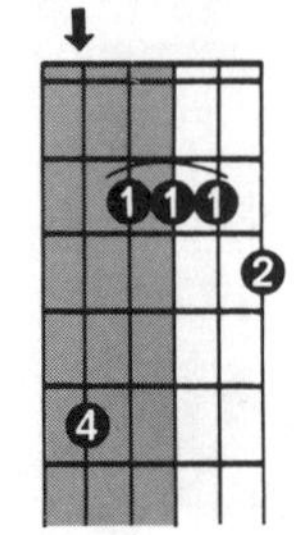

E D E A C♯G

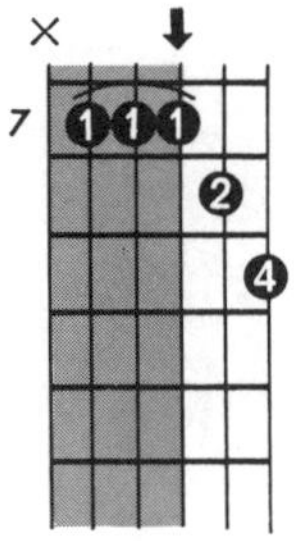

E A D G C♯

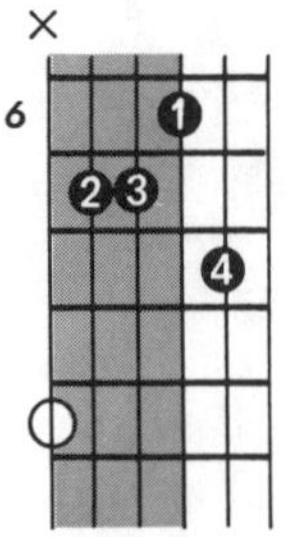

E A C♯G E

D7−5

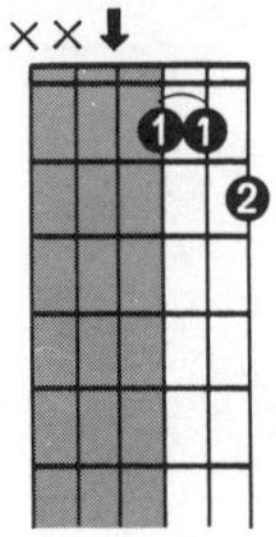

D A♭C F♯

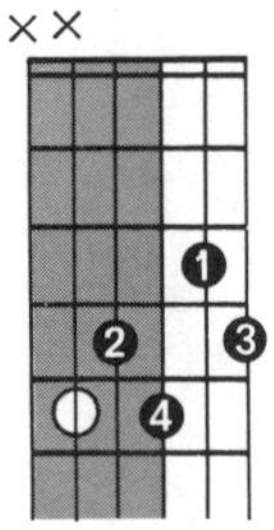

F♯C D A♭

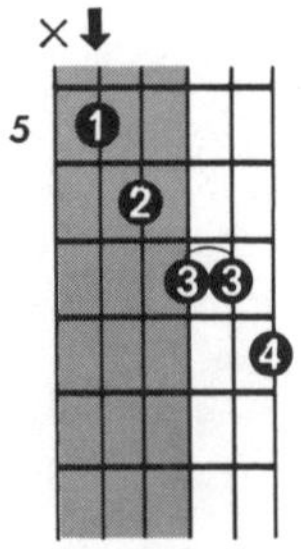

D A♭D F♯C

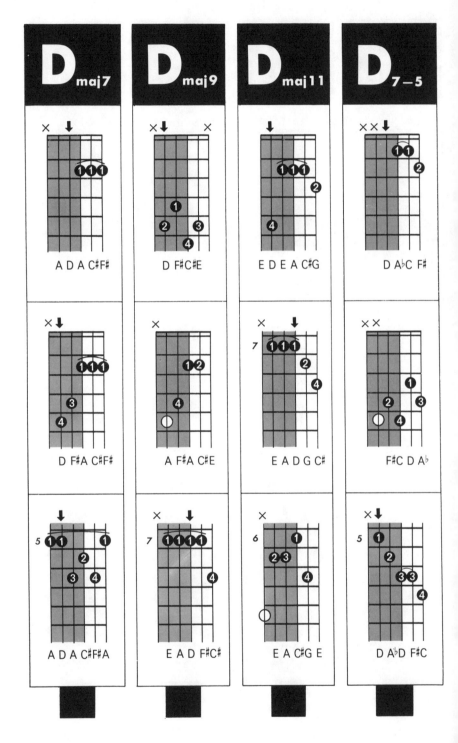

D$_{7-9}$

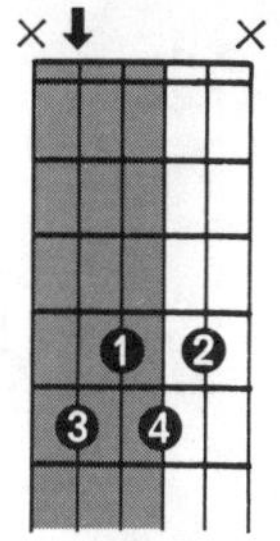

D F#C E♭

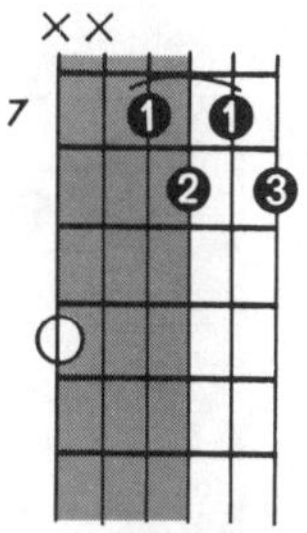

A E♭F#C

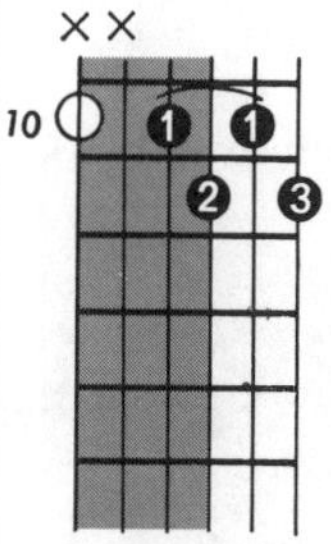

C F#A E♭

D$_{7-10}$

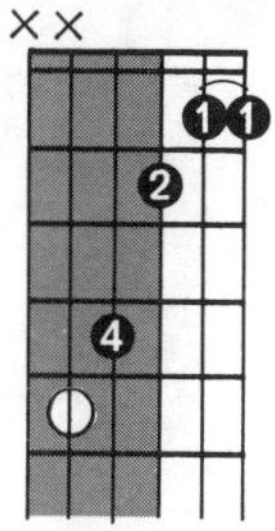

F#A C F

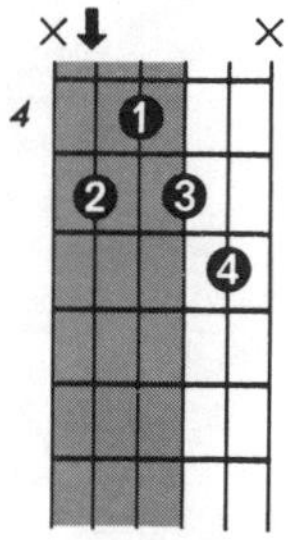

D F#C F

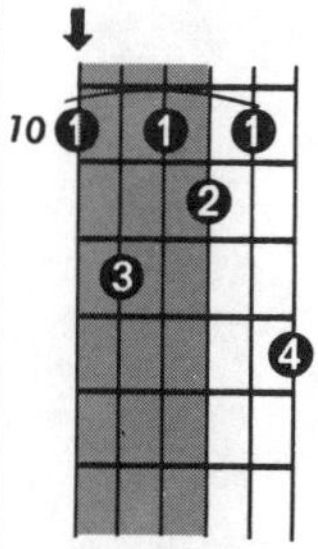

D A C F#A F

D$_{7+5}$

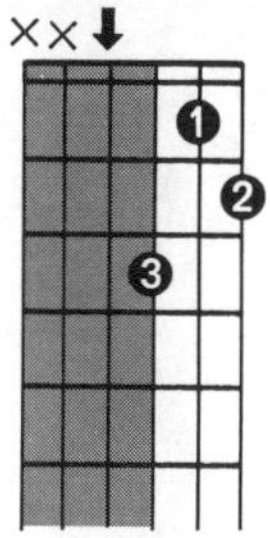

D A#C F#

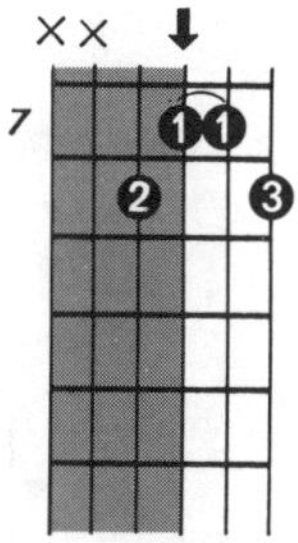

A#D F#C

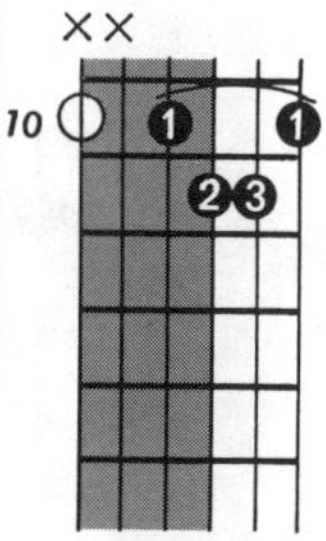

C F#A#D

D$_{9+5}$

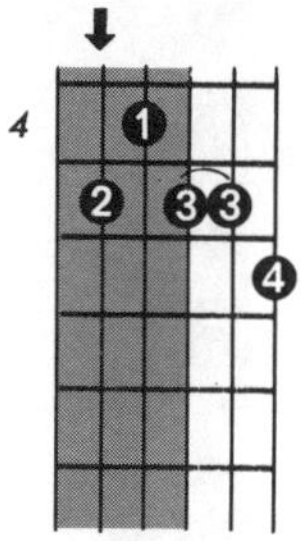

E D F#C E A#

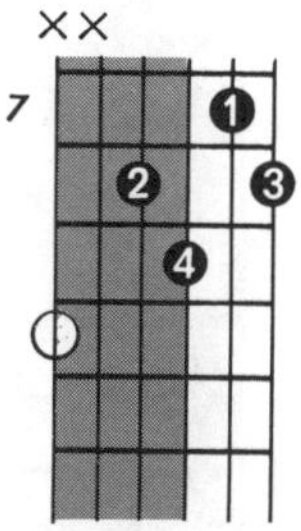

A#E F#C

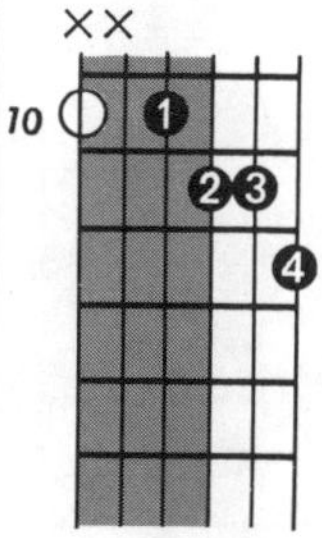

C F#A#E

D

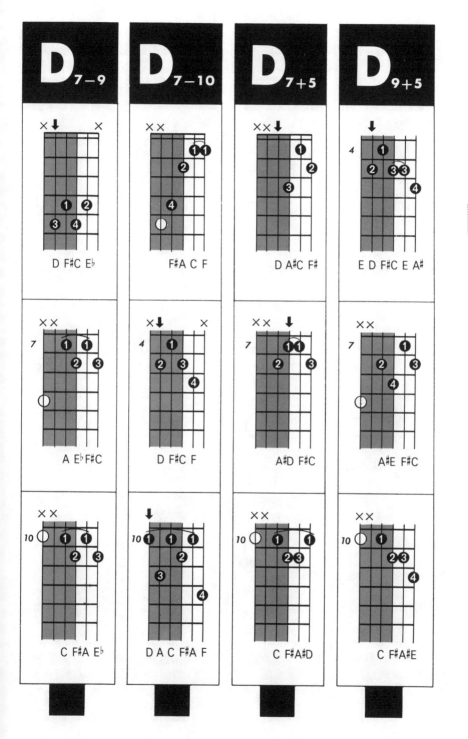

D

D^{-9}_{7+5}

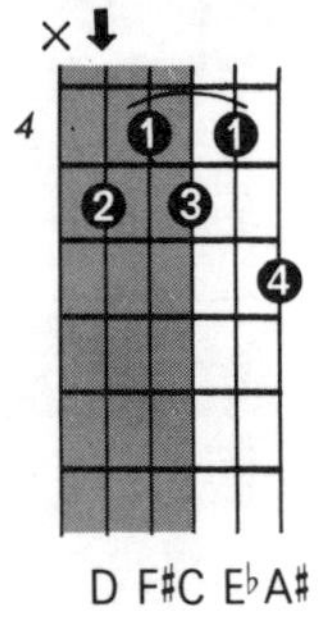

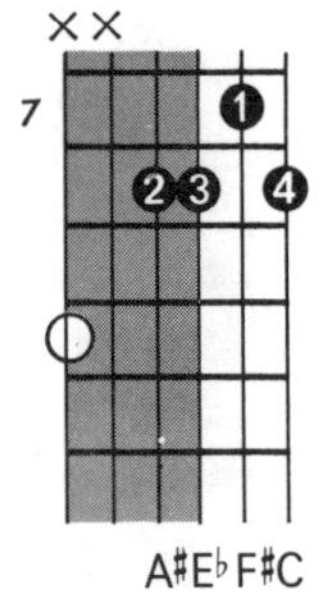

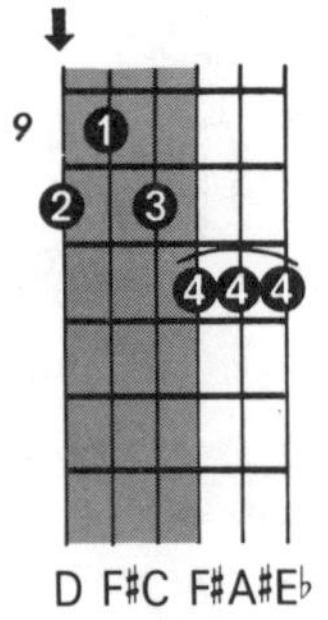

$D_{6 \cdot 9}$

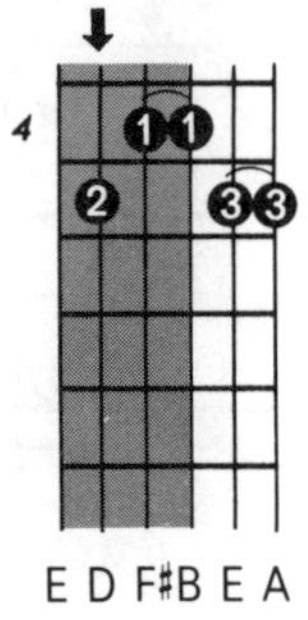

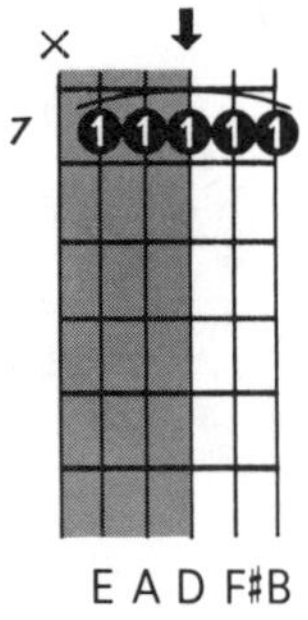

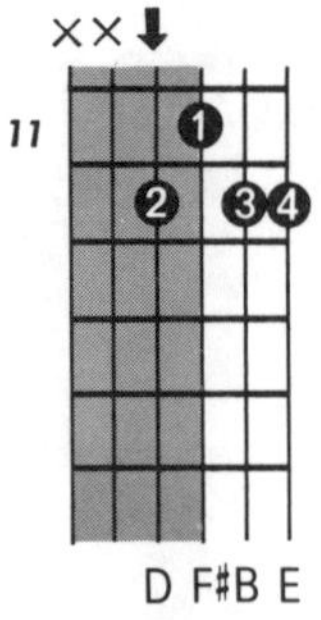

D_{dim}

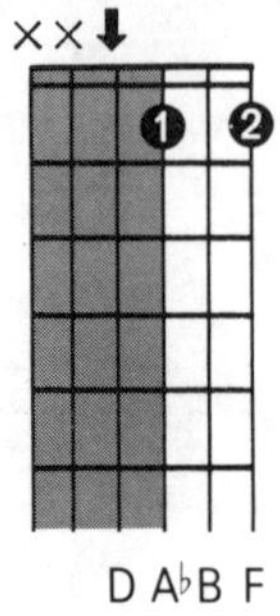

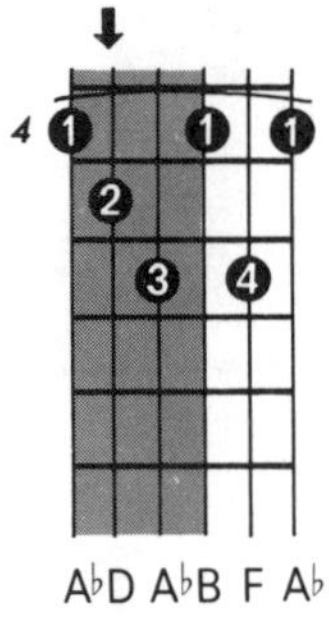

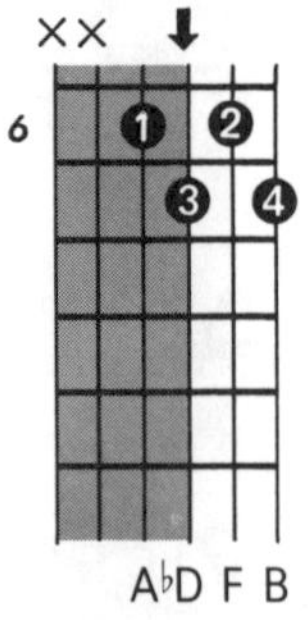

D_{+5}

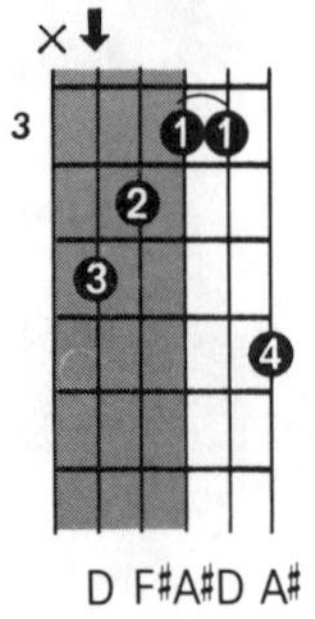

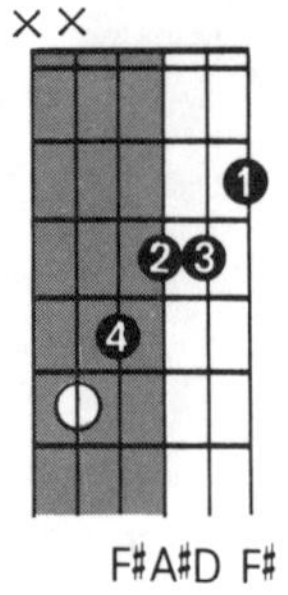

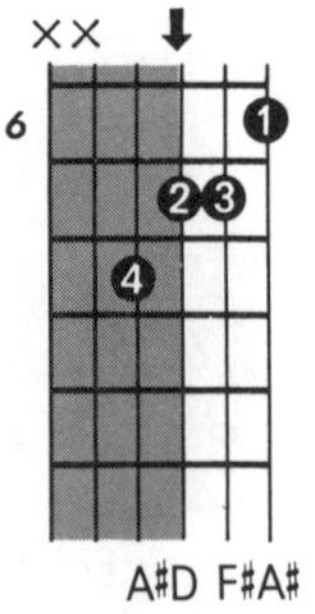

Dsus4

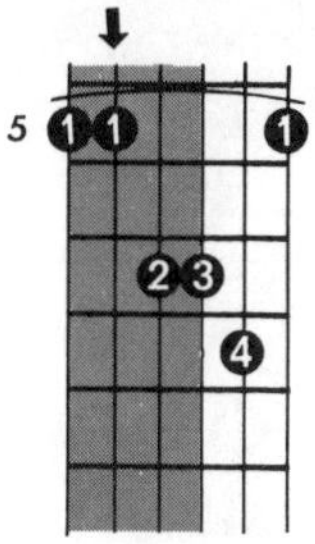

A D A D G A

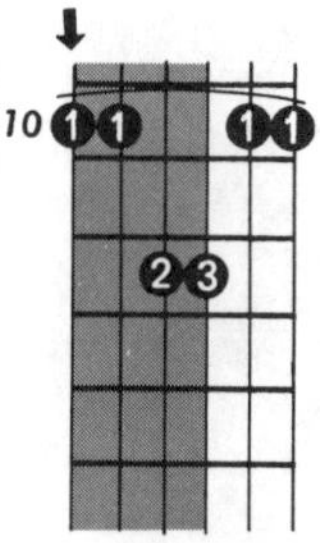

D G D G A D

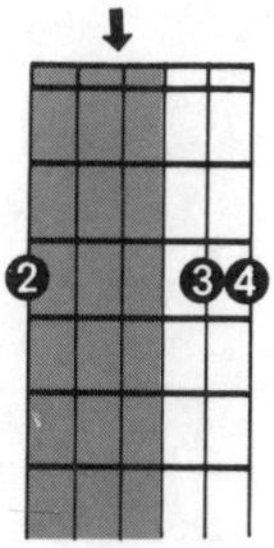

G A D G D G

D7sus4

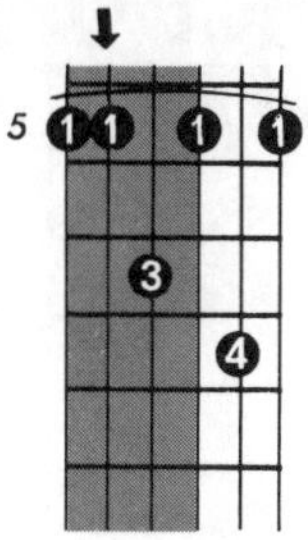

A D A C G A

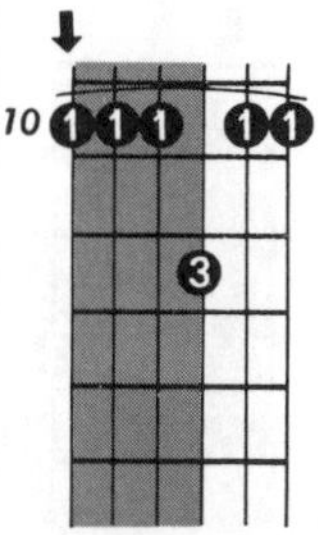

D G C G A D

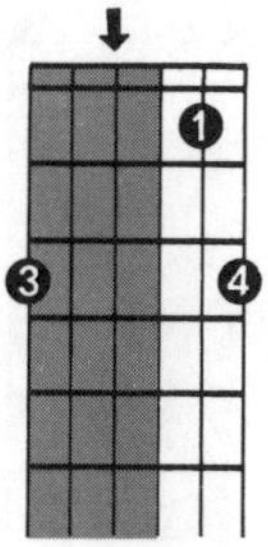

G A D G C G

Dm

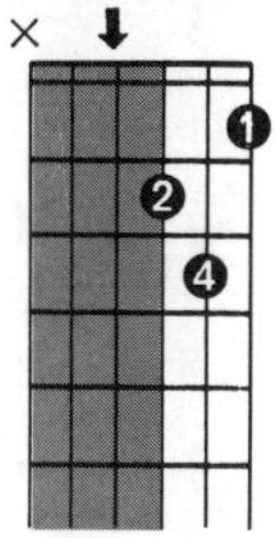

A D A D F

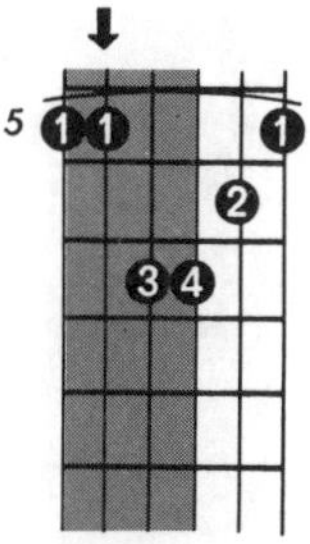

A D A D F A

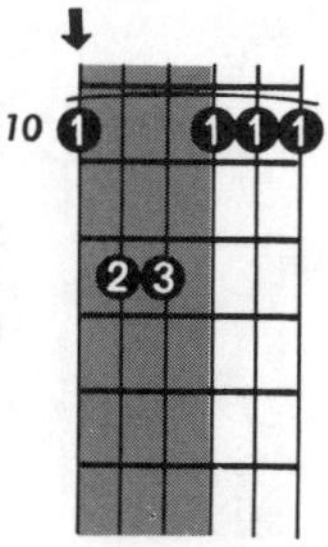

D A D F A D

Dm6

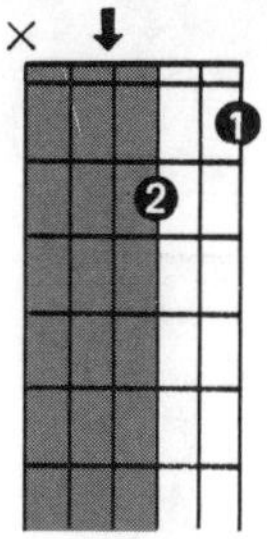

A D A B F

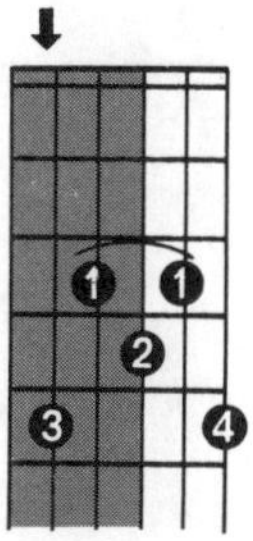

D F B D A

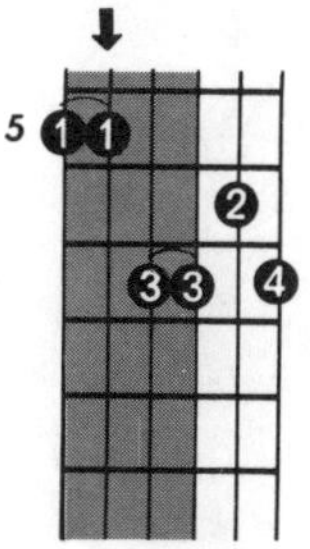

A D A D F B

D

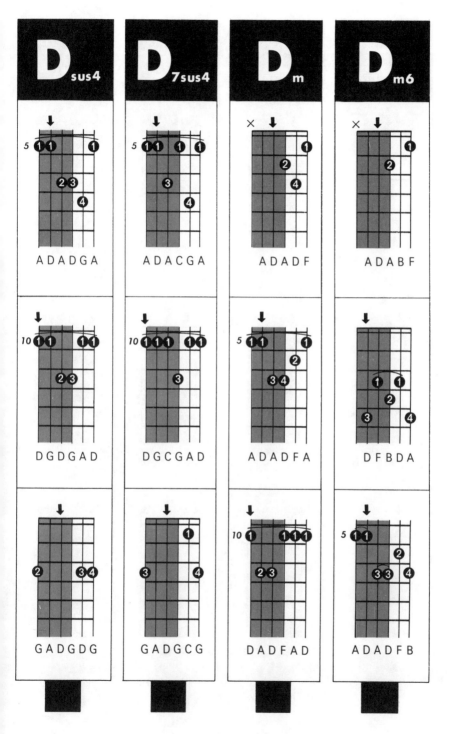

D

Dm7

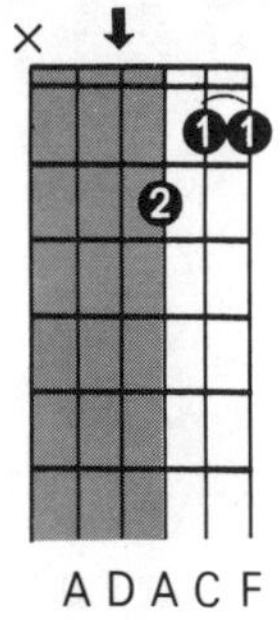

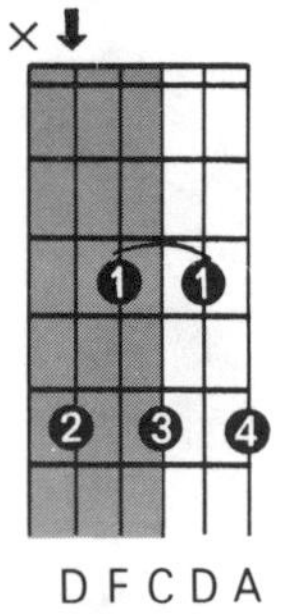

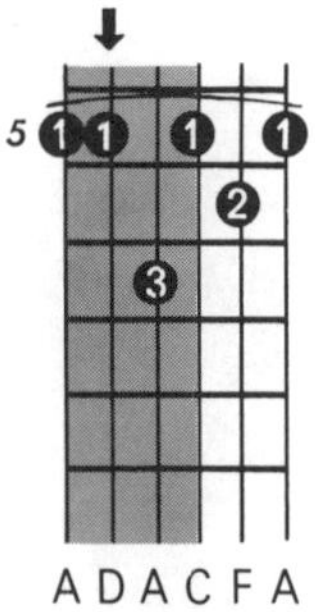

Dm9

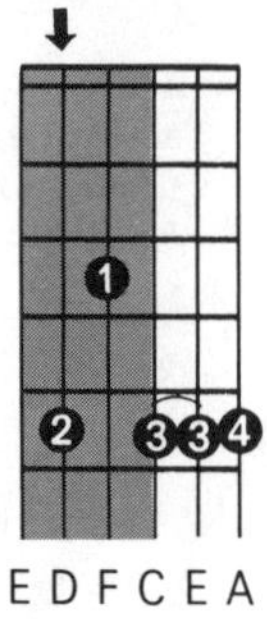

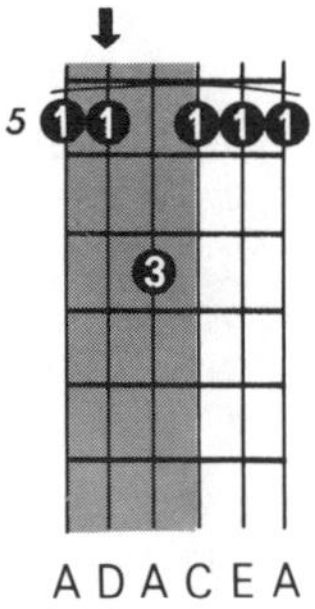

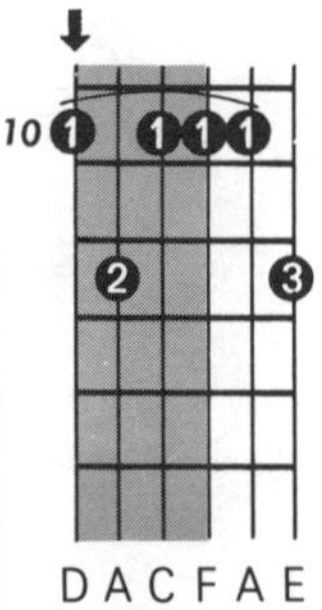

Dm7–♭5

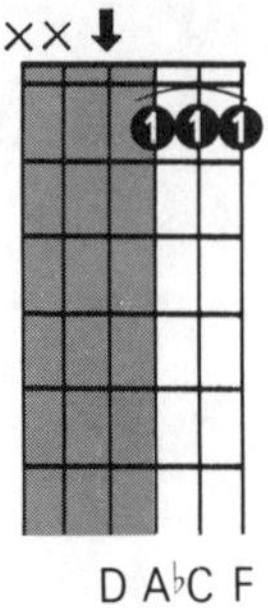

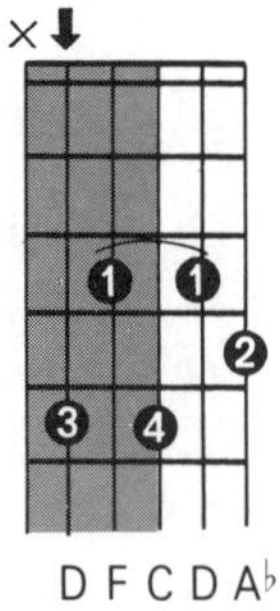

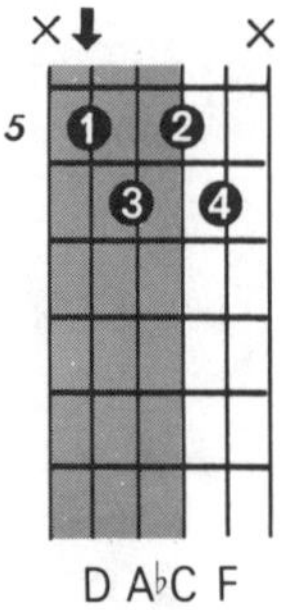

Dm7–9

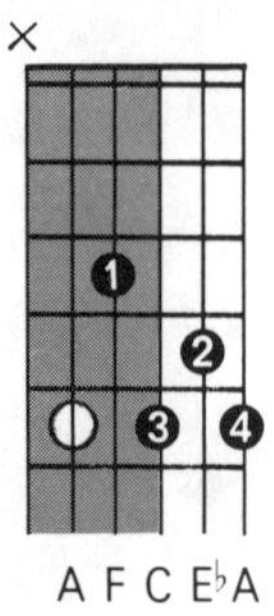

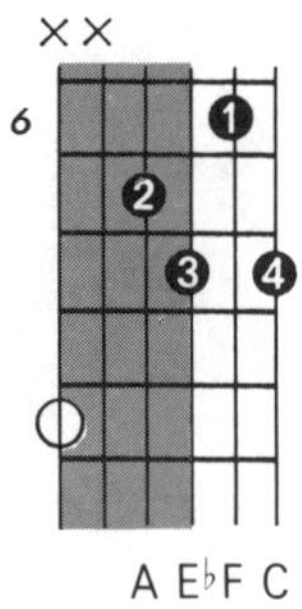

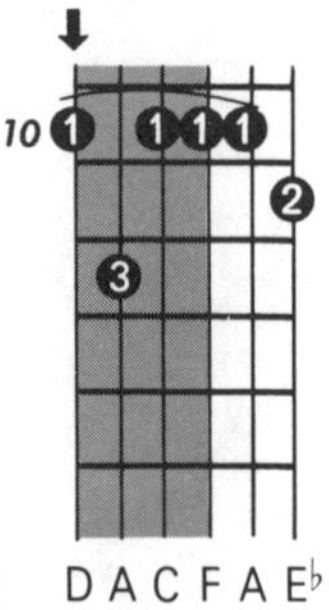

Dm+7

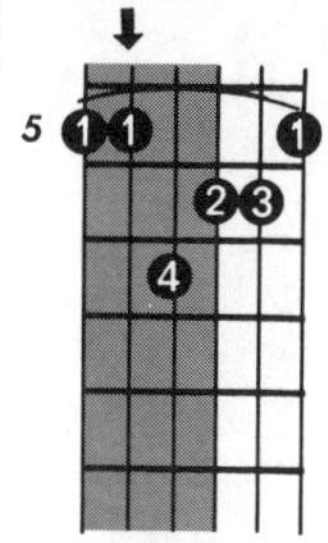

A D A C♯F A

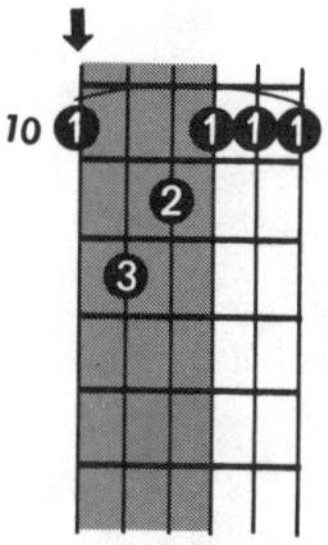

D A C♯F A D

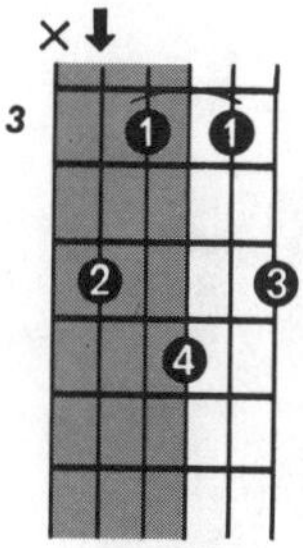

D F C♯D A

Dm9+7

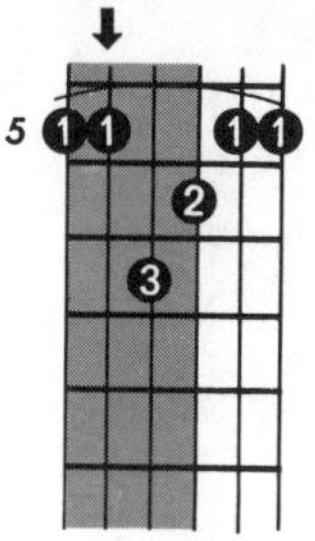

A D A C♯E A

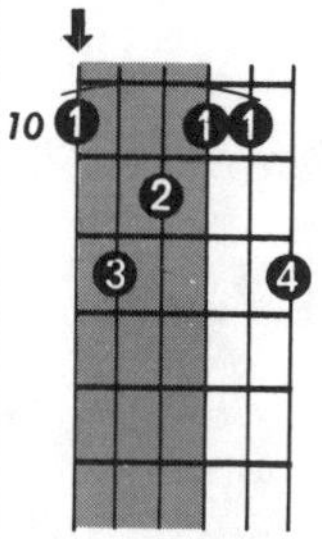

D A C♯F A E

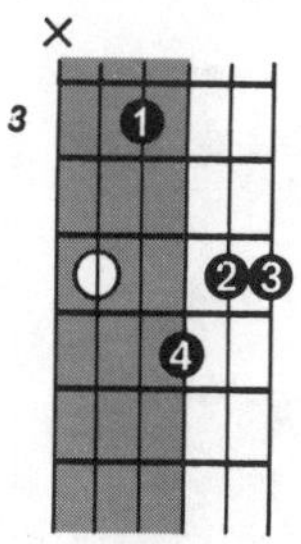

A F C♯E A

Dm+5

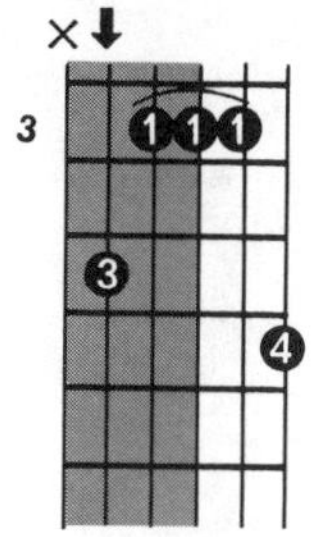

D F A♯D A♯

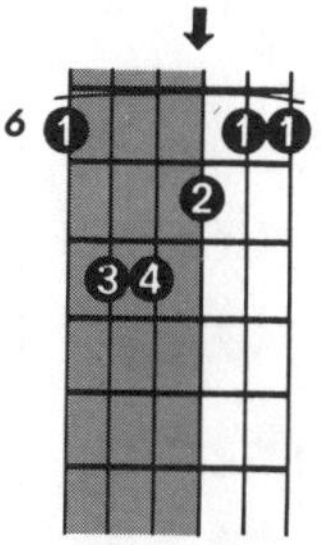

A♯F A♯D F A♯

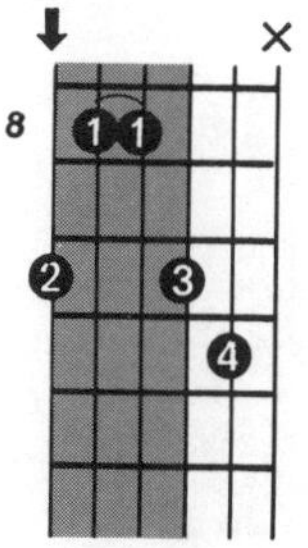

D F A♯F A♯

Dm6 · 9

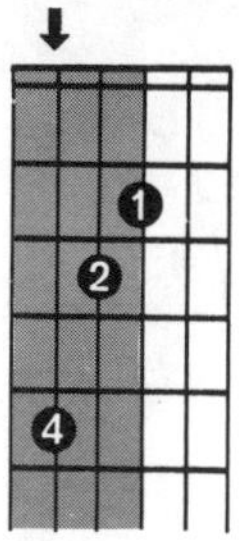

E D F A B E

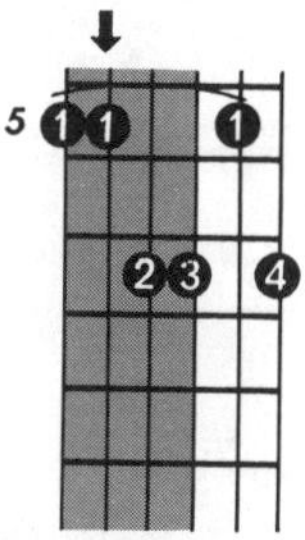

A D A D E B

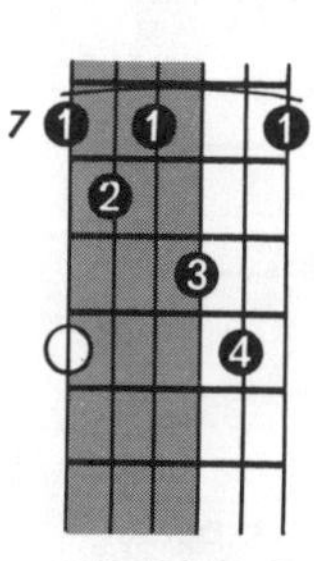

B F A E A B

E♭

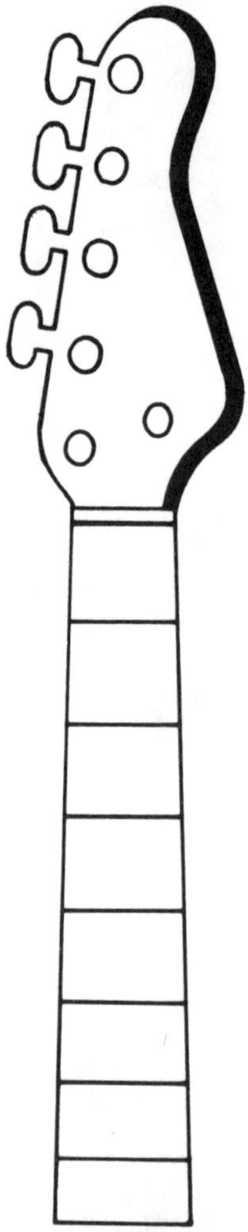

D♯

E♭

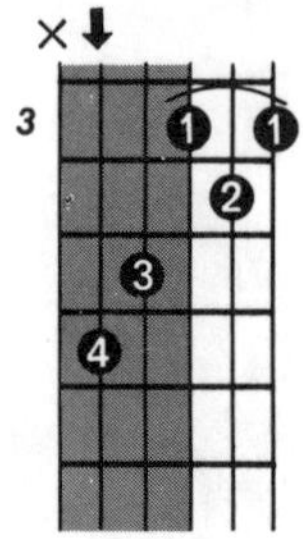

E♭G B♭E♭G

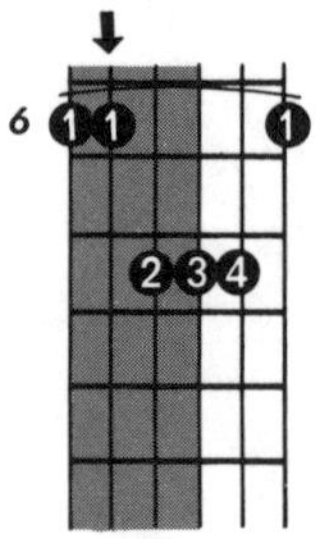

B♭E♭B♭E♭G B♭

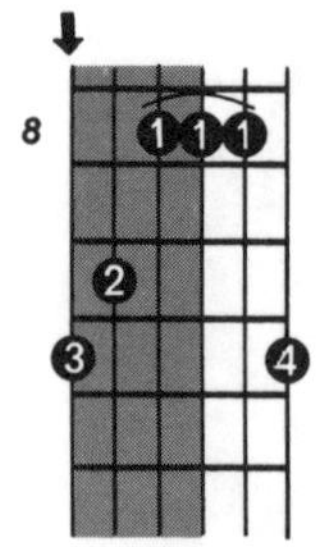

E♭G B♭E♭G E♭

D♯

E♭6

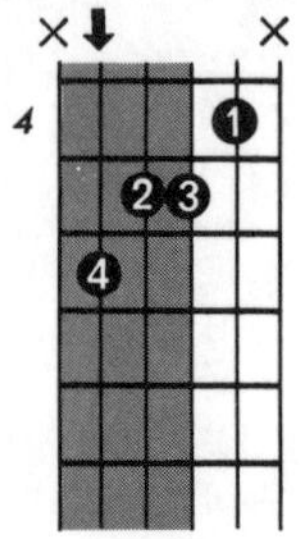

E♭G C E♭

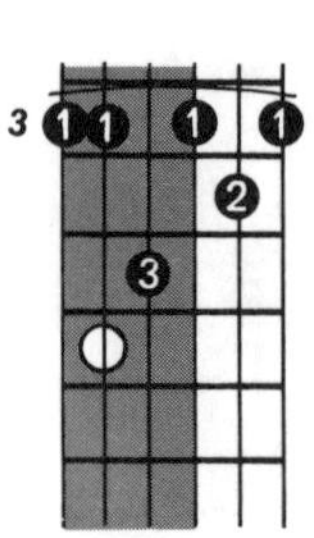

G C G B♭E♭G

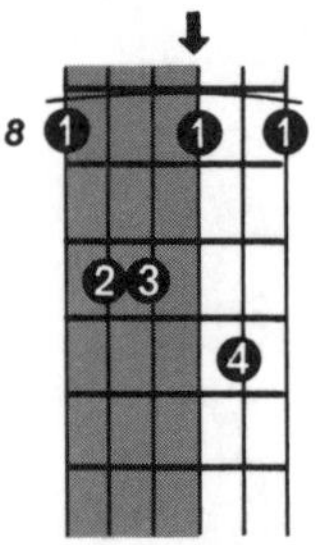

C G C E♭B♭C

D♯6

E♭7

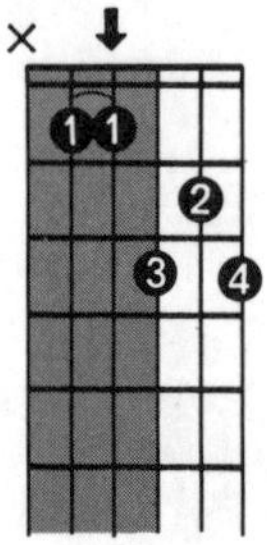

B♭E♭B♭D♭G

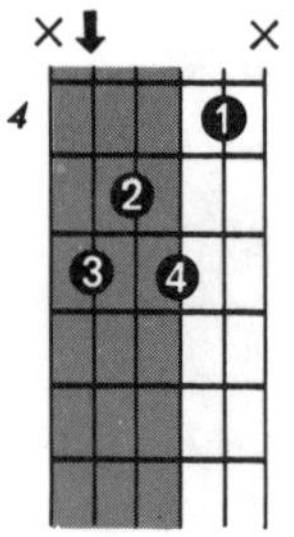

E♭G D♭E♭

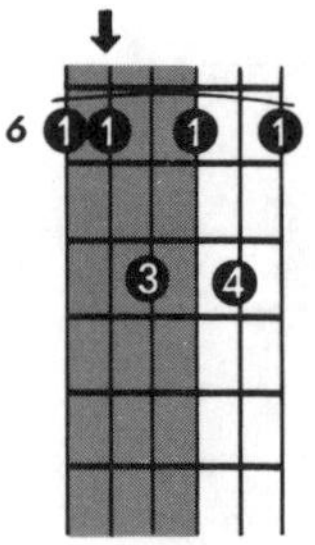

B♭E♭B♭D♭G B♭

D♯7

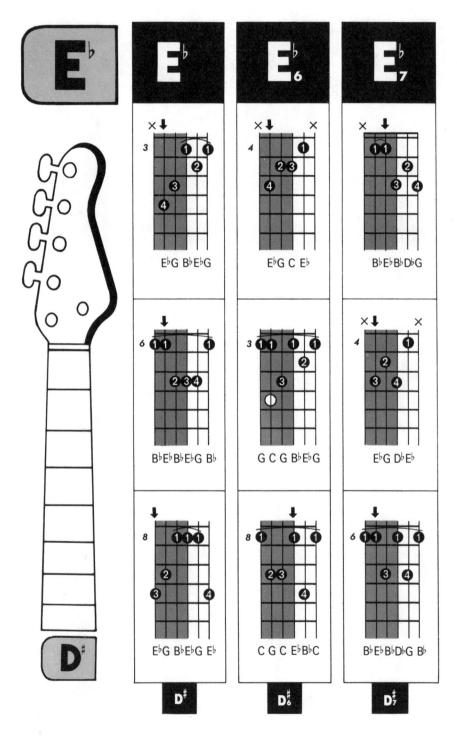

E♭9

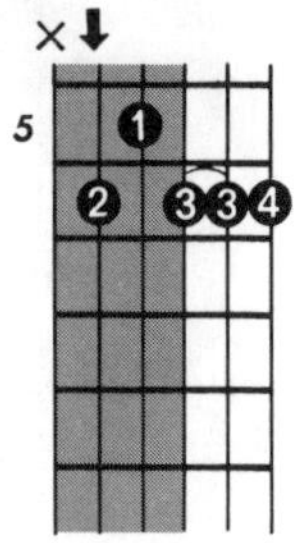

E♭G D♭F B♭

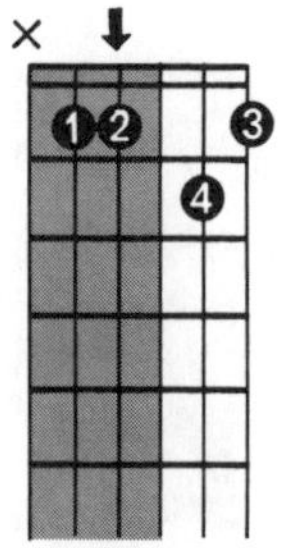

B♭E♭G D♭F

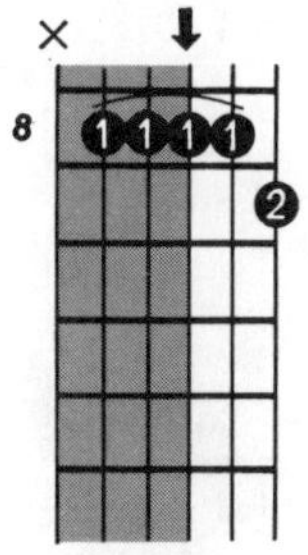

F B♭E♭G D♭

D♯9

E♭11

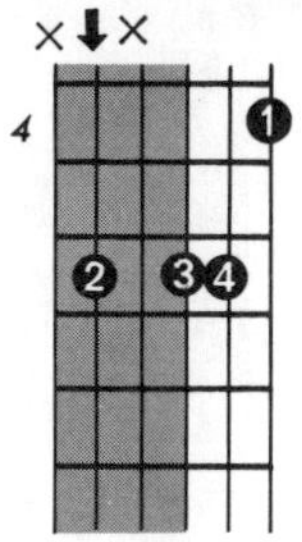

E♭ D♭F A♭

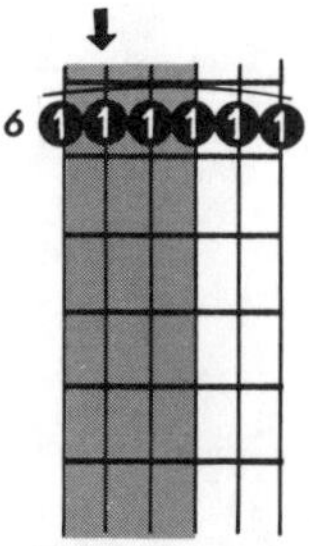

B♭E♭A♭D♭F B♭

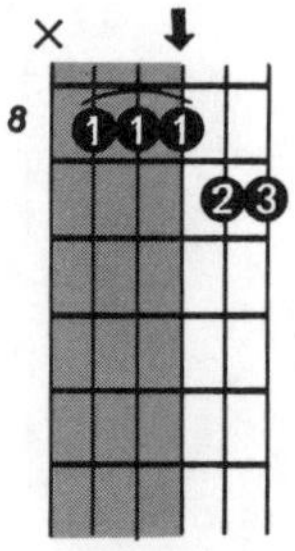

F B♭E♭A♭D♭

D♯11

E♭11+

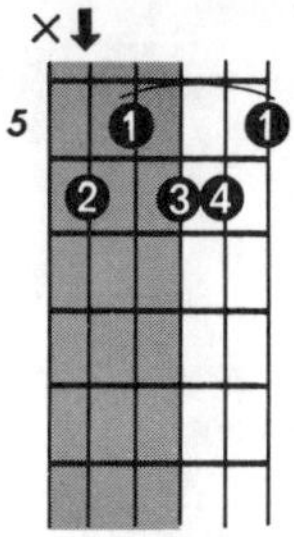

E♭G D♭F A

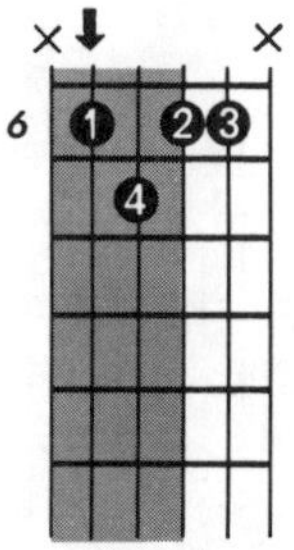

E♭A D♭F

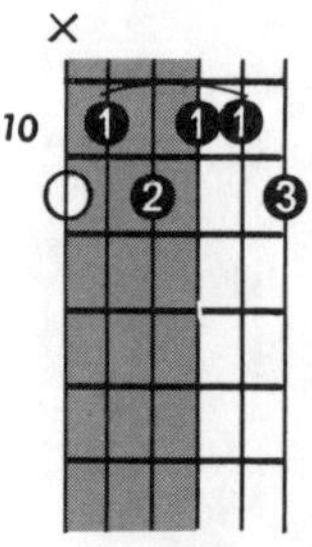

G D♭F A E♭

D♯11+

E♭13

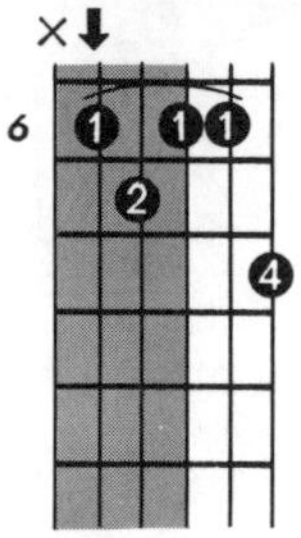

E♭A D♭F C

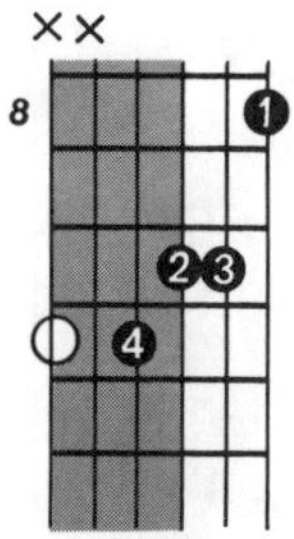

D♭F A C

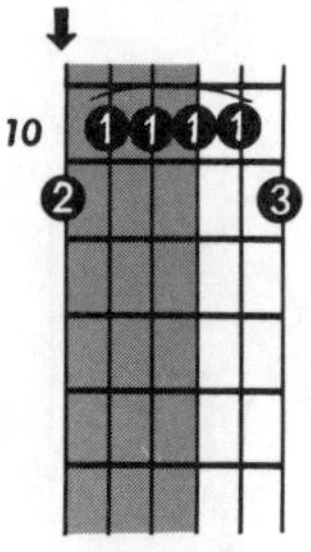

E♭G C F A E♭

D♯13

E♭

D♯

$E^{\flat}_{maj7}$

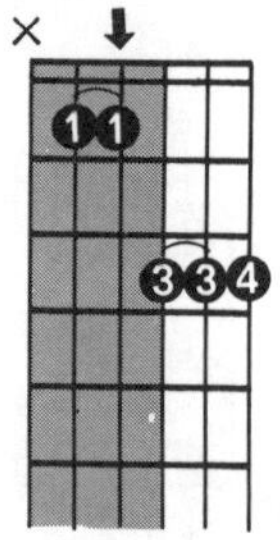

B♭E♭B♭D G

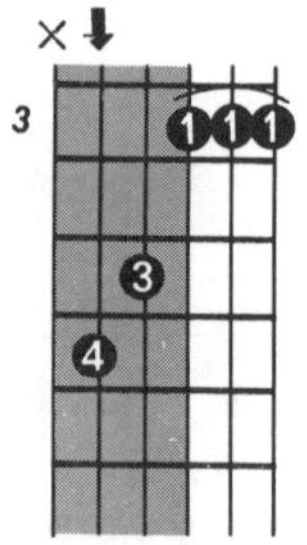

E♭G B♭D G

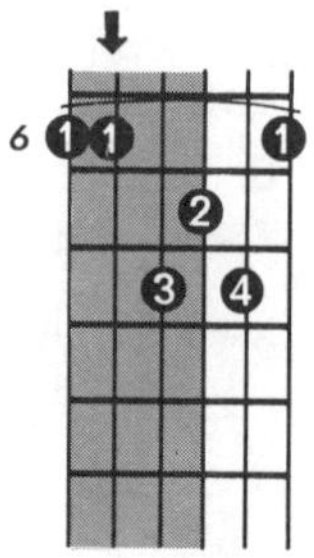

B♭E♭B♭D G B♭

$D^{\sharp}_{maj7}$

$E^{\flat}_{maj9}$

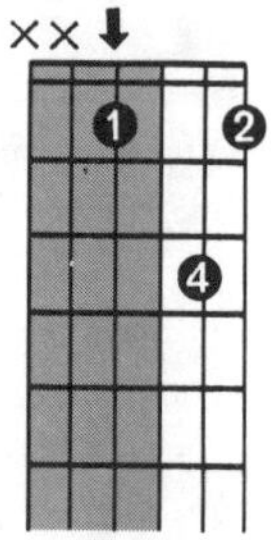

E♭G D F

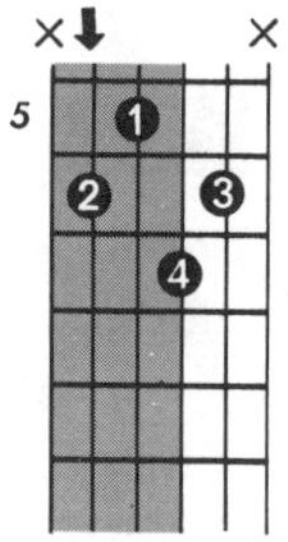

E♭G D F

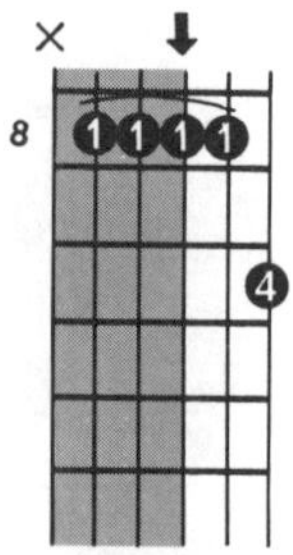

F B♭E♭G D

$D^{\sharp}_{maj9}$

$E^{\flat}_{maj11}$

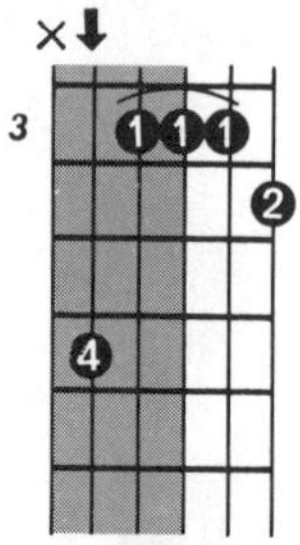

E♭F B♭D A♭

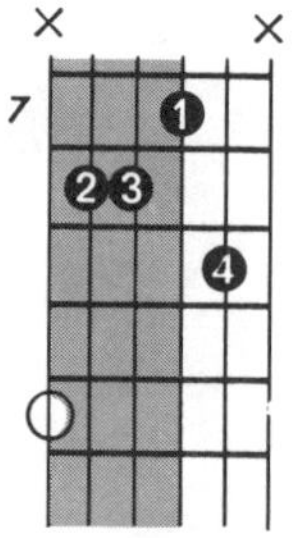

F B♭D A♭

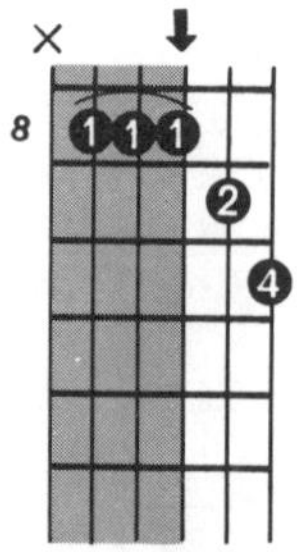

F B♭E♭A♭D

$D^{\sharp}_{maj11}$

$E^{\flat}_{7-5}$

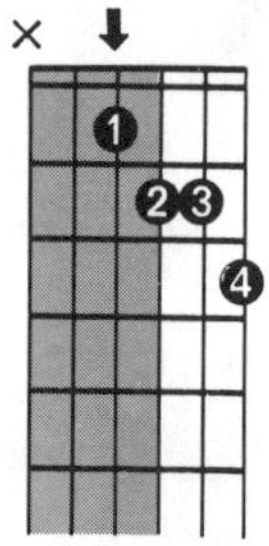

A E♭A D♭G

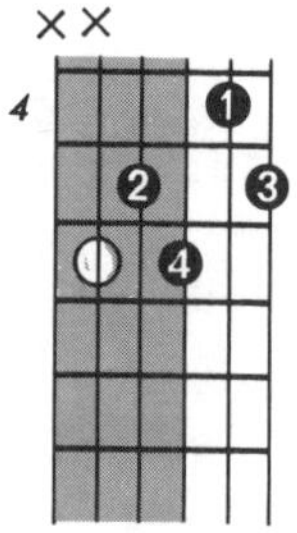

G D♭E♭A

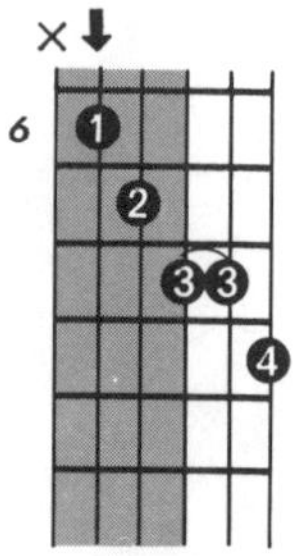

E♭A E♭G D♭

$D^{\sharp}_{7-5}$

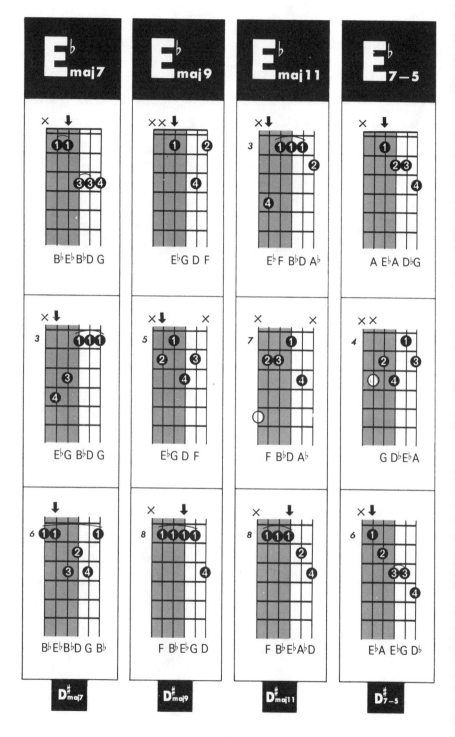

E♭ 7−9

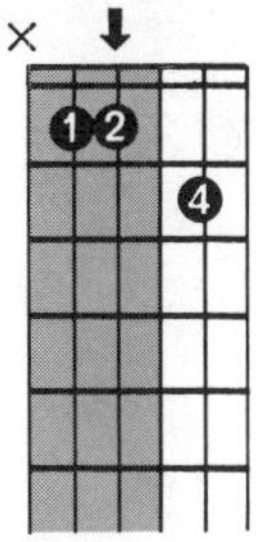

B♭E♭G D♭E

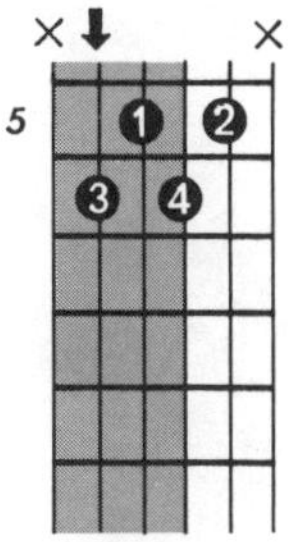

E♭G D♭E

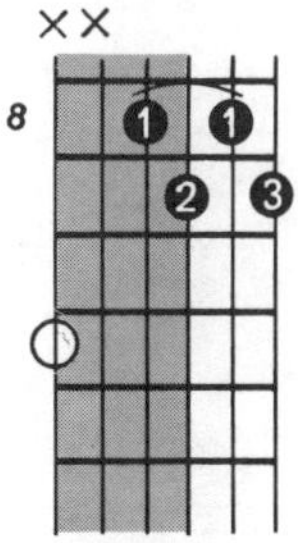

B♭E G D♭

D♯ 7−9

E♭ 7−10

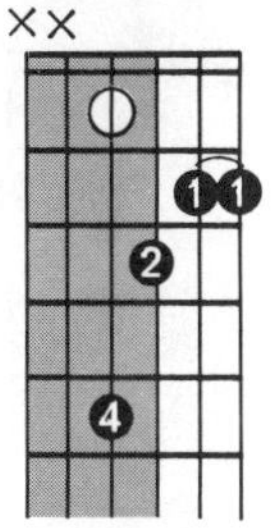

G B♭D♭G♭

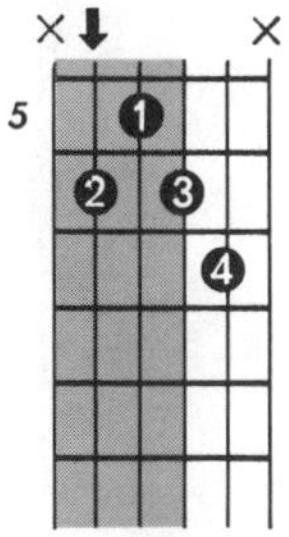

E♭G D♭G♭

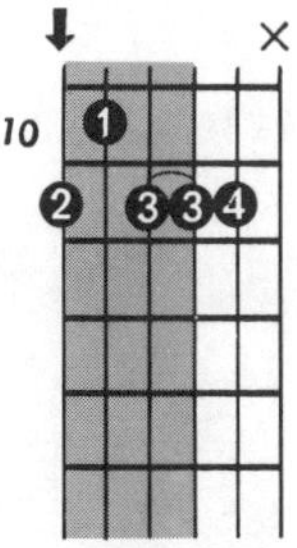

E♭G D♭G♭B♭

D♯ 7−10

E♭ 7+5

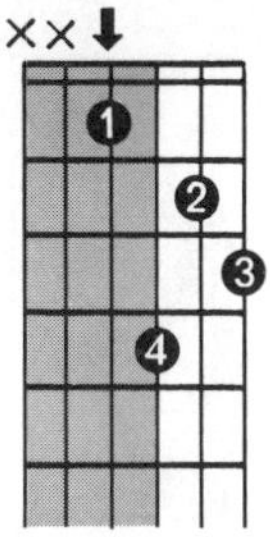

E♭B D♭G

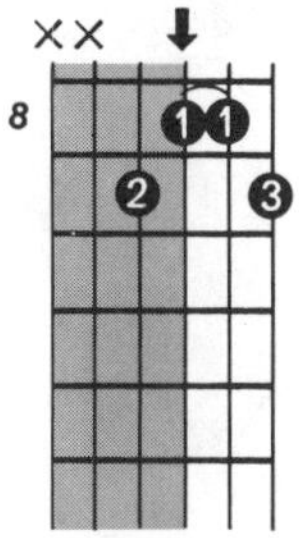

B E♭G D♭

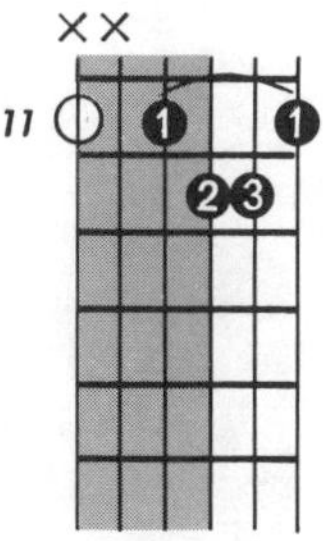

D♭G B E♭

D♯ 7+5

E♭ 9+5

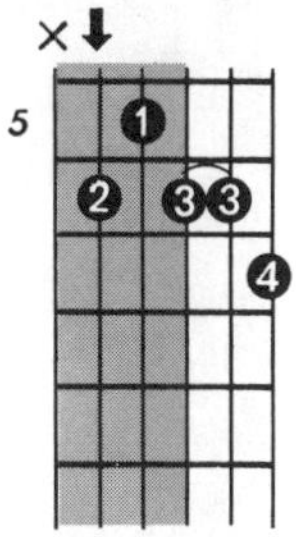

E♭G D♭F B

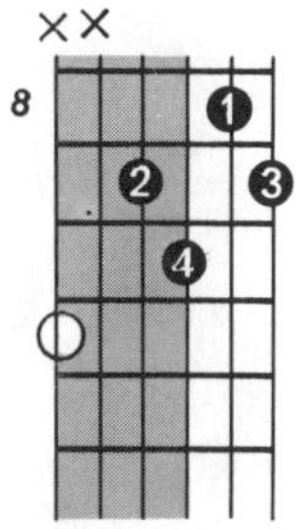

B F G D♭

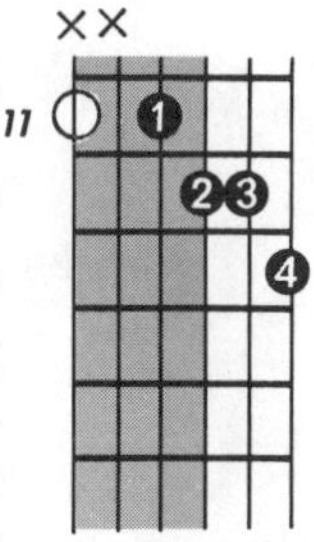

D♭G B F

D♯ 9+5

E♭

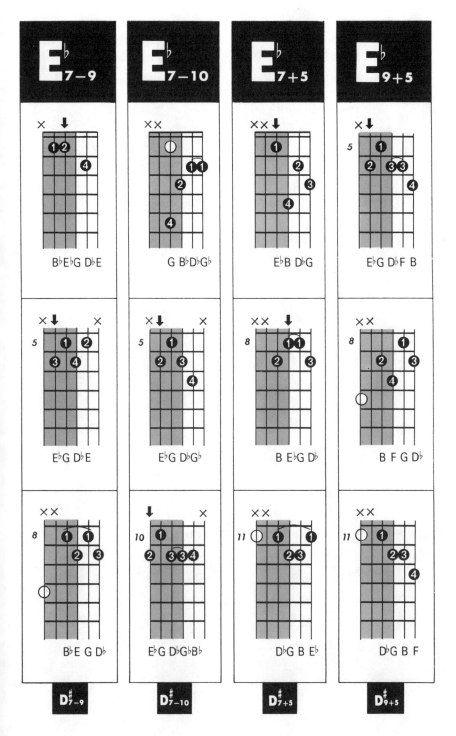

$E^{\flat\,-9}_{7+5}$

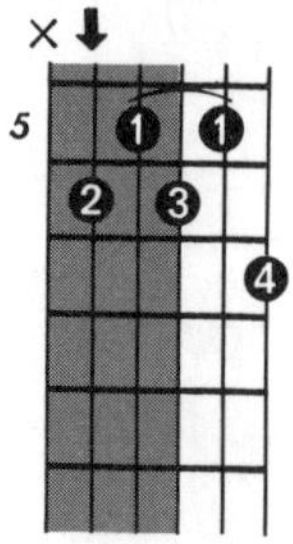

E♭G D♭E B

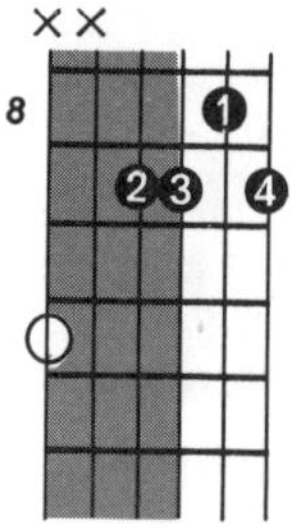

B E G D♭

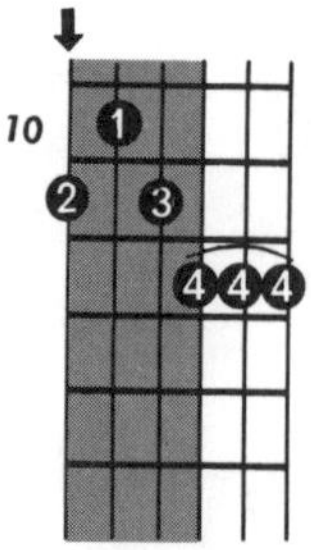

E♭G D♭G B E

$D^{\sharp\,-9}_{7+5}$

$E^{\flat}_{6\cdot 9}$

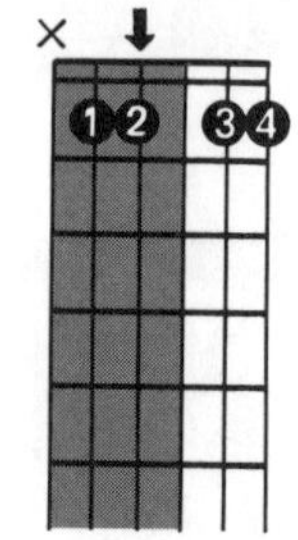

B♭E♭G C F

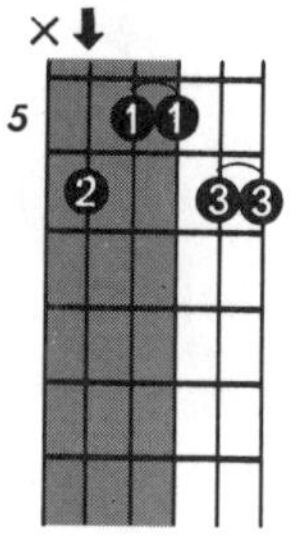

E♭G C F B♭

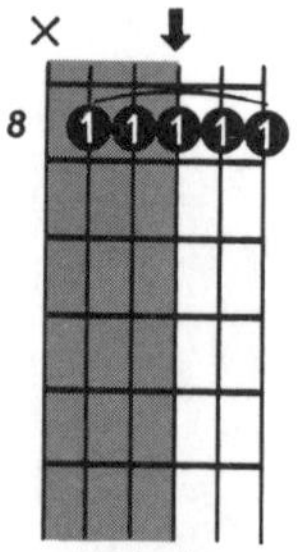

F B♭E♭G C

$D^{\sharp}_{6\cdot 9}$

$E^{\flat}_{dim}$

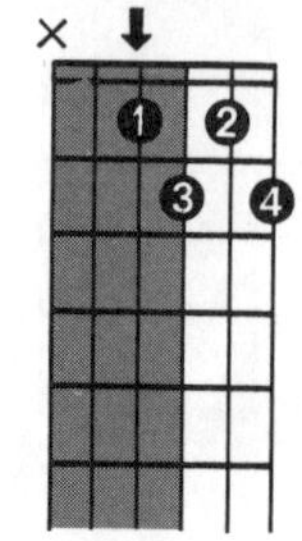

A E♭A C F♯

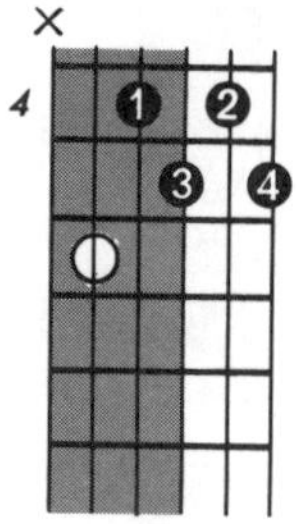

A F♯C E♭A

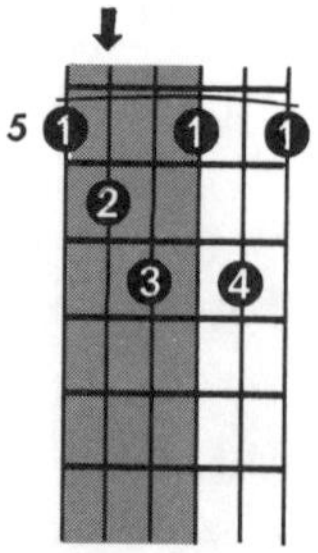

A E♭A C F♯A

$D^{\sharp}_{dim}$

$E^{\flat}_{+5}$

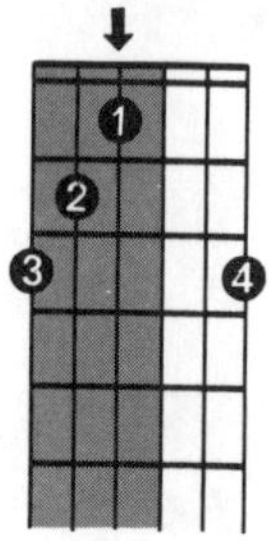

G B E♭G B G

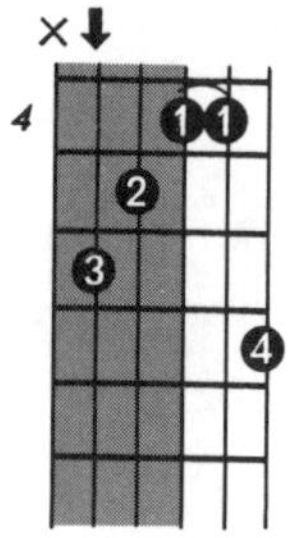

E♭G B E♭B

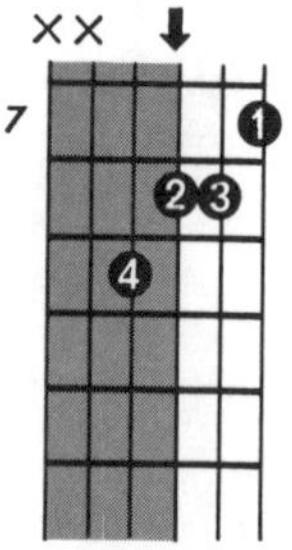

B E♭G B

$D^{\sharp}_{+5}$

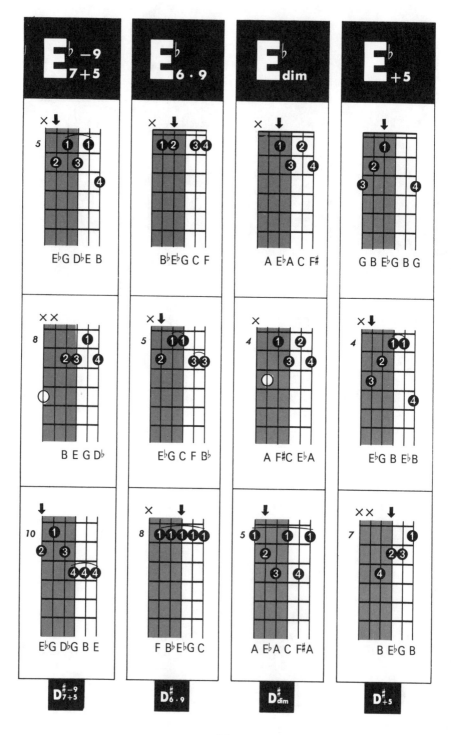

E♭sus4

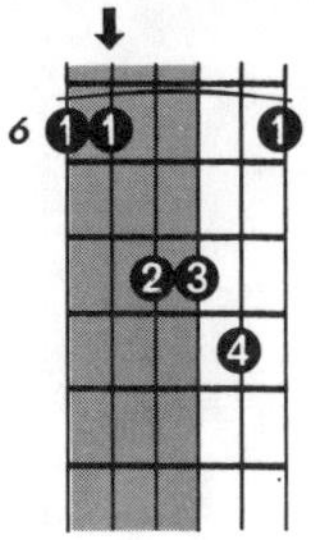

B♭E♭B♭E♭A♭B♭

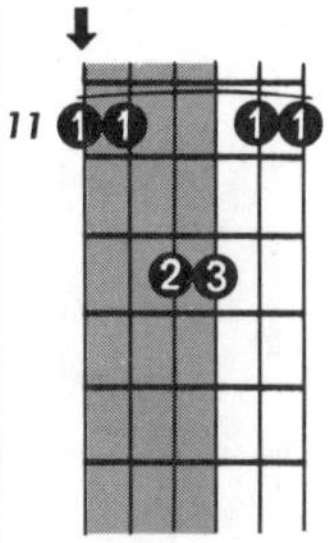

E♭A♭E♭A♭B♭E♭

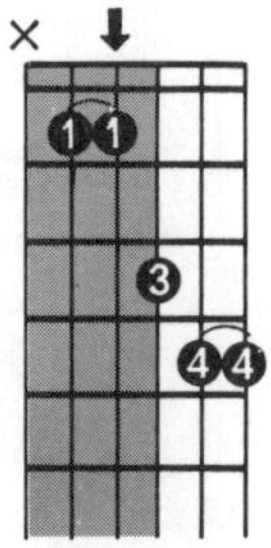

B♭E♭B♭E♭A♭

D♯sus4

E♭7sus4

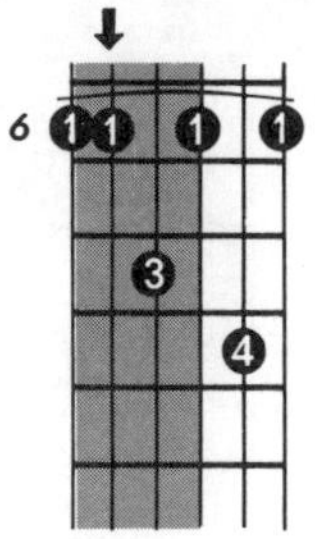

B♭E♭B♭D♭A♭B♭

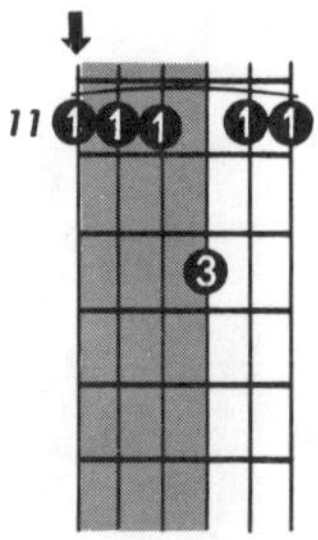

E♭A♭D♭A♭B♭E♭

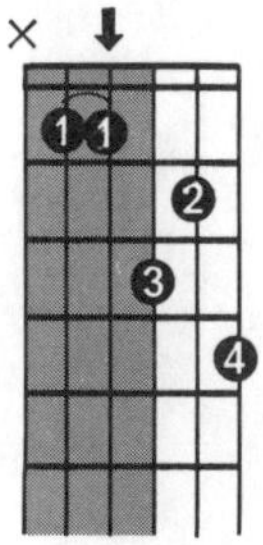

B♭E♭B♭D♭A♭

D♯7sus4

E♭m

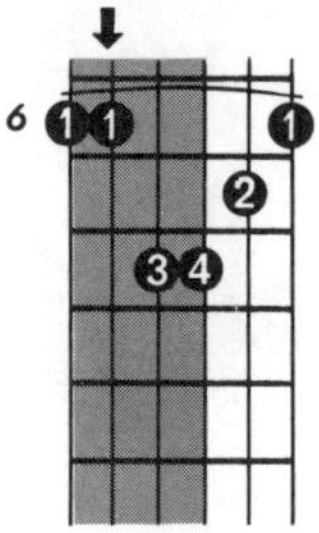

B♭E♭B♭E♭G♭B♭

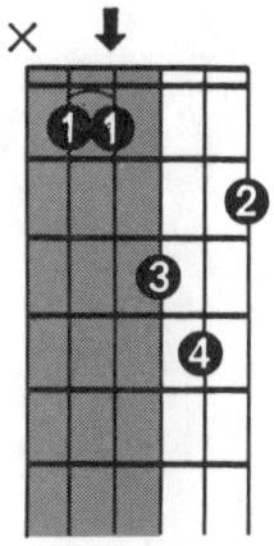

B♭E♭B♭E♭G♭

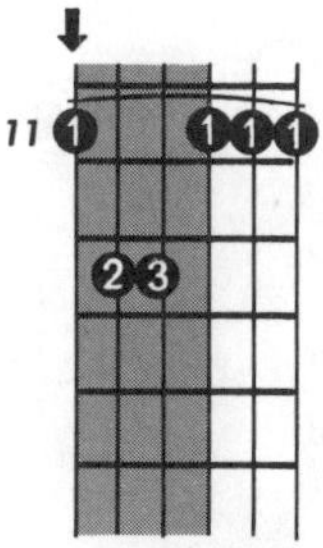

E♭B♭E♭G♭B♭E♭

D♯m

E♭m6

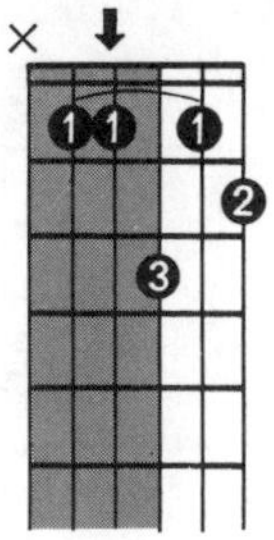

B♭E♭B♭C G♭

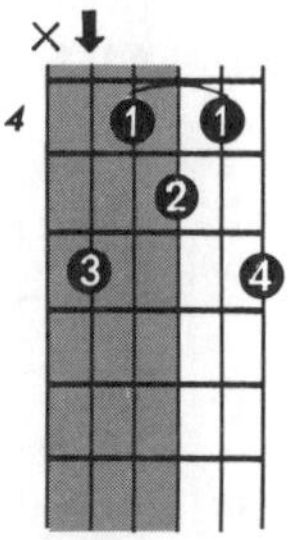

E♭G♭C E♭B♭

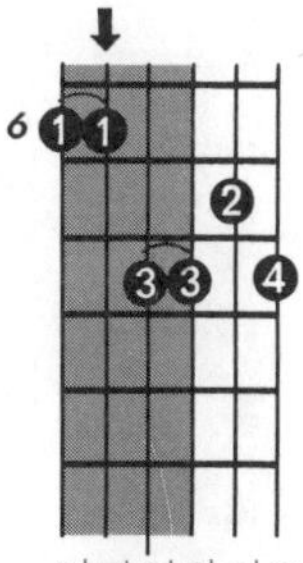

B♭E♭B♭E♭G♭C

D♯m6

E♭

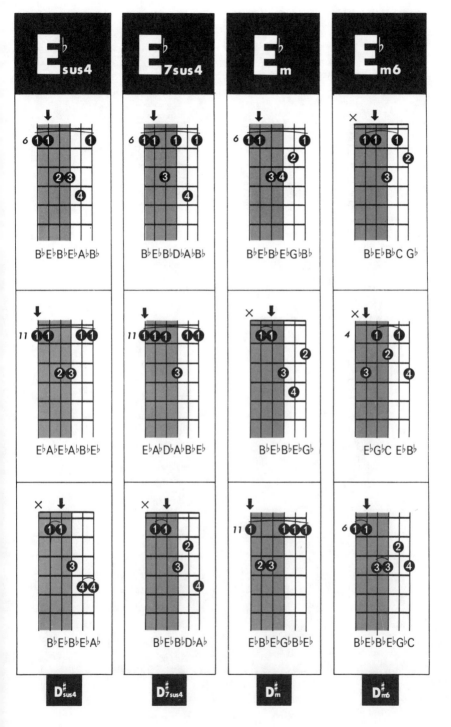

D♯

E♭m7

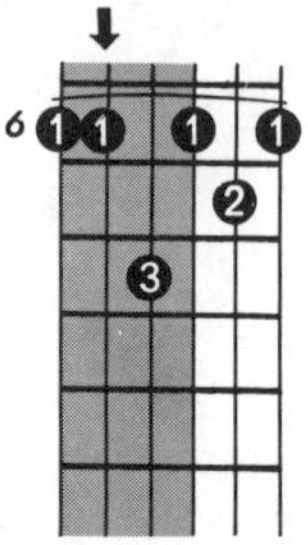

B♭E♭B♭D♭G♭B♭

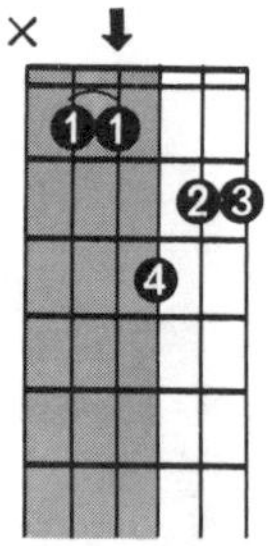

B♭E♭B♭D♭G♭

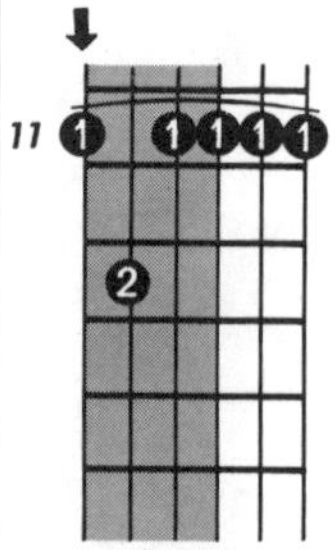

E♭B♭D♭G♭B♭E♭

D♯m7

E♭m9

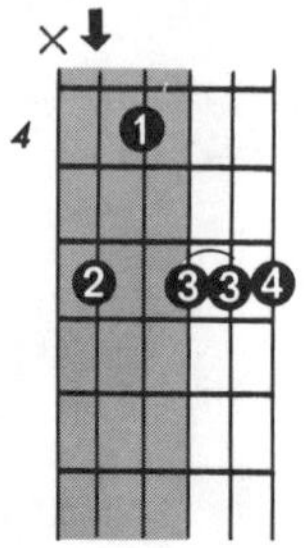

E♭G♭D♭F B♭

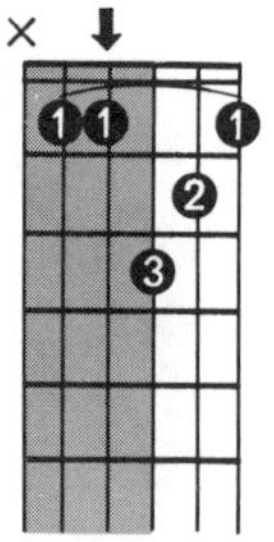

B♭E♭B♭D♭F

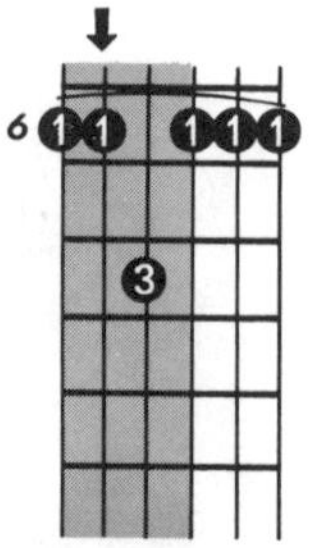

B♭E♭B♭D♭F B♭

D♯m9

E♭m7−5

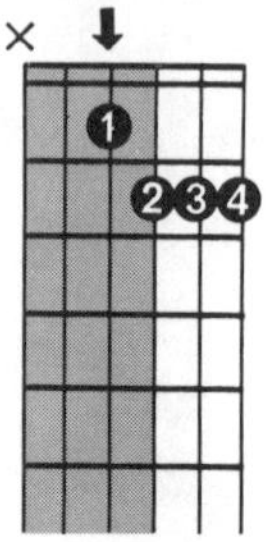

A E♭A D♭G♭

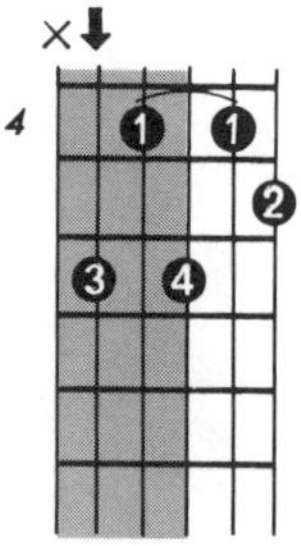

E♭G♭D♭E♭A

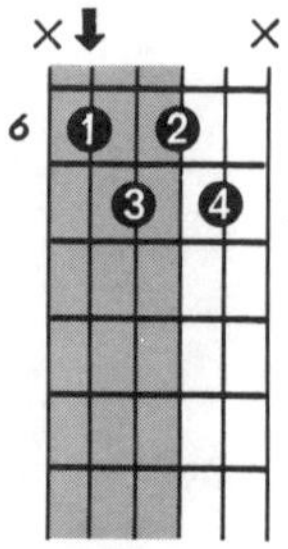

E♭A D♭G♭

D♯m7−5

E♭m7−9

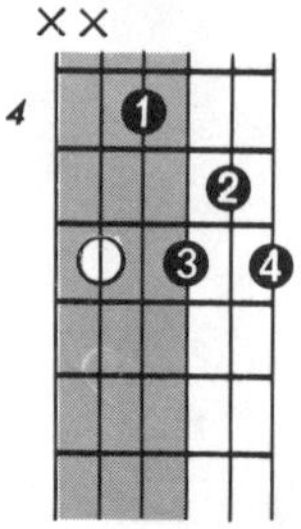

G♭D♭E B♭

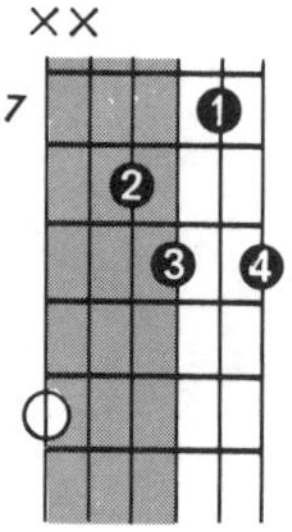

B♭E G♭D♭

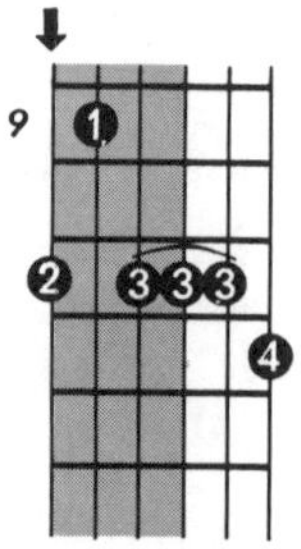

E♭G♭D♭G♭B♭E

D♯m7−9

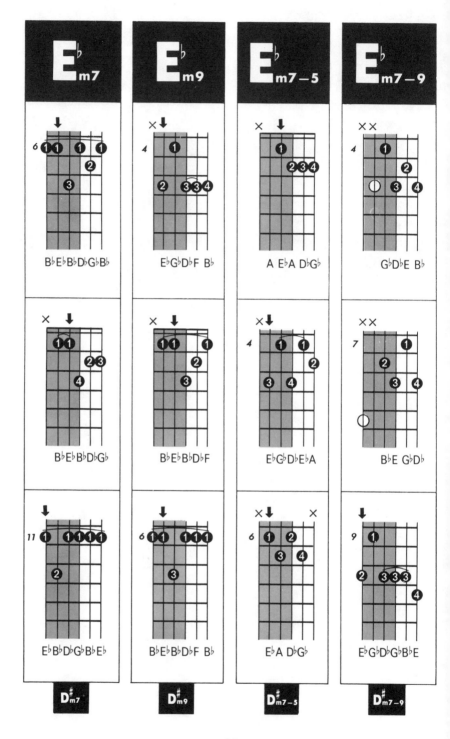

E♭m+7

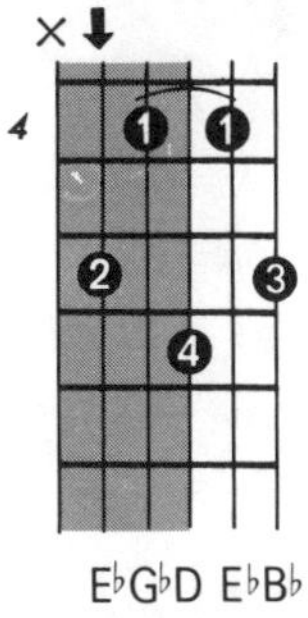

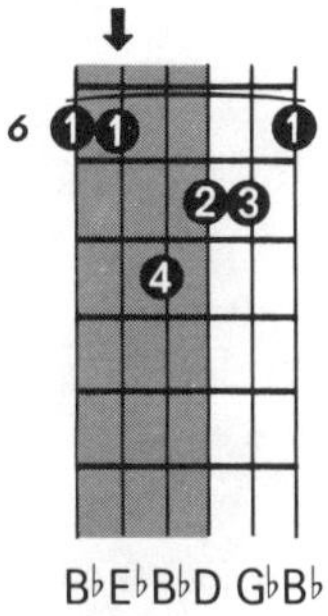

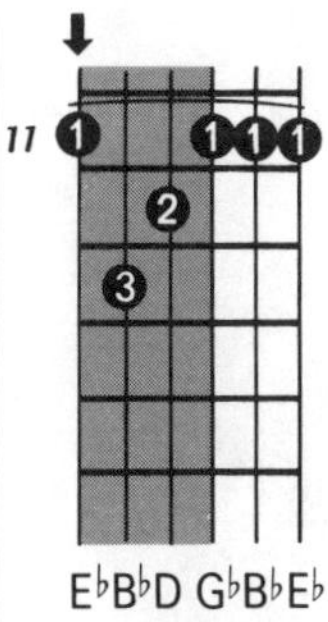

D♯m+7

E♭m9+7

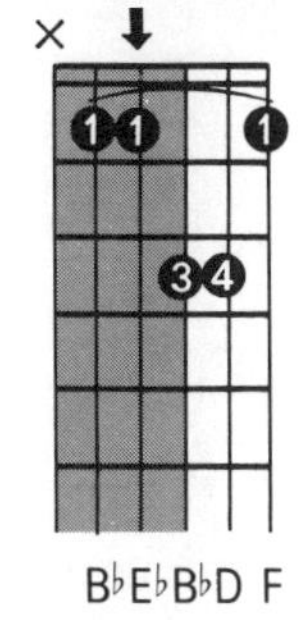

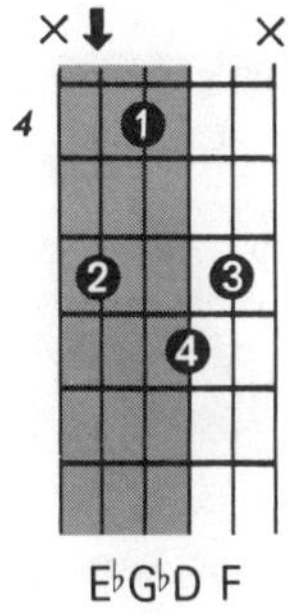

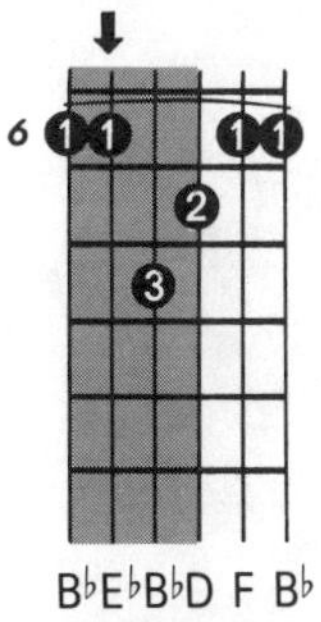

D♯m9+7

E♭m+5

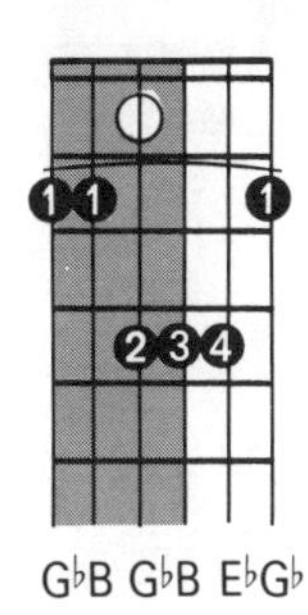

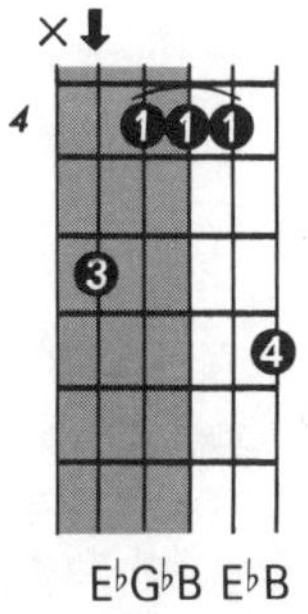

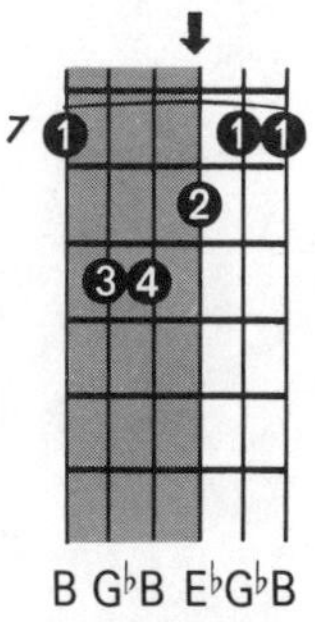

D♯m+5

E♭m6 · 9

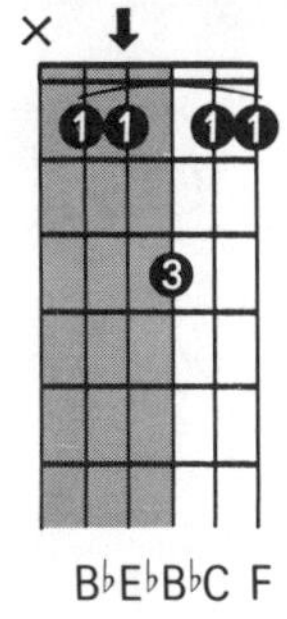

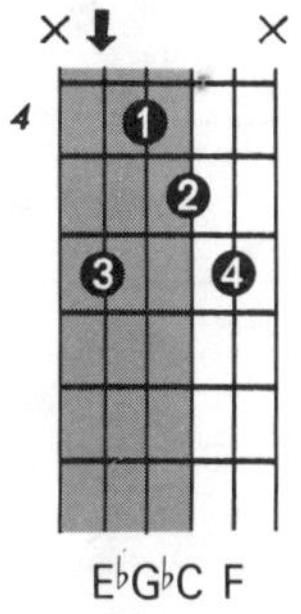

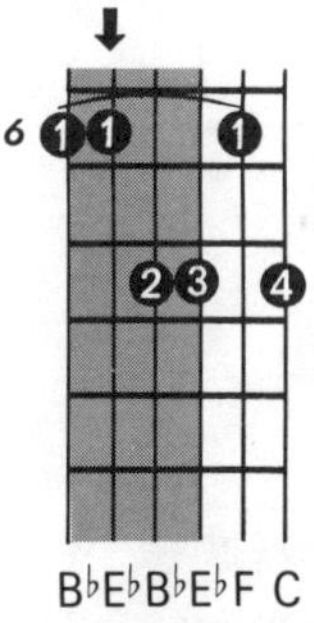

D♯m6 · 9

E♭

E

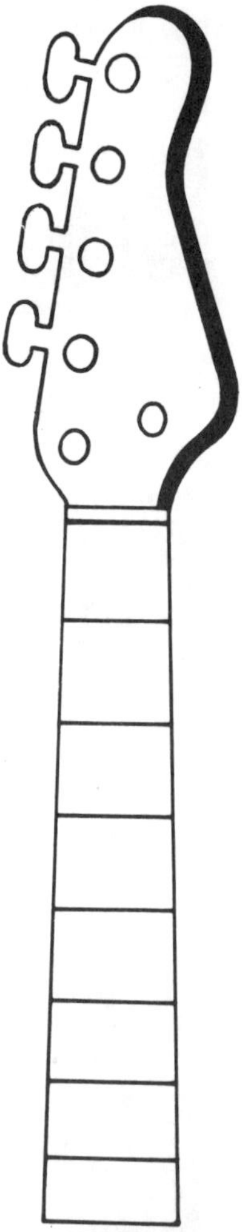

E

E

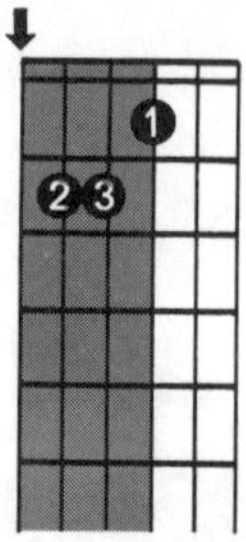
E B E G#B E

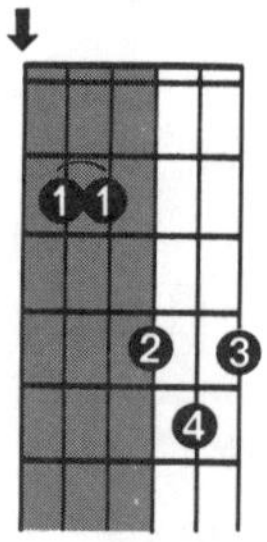
E B E B E G#

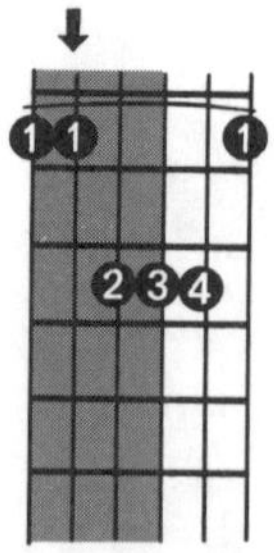
7
B E B E G#B

E6

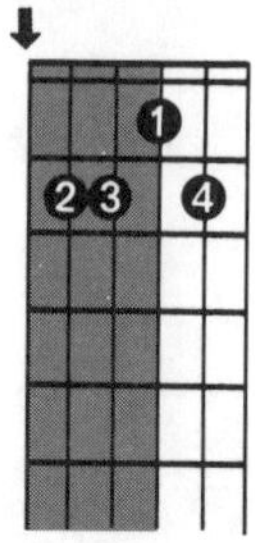
E B E G#C#E

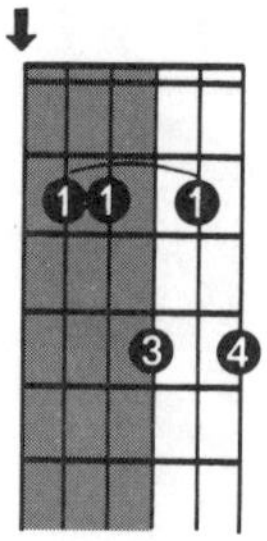
E B E B C#G#

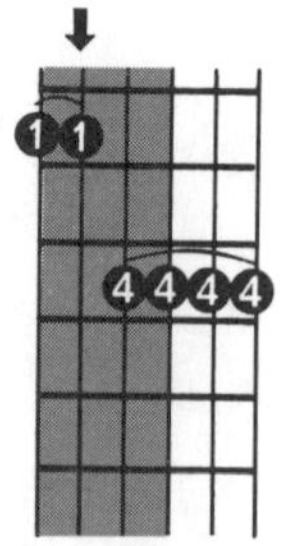
7
B E B E G#C#

E7

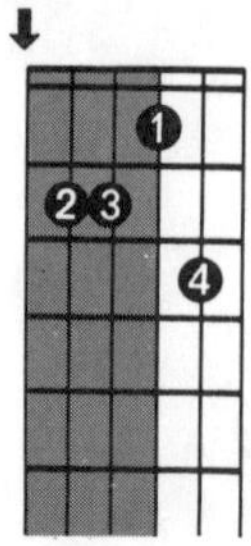
E B E G#D E

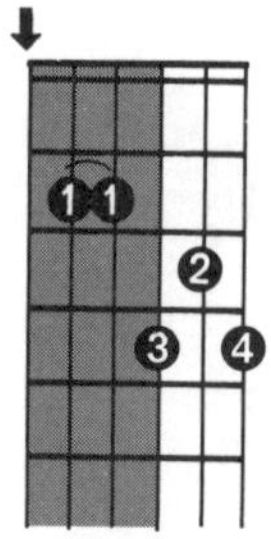
E B E B D G#

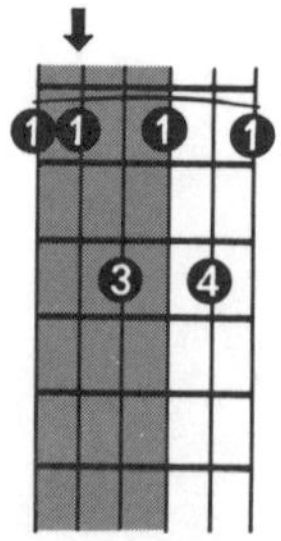
7
B E B D G#B

E_9

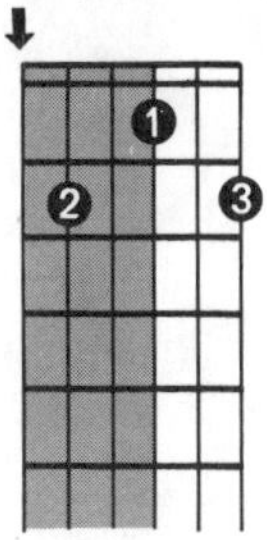

E B D G♯B F♯

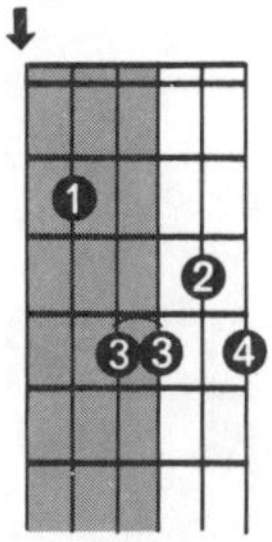

E B F♯B D G♯

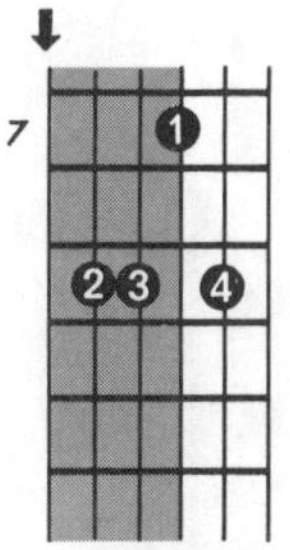

E F♯B D G♯E

E_{11}

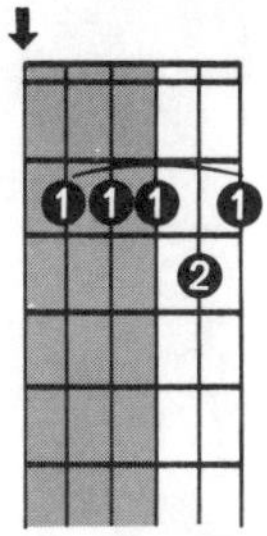

E B E A D F♯

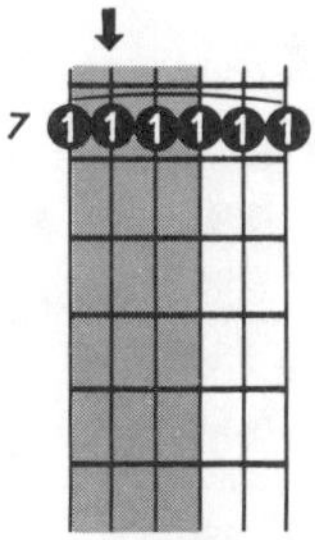

B E A D F♯B

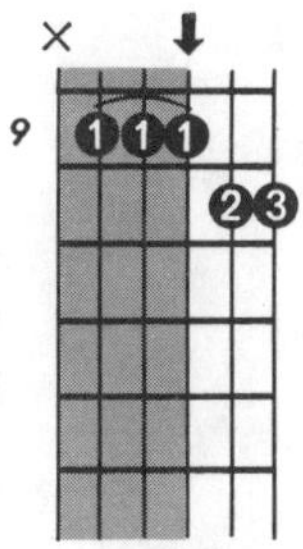

F♯B E A D

E_{11+}

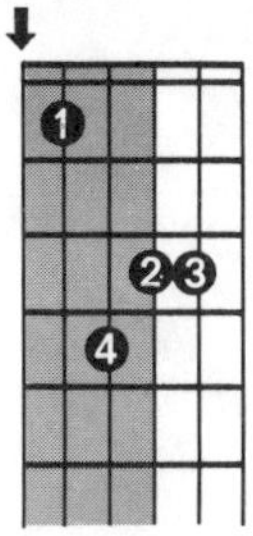

E A♯F♯A♯D E

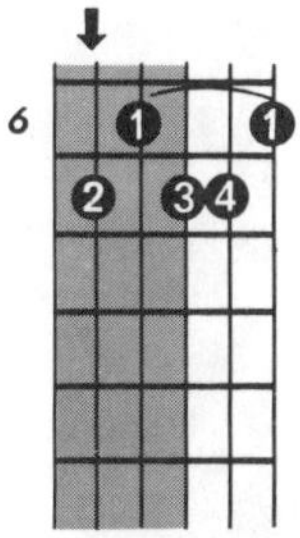

E E G♯D F♯A♯

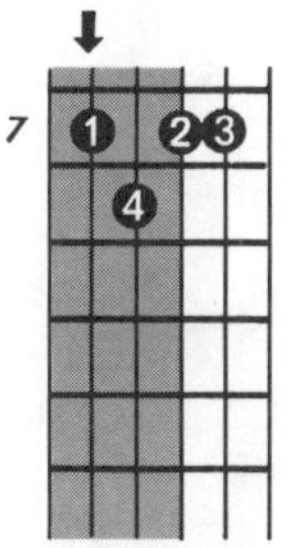

E E A♯D F♯E

E_{13}

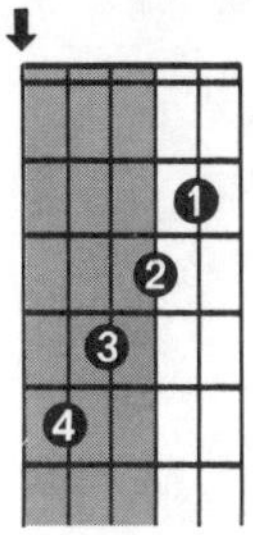

E D F♯A♯C♯E

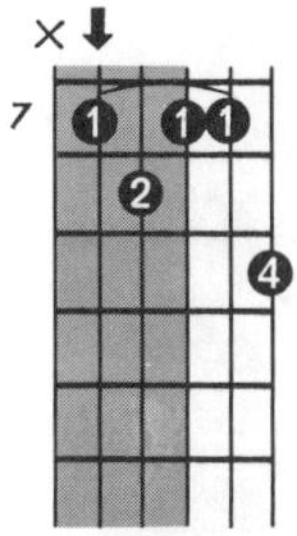

E A♯D F♯C♯

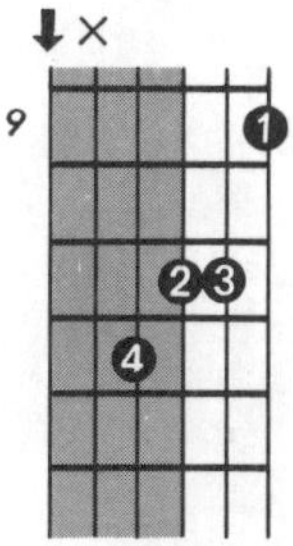

E D F♯A♯C♯

E

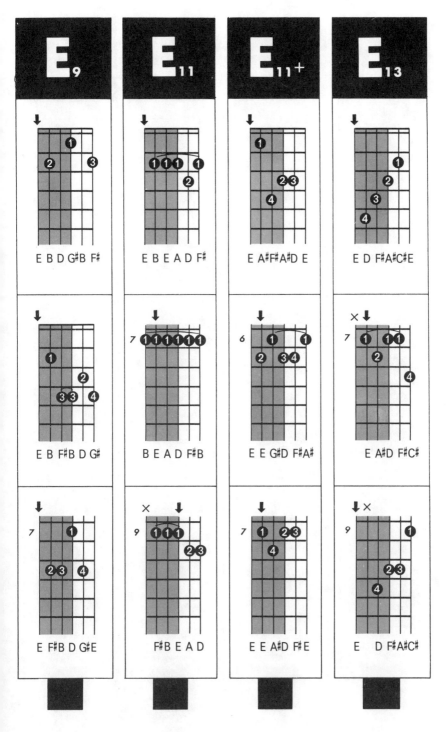

E

Emaj7

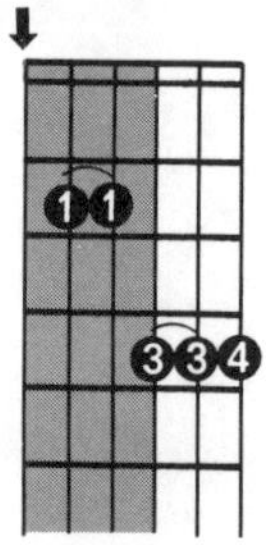

E B E B D♯G♯

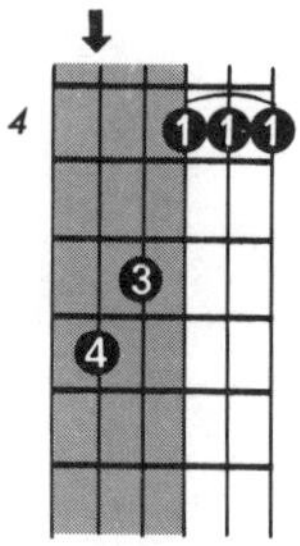

E E G♯B D♯G♯

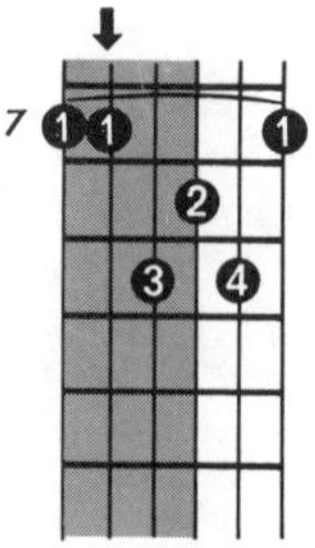

B E B D♯G♯B

Emaj9

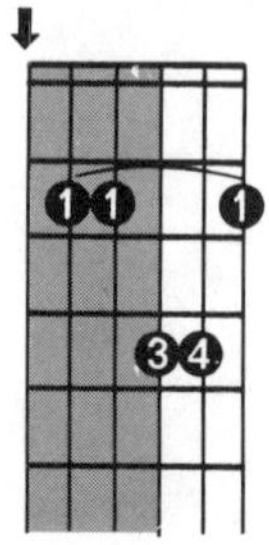

E B E B D♯F♯

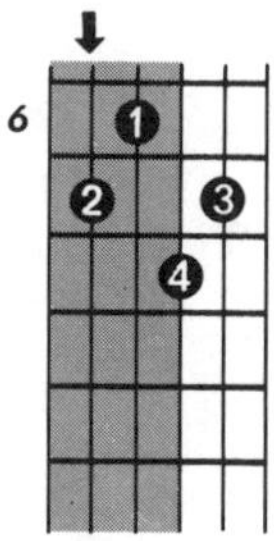

E E G♯D♯F♯E

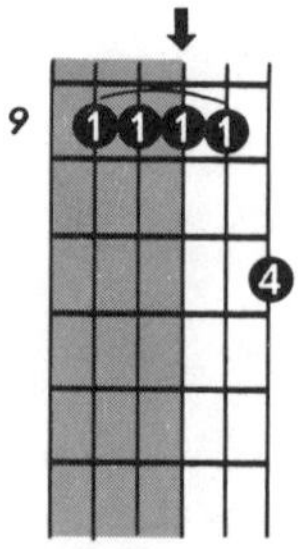

E F♯B E G♯D♯

Emaj11

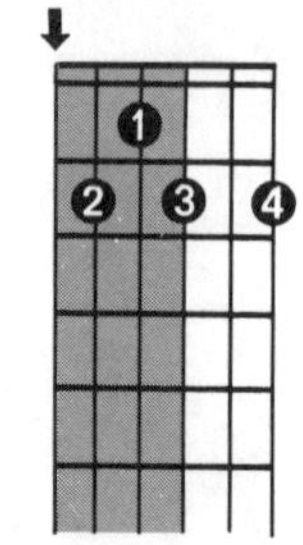

E B D♯A B F♯

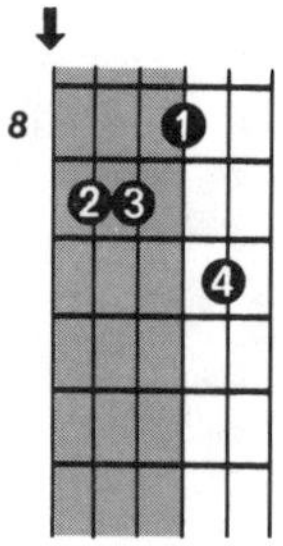

E F♯B D♯A E

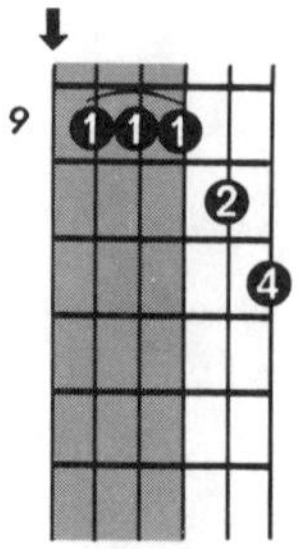

E F♯B E A D♯

E7–5

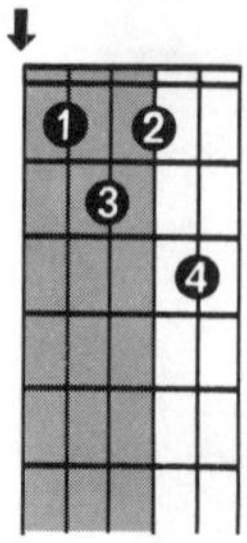

E B♭E G♯D E

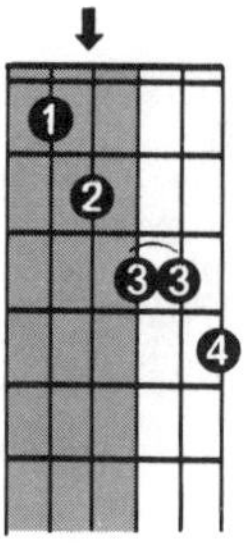

E B♭E B♭D G♯

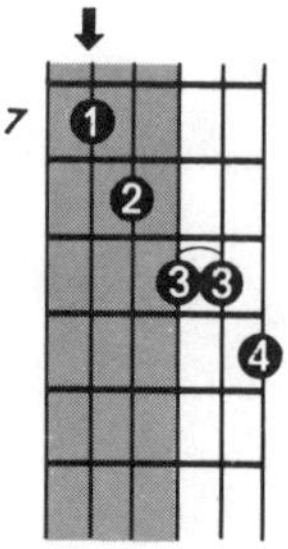

E E B♭E G♯D

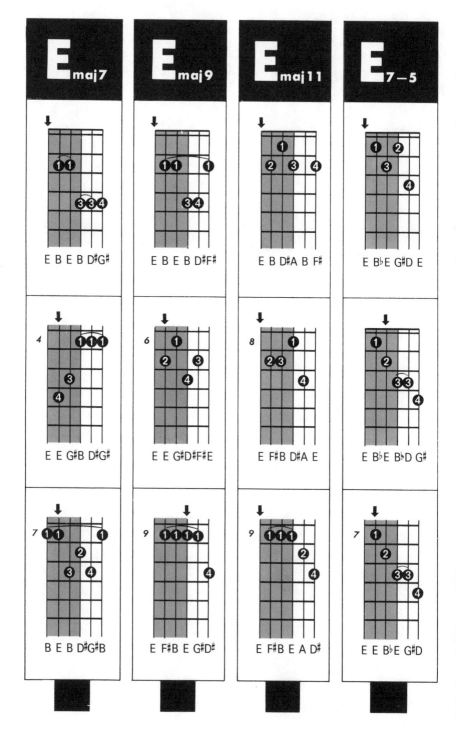

E_{7-9}

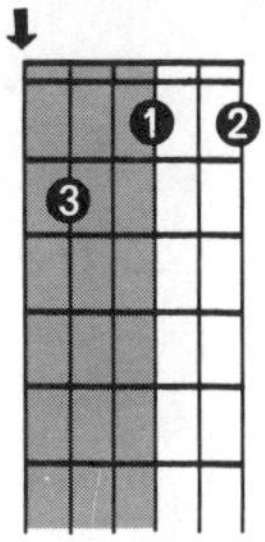

E B D G♯B F

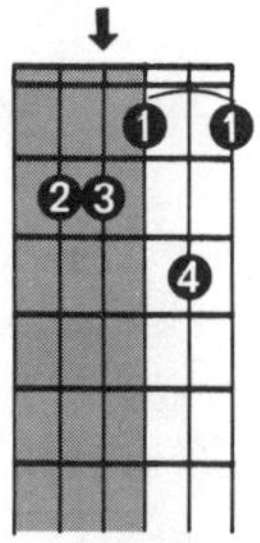

E B E G♯D F

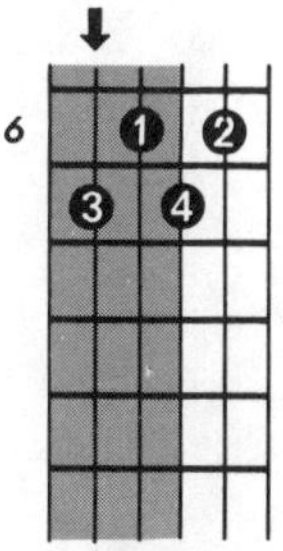

E E G♯D F E

E_{7-10}

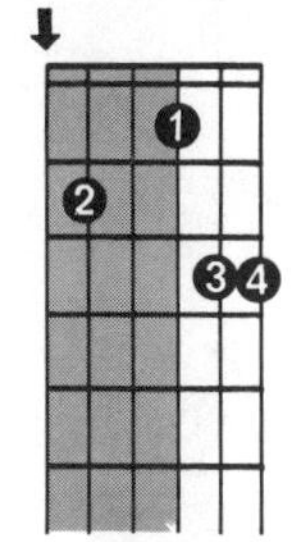

E B D G♯D G

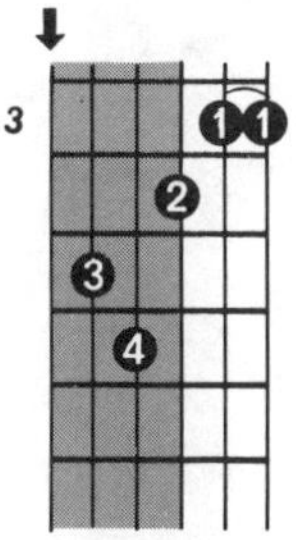

E D G♯B D G

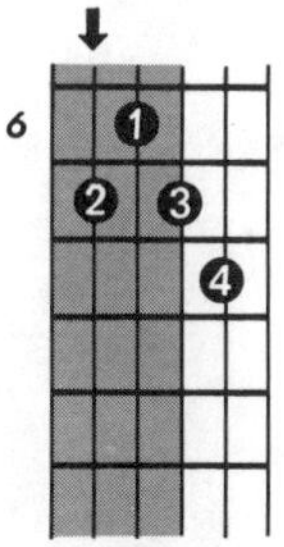

E E G♯D G E

E_{7+5}

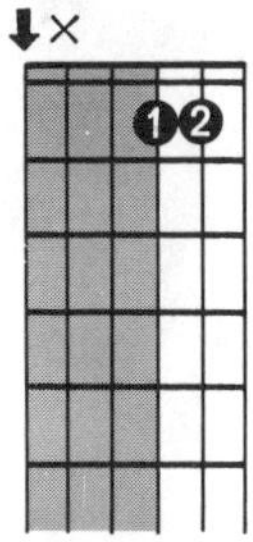

E D G♯C E

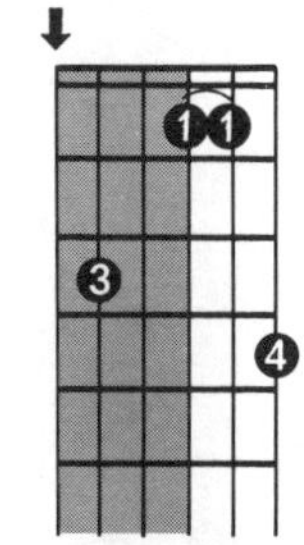

E C D G♯C G♯

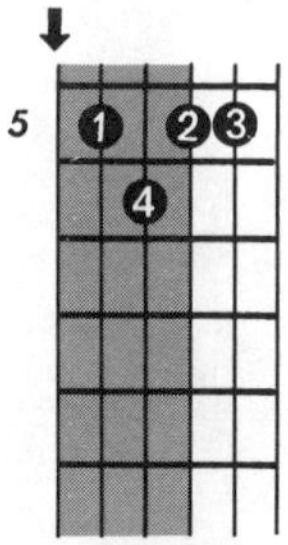

E D G♯C E E

E_{9+5}

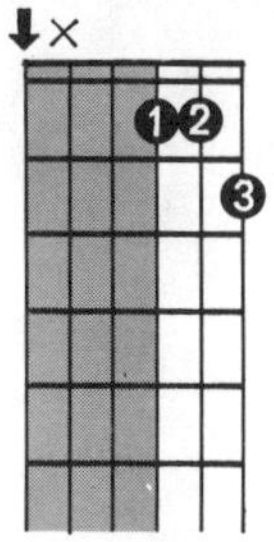

E D G♯C F♯

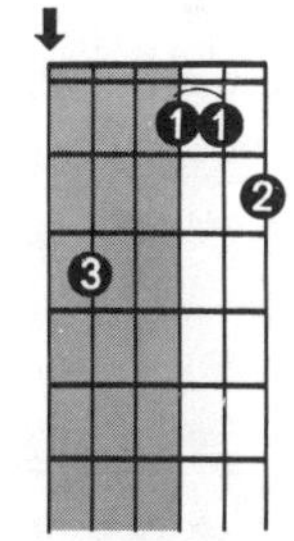

E C D G♯C F♯

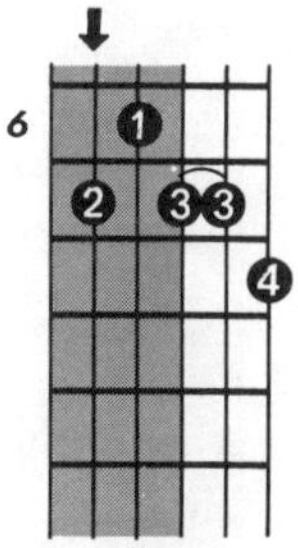

E E G♯D F♯C

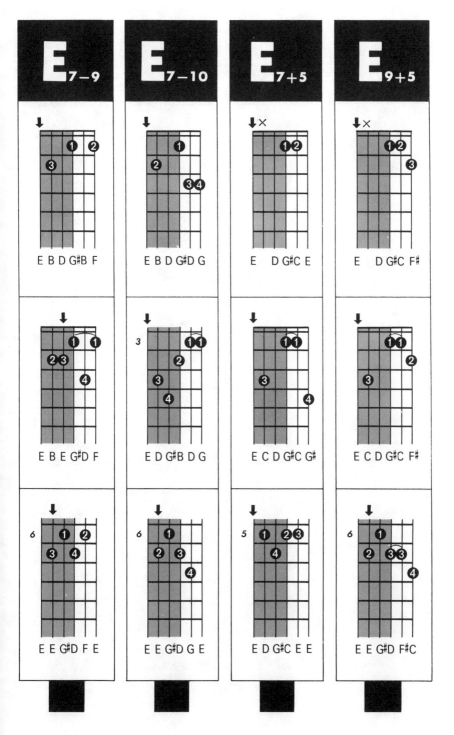

E

E^{-9}_{7+5}

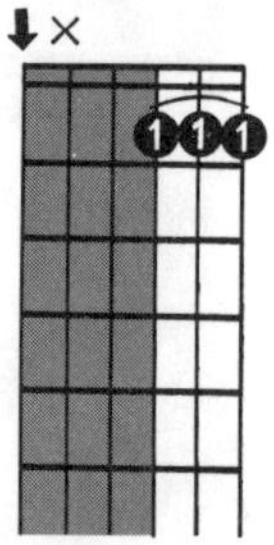

E D G♯C F

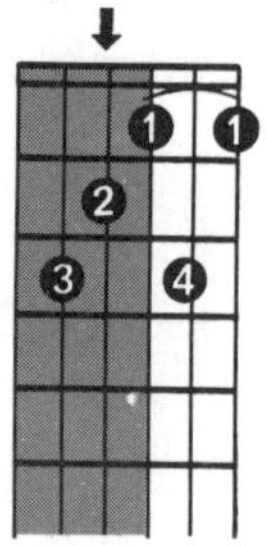

E C E G♯D F

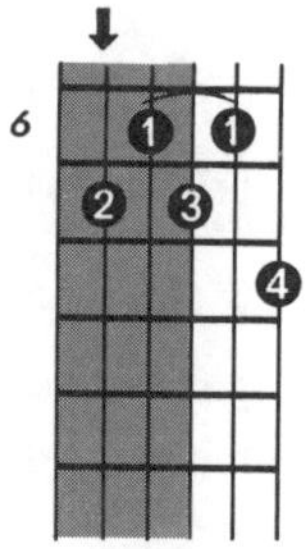

E E G♯D F C

$E_{6 \cdot 9}$

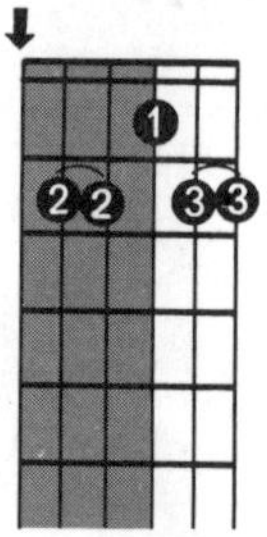

E B E G♯C♯F♯

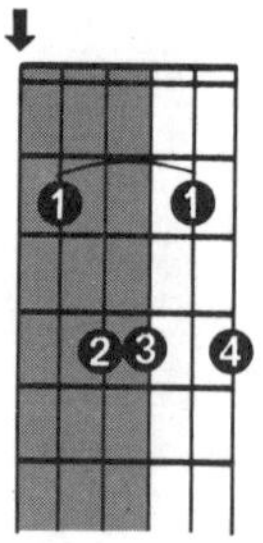

E B F♯B C♯G♯

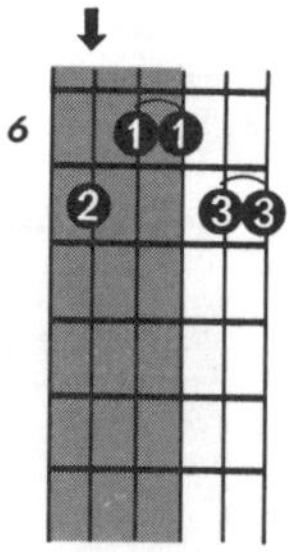

E E G♯C♯F♯B

E_{dim}

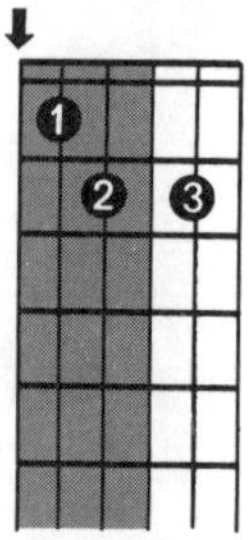

E B♭E G C♯E

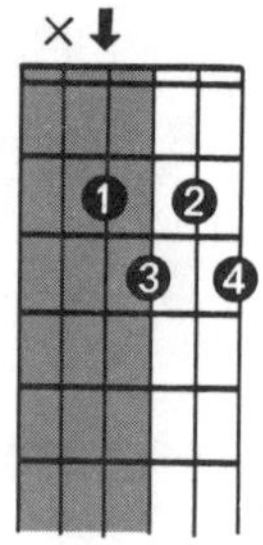

E E B♭C♯G

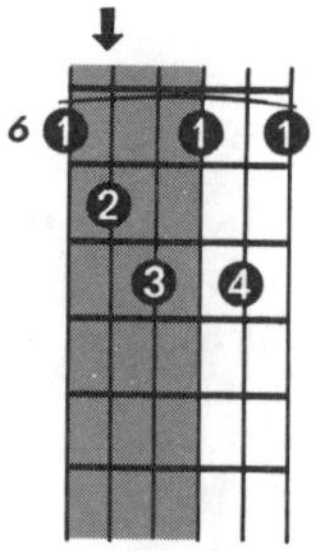

B♭E B♭C♯G B♭

E_{+5}

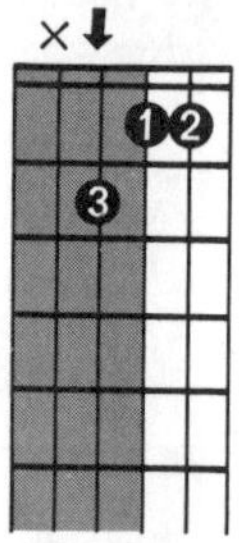

E E G♯C E

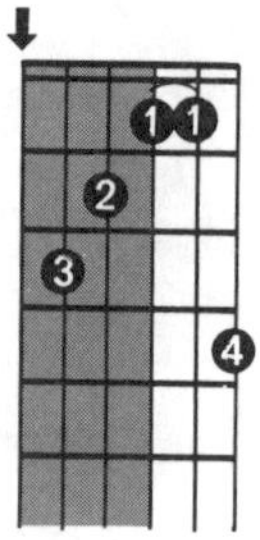

E C E G♯C G♯

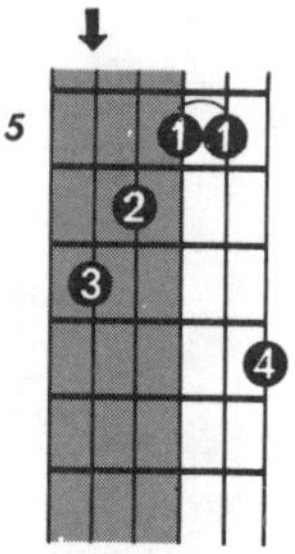

E E G♯C E C

E sus4

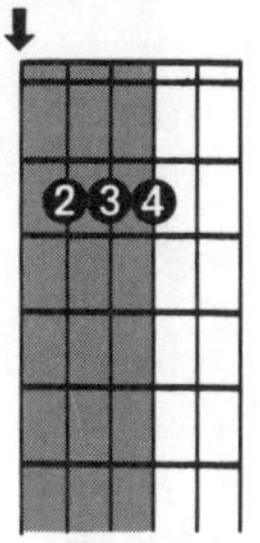

E B E A B E

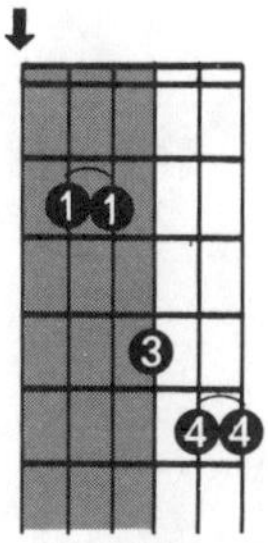

E B E B E A

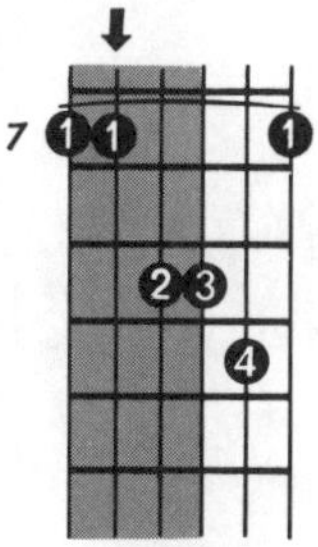

B E B E A B

E 7sus4

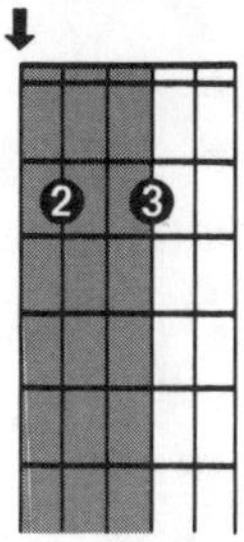

E B D A B E

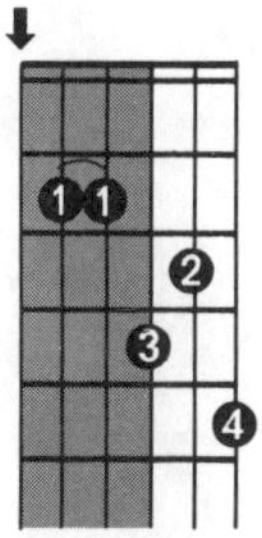

E B E B D A

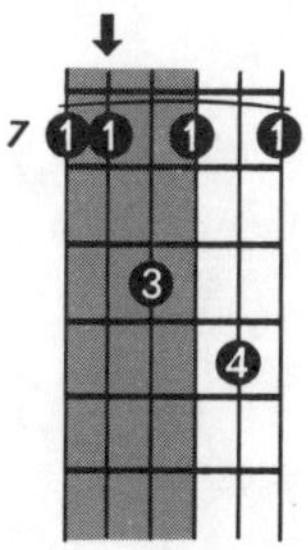

B E B D A B

E m

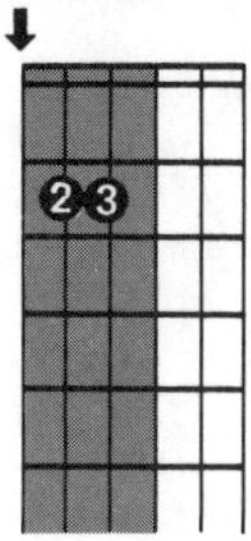

E B E G B E

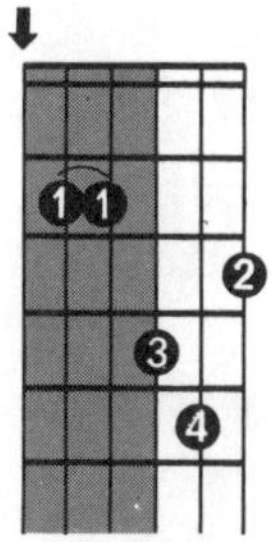

E B E B E G

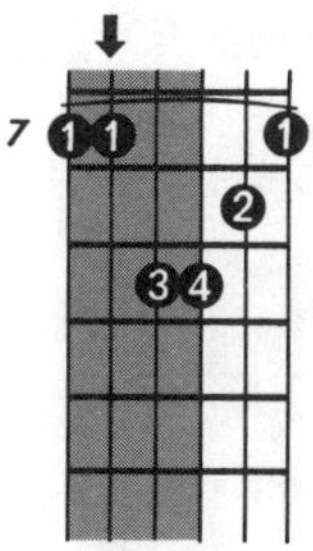

B E B E G B

E m6

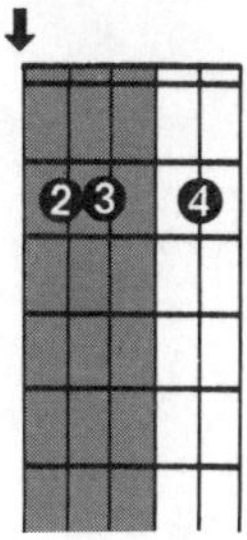

E B E G C♯E

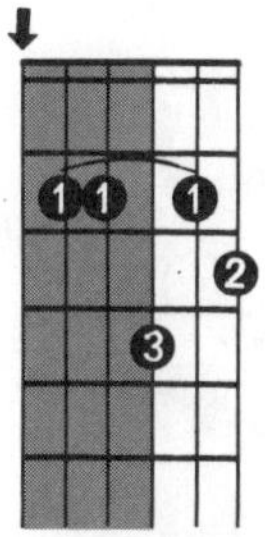

E B E B C♯G

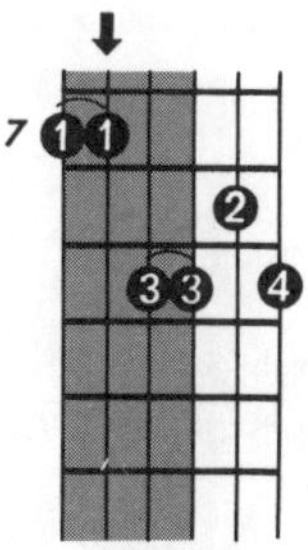

B E B E G C♯

E

Em7

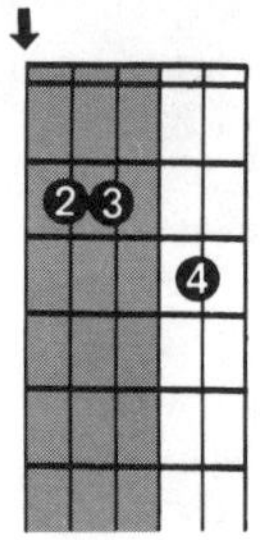

E B E G D E

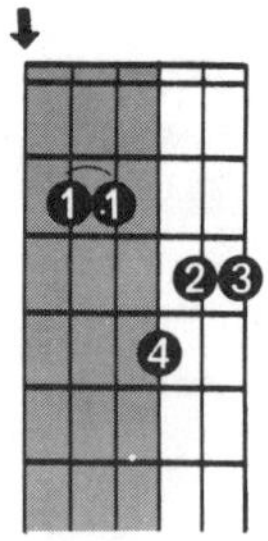

E B E B D G

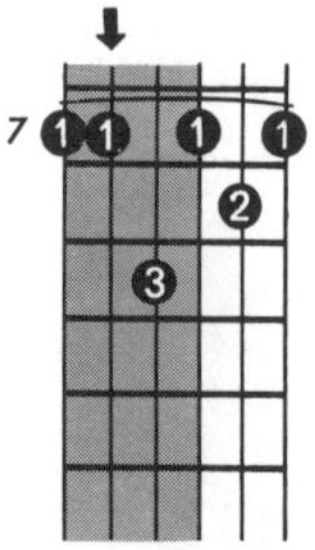

B E B D G B

Em9

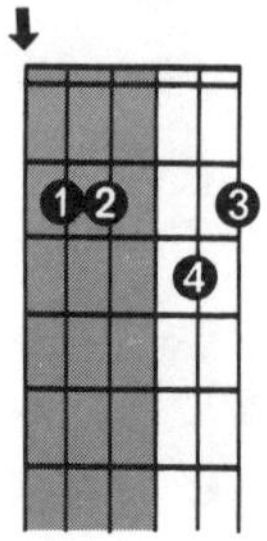

E B E G D F♯

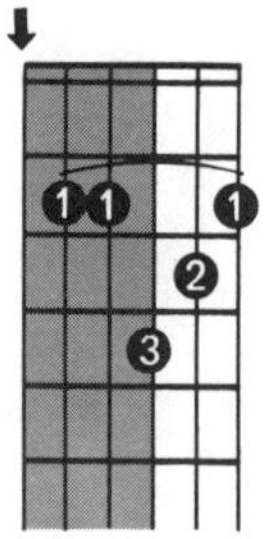

E B E B D F♯

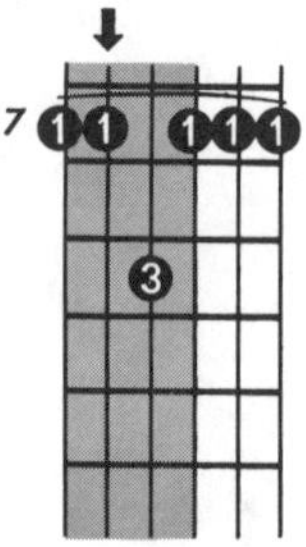

B E B D F♯B

Em7–5

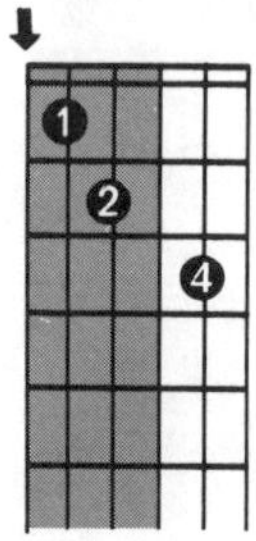

E B♭E G D E

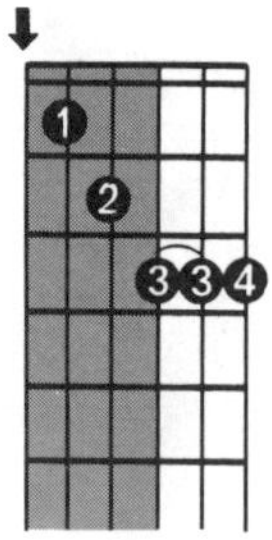

E B♭E B♭D G

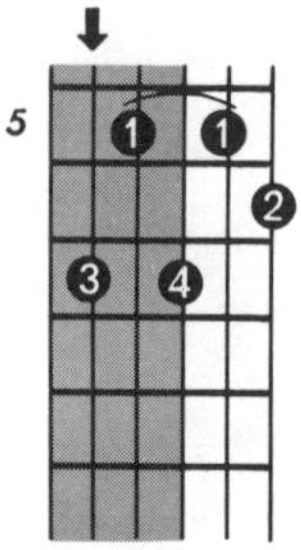

E E G D E B♭

Em7–9

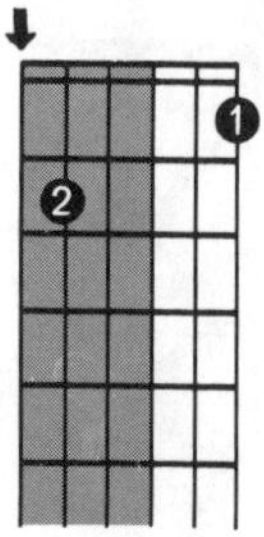

E B D G B F

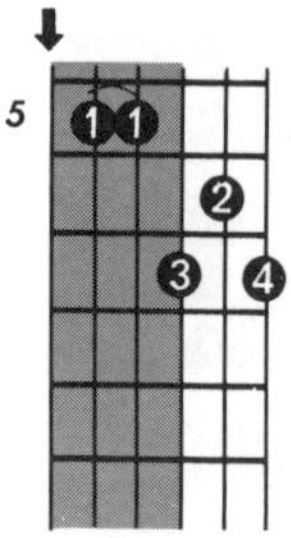

E D G D F B

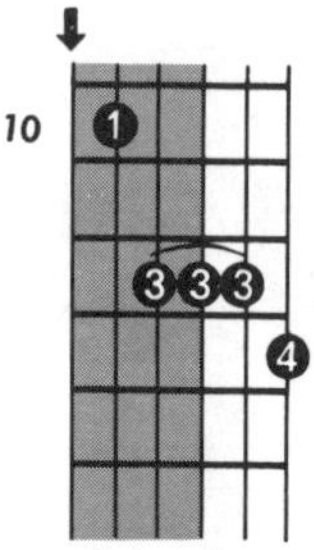

E G D G B F

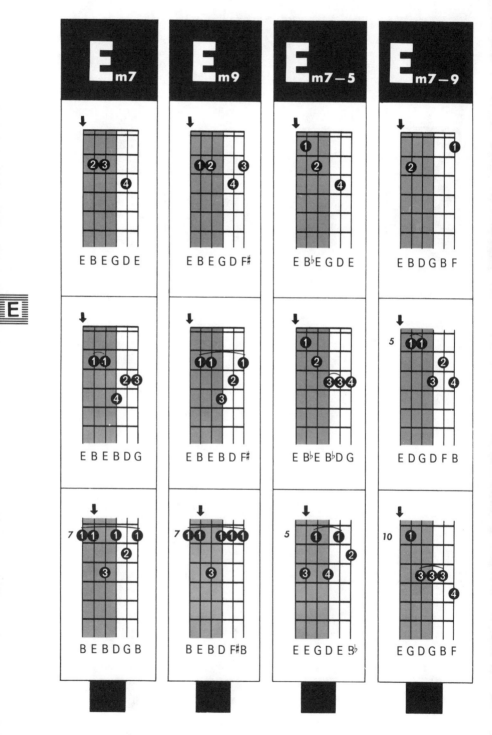

Em+7

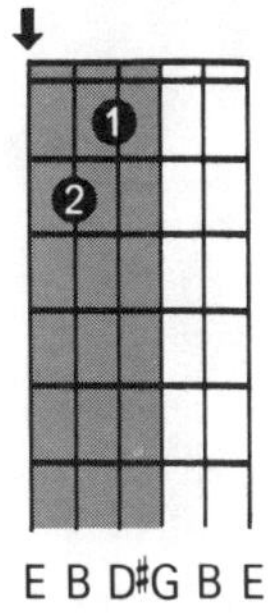

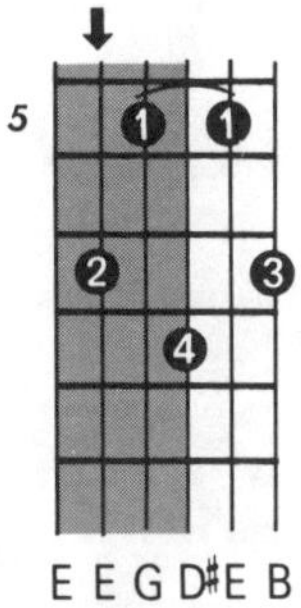

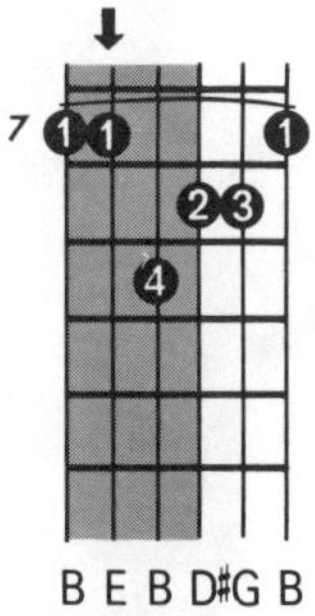

Em9+7

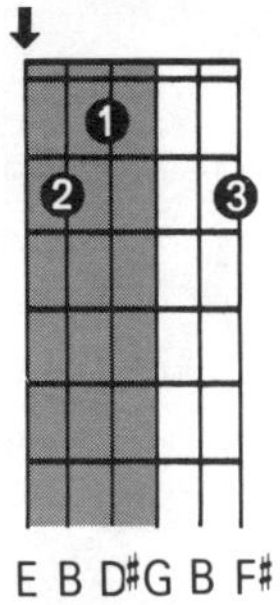

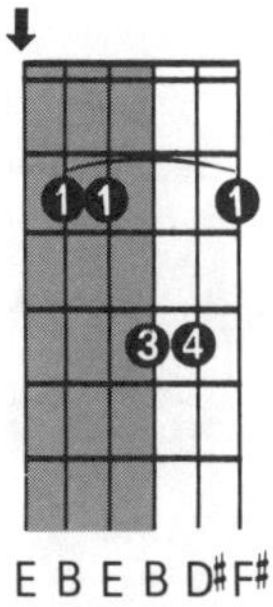

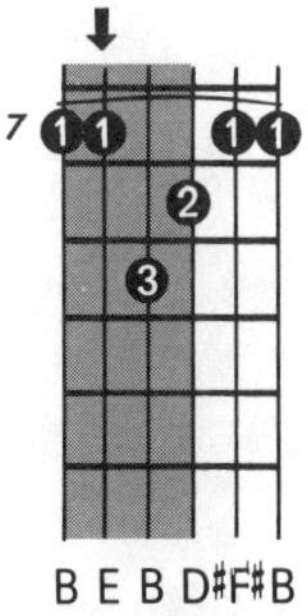

Em+5

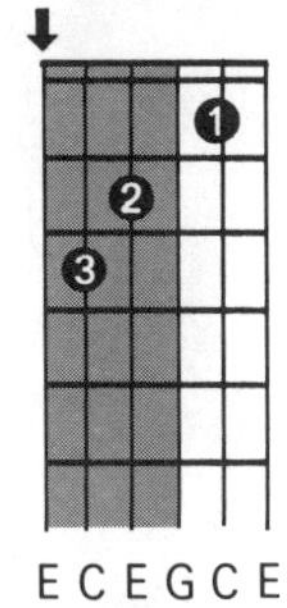

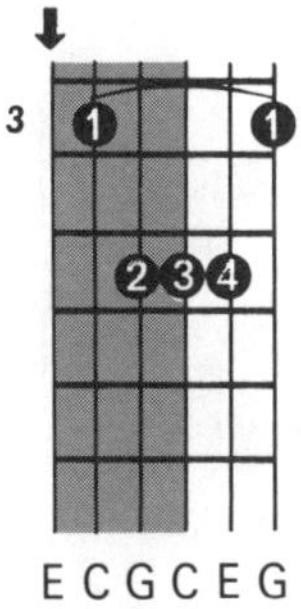

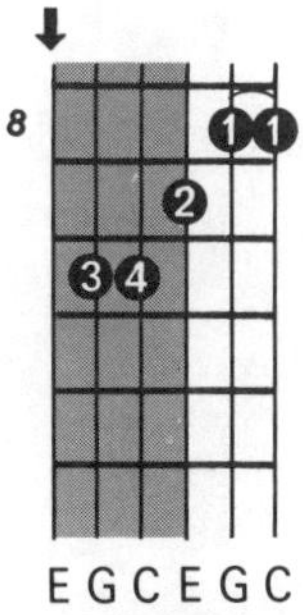

Em6 · 9

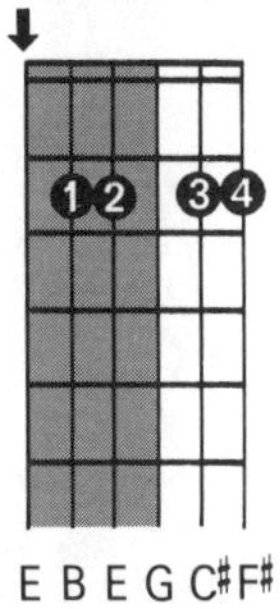

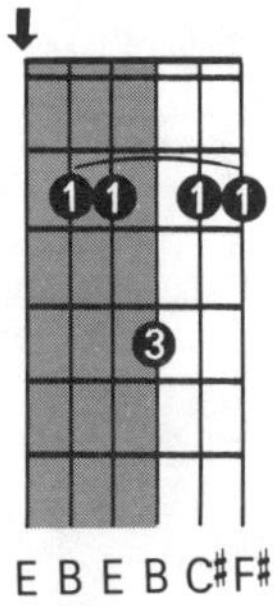

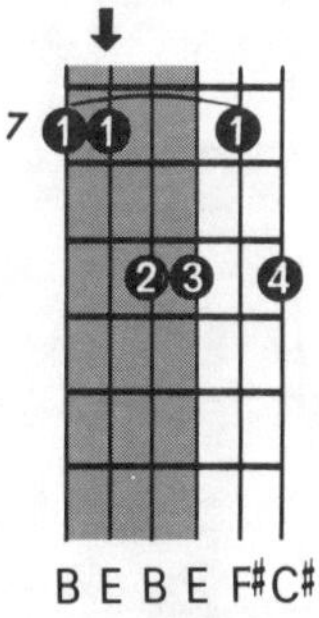

E

F

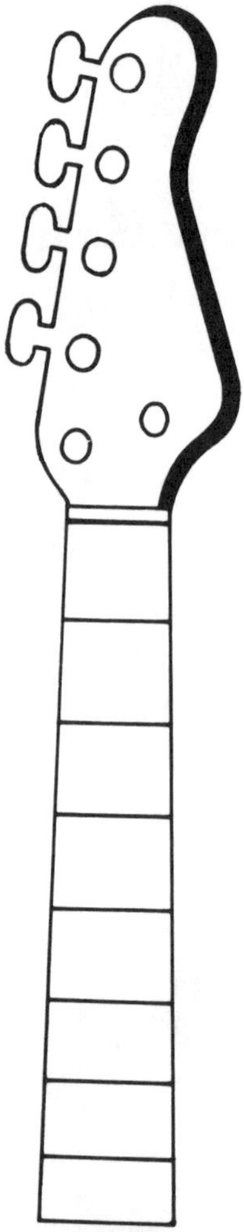

F

F

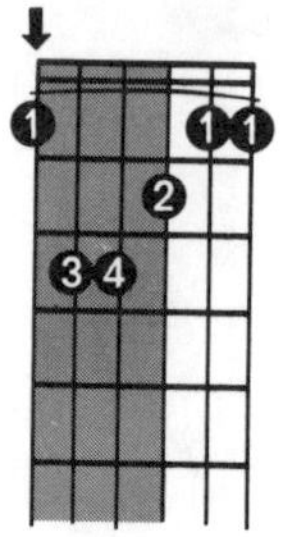

F C F A C F

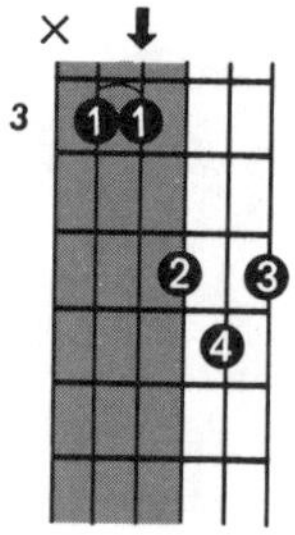

C F C F A

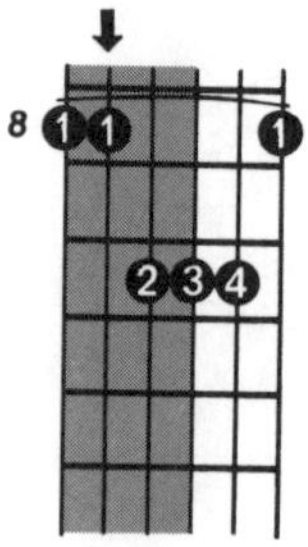

C F C F A C

F6

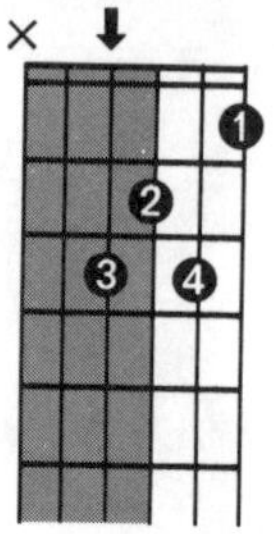

A F A D F

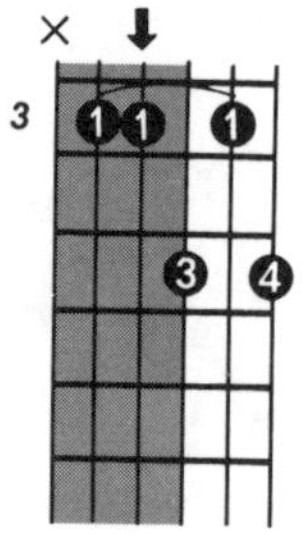

C F C D A

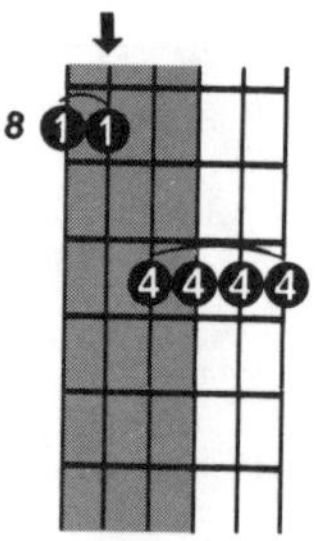

C F C F A D

F7

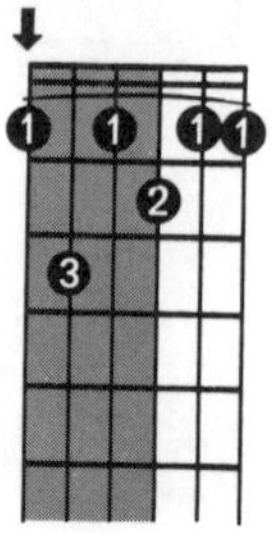

F C E♭ A C F

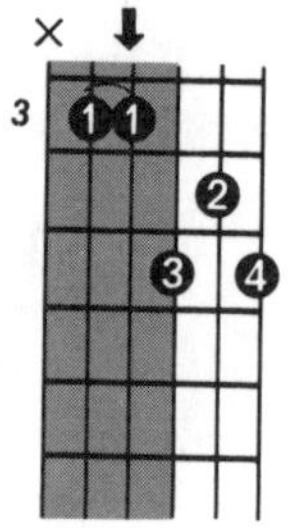

C F C E♭ A

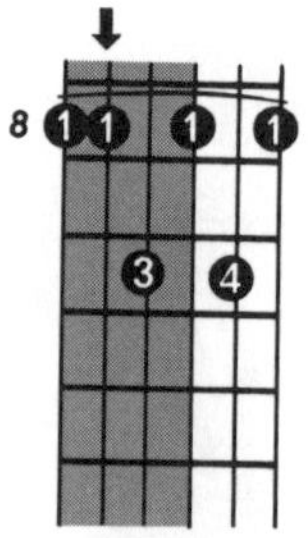

C F C E♭ A C

F9

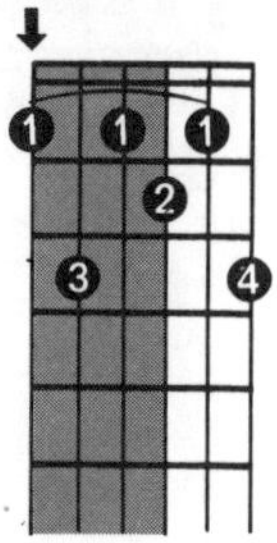

F C E♭A C G

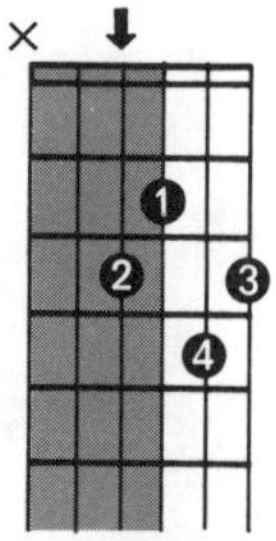

A F A E♭G

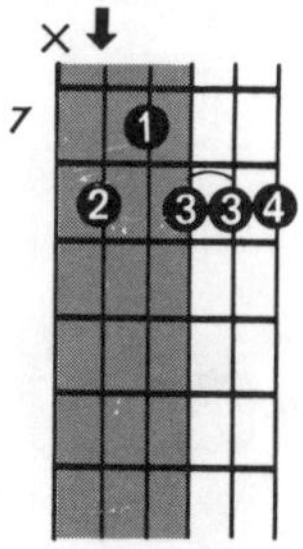

F A E♭G C

F11

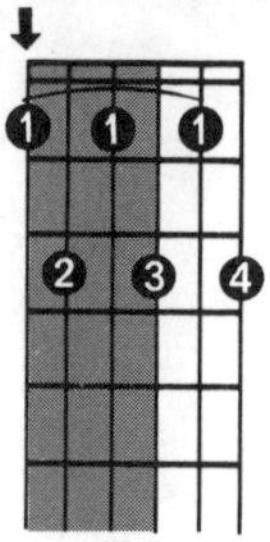

F C E♭B♭C G

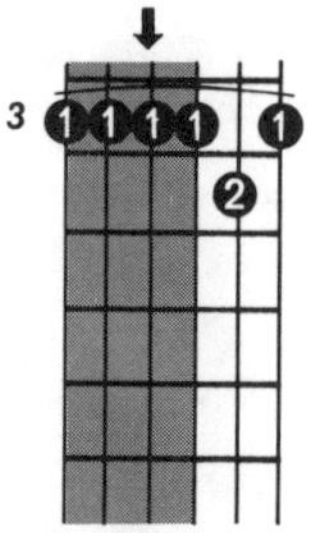

G C F B♭E♭G

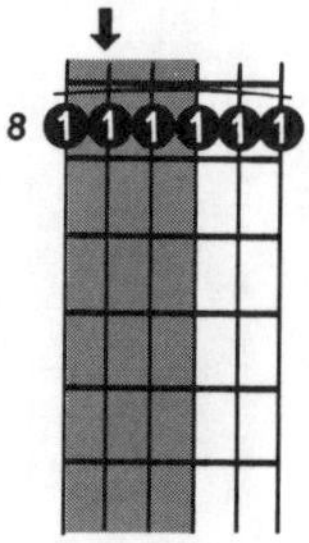

C F B♭E♭G C

F11+

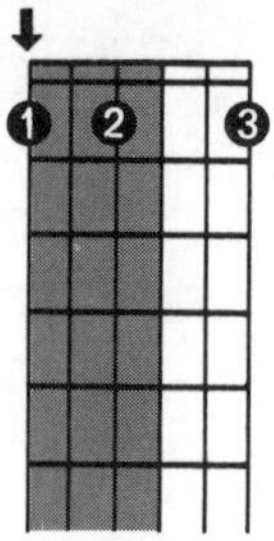

F A E♭G B F

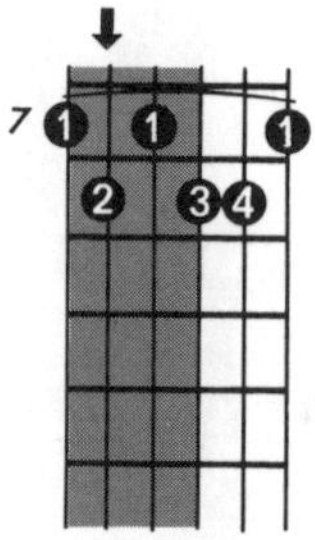

B F A E♭G B

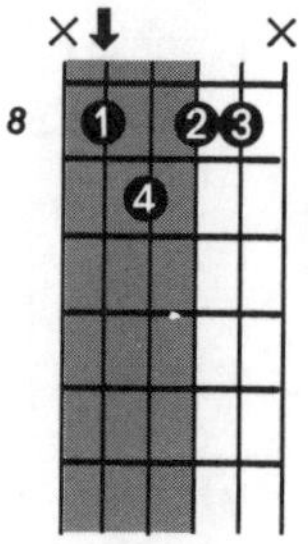

F B E♭G

F13

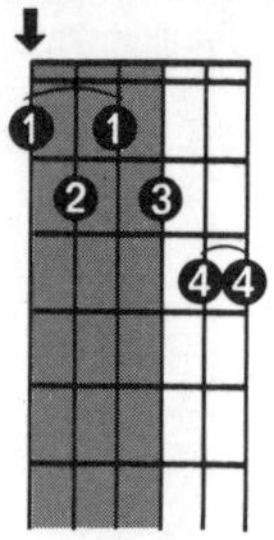

F B E♭A D G

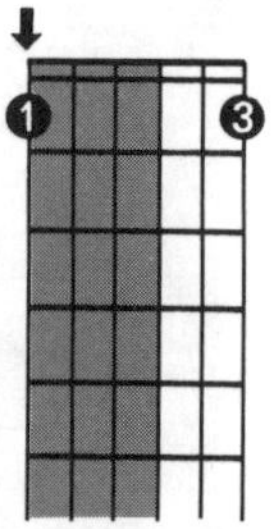

F A D G B F

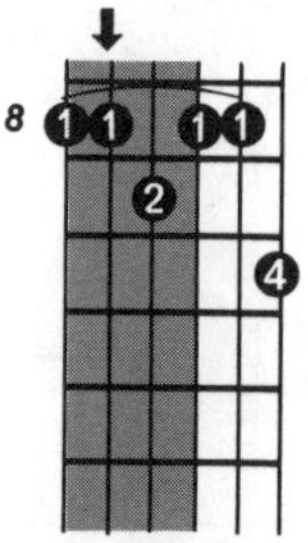

C F B E♭G D

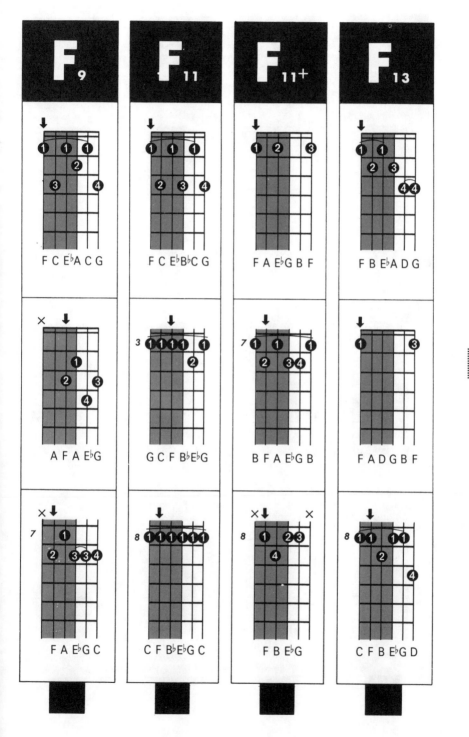

Fmaj7

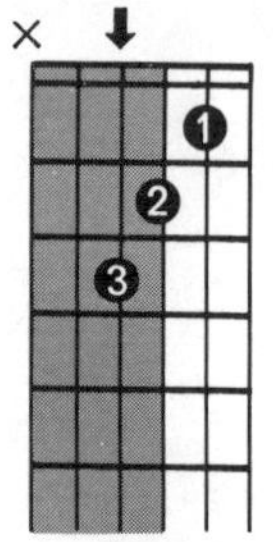

A F A C E

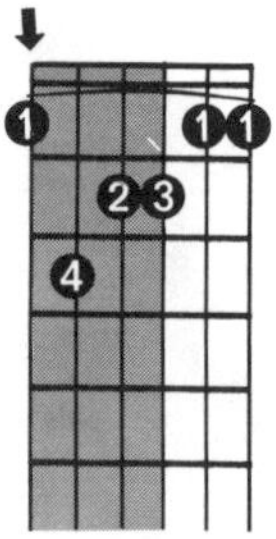

F C E A C F

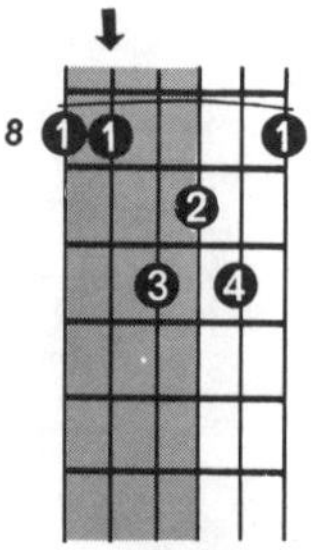

C F C E A C

Fmaj9

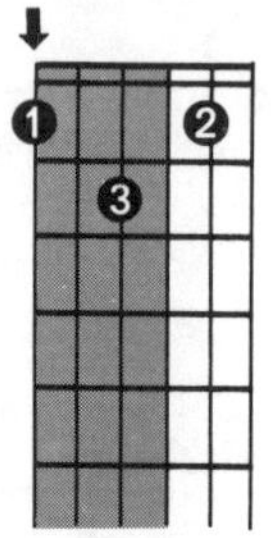

F A E G C E

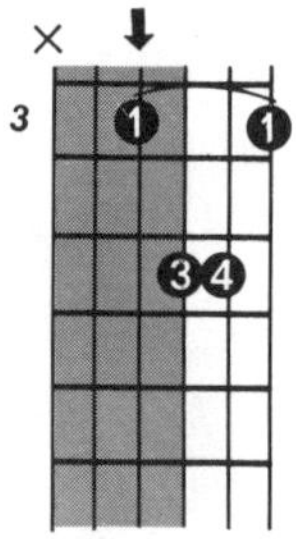

A F C E G

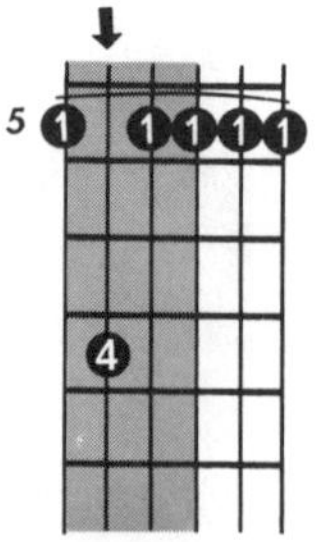

A F G C E A

Fmaj11

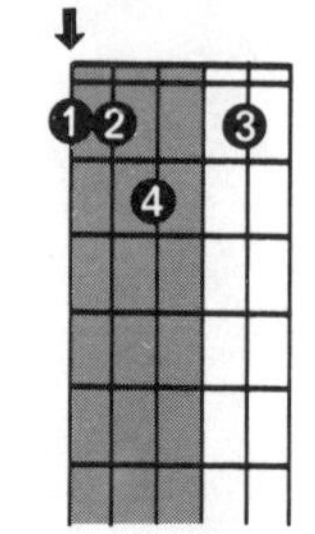

F B♭ E G C E

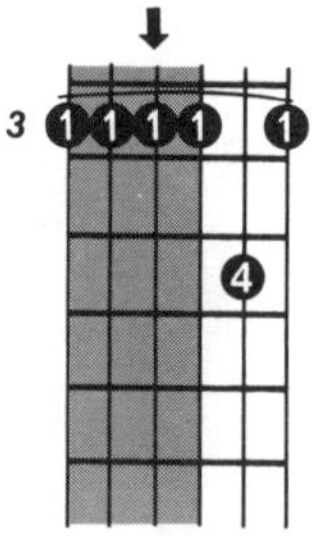

G C F B♭ E G

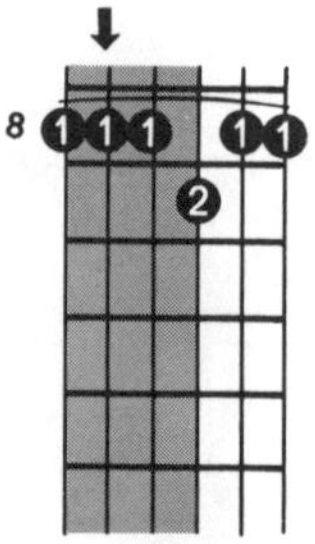

C F B♭ E G C

F7–5

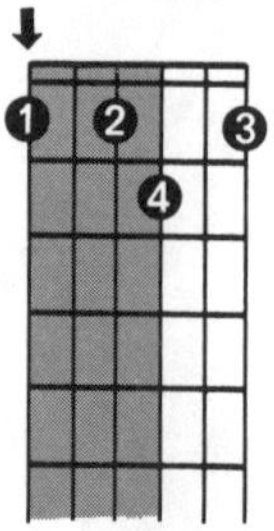

F A E♭ A B F

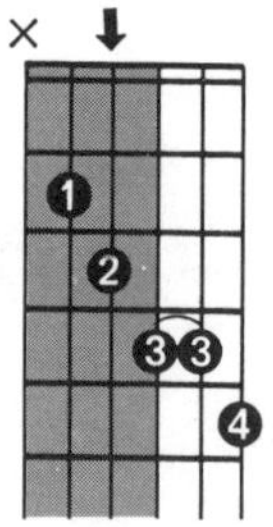

B F B E♭ A

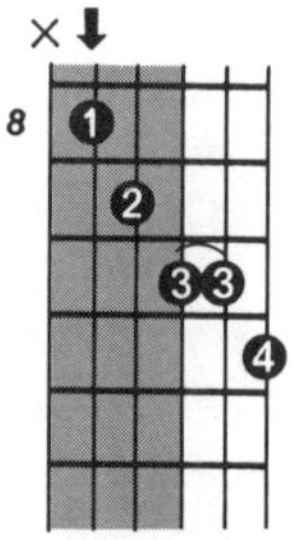

F B F A E♭

F7–9

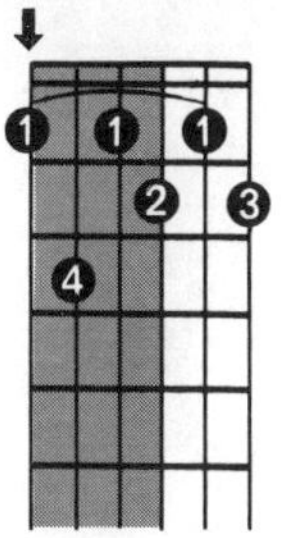

F C E♭A C G♭

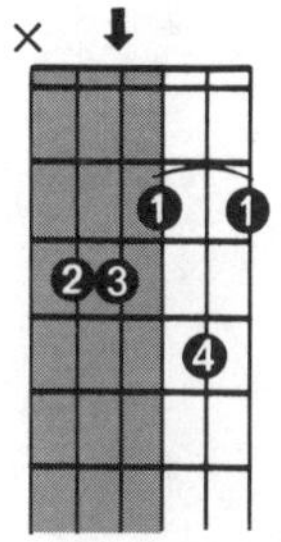

C F A E♭G♭

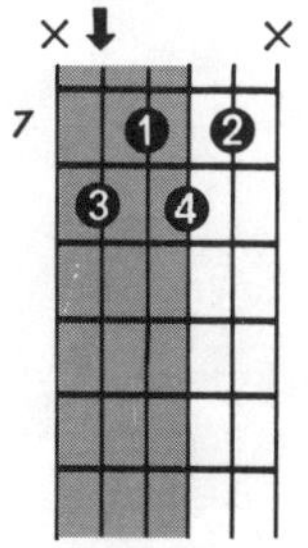

F A E♭G♭

F7–10

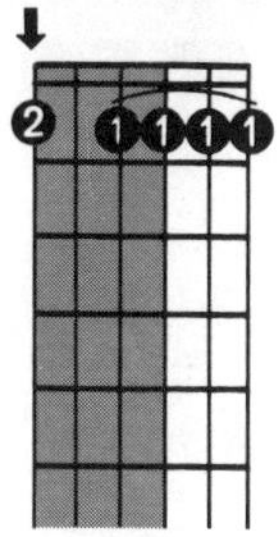

F A E♭A♭C F

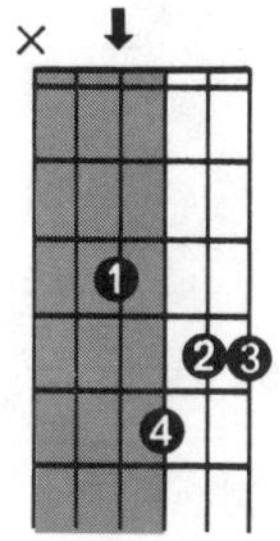

A F C E♭A♭

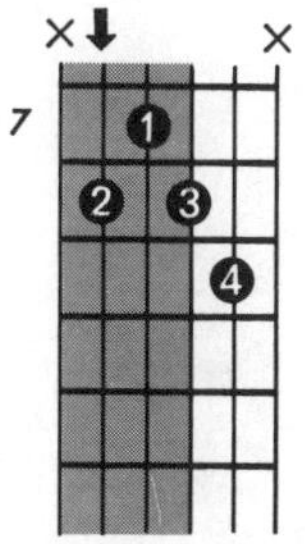

F A E♭A♭

F7+5

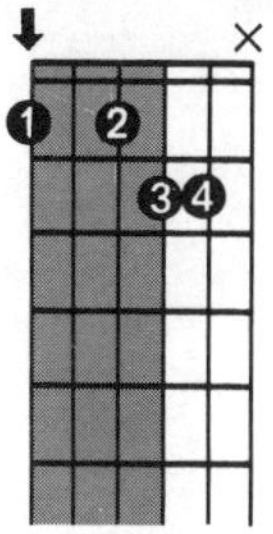

F A E♭A C♯

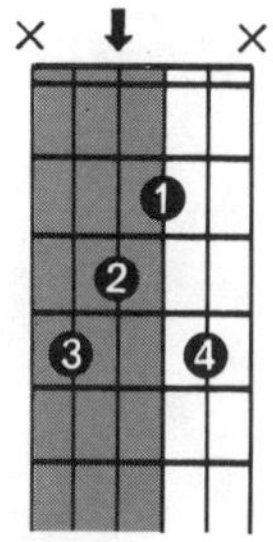

C♯F A E♭

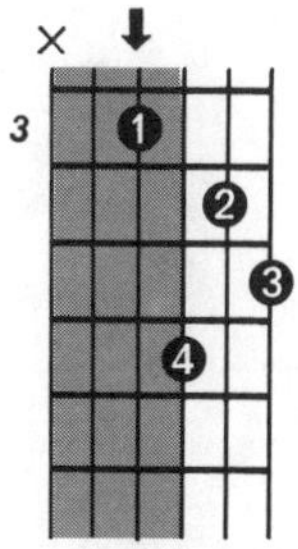

A F C♯E♭A

F9+5

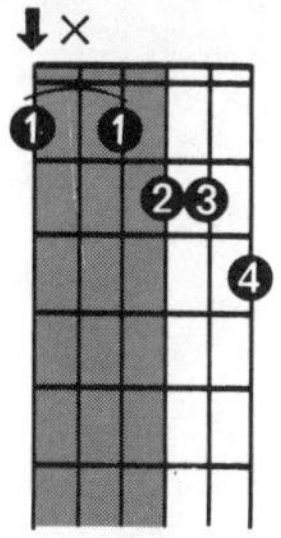

F E♭A C♯G

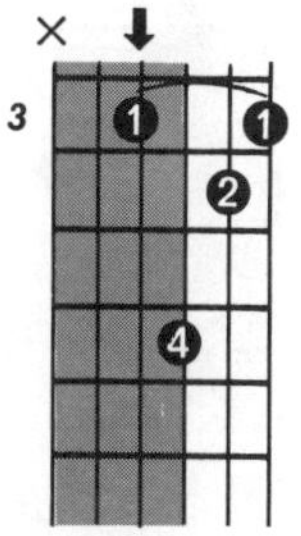

A F C♯E♭G

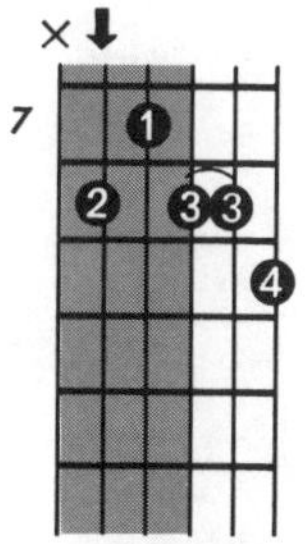

F A E♭G C♯

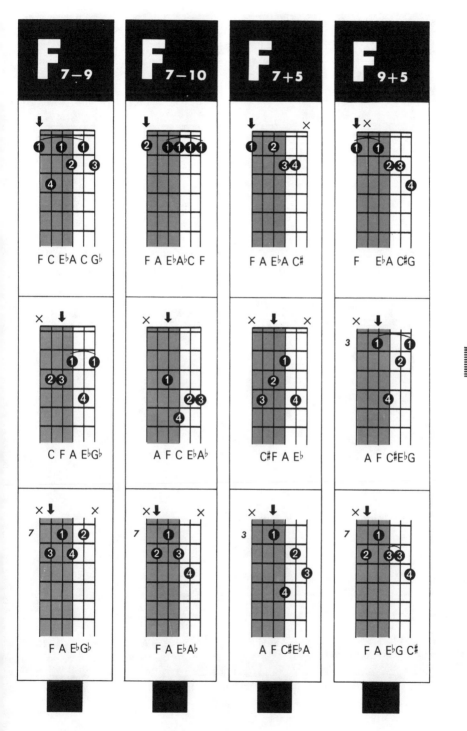

F

F 7+5 −9

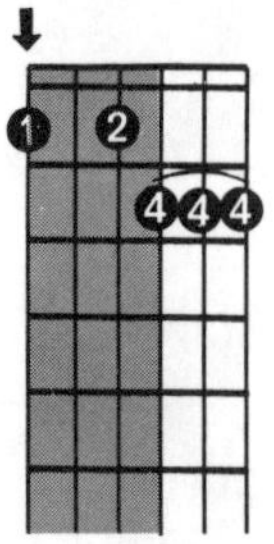

F A E♭A C♯G♭

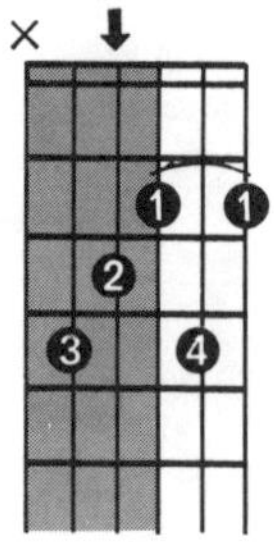

C♯F A E♭G♭

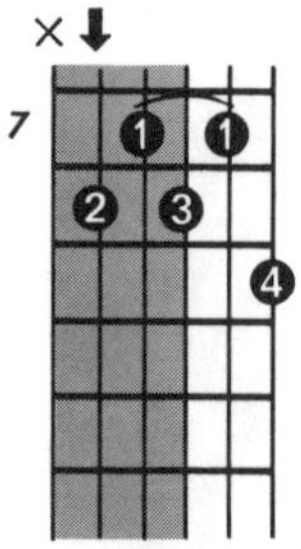

F A E♭G♭C♯

F 6·9

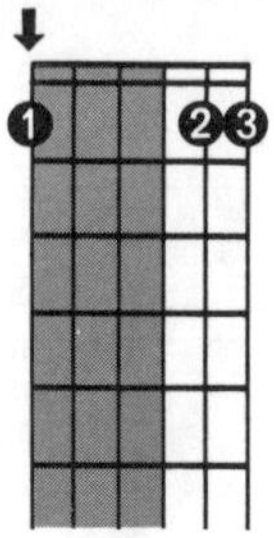

F A D G C F

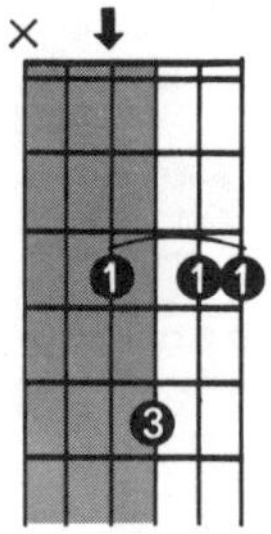

A F C D G

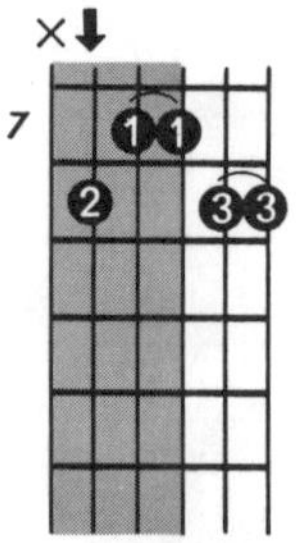

F A D G C

F dim

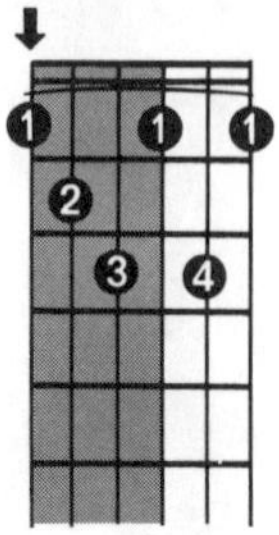

F B F A♭D F

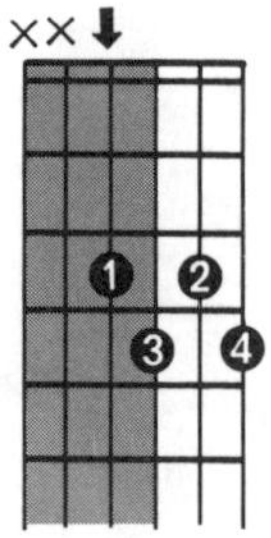

F B D A♭

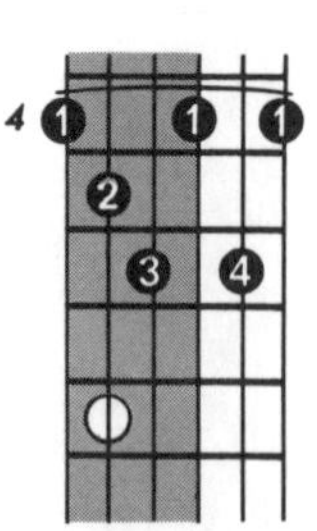

A♭D A♭B F A♭

F +5

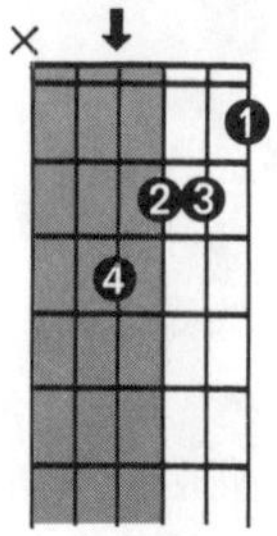

A F A C♯F

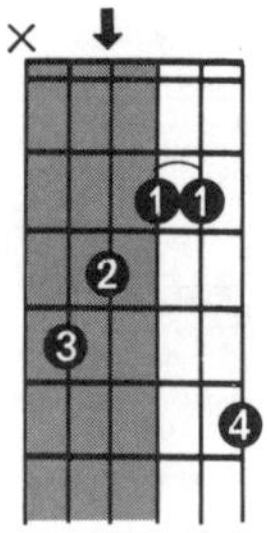

C♯F A C♯A

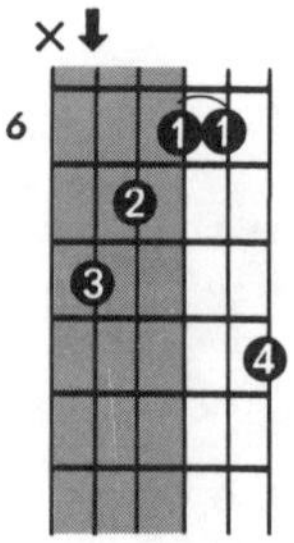

F A C♯F C♯

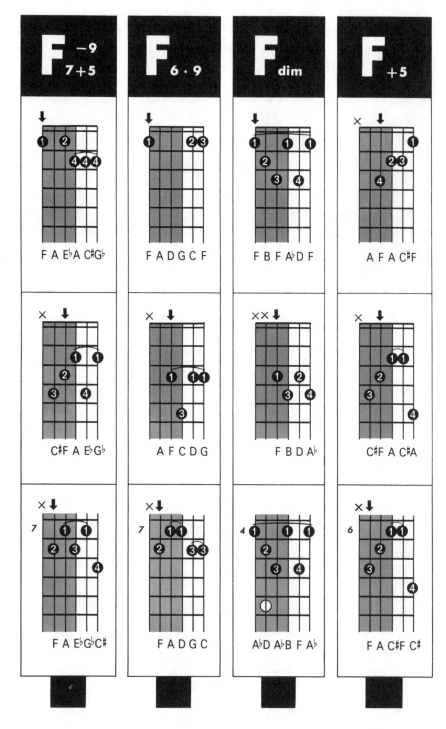

Fsus4

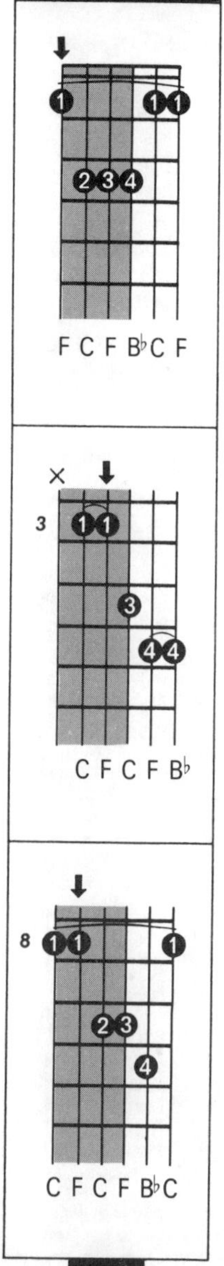

F7sus4

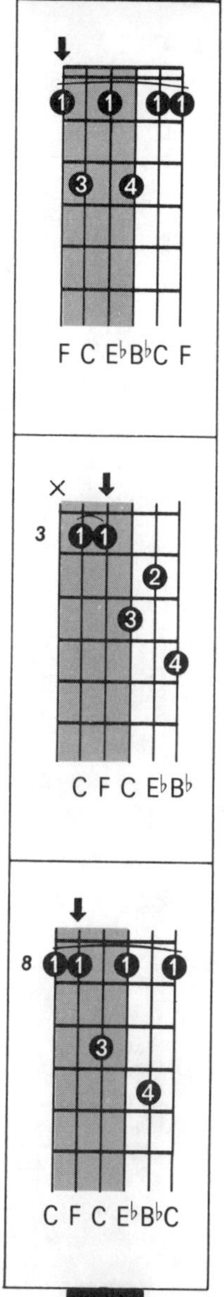

Fm

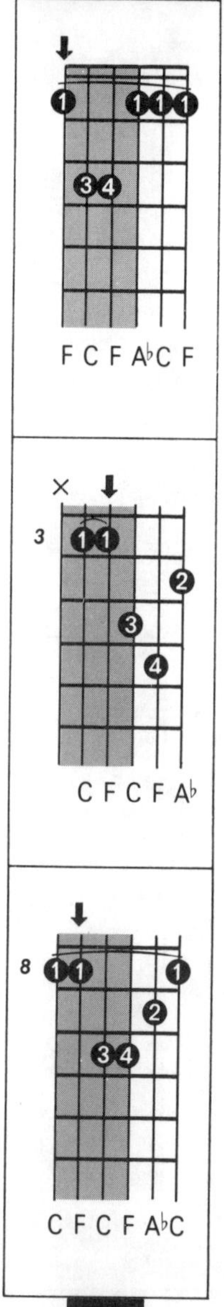

Fm6

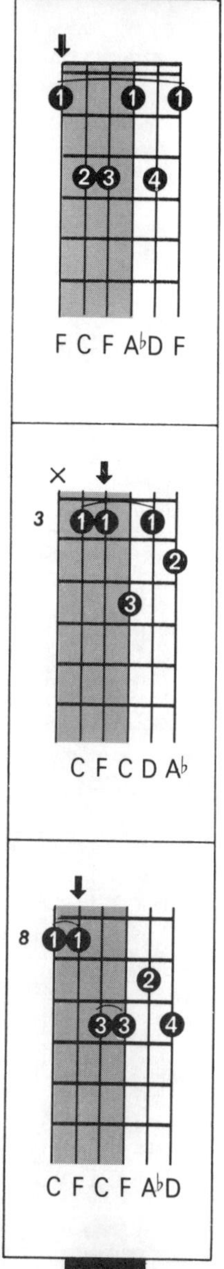

F m7

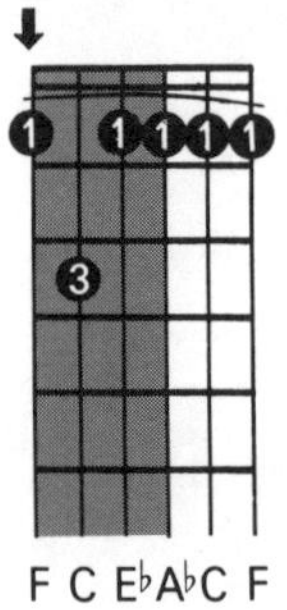

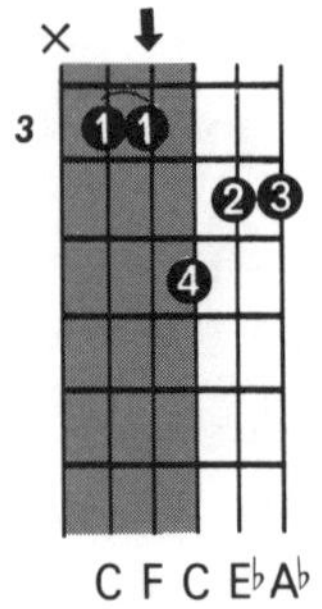

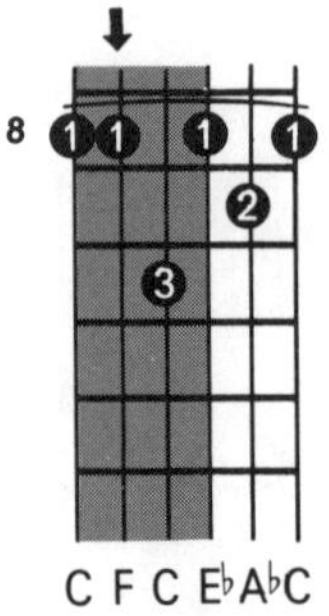

F m9

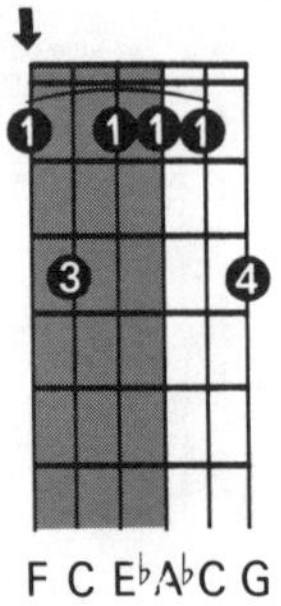

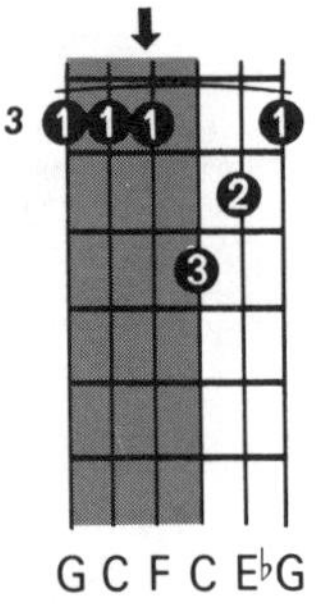

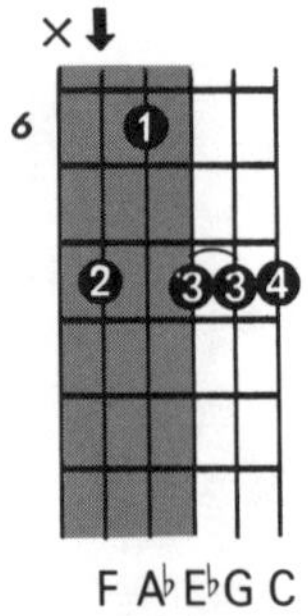

F m7 – 5

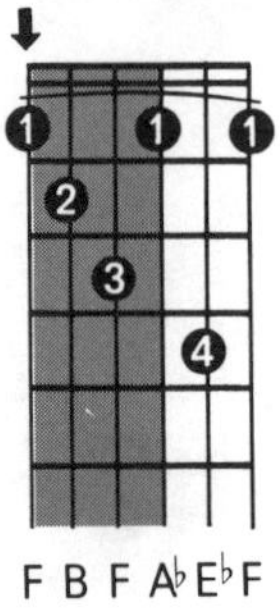

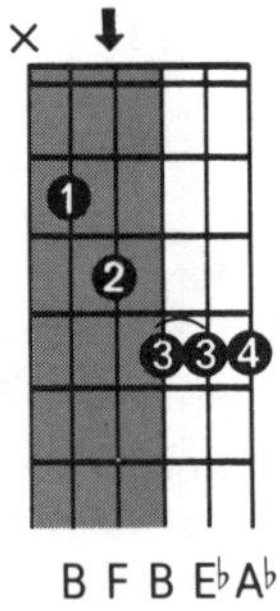

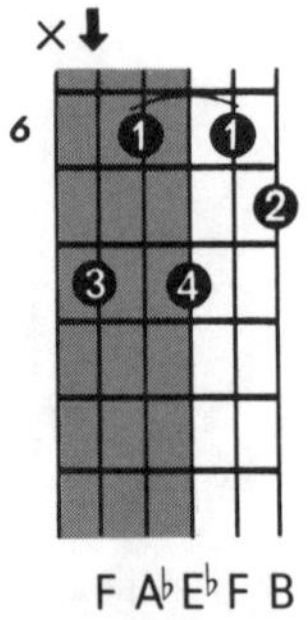

F m7 – 9

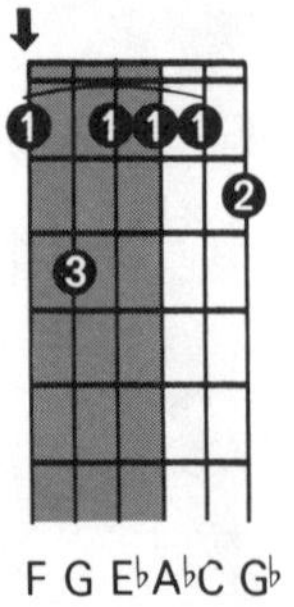

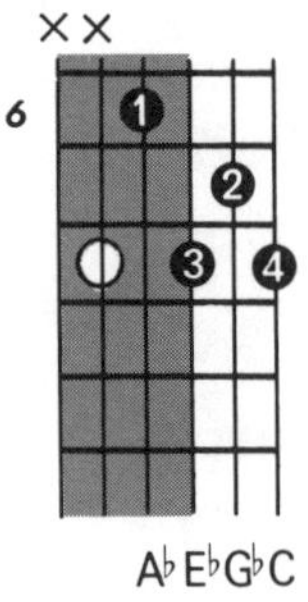

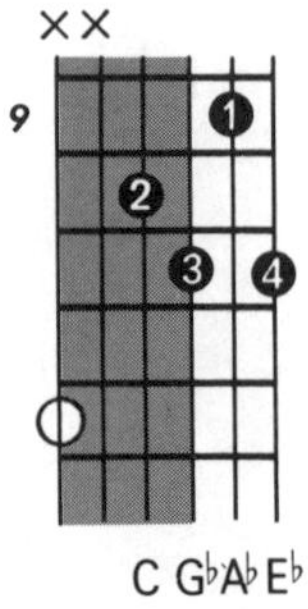

F m+7

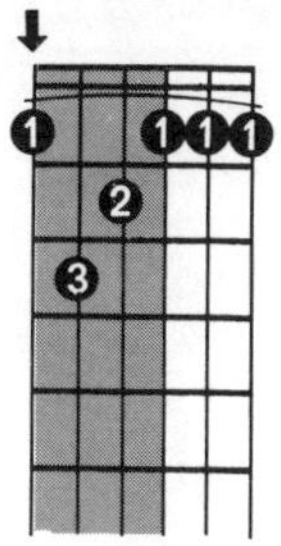

F C E A♭C F

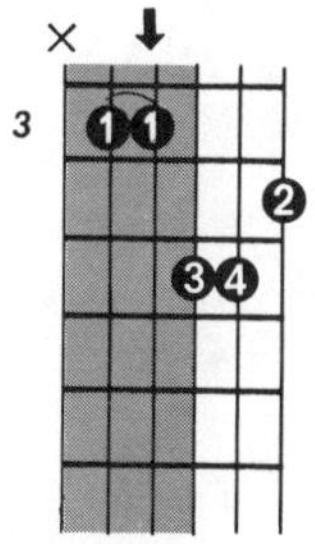

C F C E A♭

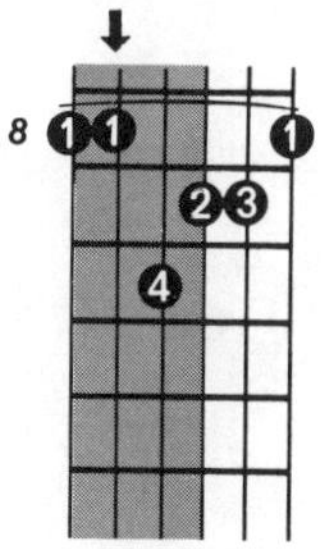

C F C E A♭C

F m9+7

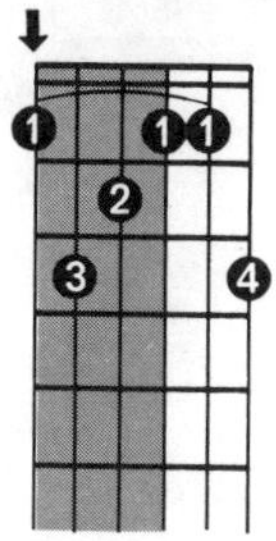

F C E A♭C G

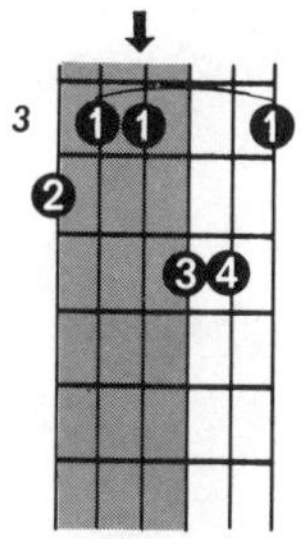

A♭C F C E G

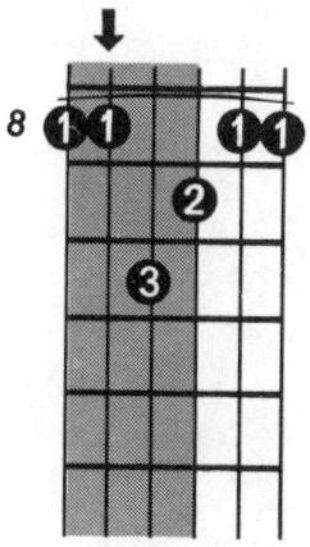

C F C E G C

F m+5

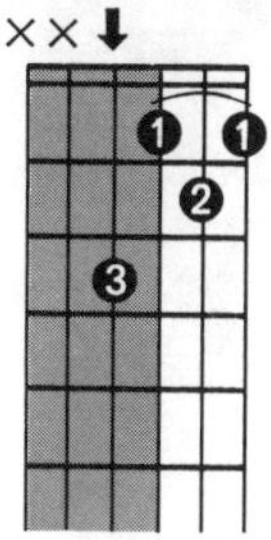

F A♭C♯F

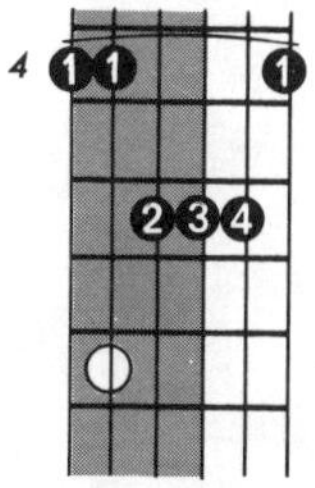

A♭C♯A♭C♯F A♭

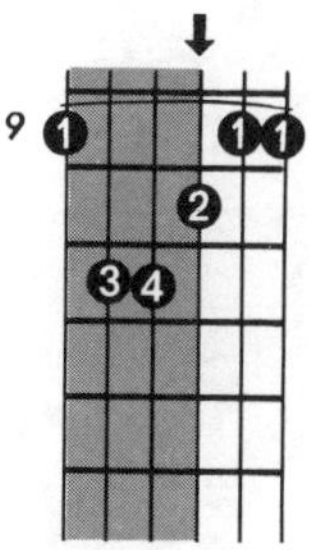

C♯A♭C♯F A♭C♯

F m6 · 9

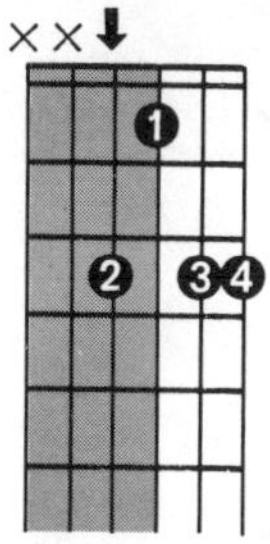

F A♭D G

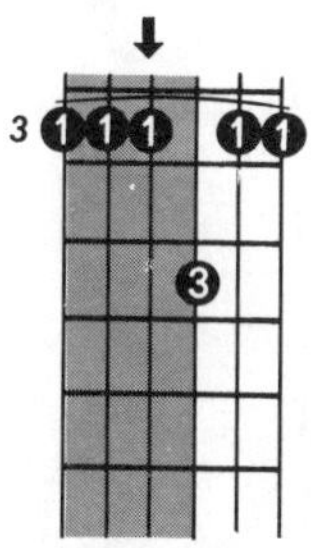

G C F C D G

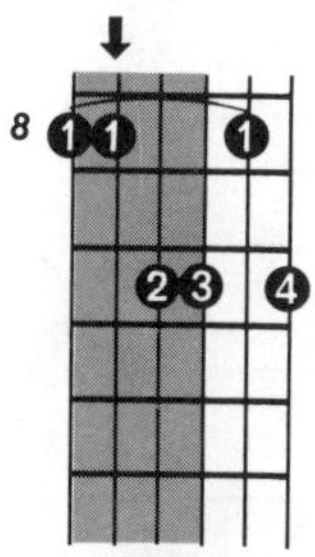

C F C F G D

F

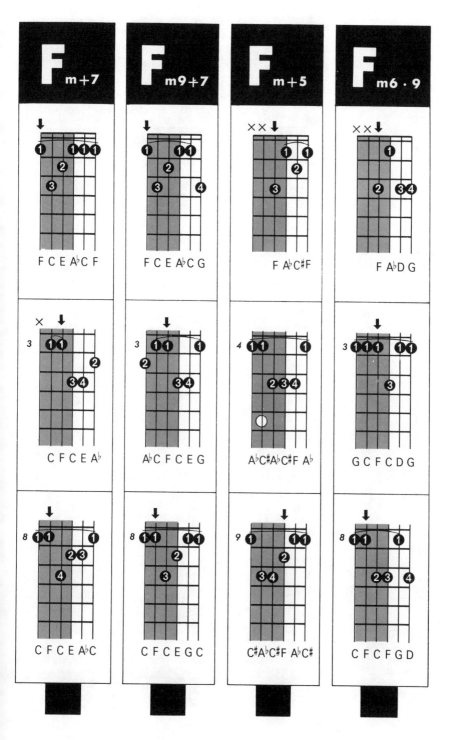

G♭

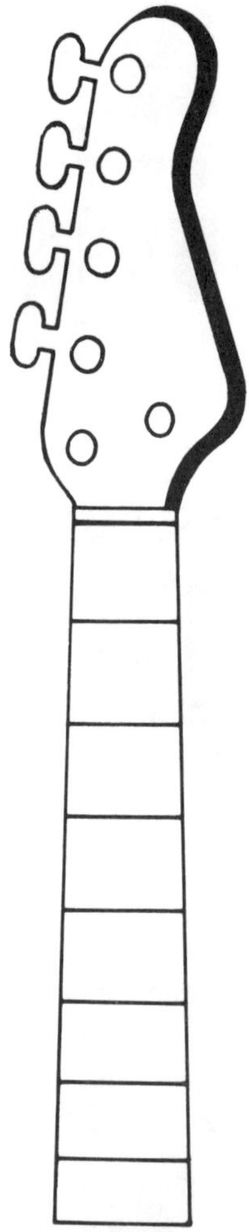

F♯

G♭

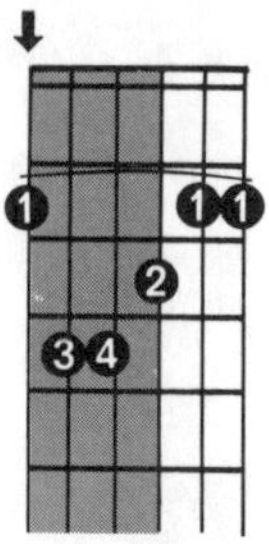

G♭D♭G♭B♭D♭G♭

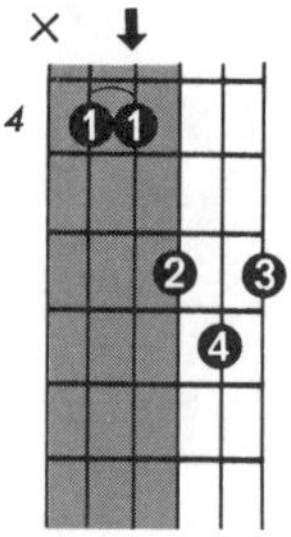

D♭G♭D♭G♭B♭

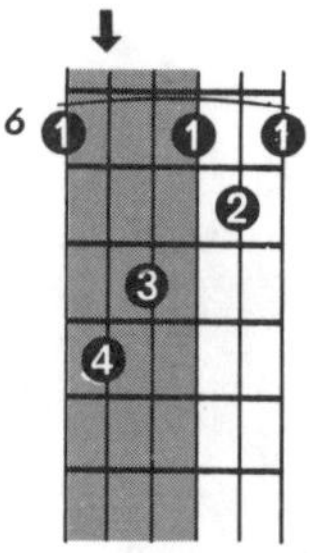

B♭G♭B♭D♭G♭B♭

F♯

G♭6

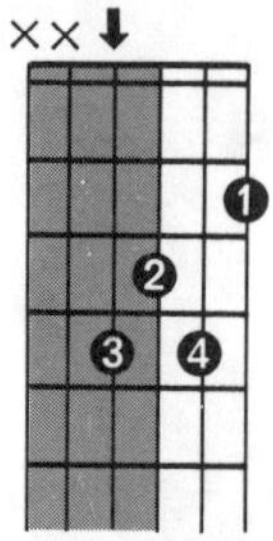

G♭B♭E♭G♭

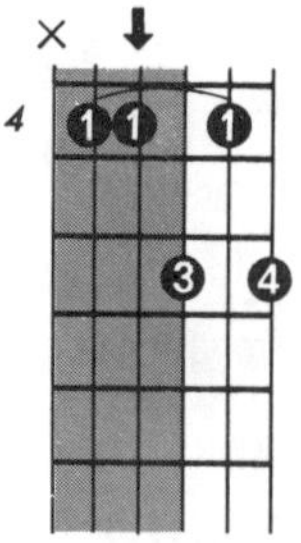

D♭G♭D♭E♭B♭

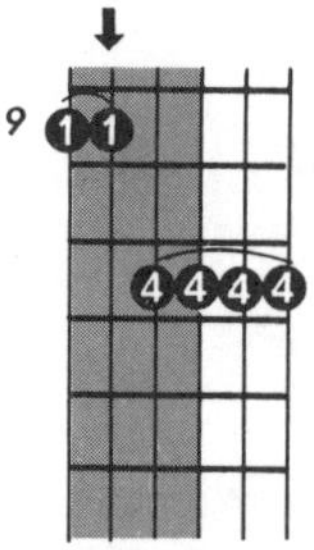

D♭G♭D♭G♭B♭E♭

F♯6

G♭7

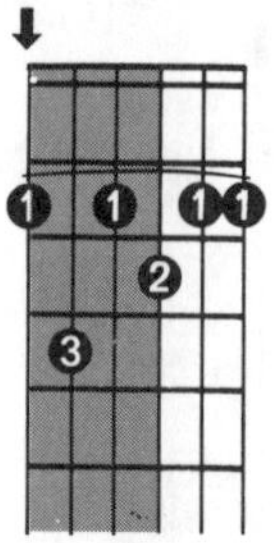

G♭D♭E B♭D♭G♭

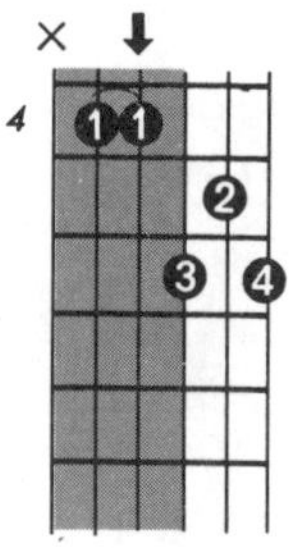

D♭G♭D♭E B♭

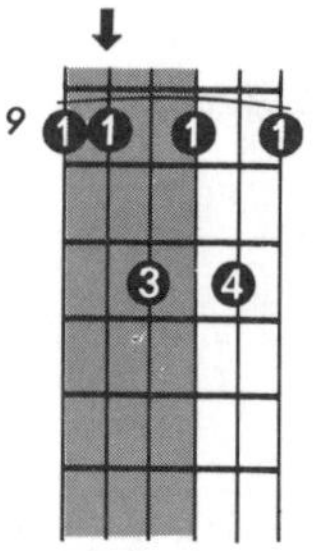

D♭G♭D♭E B♭D♭

F♯7

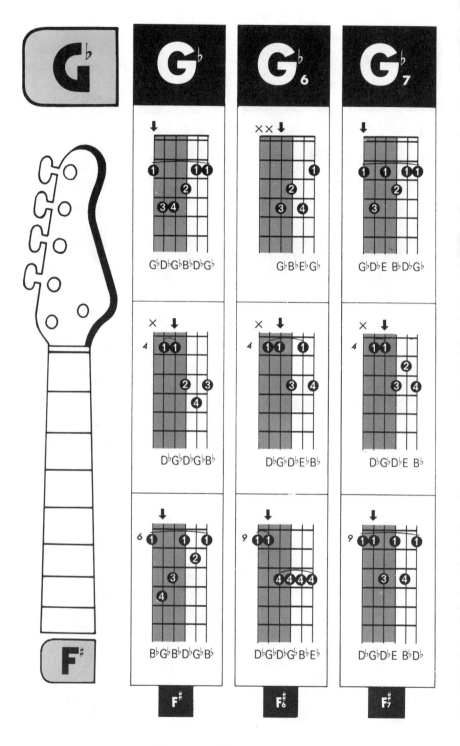

G♭9

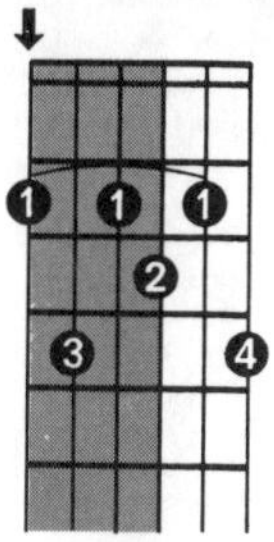

G♭D♭E B♭D♭A♭

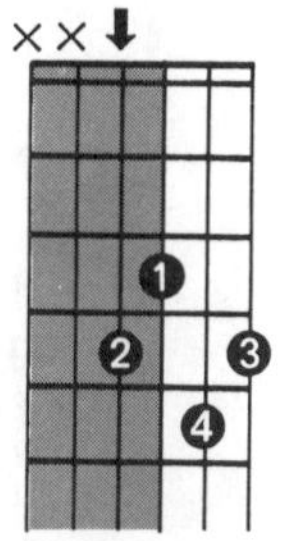

G♭B♭E A♭

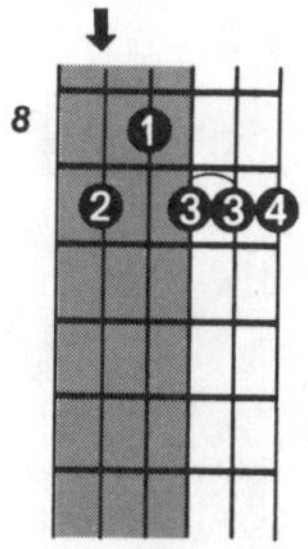

E G♭B♭E A♭D♭

F♯9

G♭11

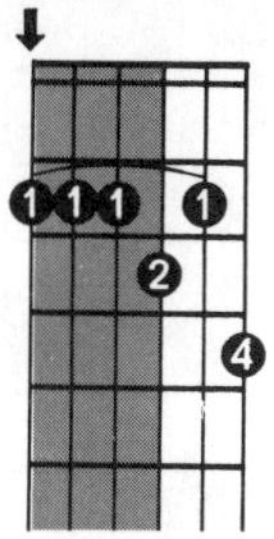

G♭B E B♭D♭A♭

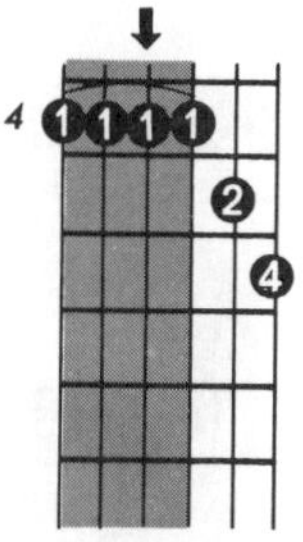

A♭D♭G♭B E B♭

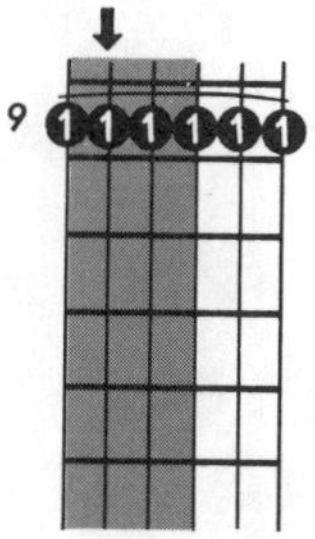

D♭G♭B E A♭D♭

F♯11

G♭11+

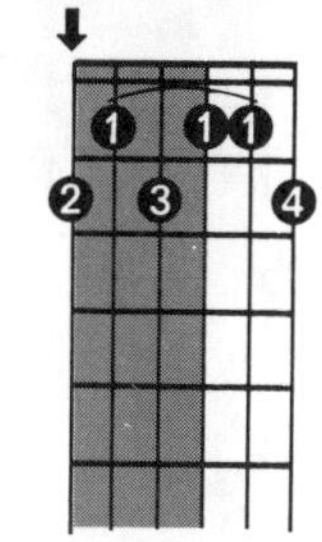

G♭B♭E A♭C G♭

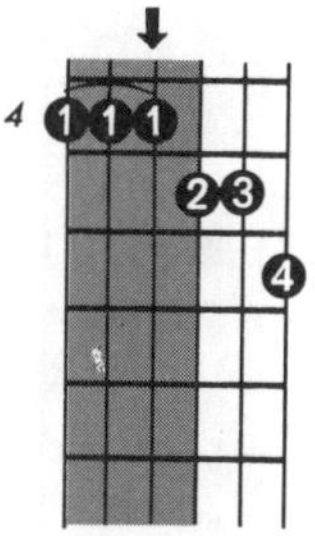

A♭D♭G♭C E B♭

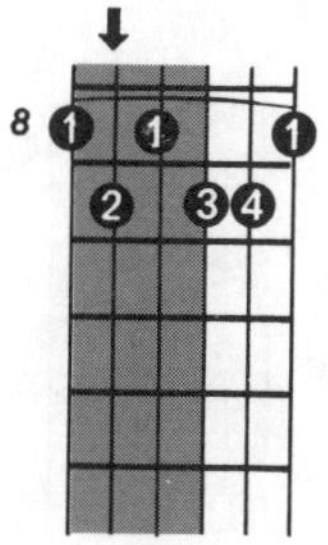

C G♭B♭E A♭C

F♯11+

G♭13

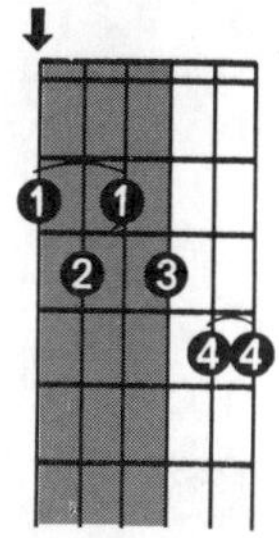

G♭C E B♭E♭A♭

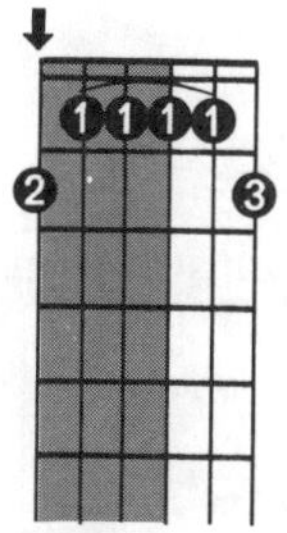

G♭B♭E♭A♭C G♭

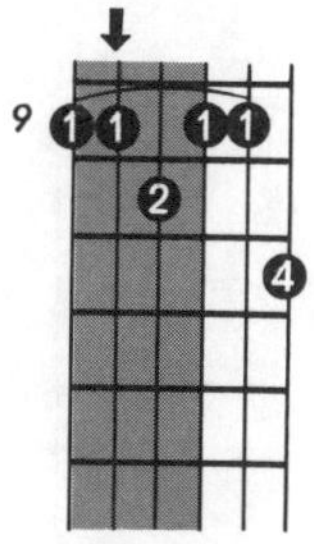

D♭G♭C E A♭E♭

F♯13

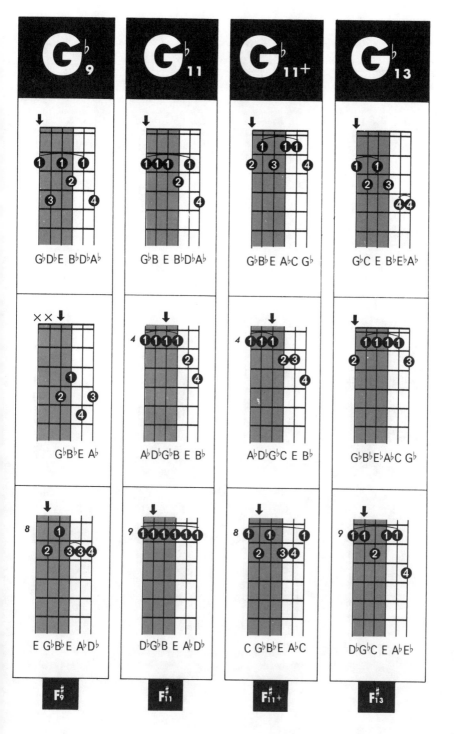

F♯

G♭maj7

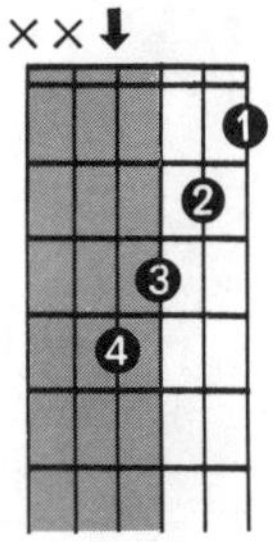

G♭B♭D♭F

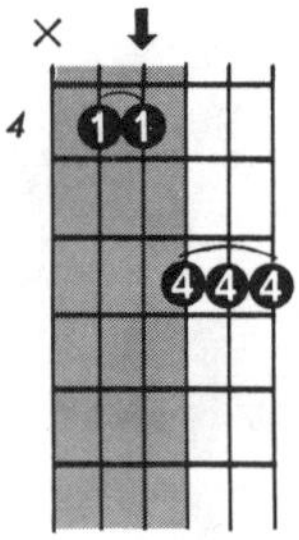

D♭G♭D♭F B♭

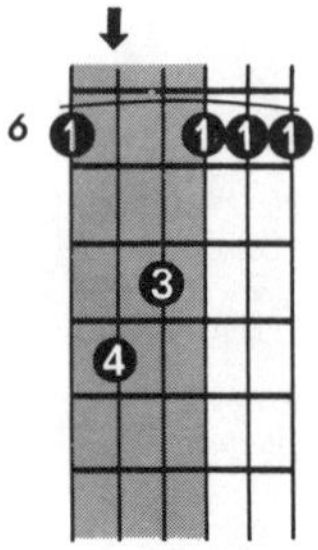

B♭G♭B♭D♭F B♭

F♯maj7

G♭maj9

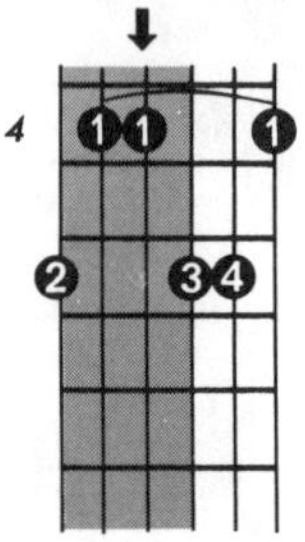

B♭D♭G♭D♭F A♭

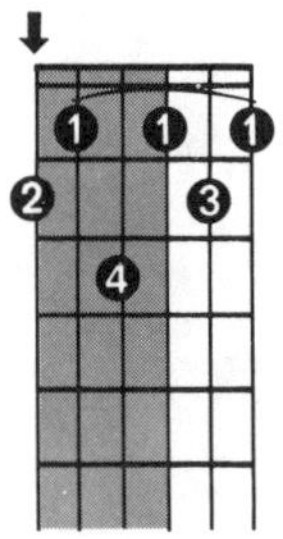

G♭B♭F A♭D♭F

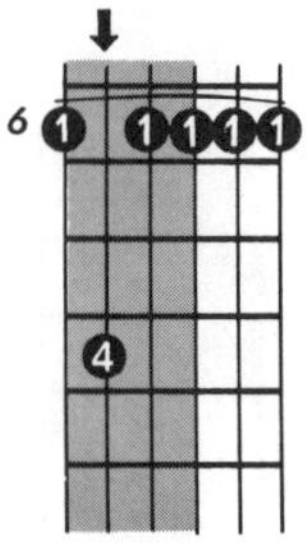

B♭G♭A♭D♭F B♭

F♯maj9

G♭maj11

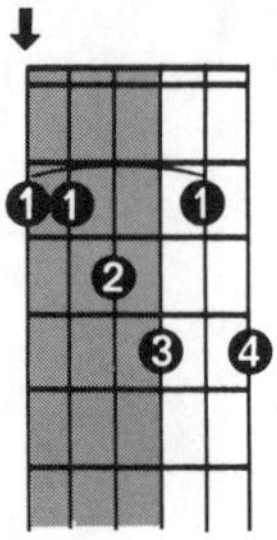

G♭B F B D♭A♭

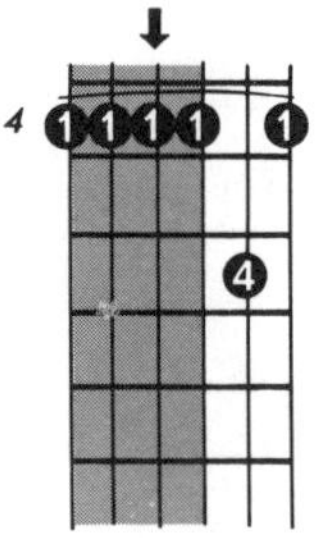

A♭D♭G♭B F A♭

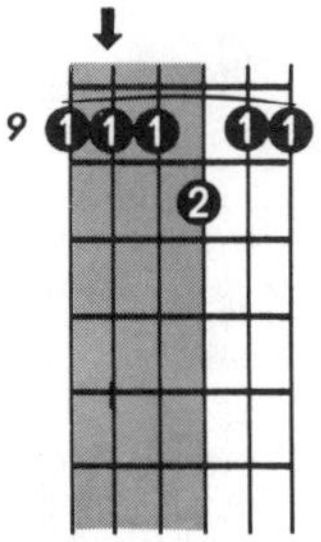

D♭G♭B F A♭D♭

F♯maj11

G♭7−5

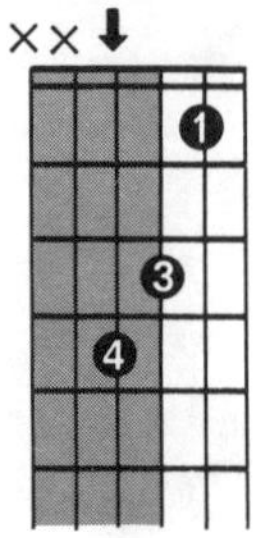

G♭B♭C E

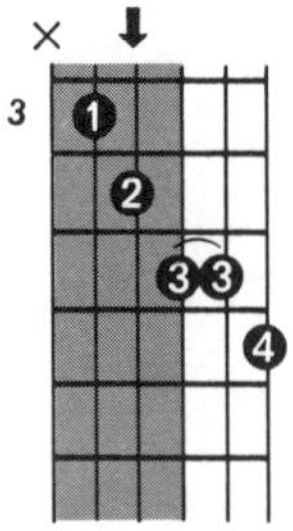

C G♭C E B♭

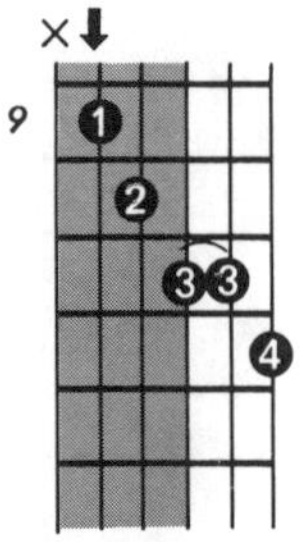

G♭C G♭B♭E

F♯7−5

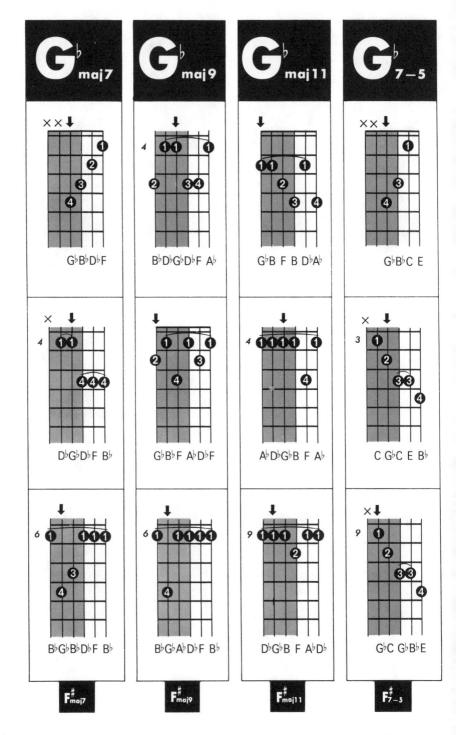

G♭7−9

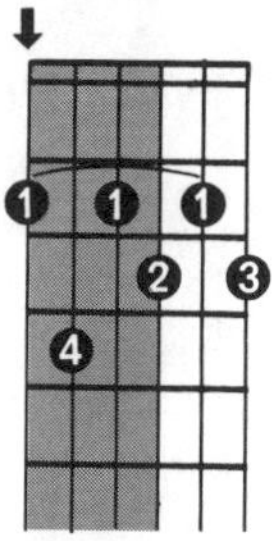

G♭D♭E B♭D♭G

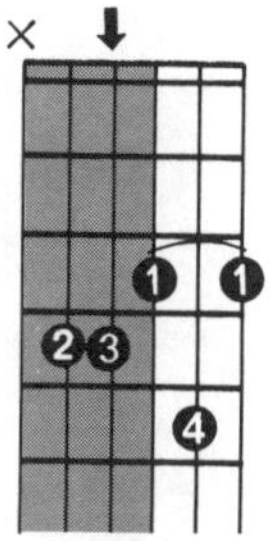

D♭G♭B♭E G

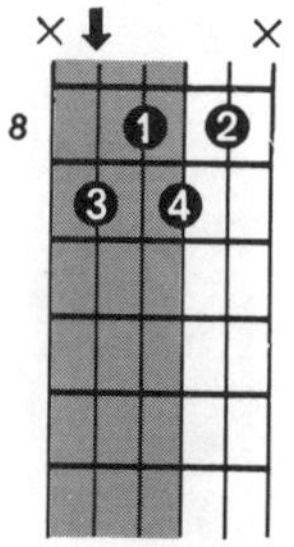

G♭B♭E G

F♯7−9

G♭7−10

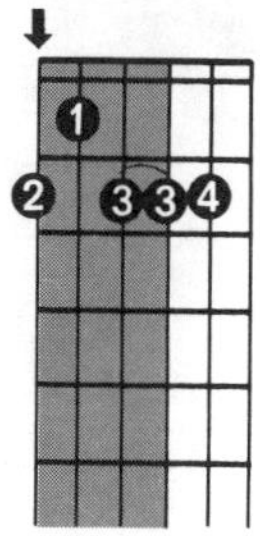

G♭B♭E A D♭E

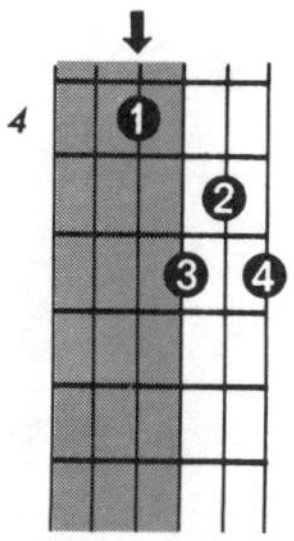

E A G♭D♭E B♭

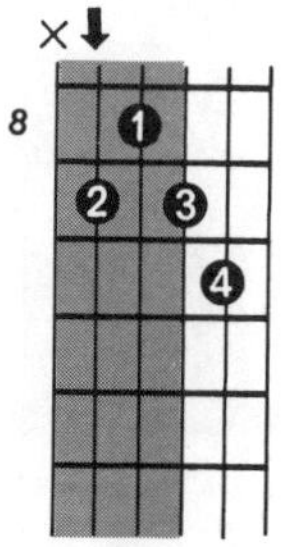

G♭B♭E A E

F♯7−10

G♭7+5

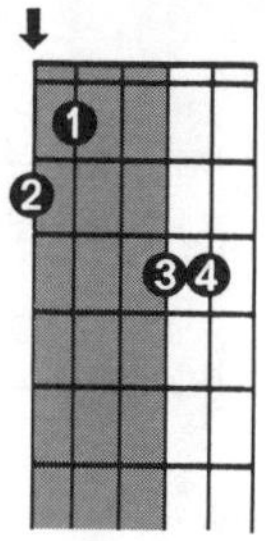

G♭B♭D B♭D E

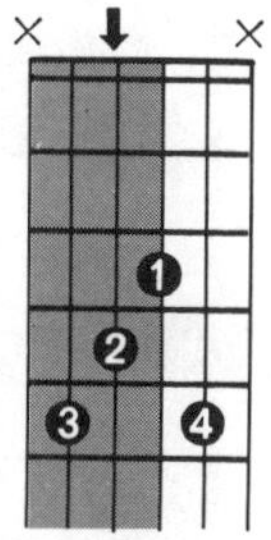

D G♭B♭E

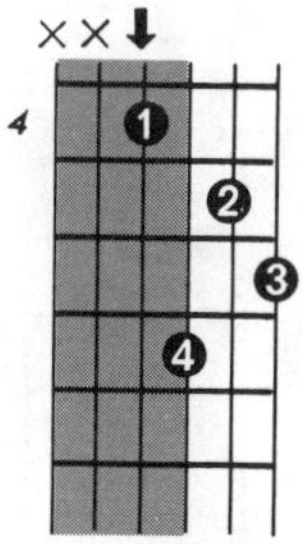

G♭D E B♭

F♯7+5

G♭9+5

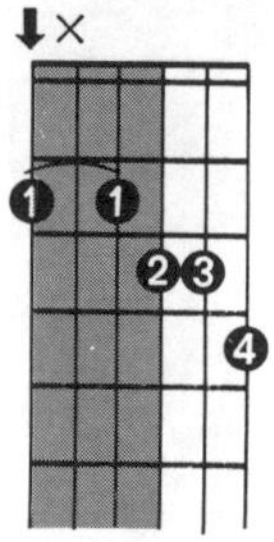

G♭ E B♭D A♭

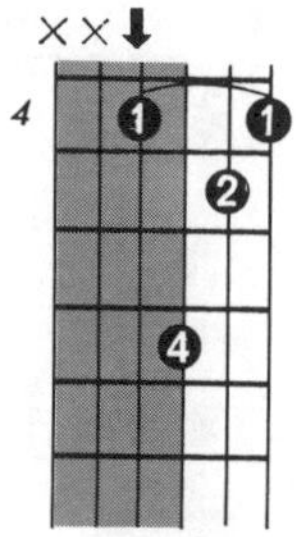

G♭D E A♭

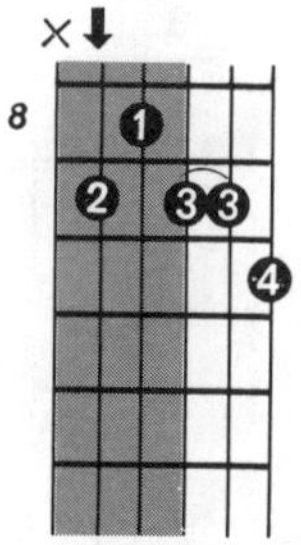

G♭B♭E A♭D

F♯9+5

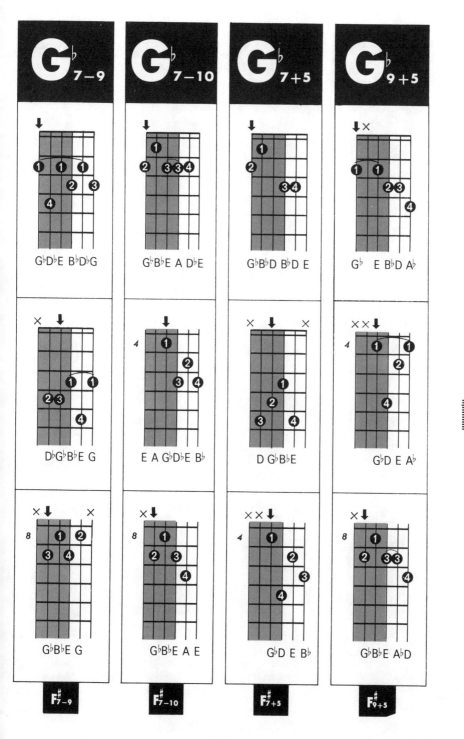

G♭ 7+5 −9

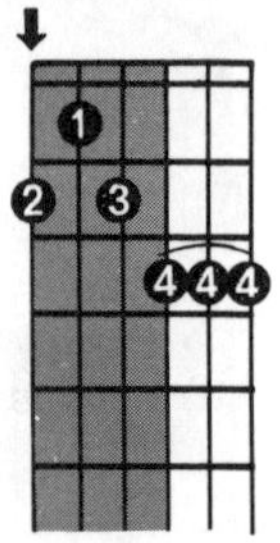

G♭B♭E B♭D G

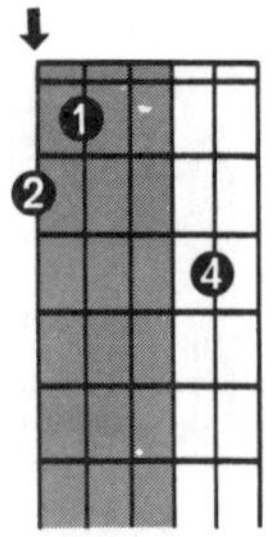

G♭B♭D G D E

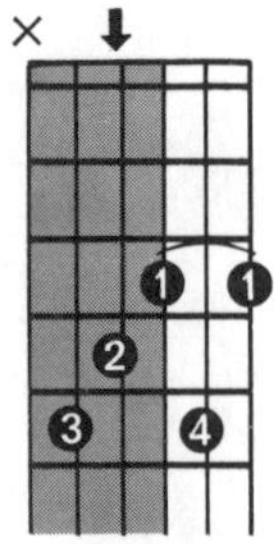

D G♭B♭E G

F♯ 7+5 −9

G♭ 6 · 9

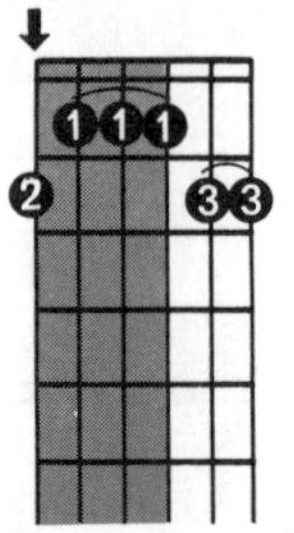

G♭B♭E♭A♭D♭G♭

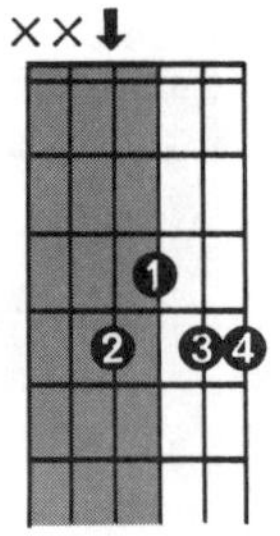

G♭B♭E♭A♭

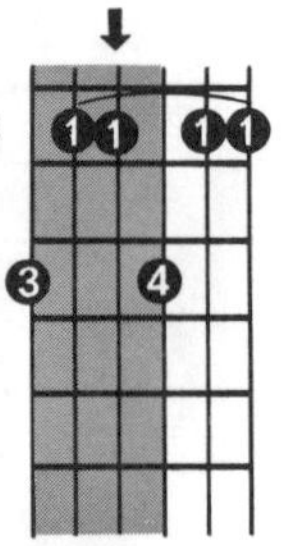

B♭D♭G♭D♭E♭A♭

F♯ 6 · 9

G♭ dim

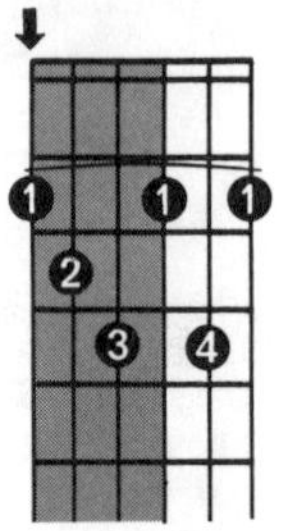

G♭C G♭A E♭G♭

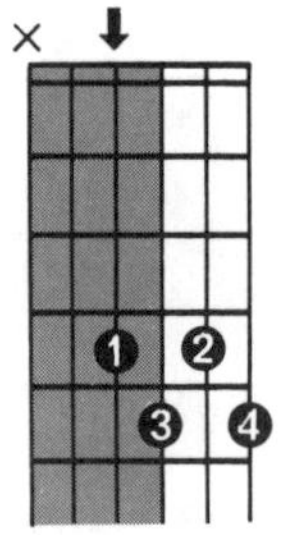

A G♭C E♭A

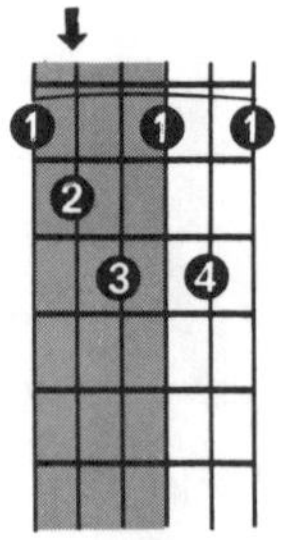

C G♭C E♭A C

F♯ dim

G♭ +5

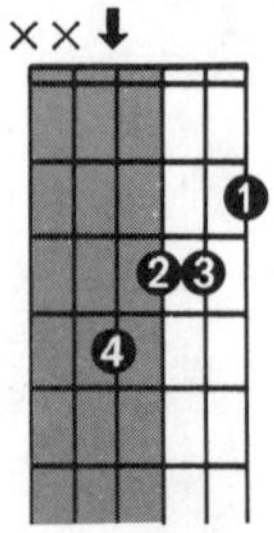

G♭B♭D G♭

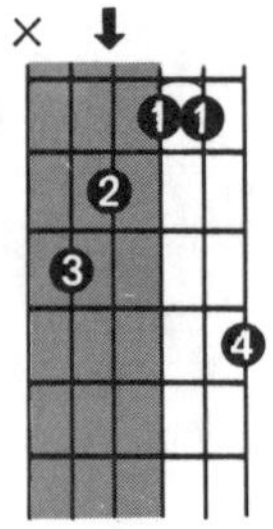

D G♭B♭D B♭

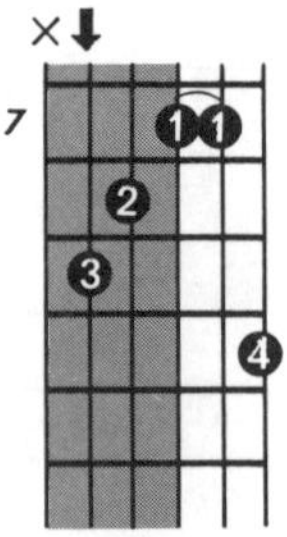

G♭B♭D G♭D

F♯ +5

F♯

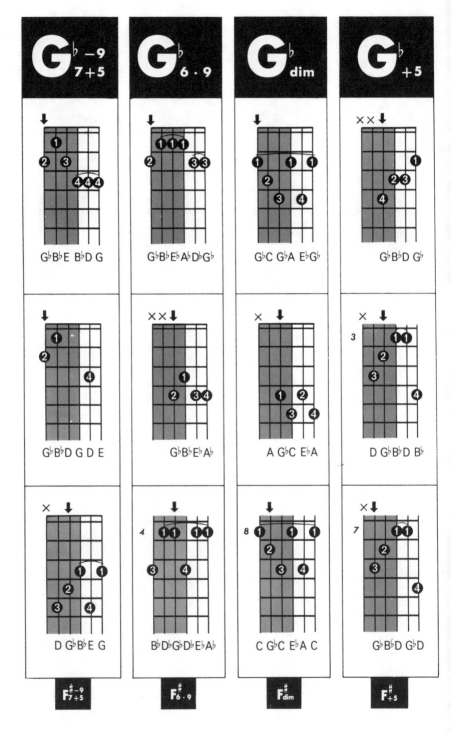

G♭sus4

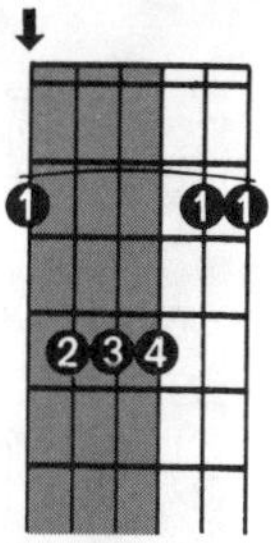

G♭D♭G♭B D♭G♭

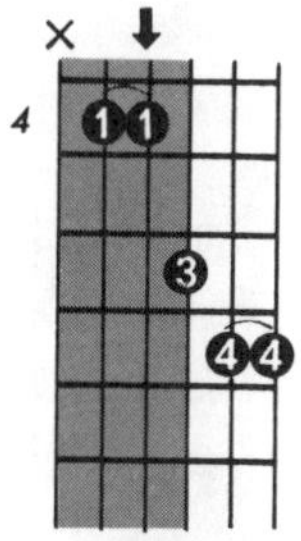

D♭G♭D♭G♭B

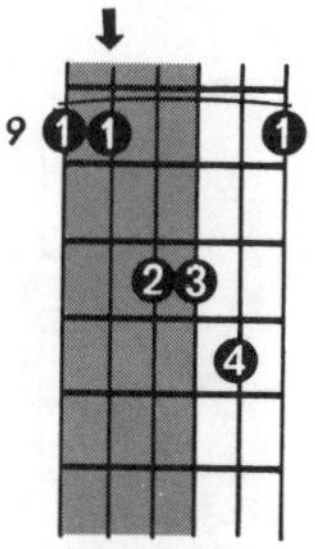

D♭G♭D♭G♭B D♭

F♯sus4

G♭7sus4

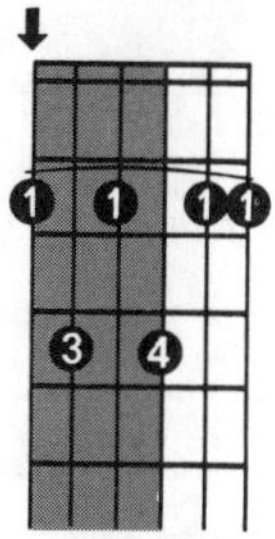

G♭D♭E B D♭G♭

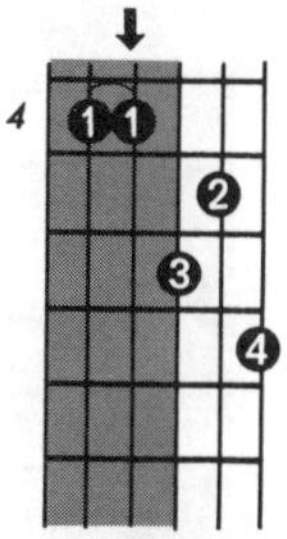

E D♭G♭D♭E B

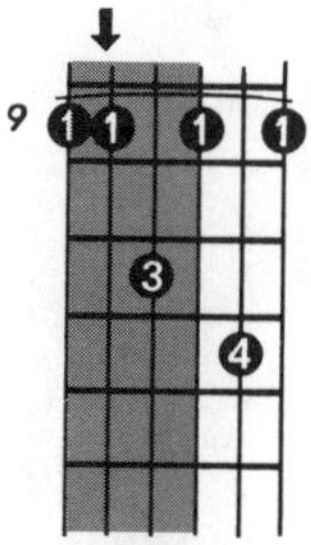

D♭G♭D♭E B D♭

F♯7sus4

G♭m

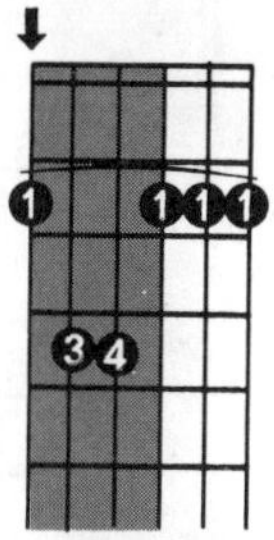

G♭D♭G♭A D♭G♭

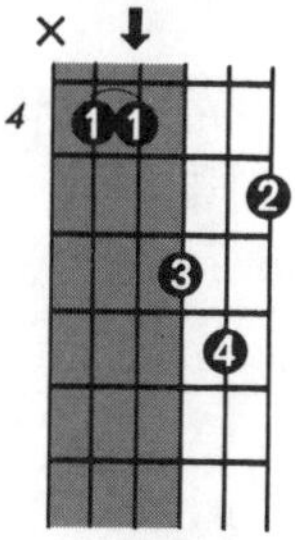

D♭G♭D♭G♭A

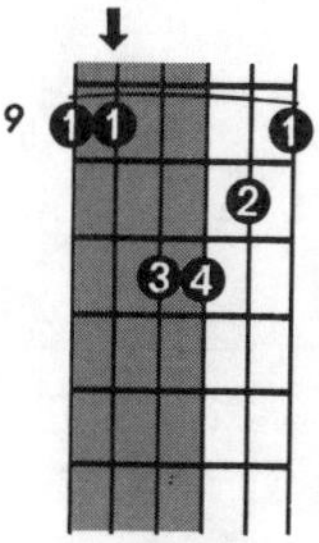

D♭G♭D♭G♭A D♭

F♯m

G♭m6

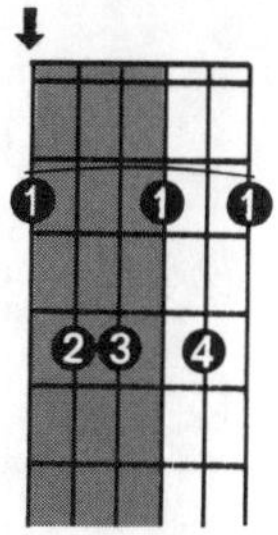

G♭D♭G♭A E♭G♭

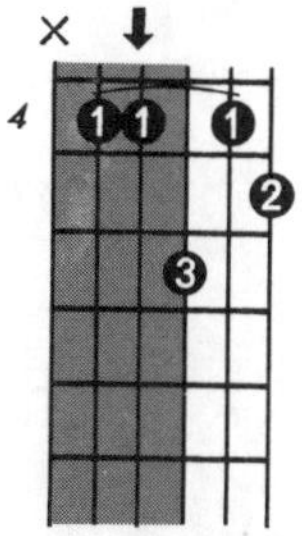

D♭G♭D♭E♭A

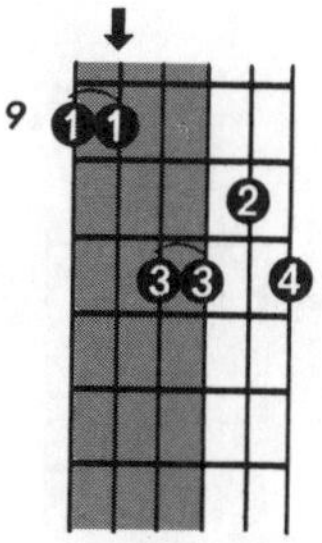

D♭G♭D♭G♭A E♭

F♯m6

G♭

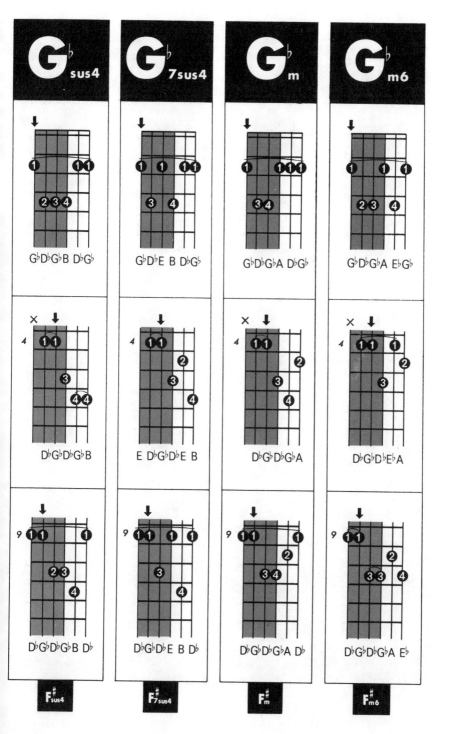

F♯

G♭m7

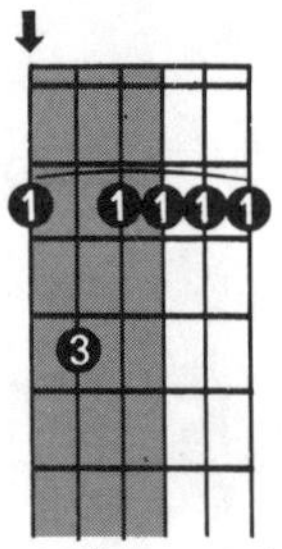

G♭D♭E A D♭G♭

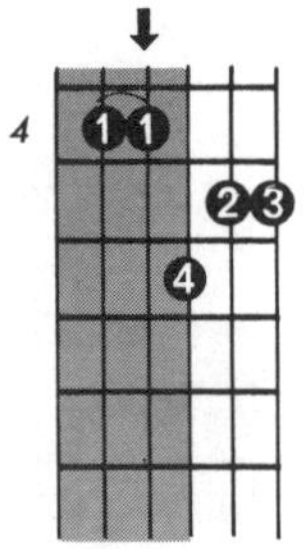

E D♭G♭D♭E A

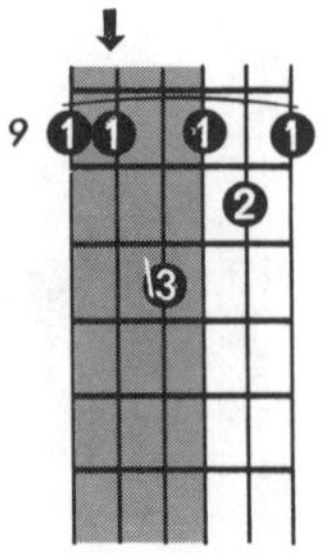

D♭G♭D♭E A D♭

F♯m7

G♭m9

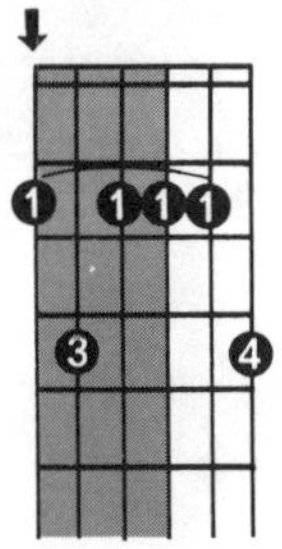

G♭D♭E A D♭A♭

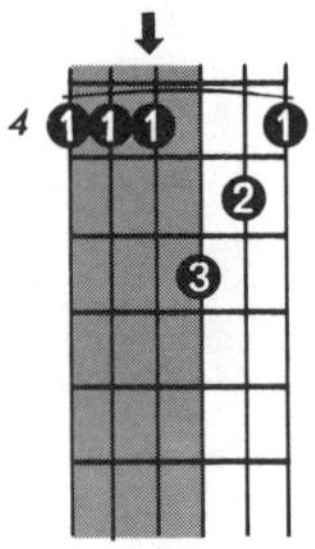

A♭D♭G♭D♭E A♭

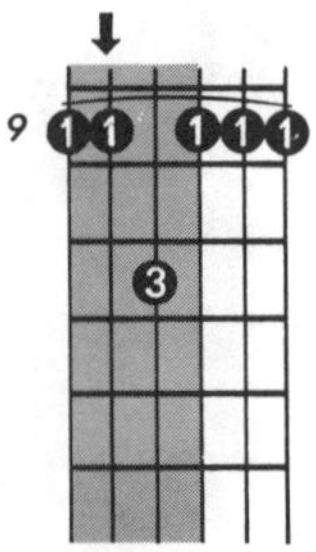

D♭G♭D♭E A♭D♭

F♯m9

G♭m7−5

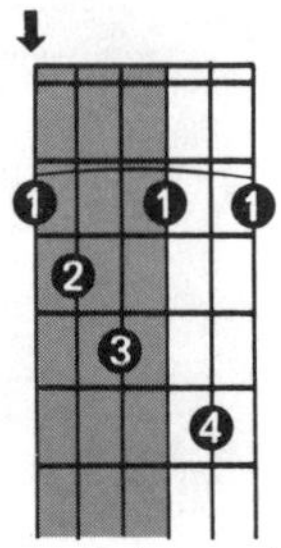

G♭C G♭A E G♭

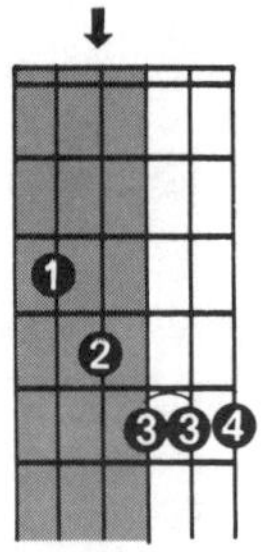

E C G♭C E A

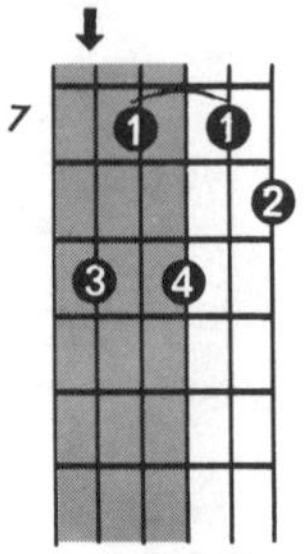

E G♭A E G♭C

F♯m7−5

G♭m7−9

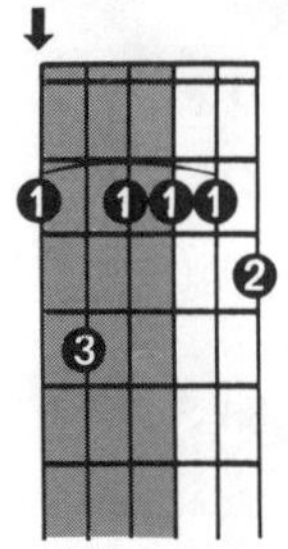

G♭D♭E A D♭G

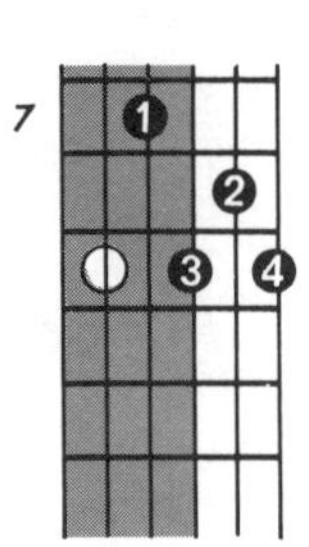

E A A E G D♭

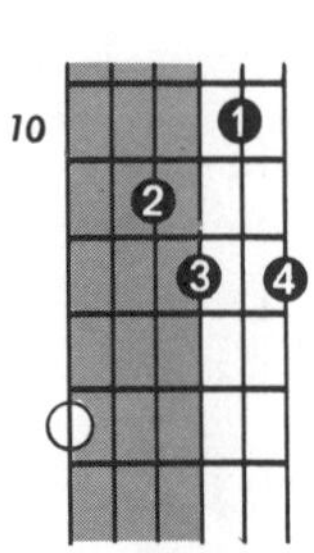

E A D♭G A E

F♯m7−9

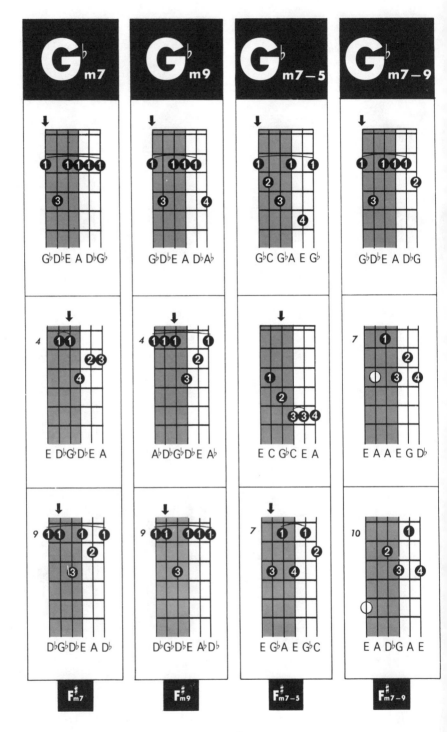

G♭m+7

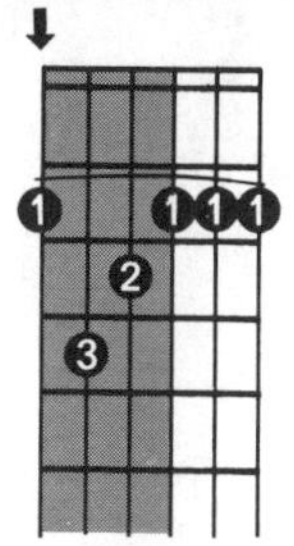

G♭D♭F A D♭G♭

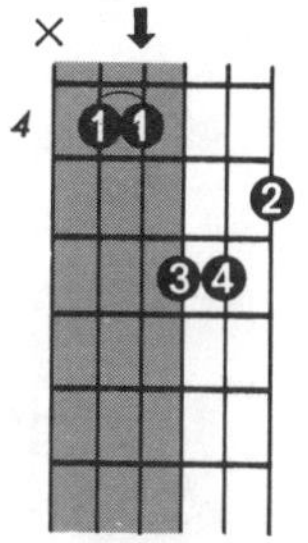

D♭G♭D♭F A

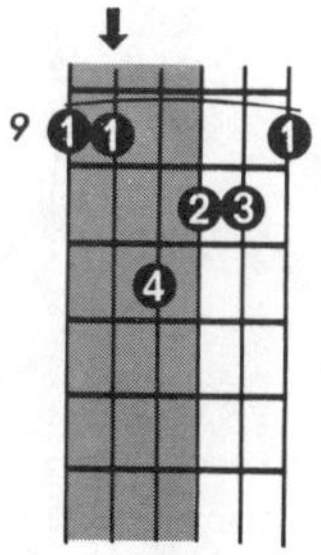

D♭G♭D♭F A D♭

F♯m+7

G♭m9+7

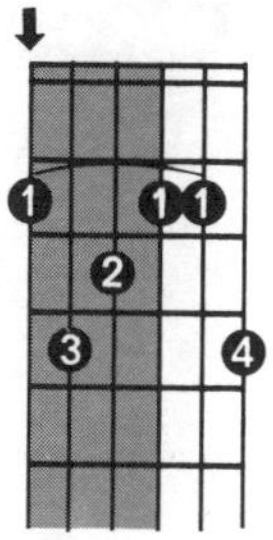

G♭D♭F A D♭A♭

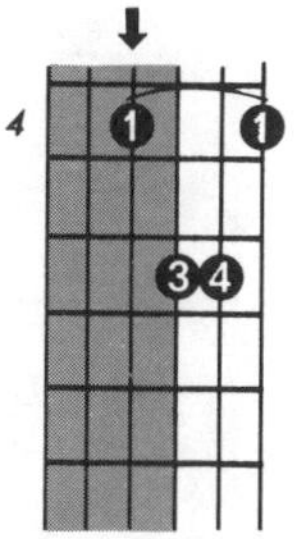

E A G♭D♭F A♭

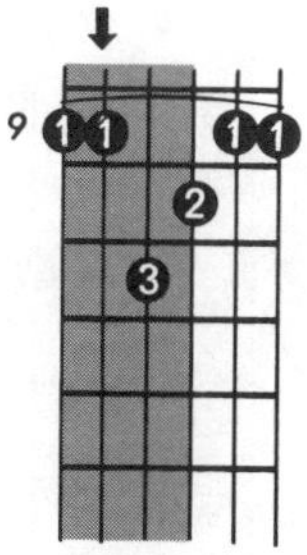

D♭G♭D♭F A♭D♭

F♯m9+7

G♭m+5

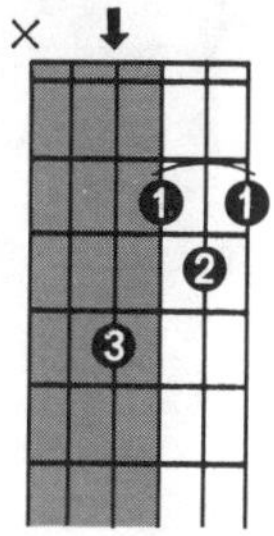

A G♭A D G♭

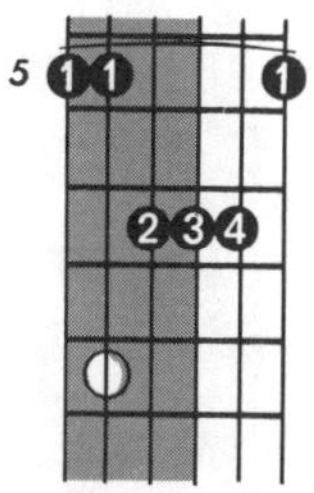

A D A D G♭A

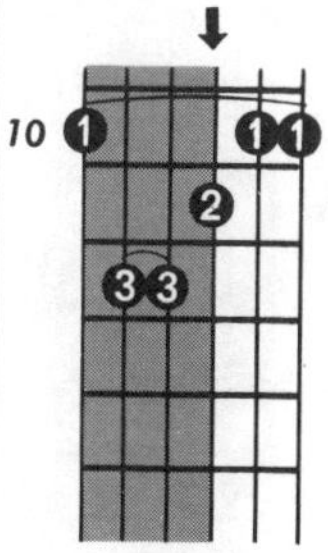

D A D G♭A D

F♯m+5

G♭m6·9

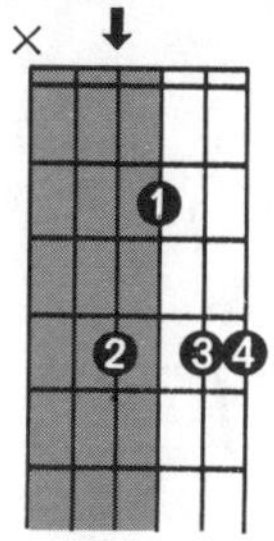

A G♭A E♭A♭

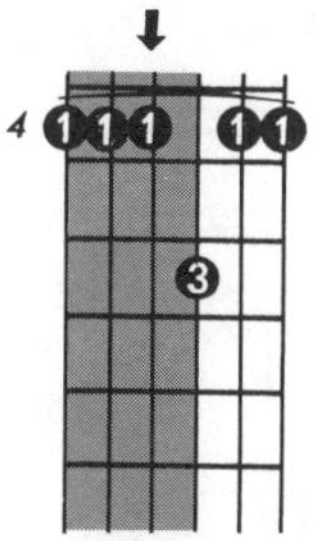

A♭D♭G♭D♭E♭A♭

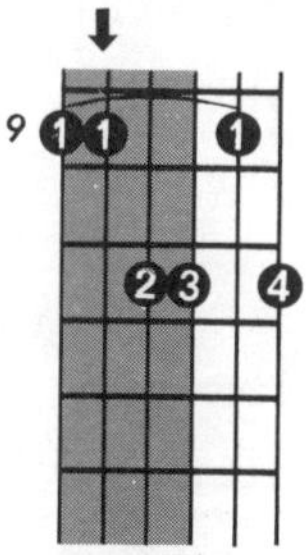

D♭G♭D♭G♭A♭E♭

F♯m6·9

G♭

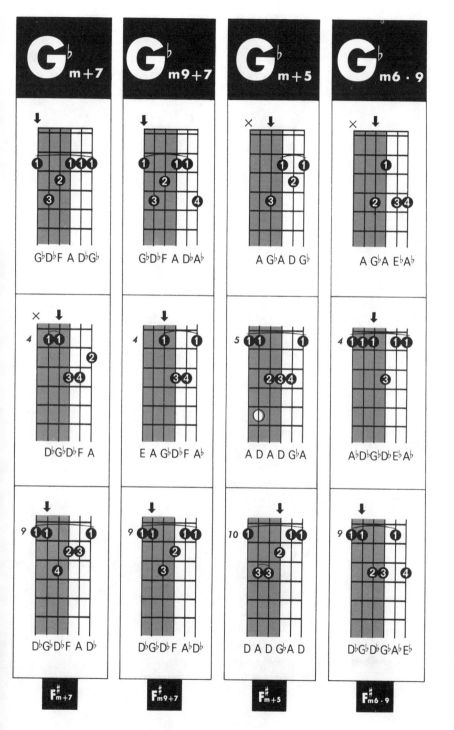

G

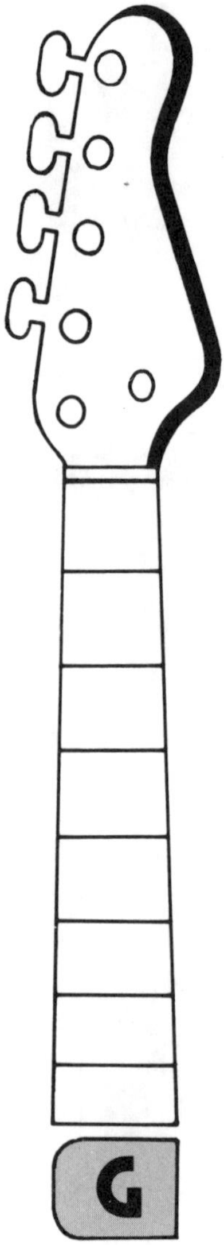

G

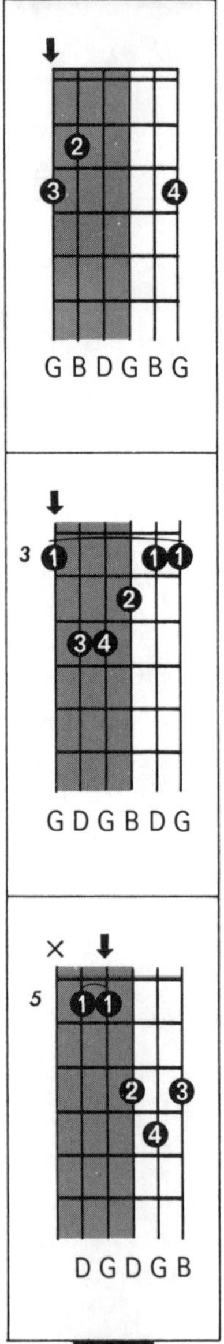
G B D G B G
3
G D G B D G
5
D G D G B

G6

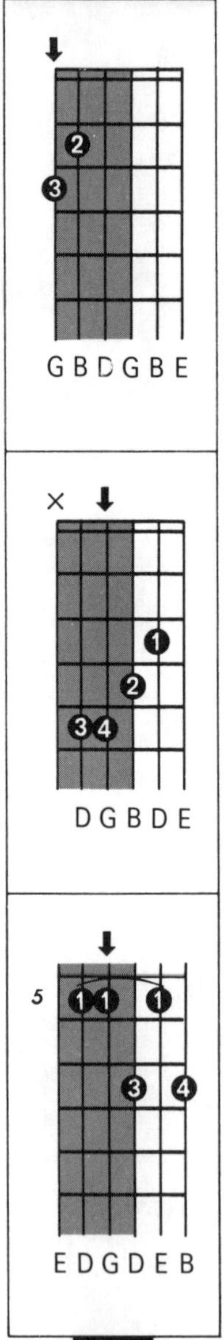
G B D G B E
D G B D E
5
E D G D E B

G7

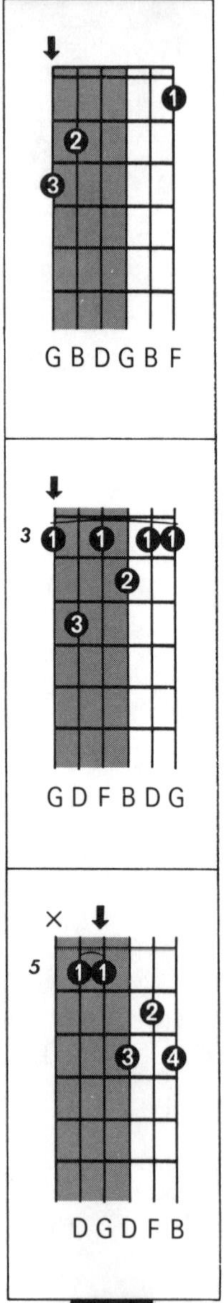
G B D G B F
3
G D F B D G
5
D G D F B

G_{9}

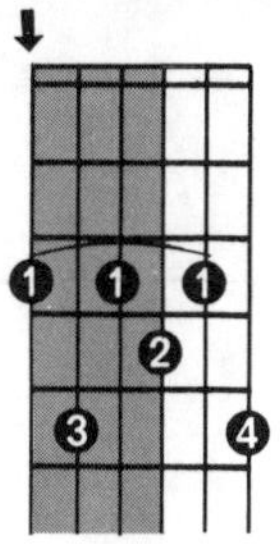

G D F B D A

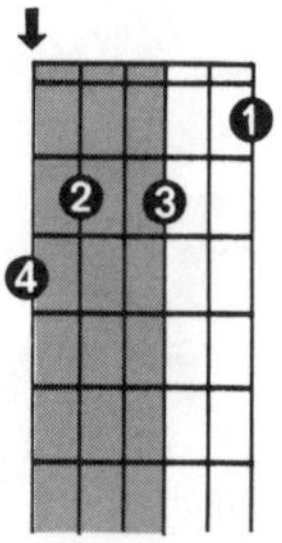

G B D A B F

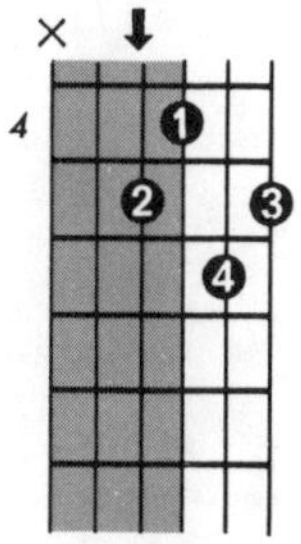

A G B F A

G_{11}

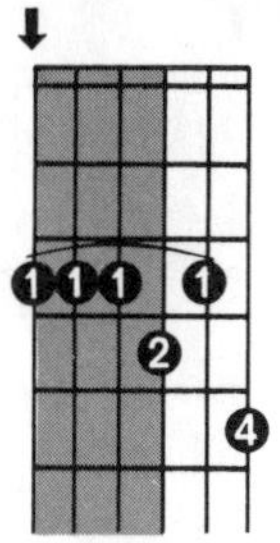

G C F B D A

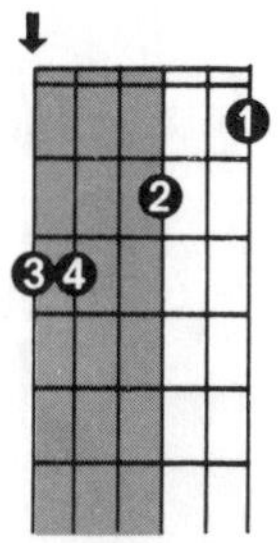

G C D A B F

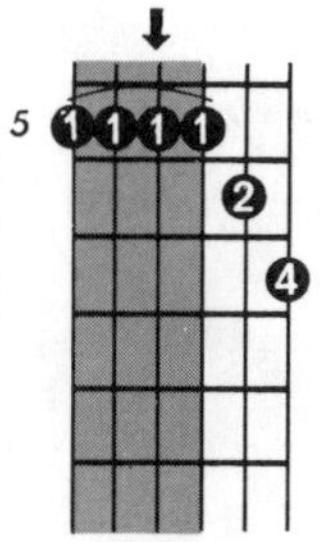

A D G C F B

G_{11+}

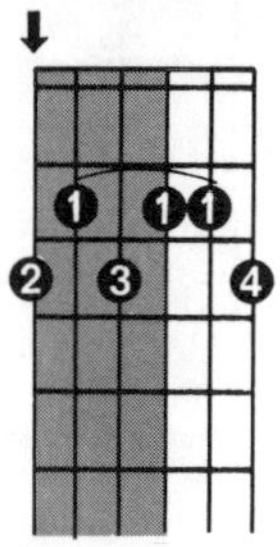

G B F A C♯G

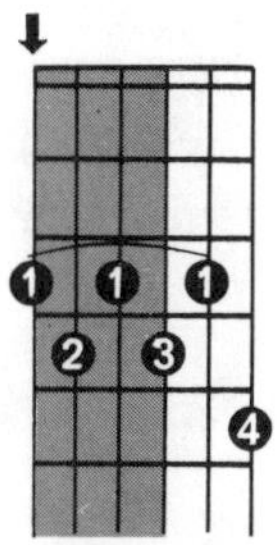

G C♯F B D A

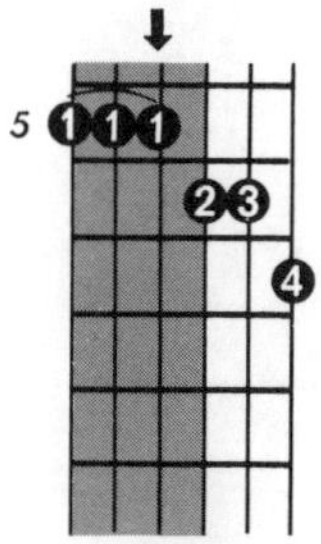

A D G C♯F B

G_{13}

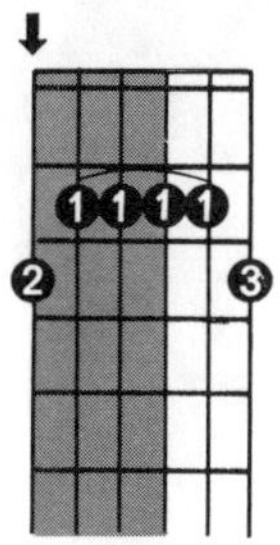

G B E A C♯G

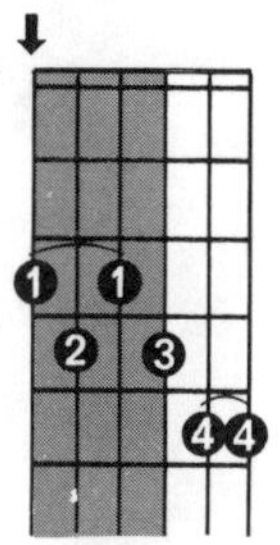

G C♯F B E A

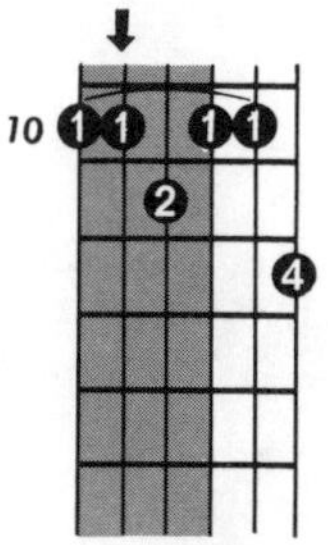

D G C♯F A E

G

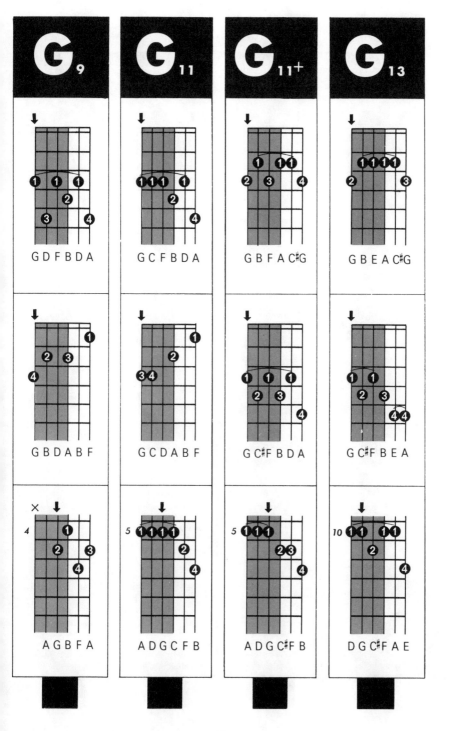

G maj7

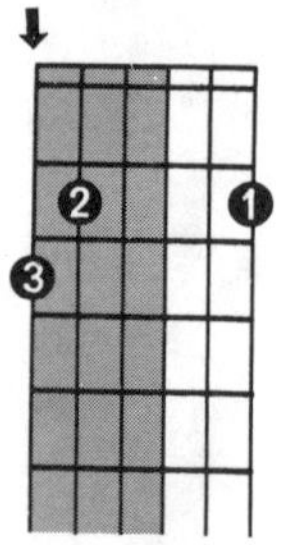

G B D G B F♯

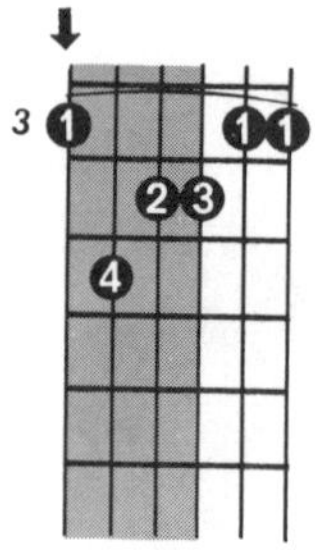

G D F♯B D G

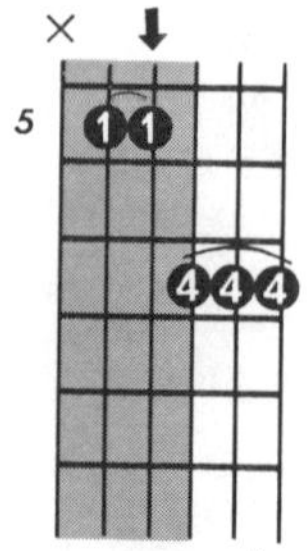

D G D F♯B

G maj9

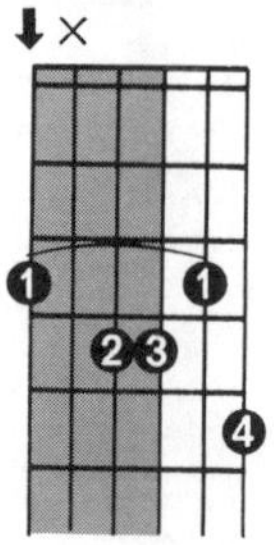

G F♯B D A

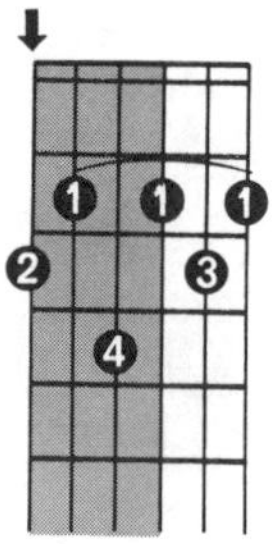

G B F♯A D F♯

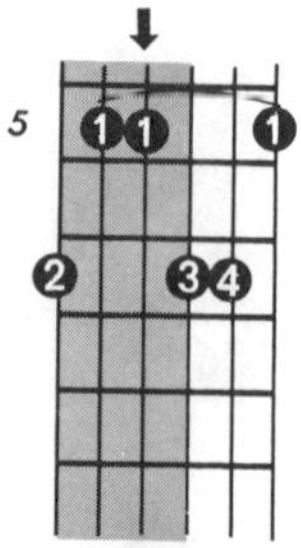

B D G D F♯A

G maj11

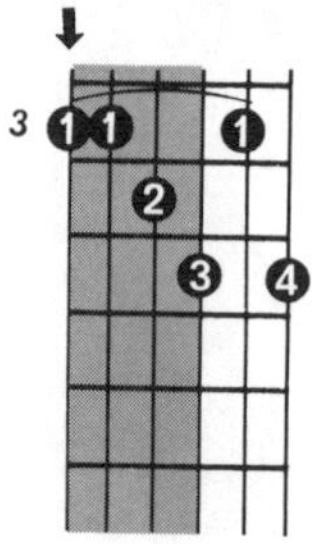

G C F♯C D A

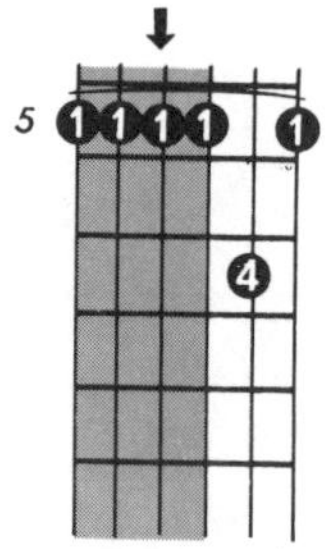

A D G C F♯A

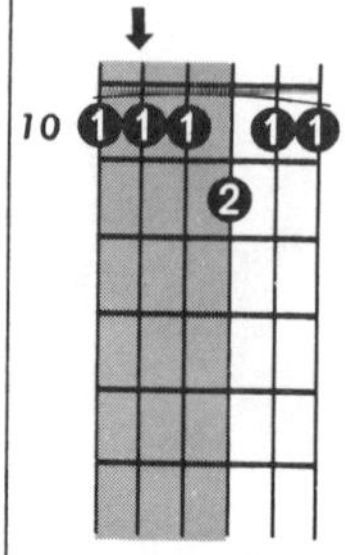

D G C F♯A D

G 7–5

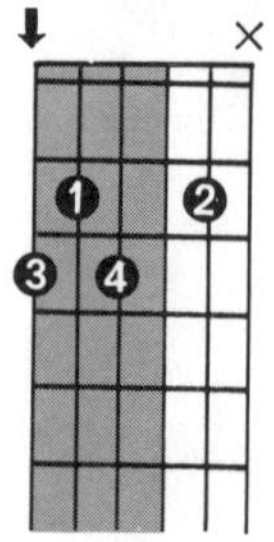

G B F G D♭

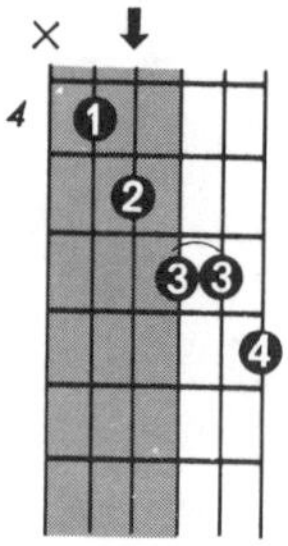

D♭G D♭F B

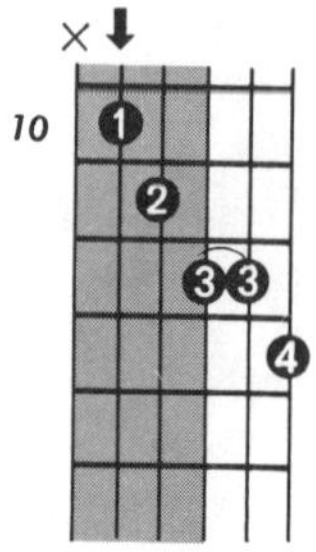

G D♭G B F

G_{7-9}

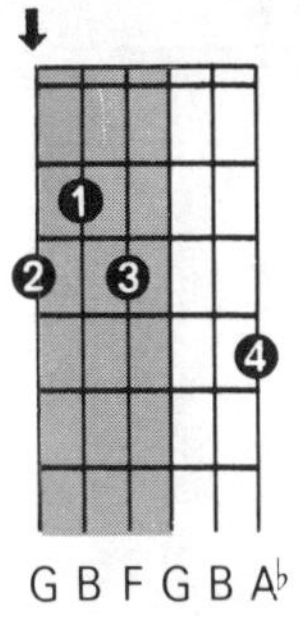

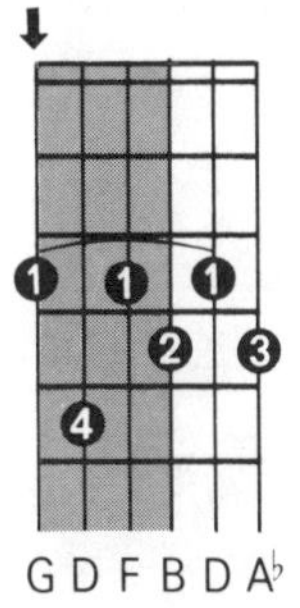

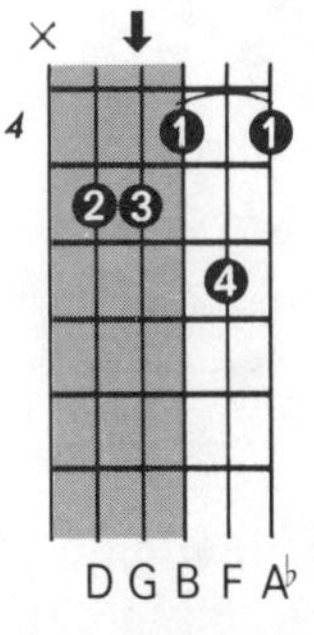

G_{7-10}

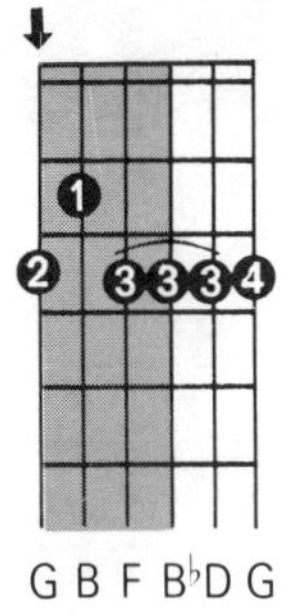

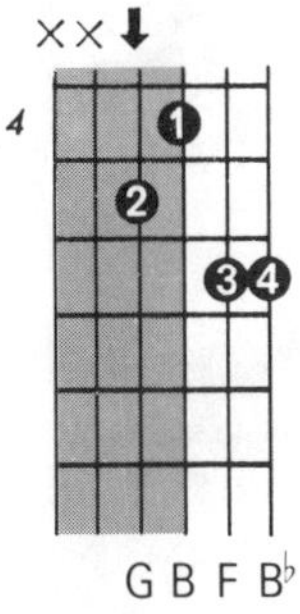

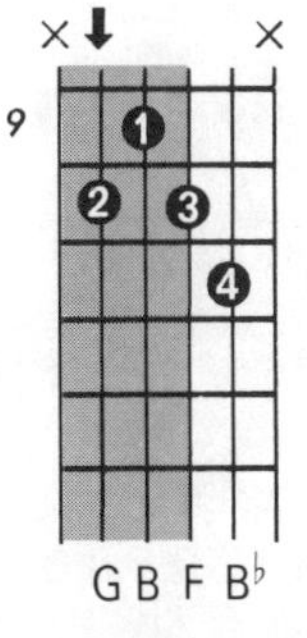

G_{7+5}

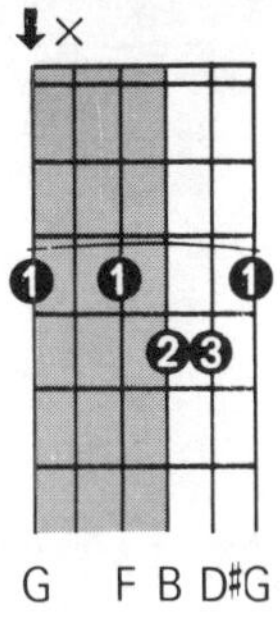

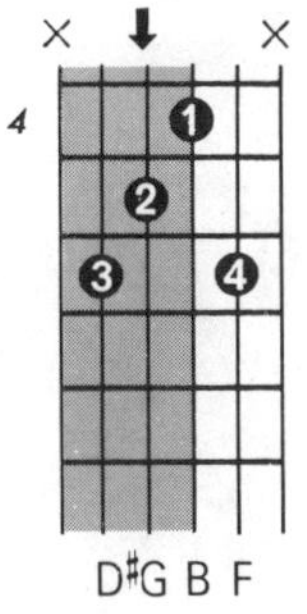

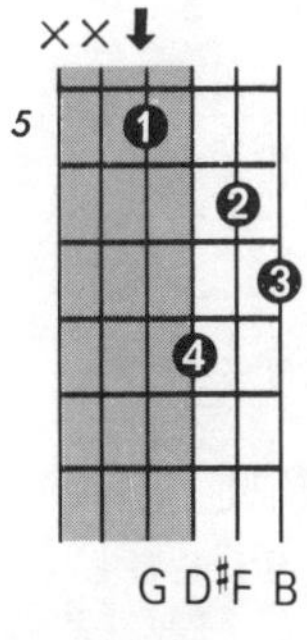

G_{9+5}

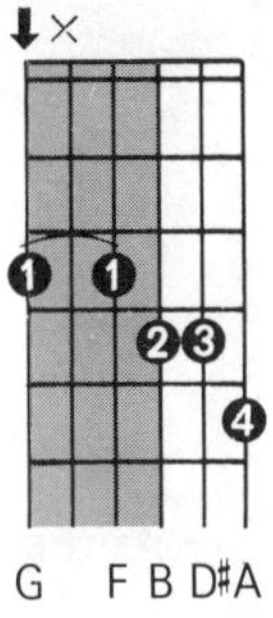

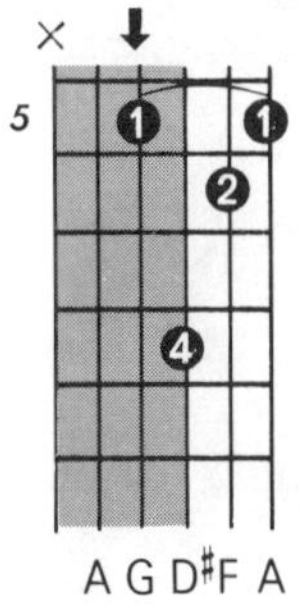

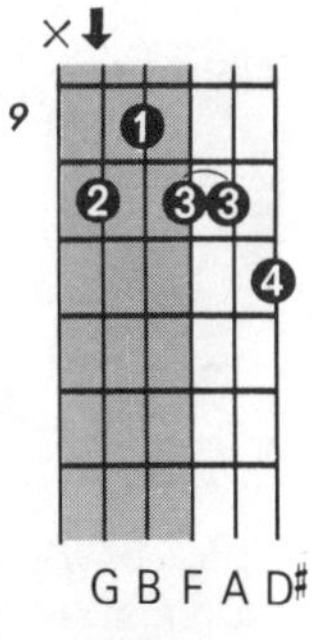

G

G

G_{7+5}^{-9}

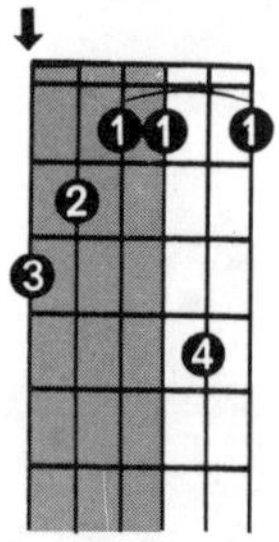

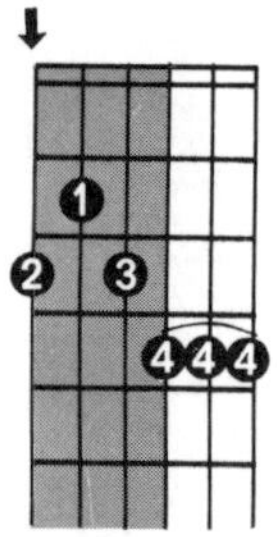

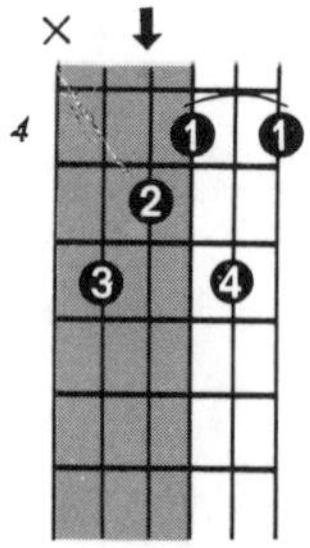

$G_{6 \cdot 9}$

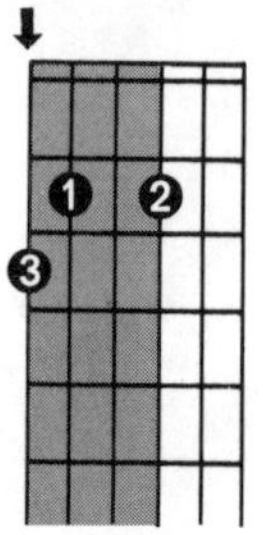

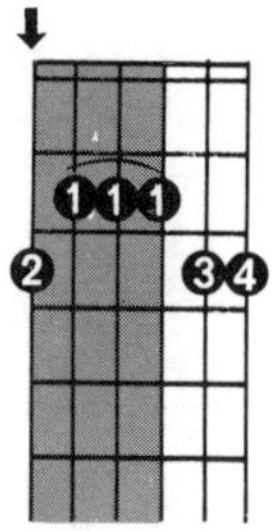

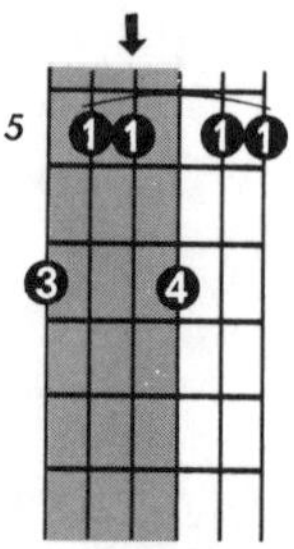

G_{dim}

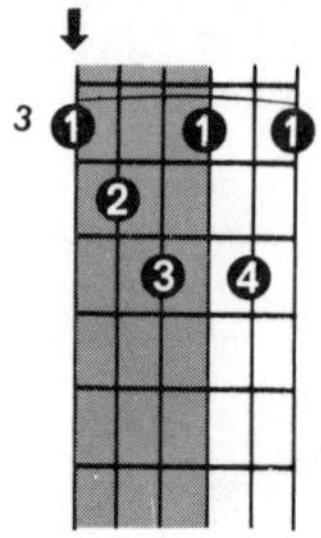

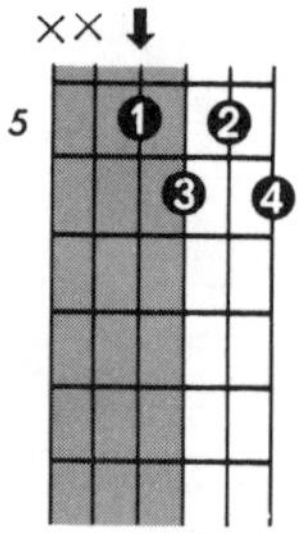

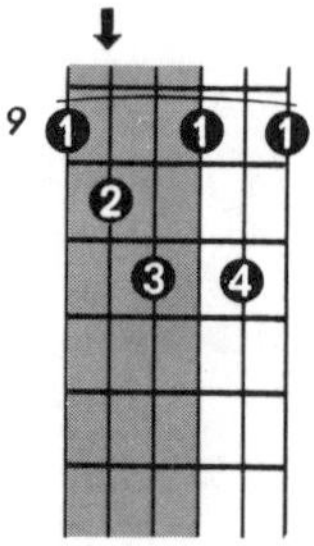

G_{+5}

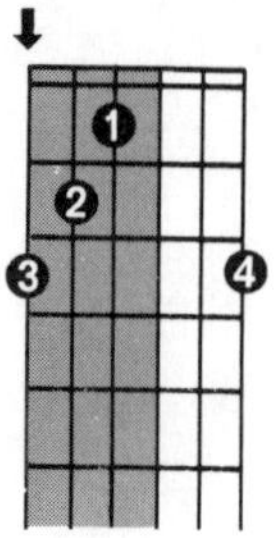

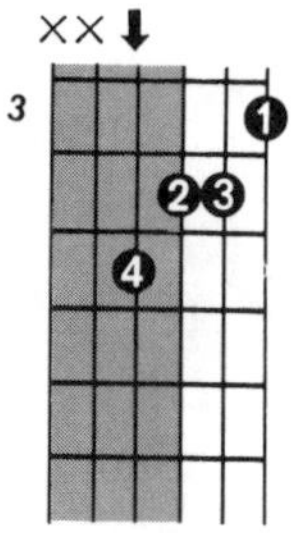

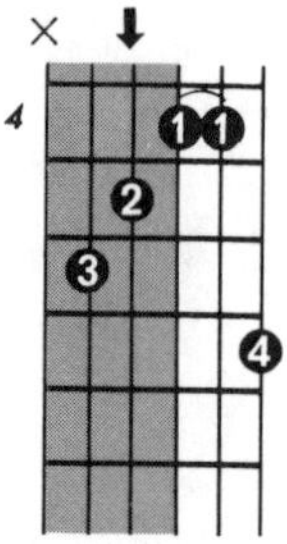

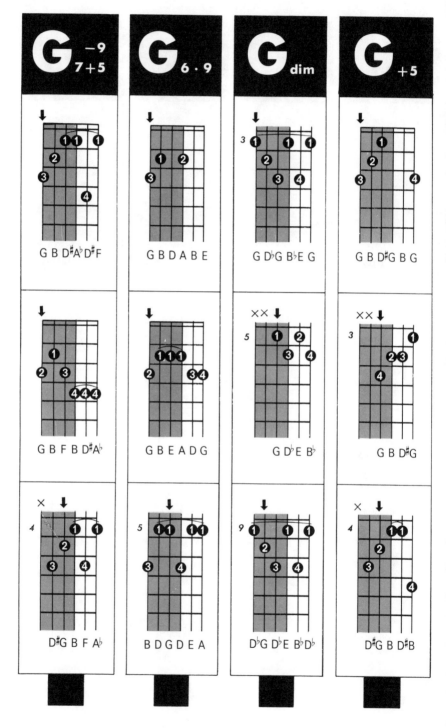

G sus4

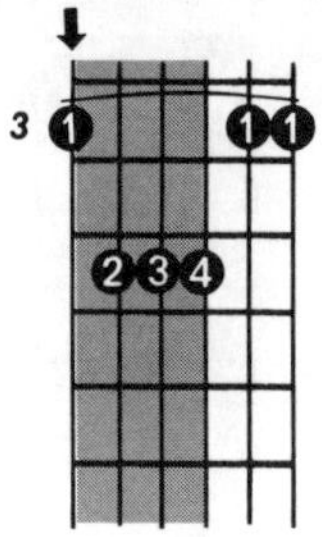

G D G C D G

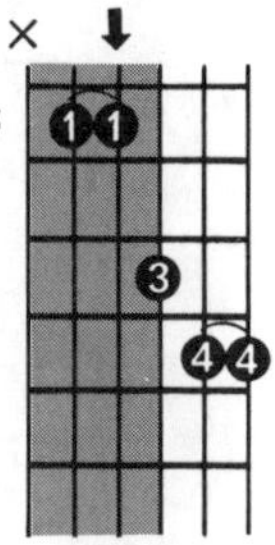

D G D G C

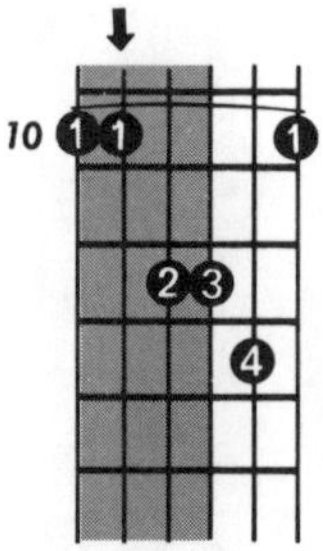

D G D G C D

G 7sus4

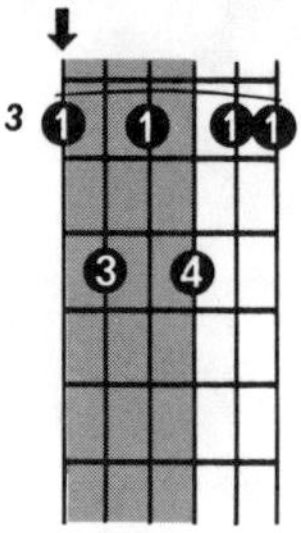

G D F C D G

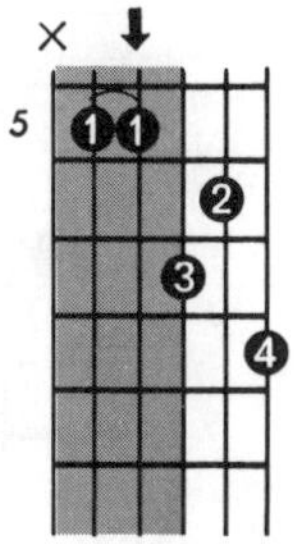

D G D F C

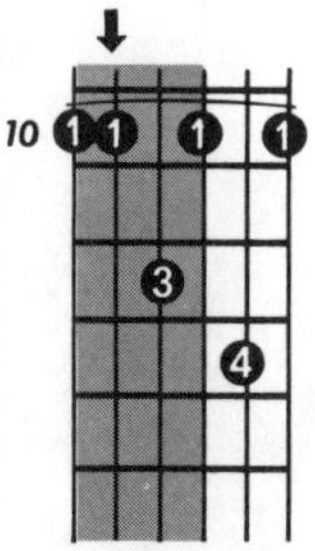

D G D F C D

G m

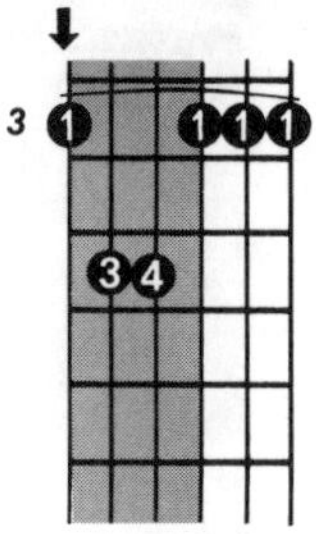

G D G B♭ D G

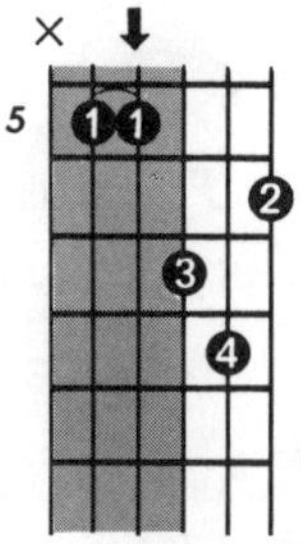

D G D G B♭

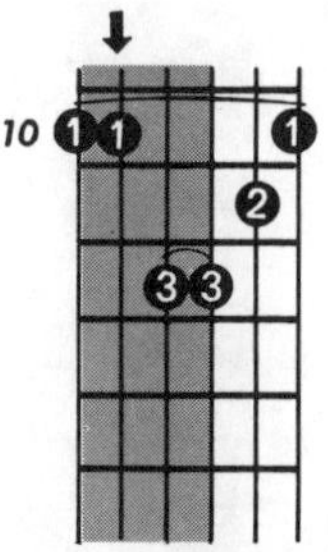

D G D G B♭ D

G m6

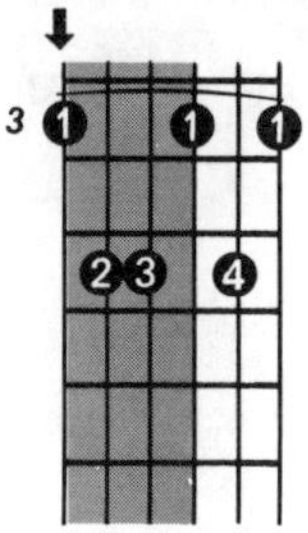

G D G B♭ E G

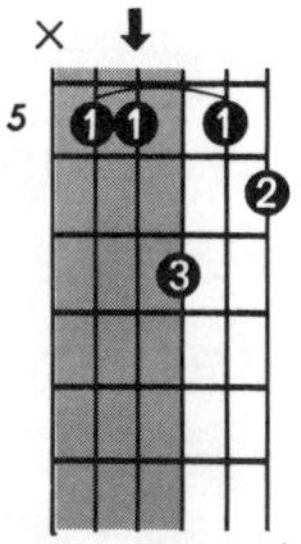

D G D E B♭

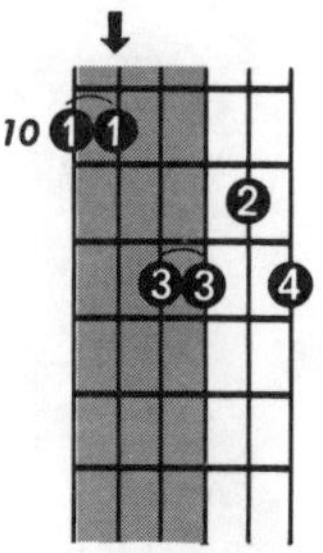

D G D G B♭ E

G

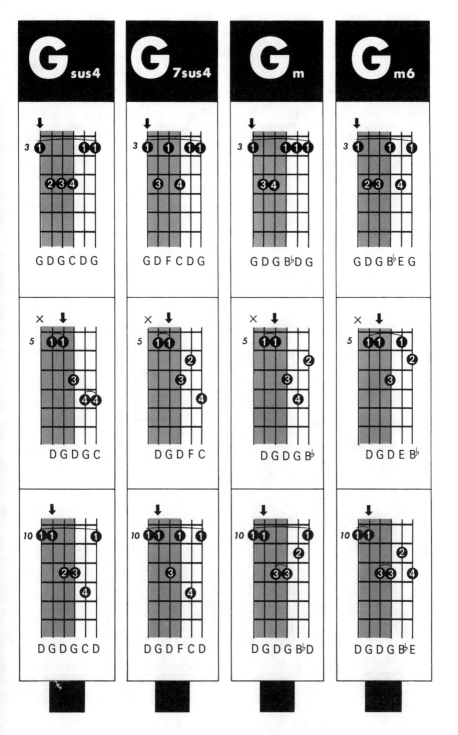

G m7

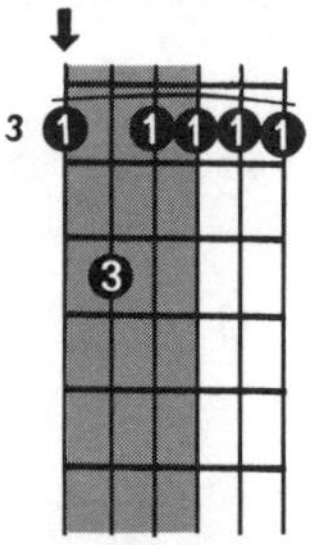

G D F B♭ D G

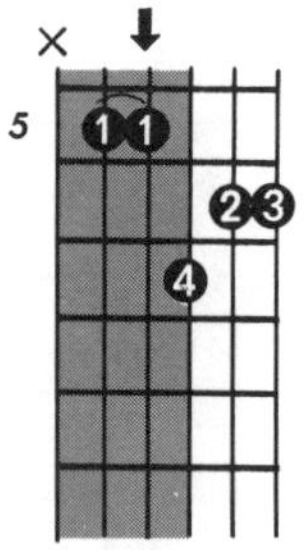

D G D F B♭

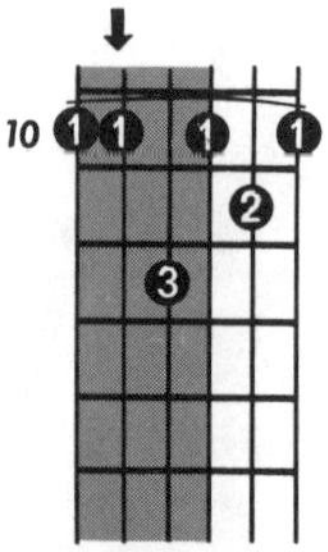

D G D F B♭ D

G m9

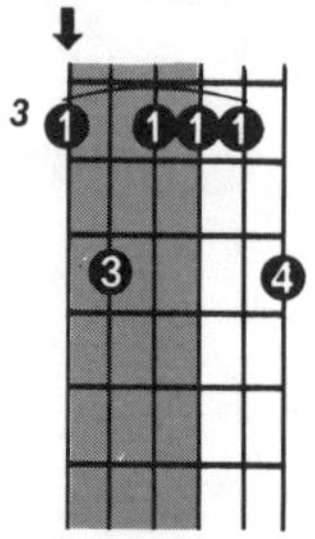

G D F B♭ D A

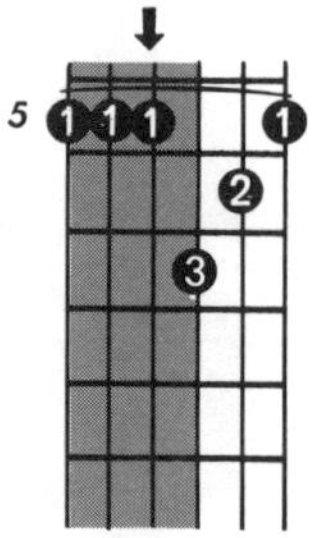

A D G D F A

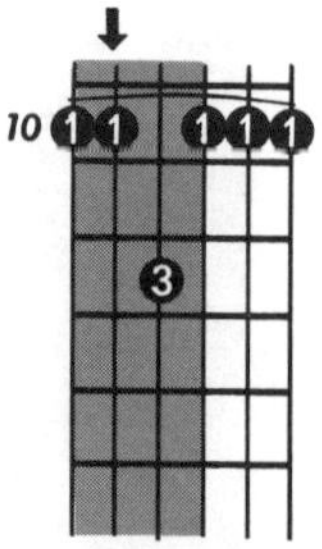

D G D F A D

G m7–5

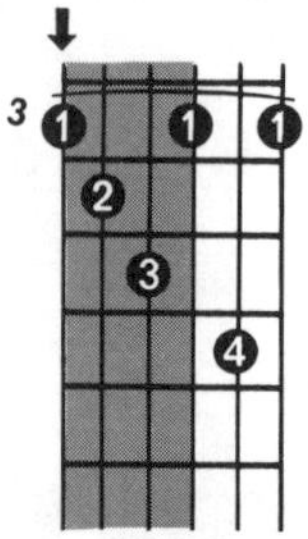

G D♭ G B♭ F G

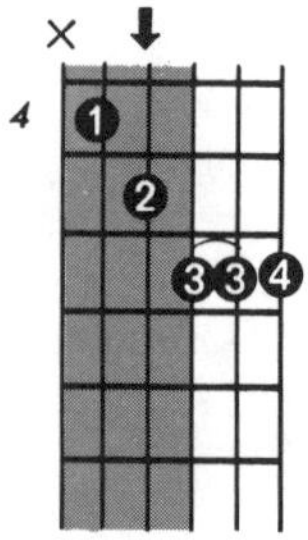

D♭ G D♭ F B♭

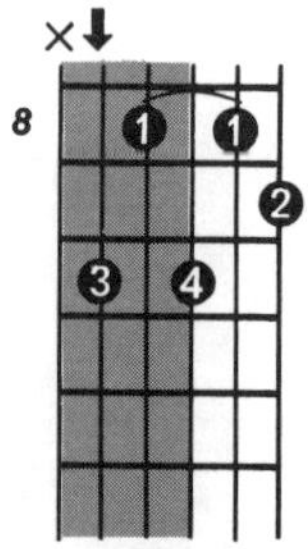

G B♭ F G D♭

G m7–9

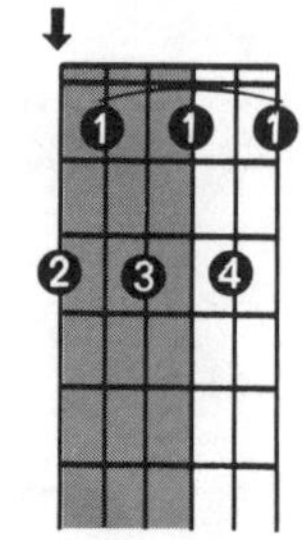

G B♭ F A♭ D F

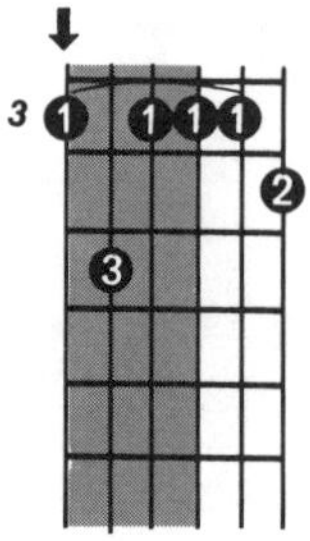

G D F B♭ D A♭

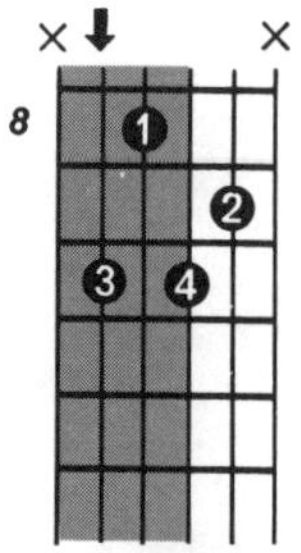

G B♭ F A♭

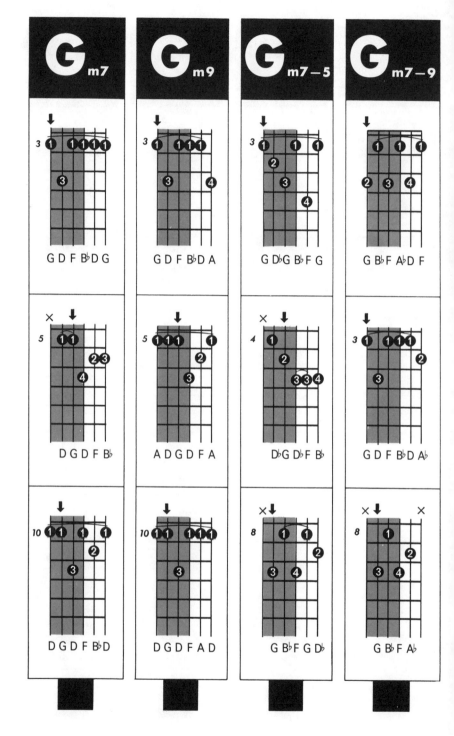

G m+7

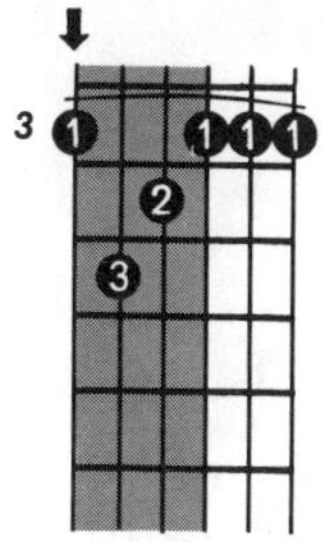

G D F♯B♭D G

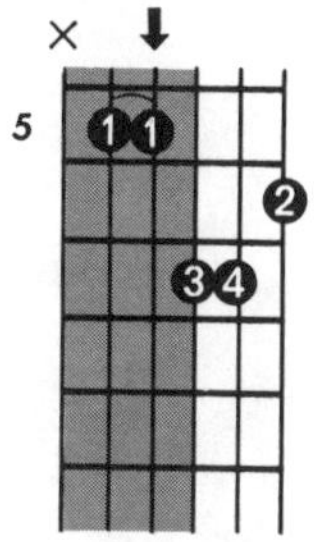

D G D F♯B♭

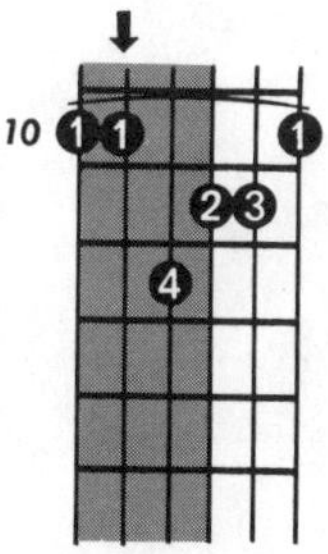

D G D F♯B♭D

G m9+7

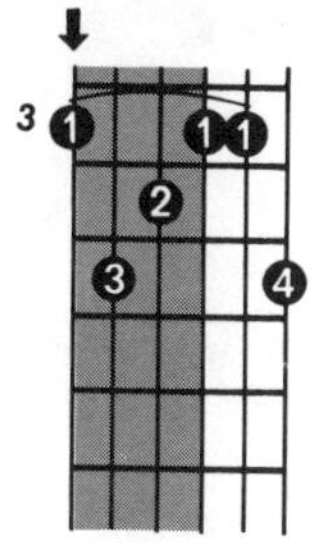

G D F♯B♭D A

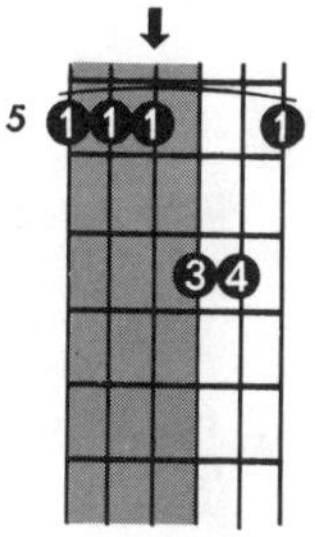

A D G D F♯A

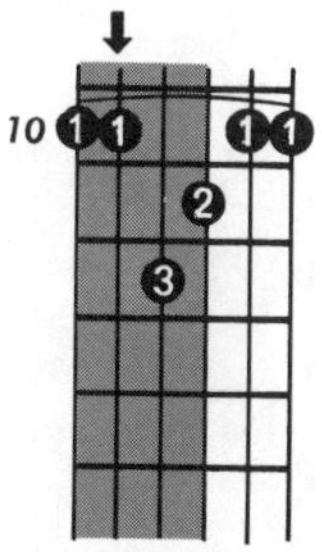

D G D F♯A D

G m+5

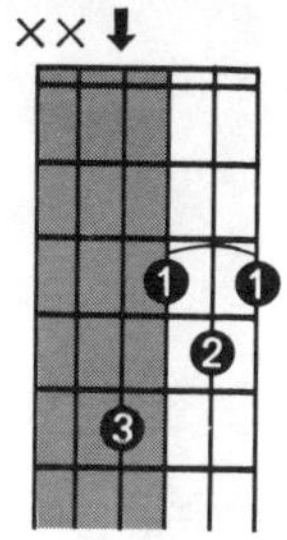

G B♭E♭G

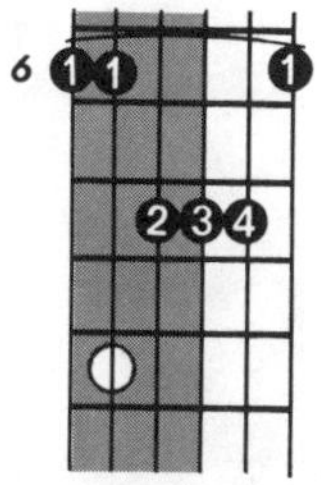

B♭D♯B♭D♯G B♭

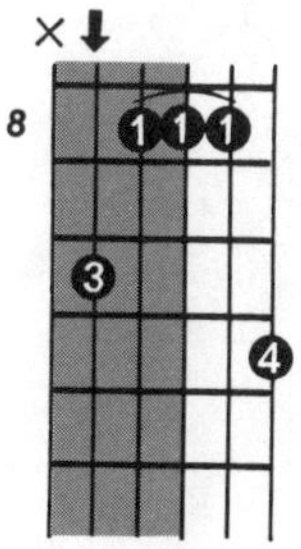

G B♭D♯G D♯

G m6 · 9

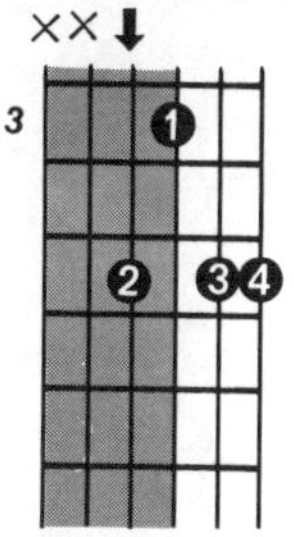

G B♭E A

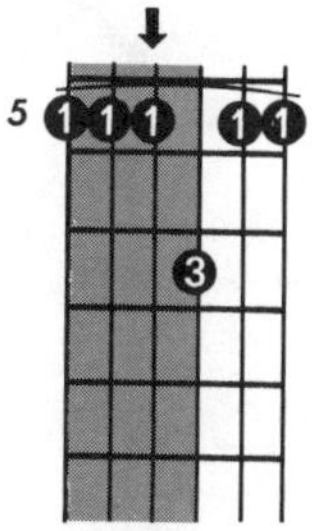

A D G D E A

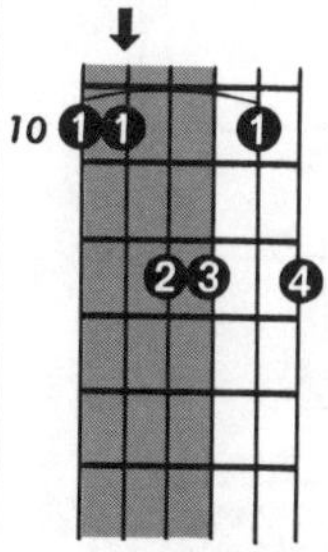

D G D G A E

G

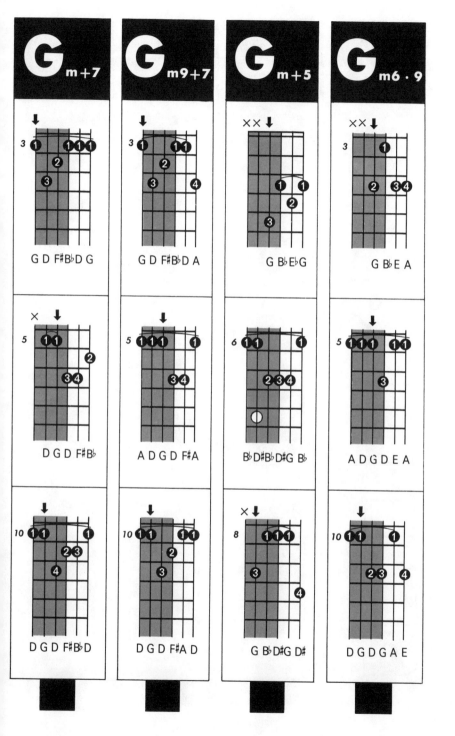

A♭

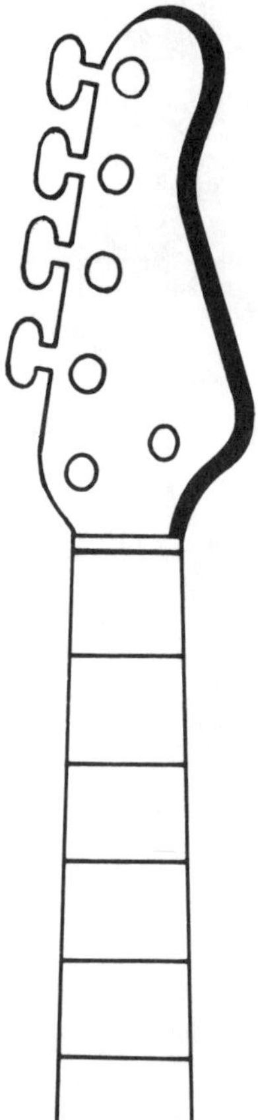

G♯

A♭	A♭6	A♭7
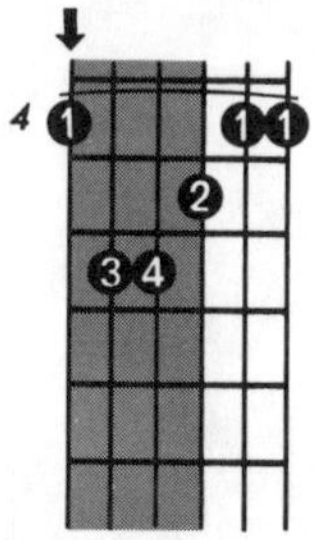 A♭ E♭ A♭ C E♭ A♭	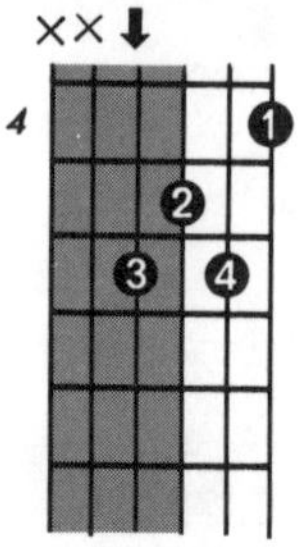 A♭ C F A♭	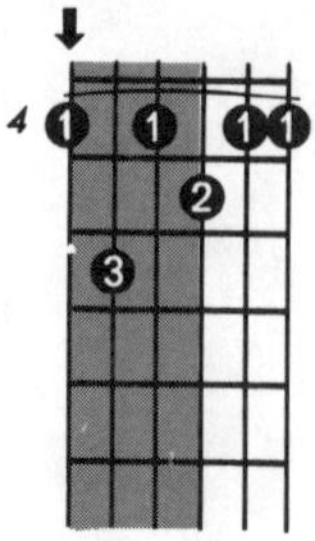 A♭ E♭ G♭ C E♭ A♭
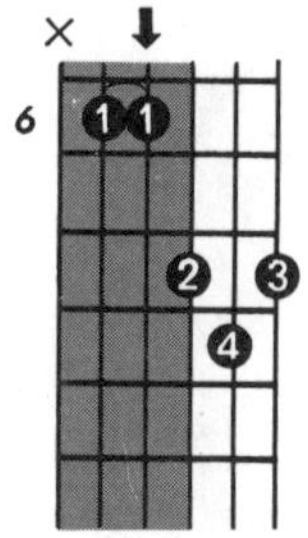 E♭ A♭ E♭ A♭ C	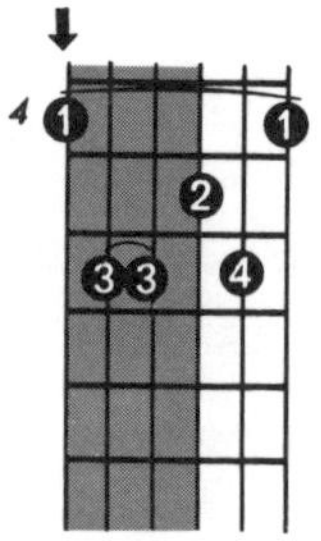 A♭ E♭ A♭ C F A♭	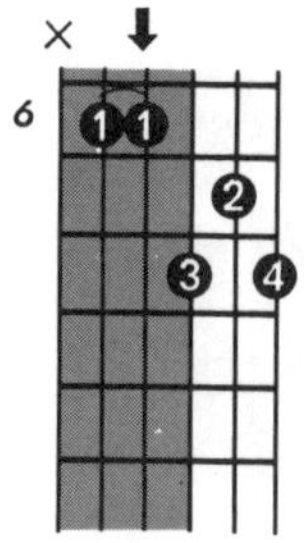 E♭ A♭ E♭ G♭ C
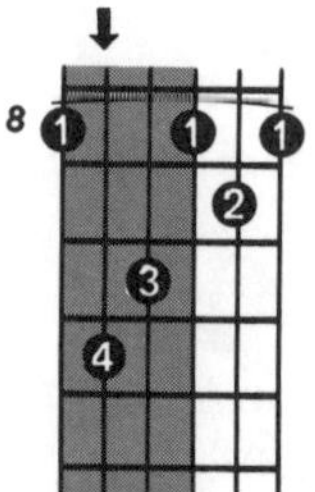 C A♭ C E♭ A♭ C	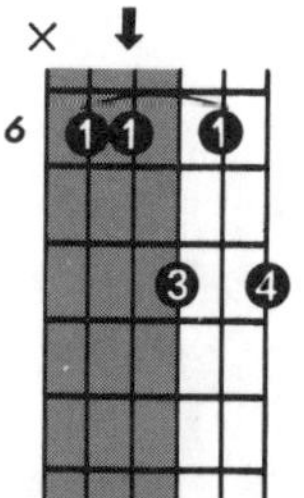 E♭ A♭ E♭ F C	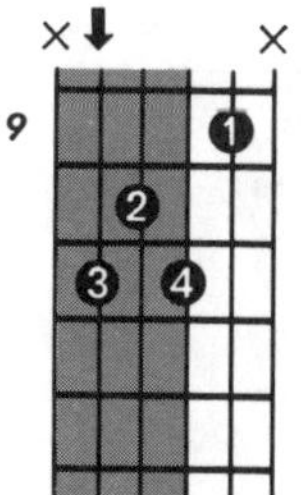 A♭ C G♭ A♭
G♯	G♯6	G♯7

A♭9

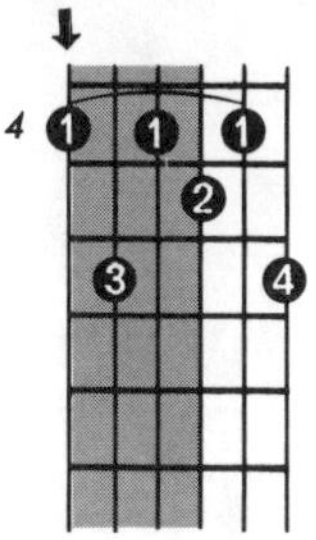

A♭ E♭ G♭ C E♭ B♭

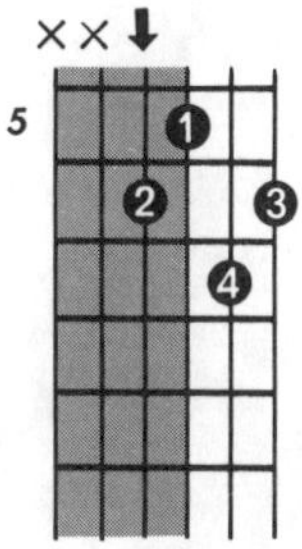

A♭ C G♭ B♭

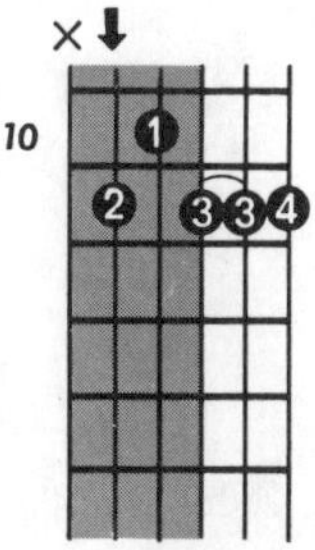

A♭ C G♭ B♭ E♭

G♯9

A♭11

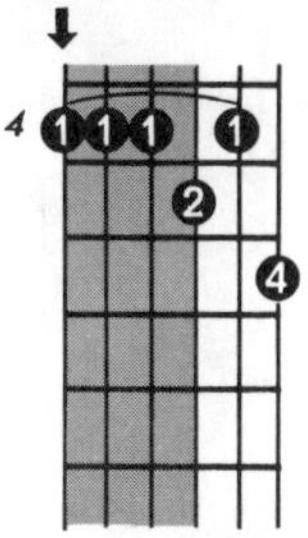

A♭ D♭ G♭ C E♭ B♭

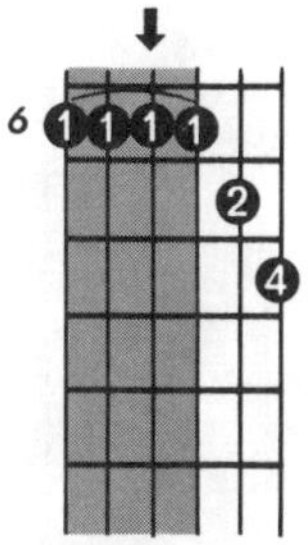

B♭ E♭ A♭ D♭ G♭ C

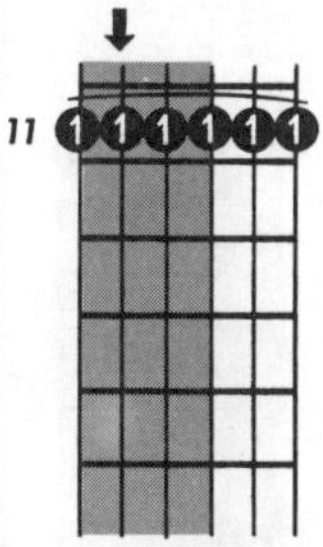

E♭ A♭ D♭ G♭ B♭ E♭

G♯11

A♭11+

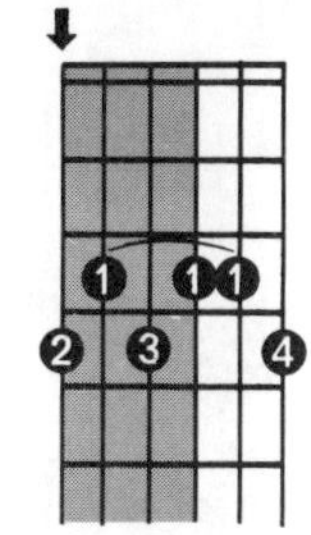

A♭ C G♭ B♭ D A♭

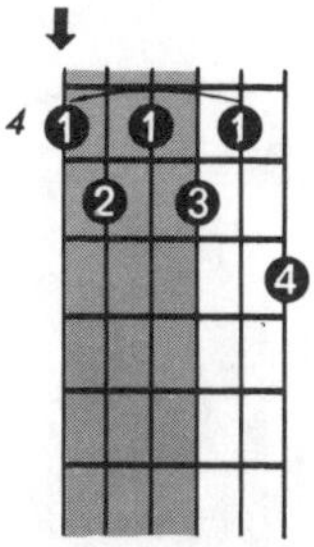

A♭ D G♭ C E♭ B♭

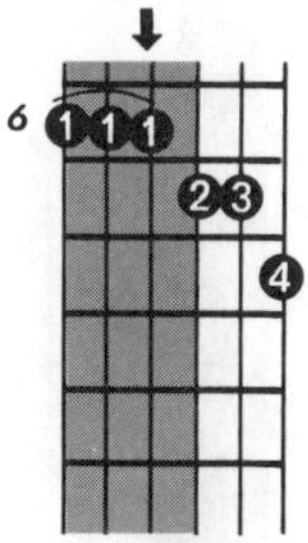

B♭ E♭ A♭ D G♭ C

G♯11+

A♭13

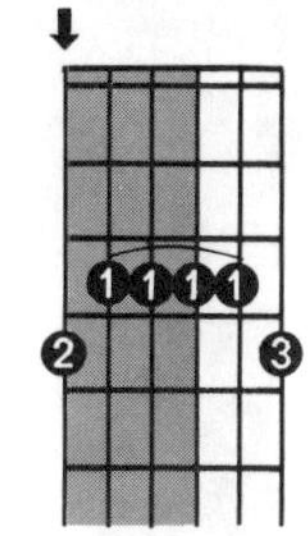

A♭ C F B♭ D A♭

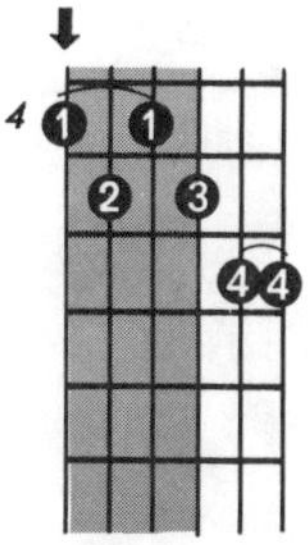

A♭ D G♭ C F B♭

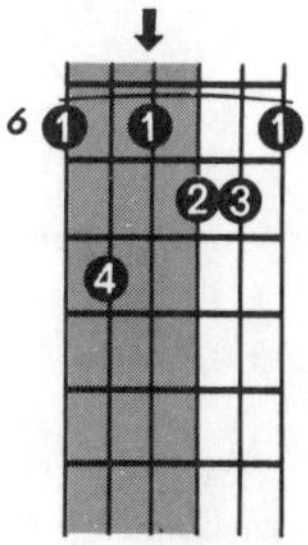

B♭ F A♭ D G♭ B♭

G♯13

A♭

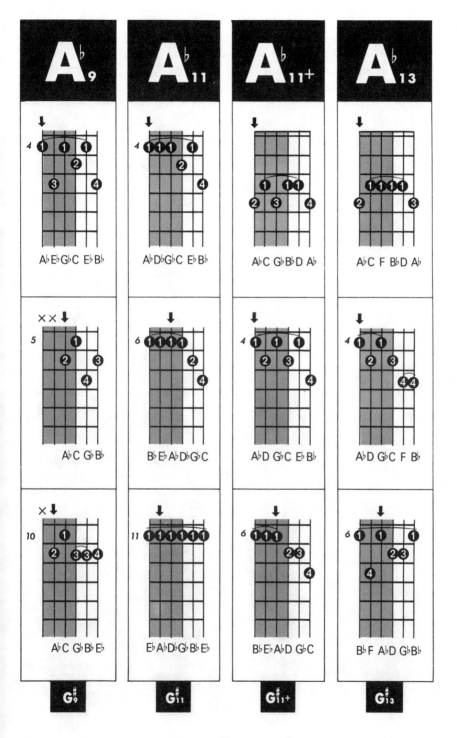

G♯

A♭ maj7

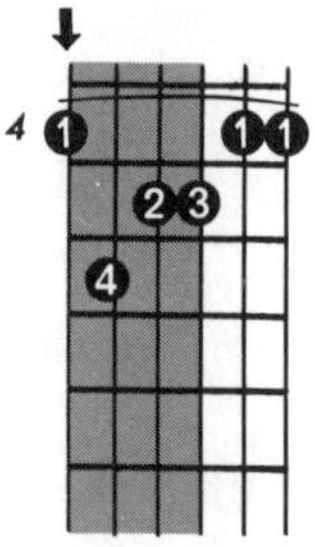

A♭E♭G C E♭A♭

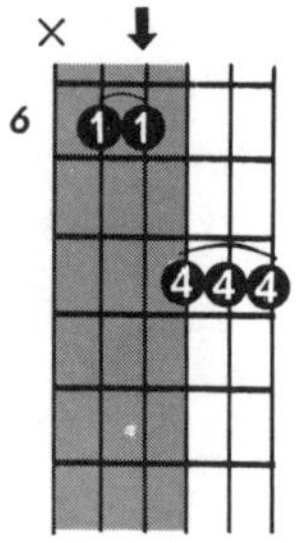

E♭A♭E♭G C

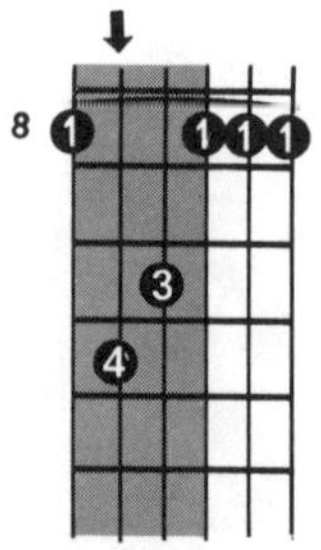

C A♭C E♭G C

G♯ maj7

A♭ maj9

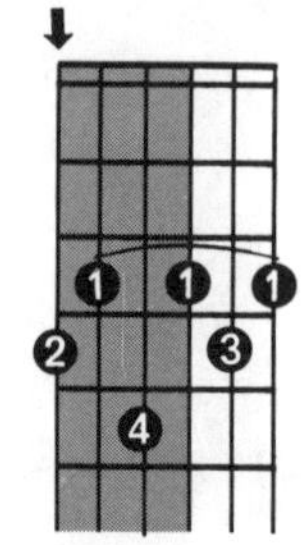

A♭C G B♭E♭G

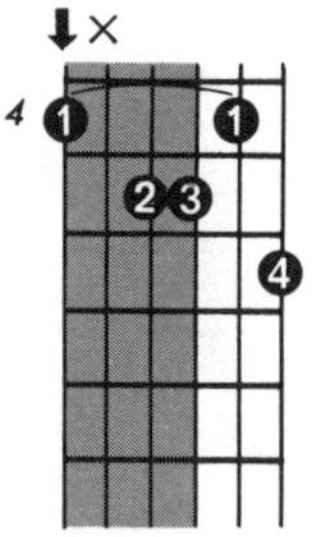

A♭ G C E♭B♭

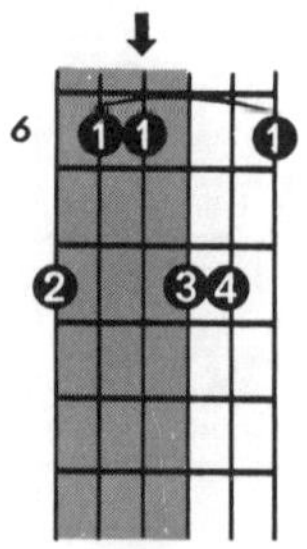

C E♭A♭E♭G B♭

G♯ maj9

A♭ maj11

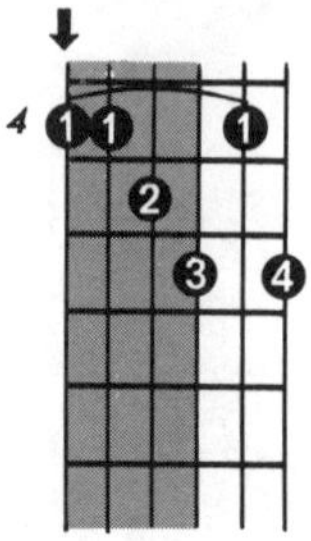

A♭D♭G D♭E♭B♭

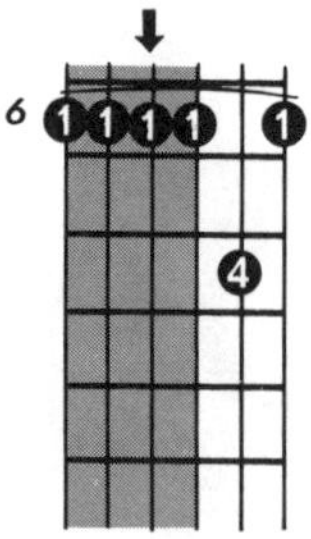

B♭E♭A♭D♭G B♭

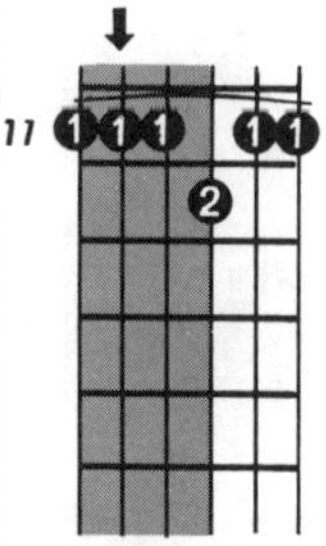

E♭A♭D♭G B♭E♭

G♯ maj11

A♭ 7–5

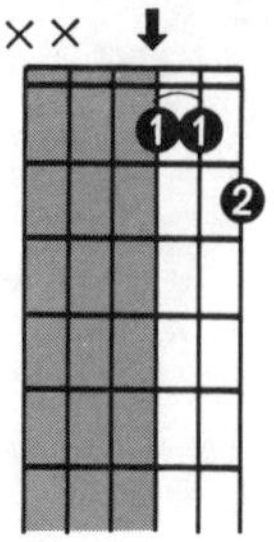

D A♭C G♭

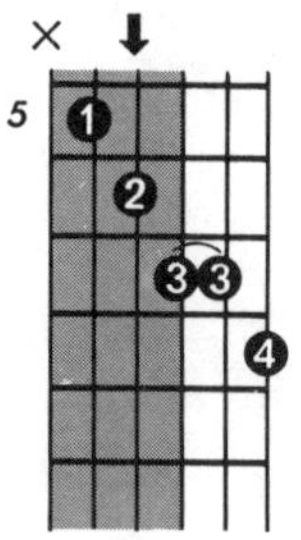

D A♭D G♭C

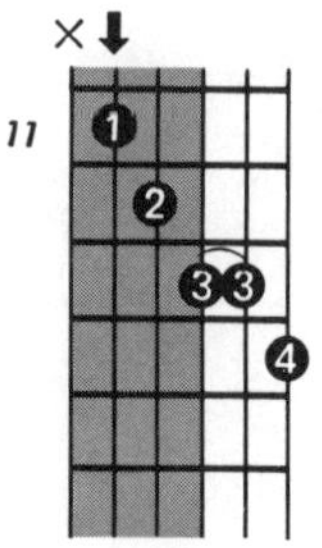

A♭D A♭C G♭

G♯ 7–5

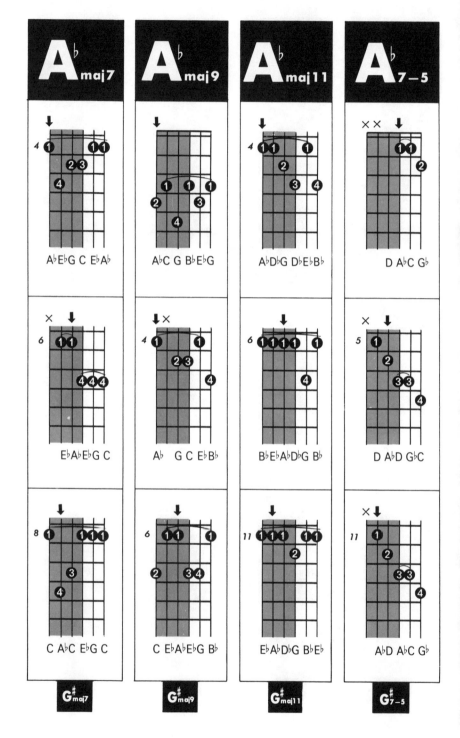

$A^{\flat}_{7-9}$

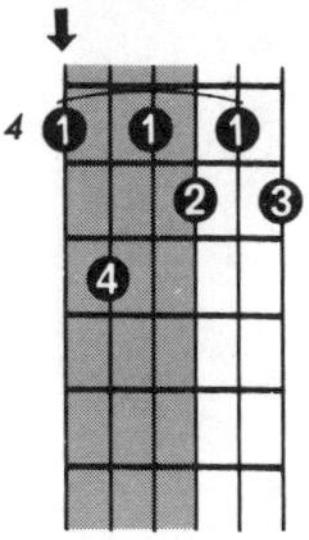

A♭E♭G♭C E♭A

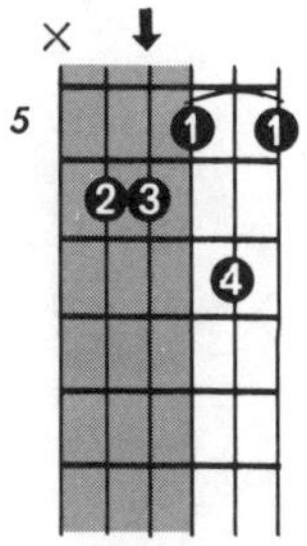

E♭A♭C G♭A

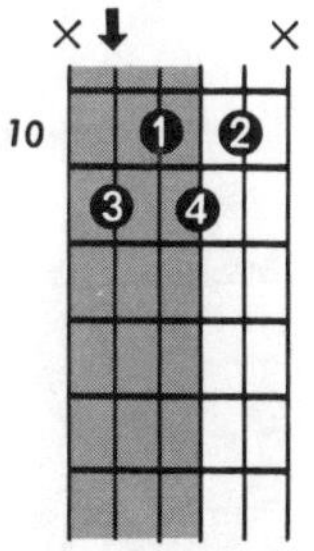

A♭C G♭A

$G^{\sharp}_{7-9}$

$A^{\flat}_{7-10}$

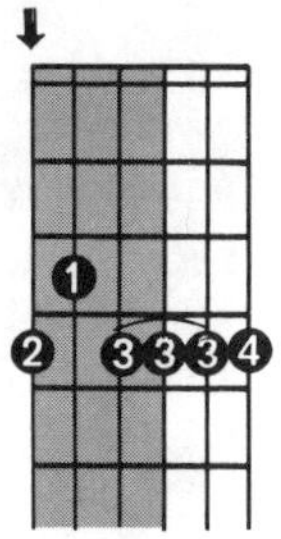

A♭C G♭B E♭A♭

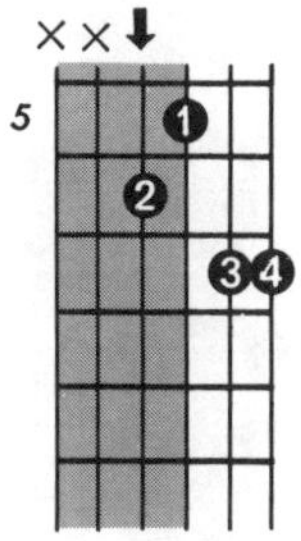

A♭C G♭B

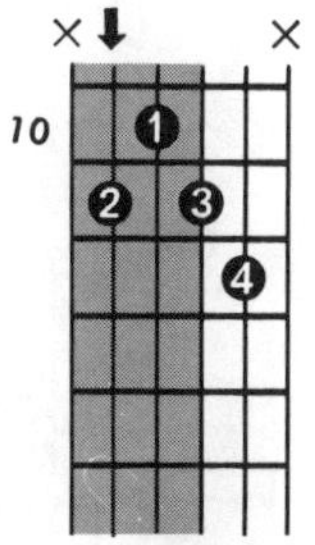

A♭C G♭B

$G^{\sharp}_{7-10}$

$A^{\flat}_{7+5}$

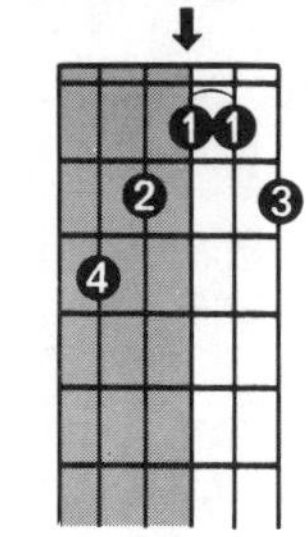

E C E A♭C G♭

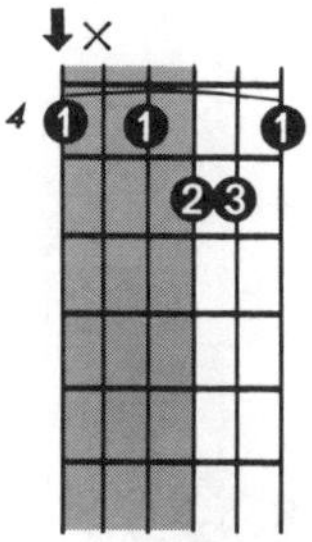

A♭ G♭C E A♭

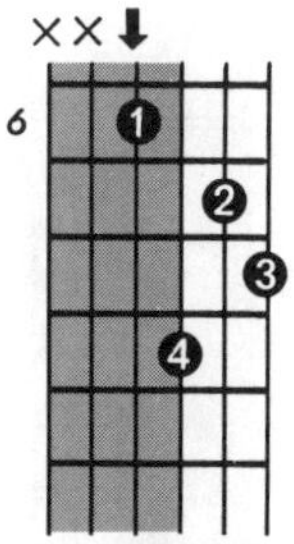

A♭E G♭C

$G^{\sharp}_{7+5}$

$A^{\flat}_{9+5}$

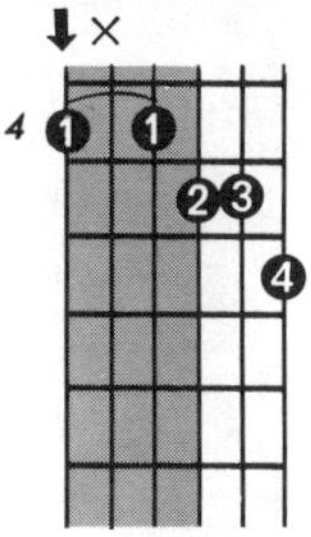

A♭ G♭C E B♭

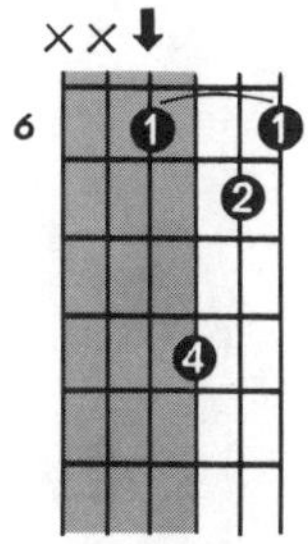

A♭E G♭B♭

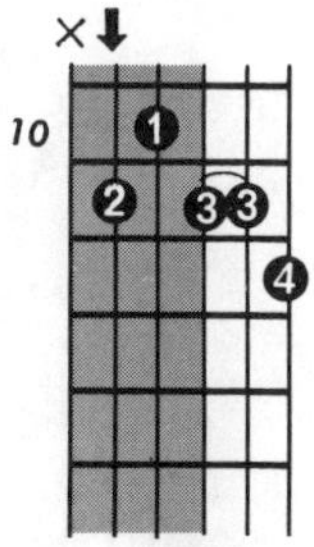

A♭C G♭B♭E

$G^{\sharp}_{9+5}$

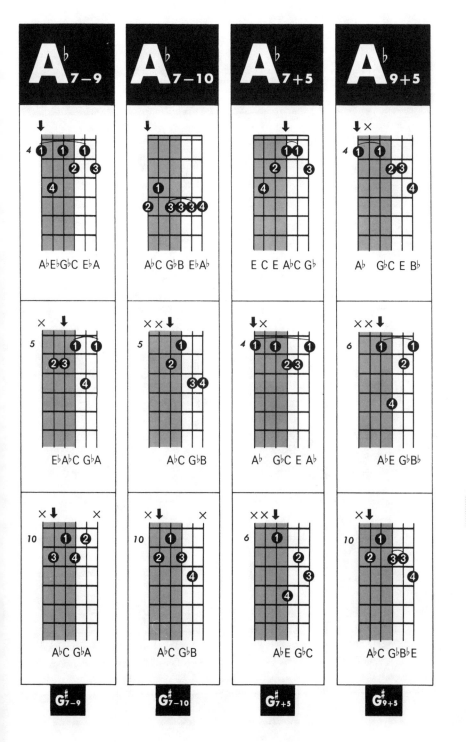

G♯

A♭ $_{7+5}^{-9}$

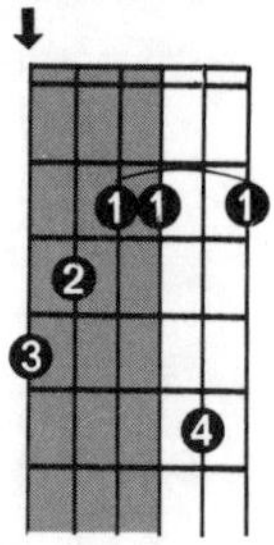

A♭C E A E G♭

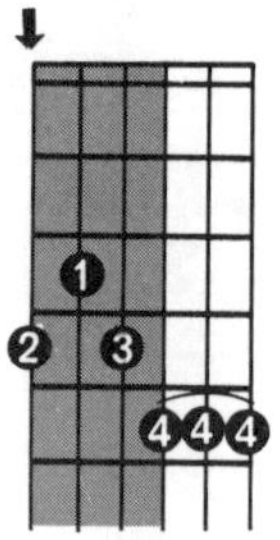

A♭C G♭C E A

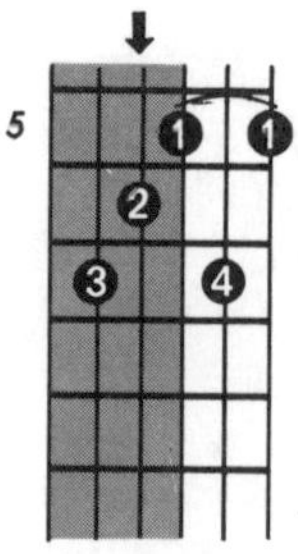

E E A♭C G♭A

G♯ $_{7+5}^{-9}$

A♭ $_{6 \cdot 9}$

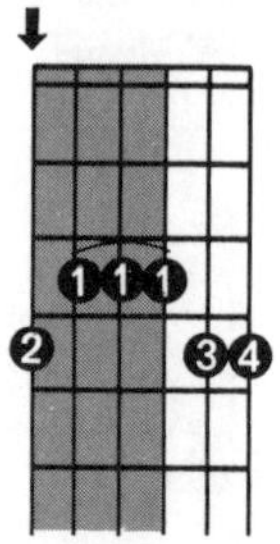

A♭C F B♭E♭A♭

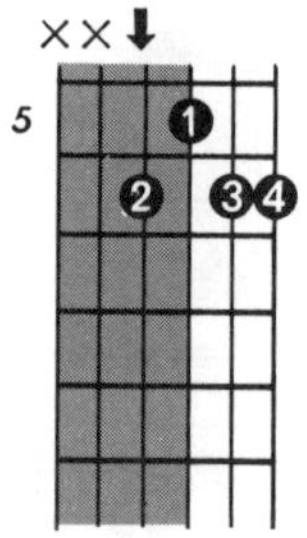

A♭C F B♭

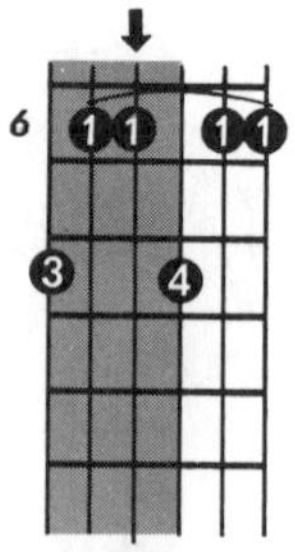

C E♭A♭E♭F B♭

G♯ $_{6 \cdot 9}$

A♭ dim

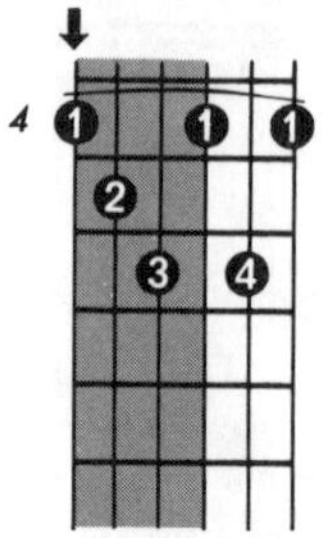

A♭D A♭B F A♭

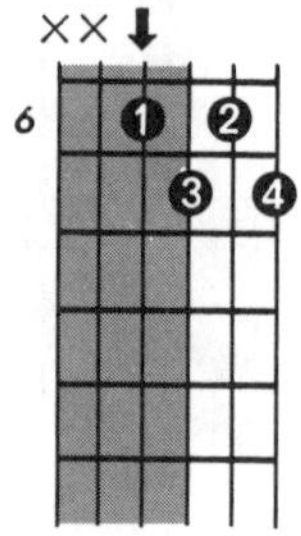

A♭D F B

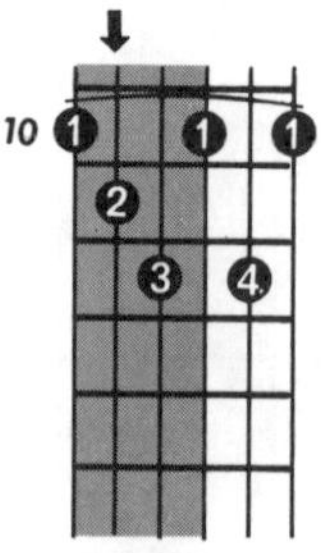

D A♭D F B D

G♯ dim

A♭ +5

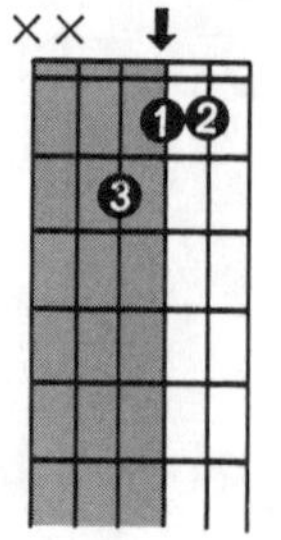

E A♭C E

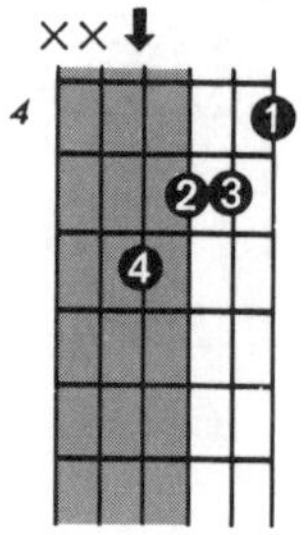

A♭C E A♭

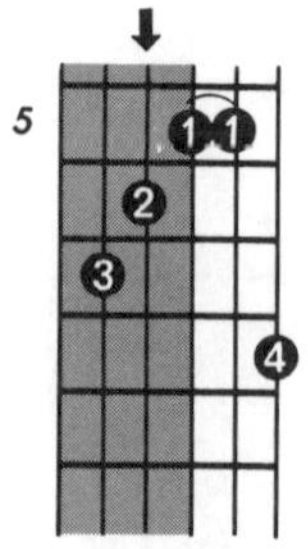

E E A♭C E C

G♯ +5

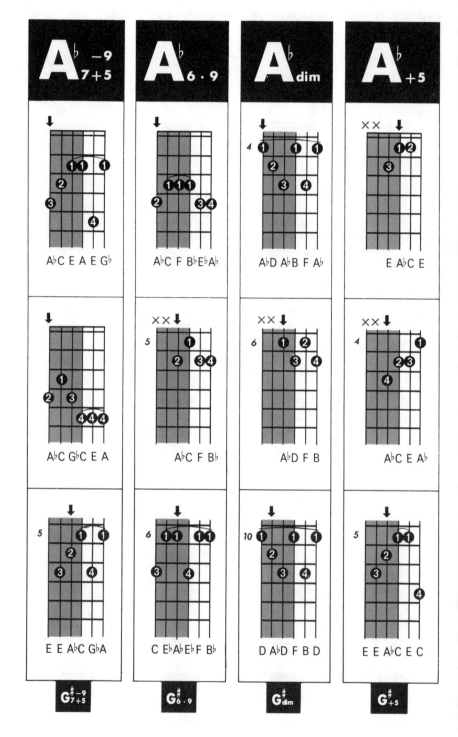

A♭sus4

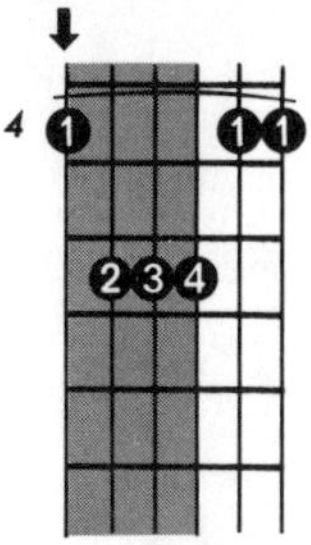

A♭E♭A♭D♭E♭A♭

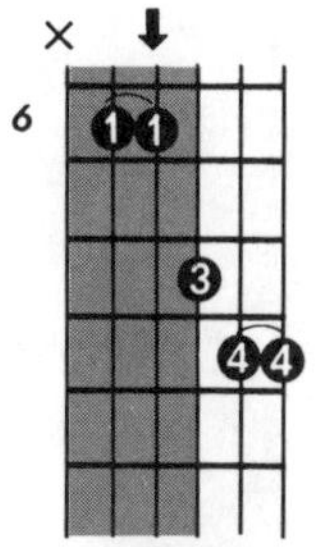

E♭A♭E♭A♭D♭

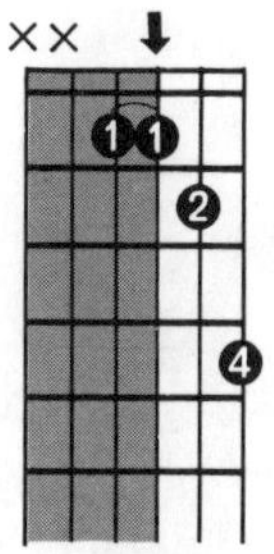

E♭A♭D♭A♭

G♯sus4

A♭7sus4

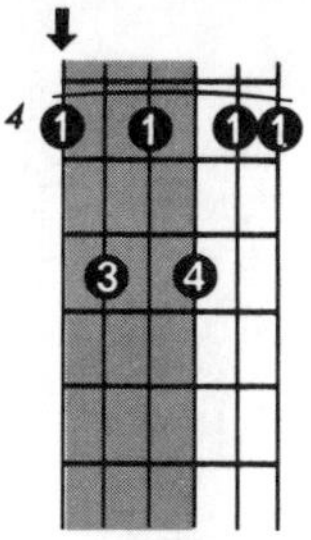

A♭E♭G♭D♭E♭A♭

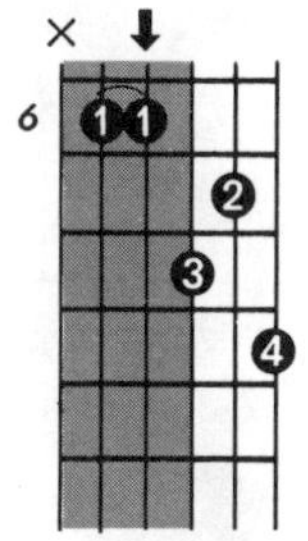

E♭A♭E♭G♭D♭

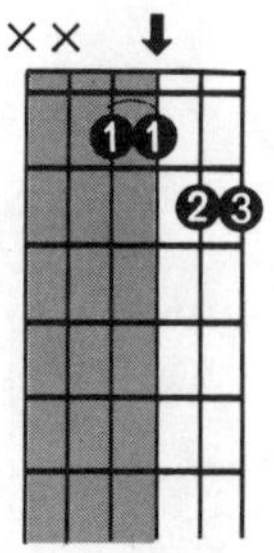

E♭A♭D♭G♭

G♯7sus4

A♭m

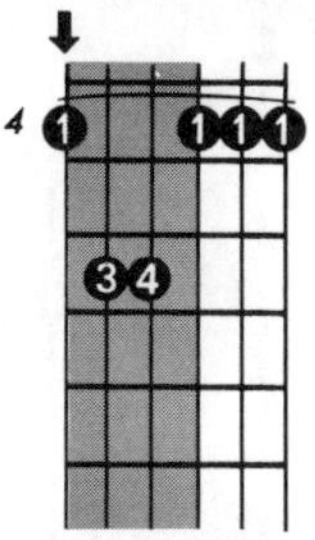

A♭E♭A♭B E♭A♭

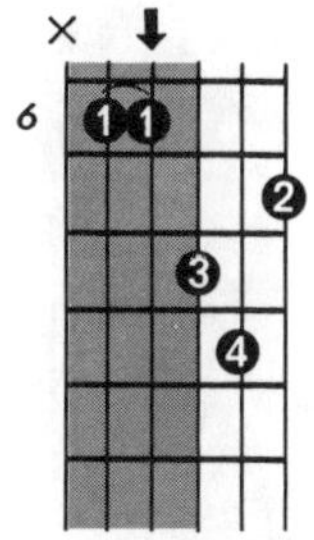

E♭A♭E♭A♭B

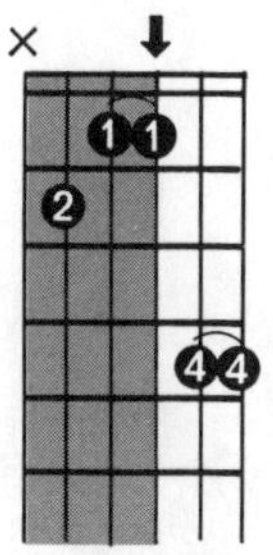

B E♭A♭E♭A♭

G♯m

A♭m6

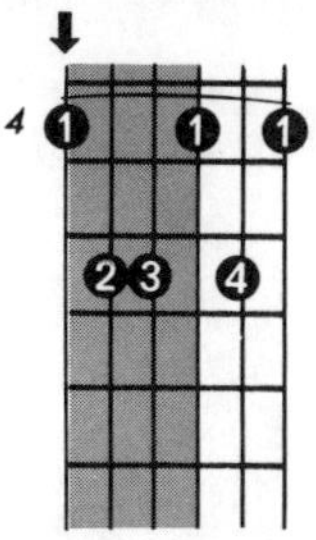

A♭E♭A♭B F A♭

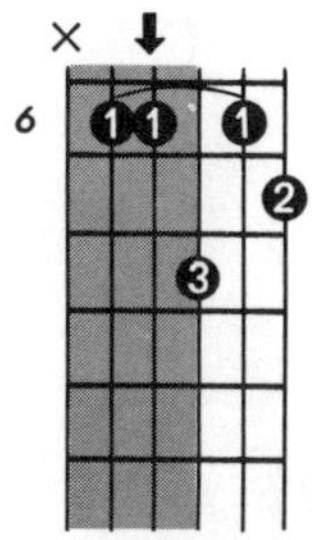

E♭A♭E♭F B

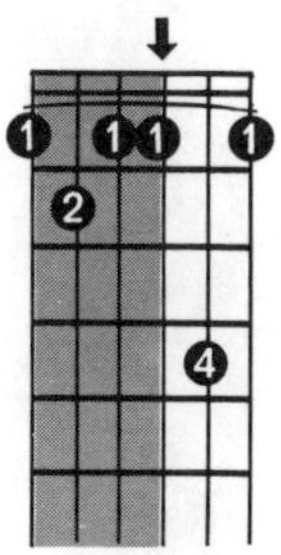

F B E♭A♭E♭F

G♯m6

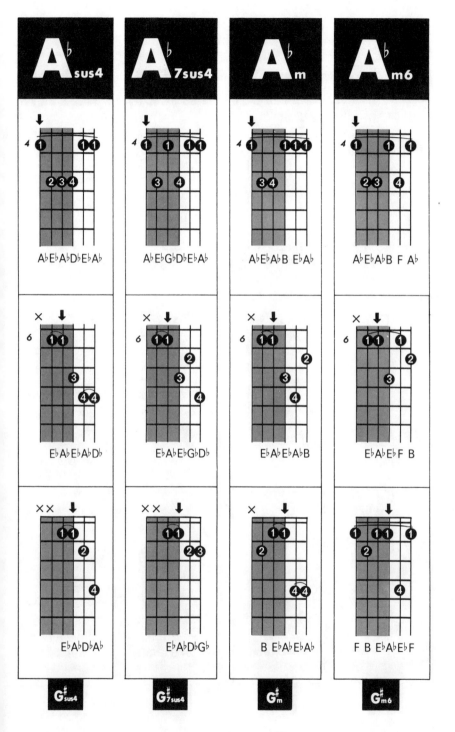

A♭m7

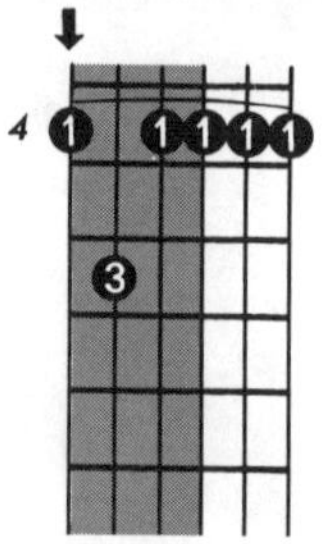

A♭E♭G♭B E♭A♭

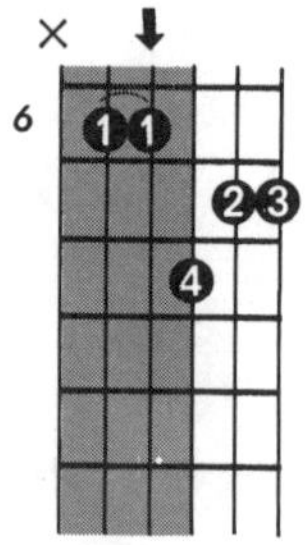

E♭A♭E♭G♭B

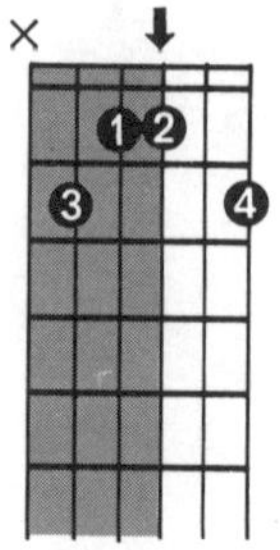

B E♭A♭B G♭

G♯m7

A♭m9

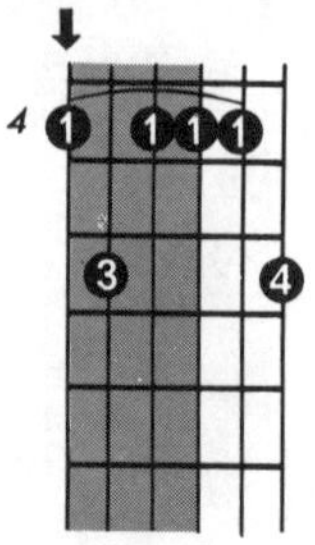

A♭E♭G♭B E♭B♭

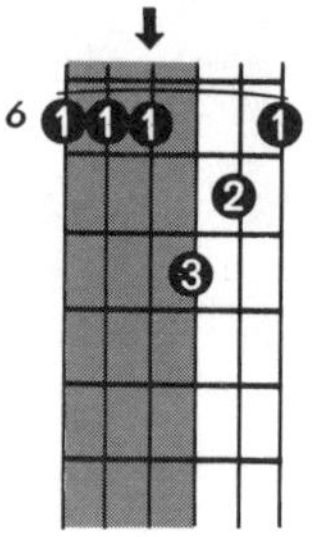

B♭E♭A♭E♭G♭B♭

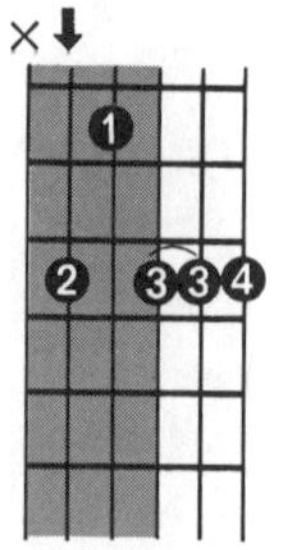

A♭B G♭B♭E♭

G♯m9

A♭m7−5

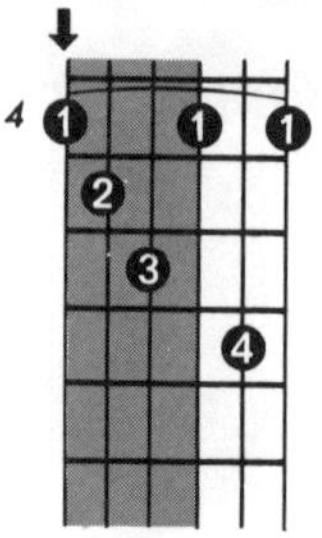

A♭D A♭B G♭A♭

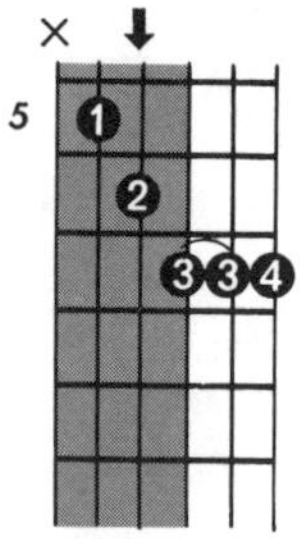

D A♭D G♭B

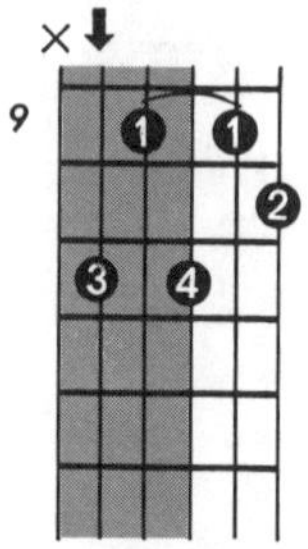

A♭B G♭A♭D

G♯m7−5

A♭m7−9

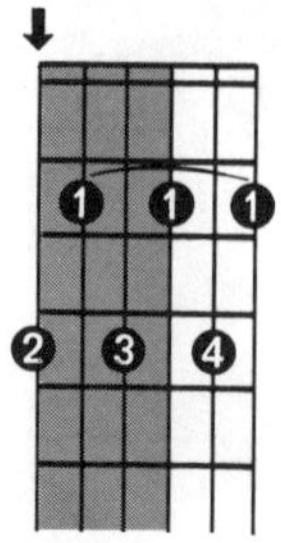

A♭B G♭A E♭G♭

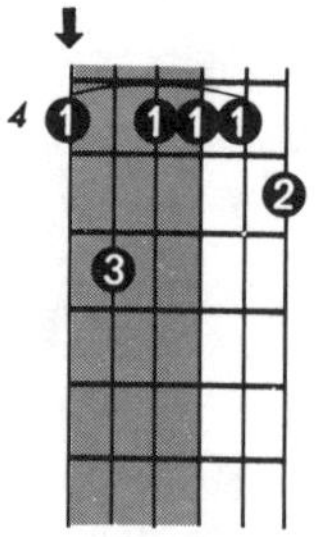

A♭E♭G♭B E♭A

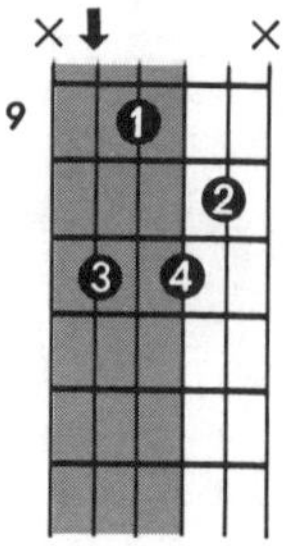

A♭B G♭A

G♯m7−9

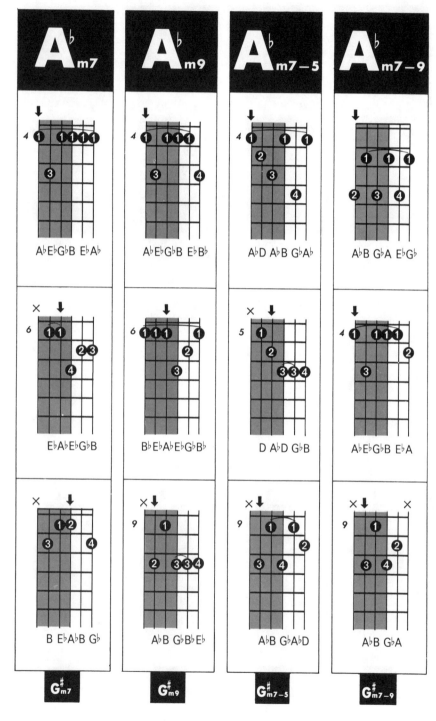

A♭m+7

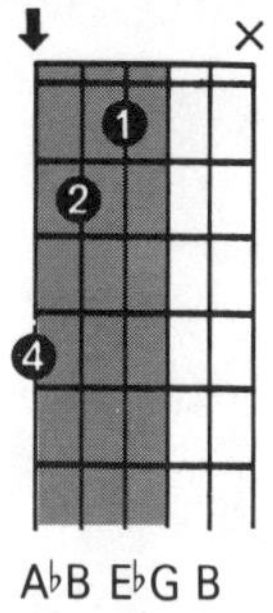

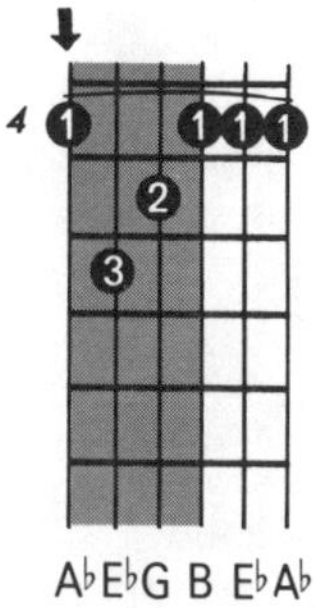

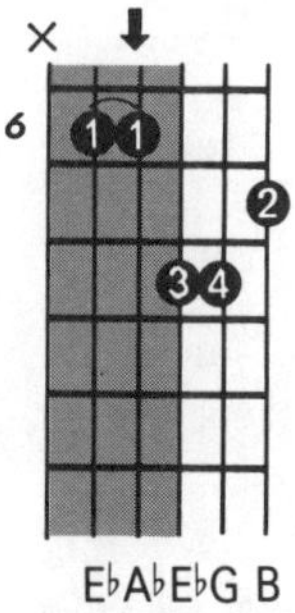

G♯m+7

A♭m9+7

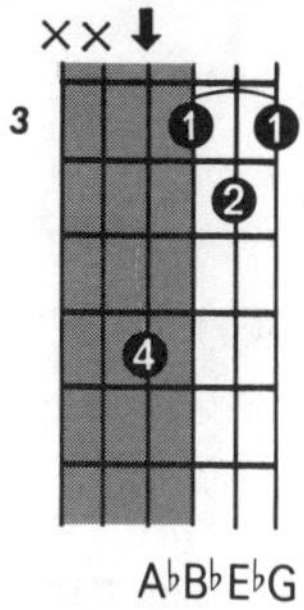

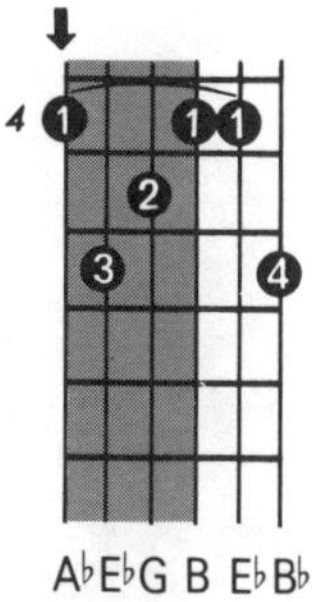

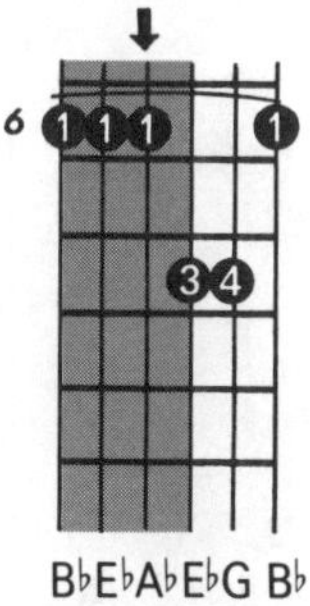

G♯m9+7

A♭m+5

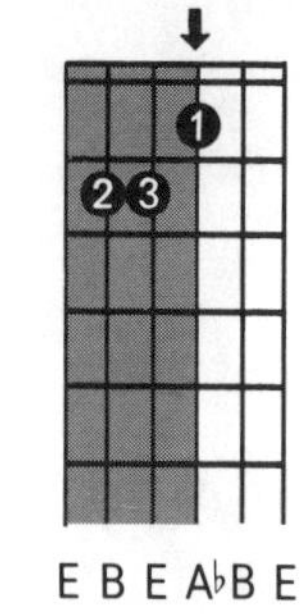

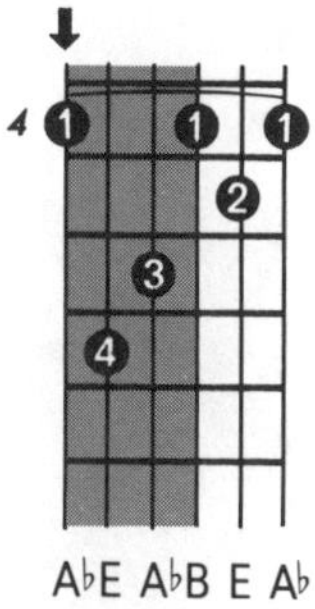

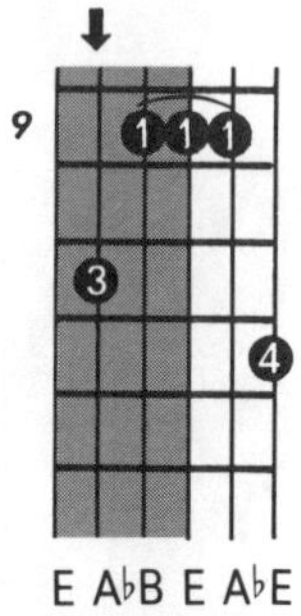

G♯m+5

A♭m6 · 9

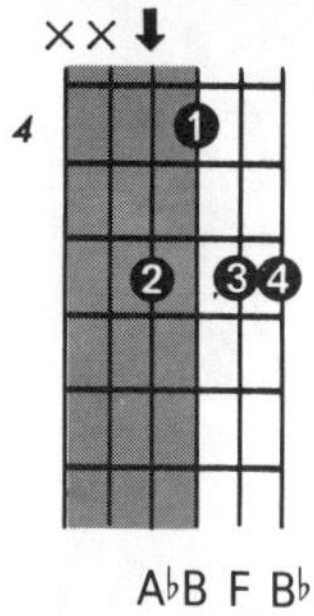

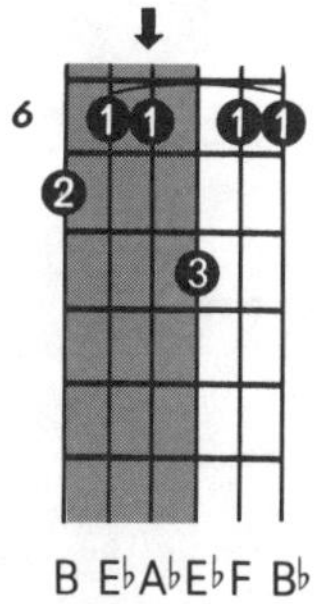

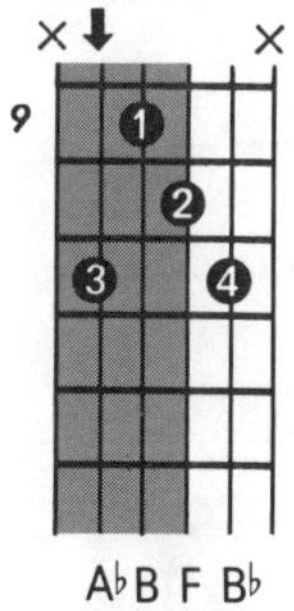

G♯m6 · 9

A♭

A

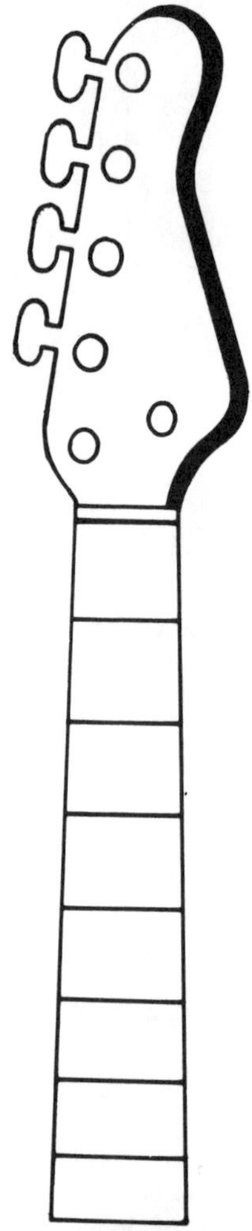

A

A

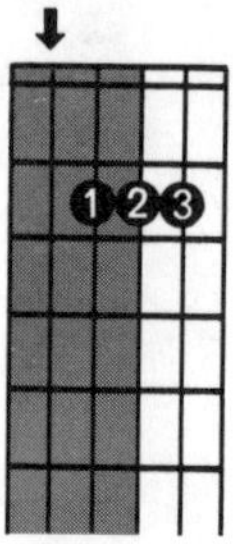

E A E A C♯E

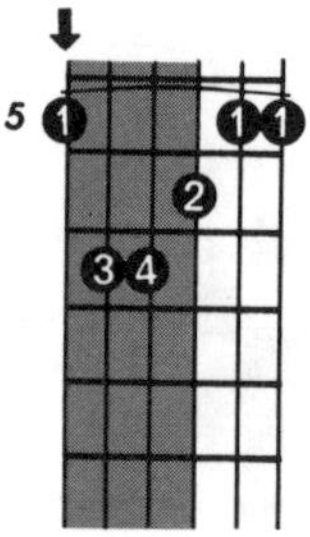

A E A C♯E A

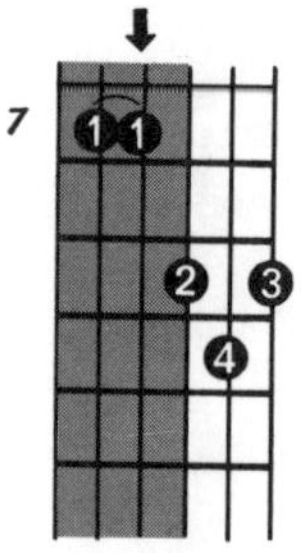

E E A E A C♯

A_6

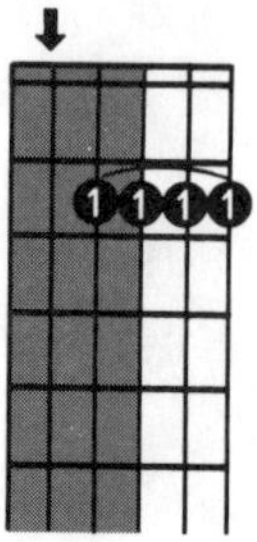

E A E A C♯F♯

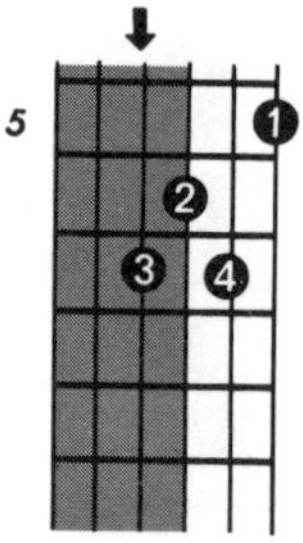

E A A C♯F♯A

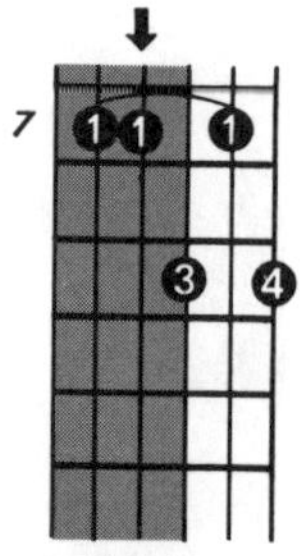

E E A E F♯C♯

A_7

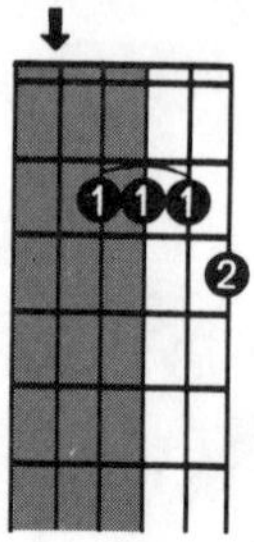

E A E A C♯G

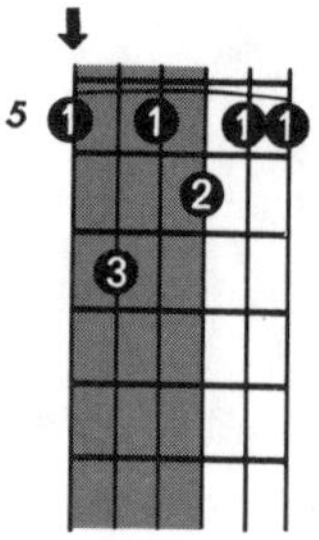

A E G C♯E A

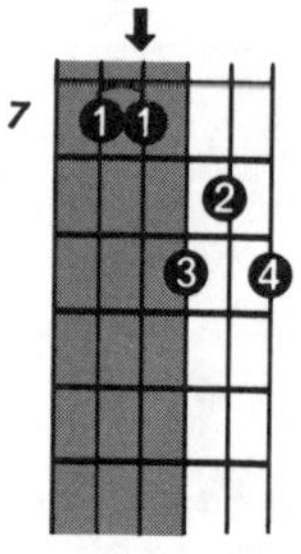

E E A E G C♯

A9

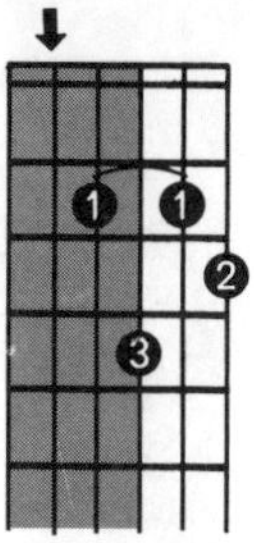

E A E B C♯G

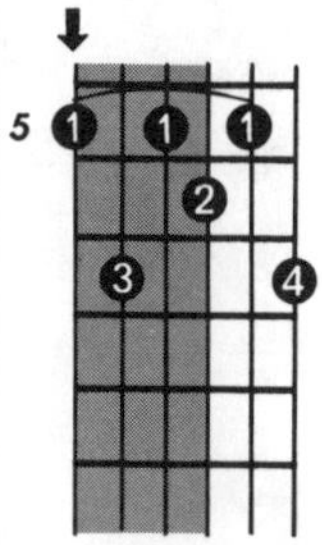

A E G C♯E B

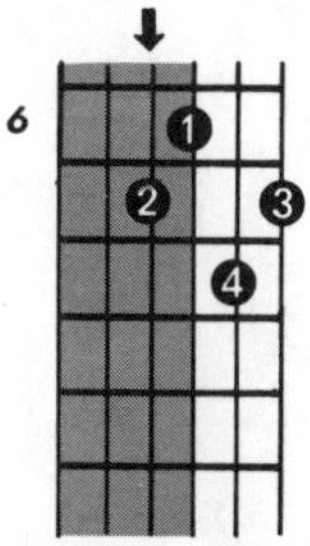

E A A C♯G B

A11

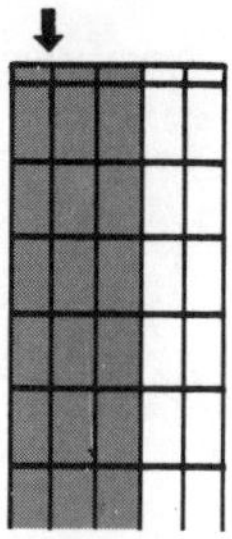

E A D G B E

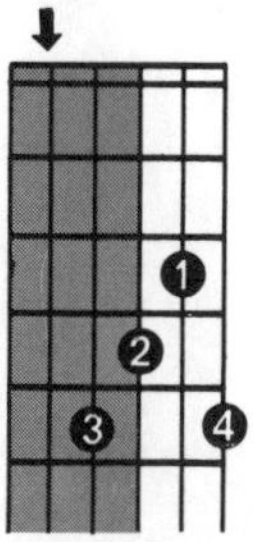

E A G B D A

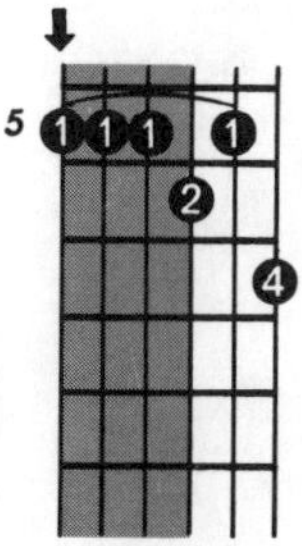

A D G C♯E B

A11+

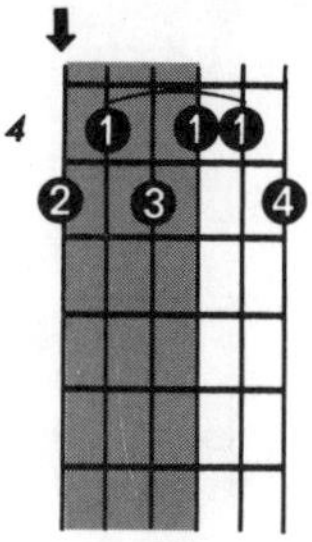

A C♯G B D♯A

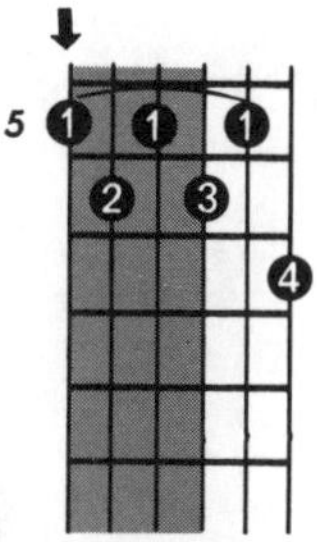

A D♯G C♯E B

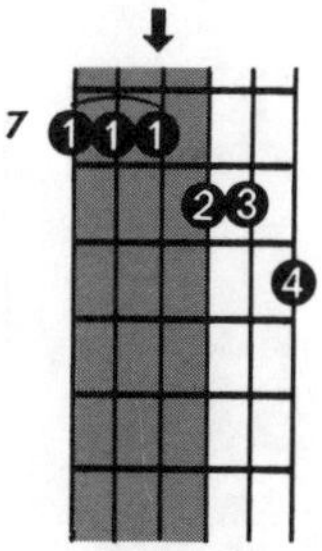

B E A D♯G C♯

A13

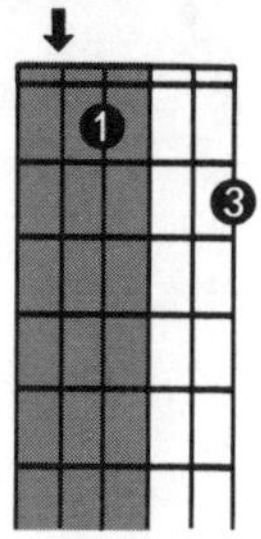

E A D♯G B F♯

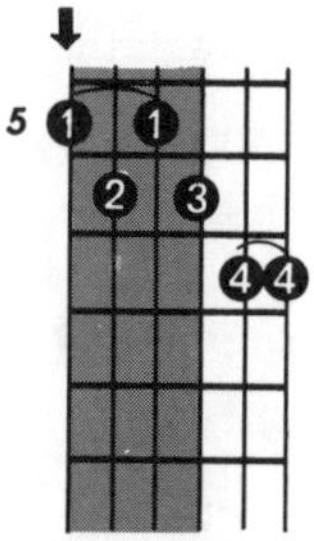

A D♯G C♯F♯B

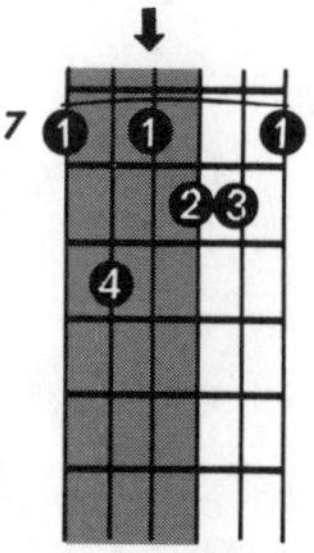

B F♯A D♯G B

A

A maj7

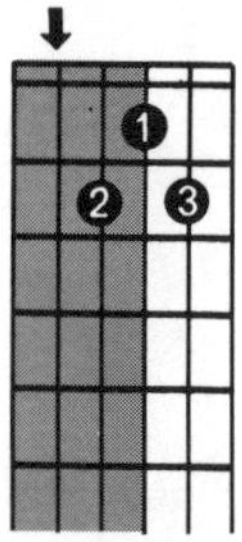

E A E G#C#E

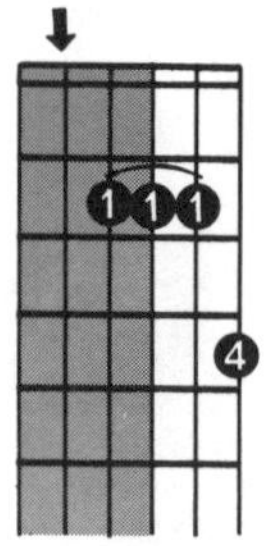

E A E A C#G#

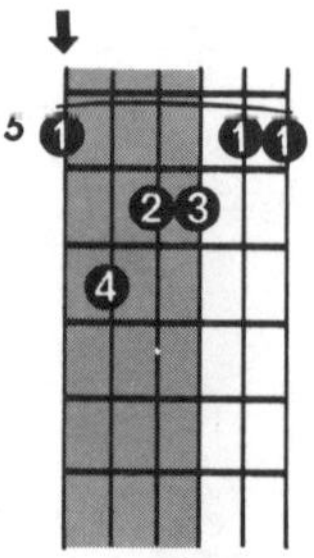

A E G#C#E A

A maj9

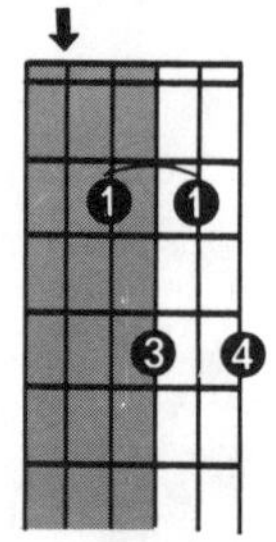

E A E B C#G#

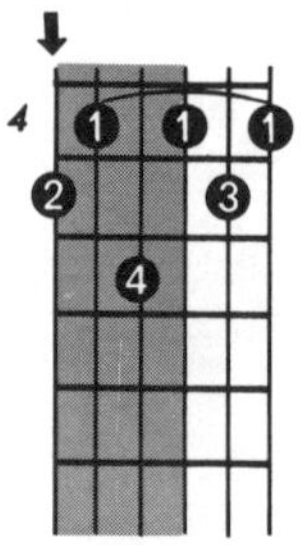

A C#G#B E G#

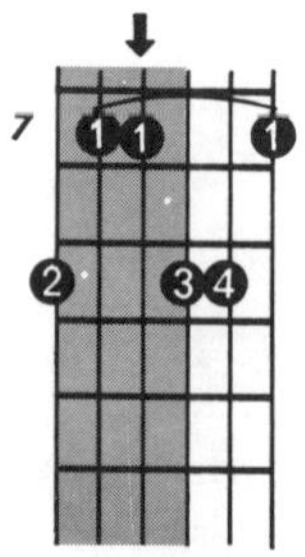

C#E A E G#B

A maj11

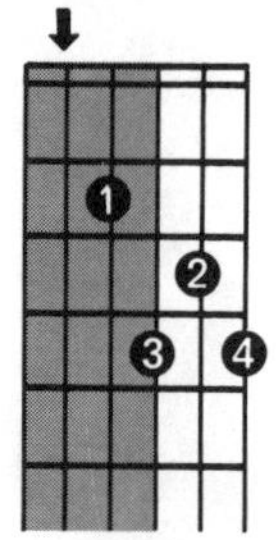

E A E B D G#

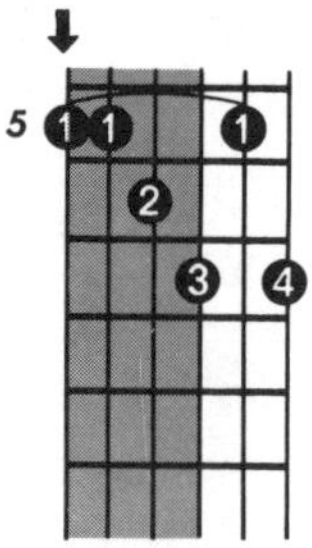

A D G#D E B

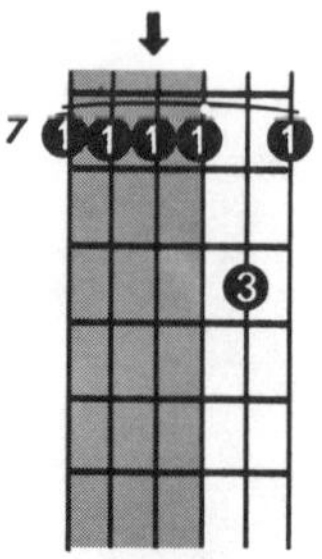

B E A D G#B

A 7−5

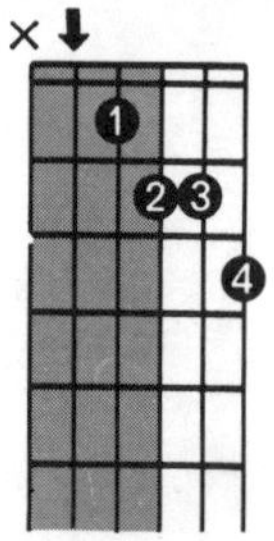

A E♭A C#G

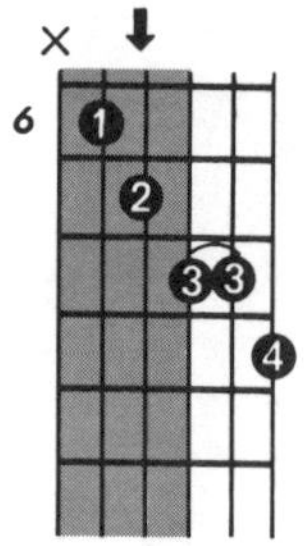

E♭A E♭G C#

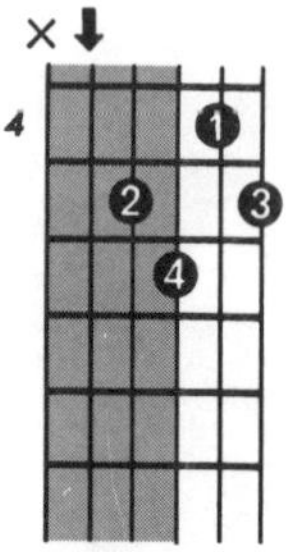

A G C#E♭A

A

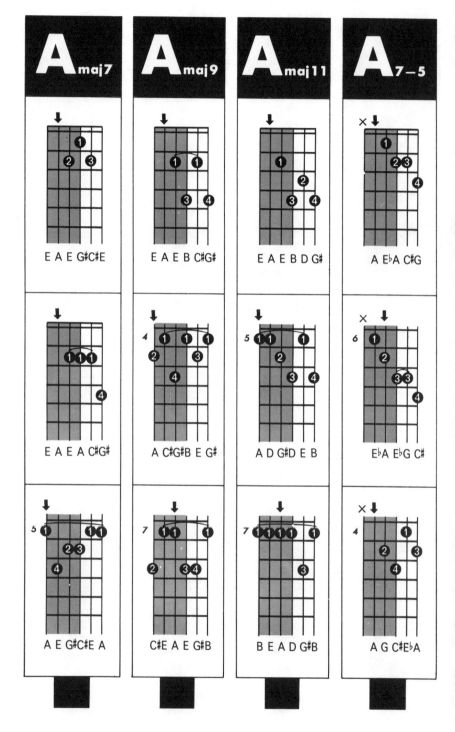

A_{7-9}

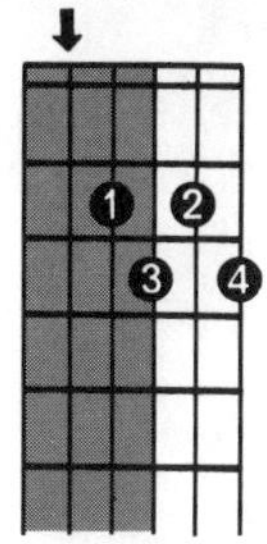

E A E B♭C♯G

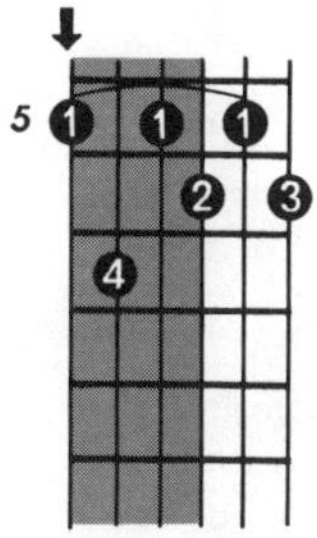

A E G C♯E B♭

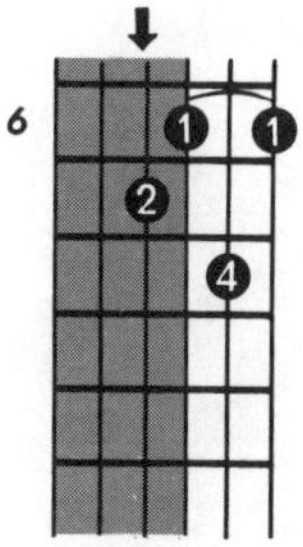

E A A C♯G B♭

A_{7-10}

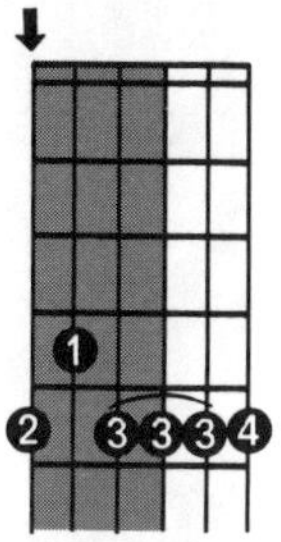

A C♯G C E A

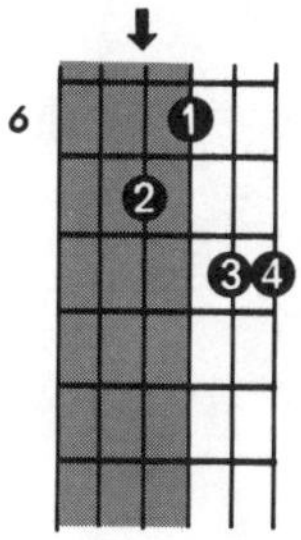

E A A C♯G C

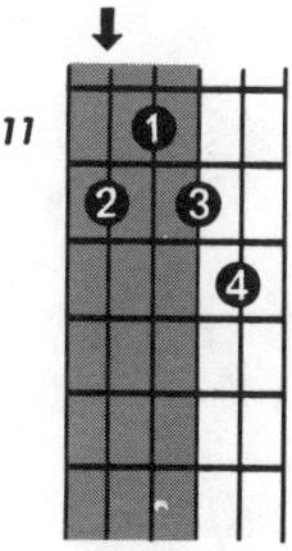

E A C♯G C E

A_{7+5}

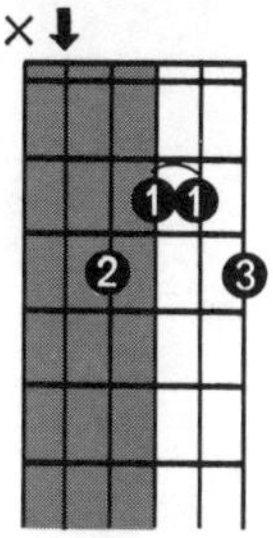

A F A C♯G

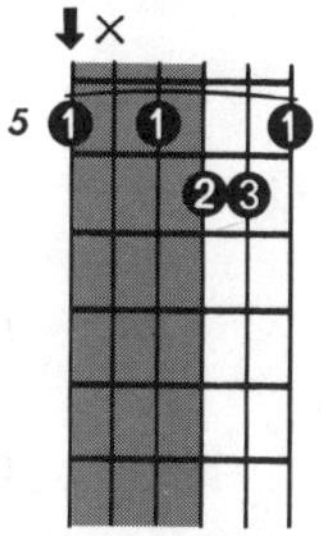

A G C♯F A

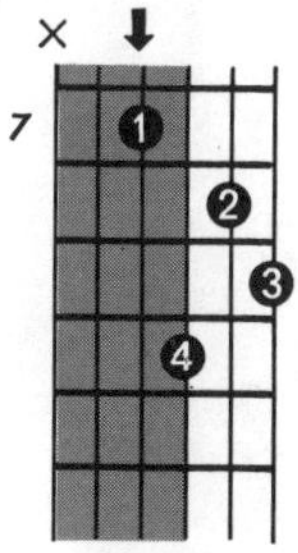

A A F G C♯

A_{9+5}

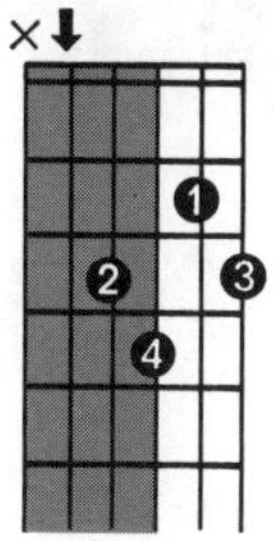

A F B C♯G

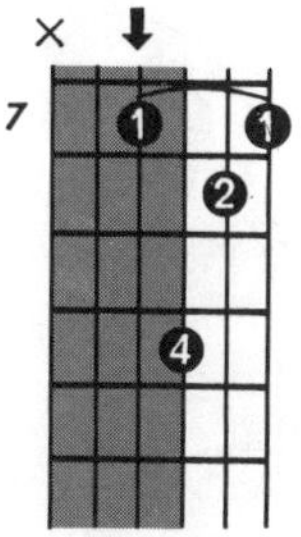

A A F G B

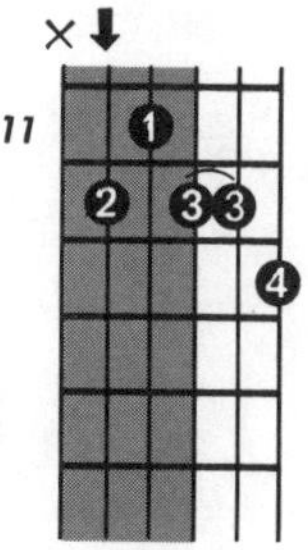

A C♯G B F

A

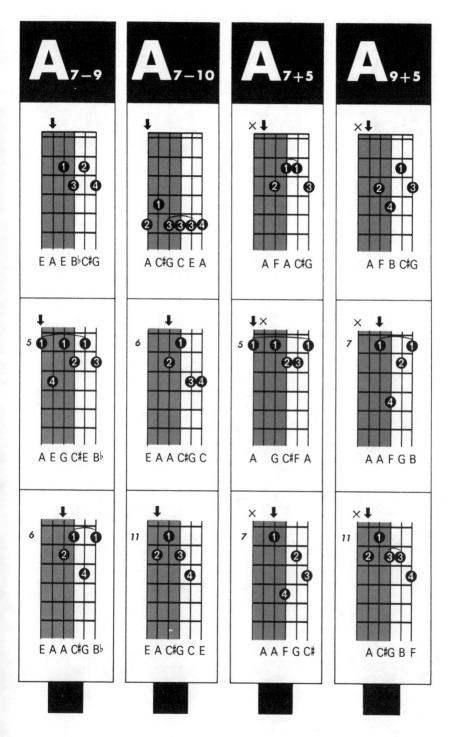

A^{-9}_{7+5}

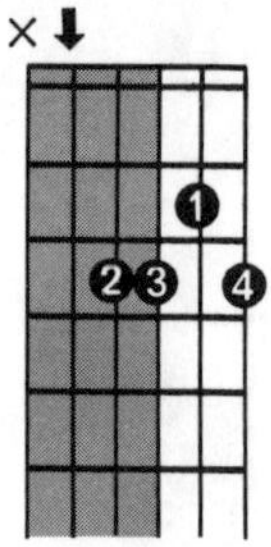

A F B♭C♯G

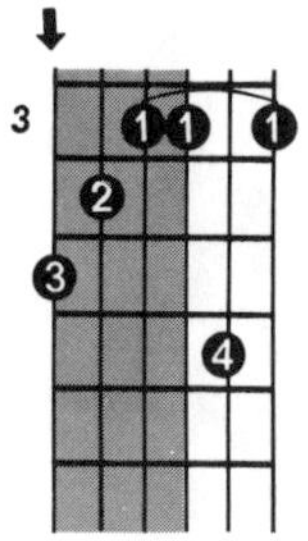

A C♯F B♭F G

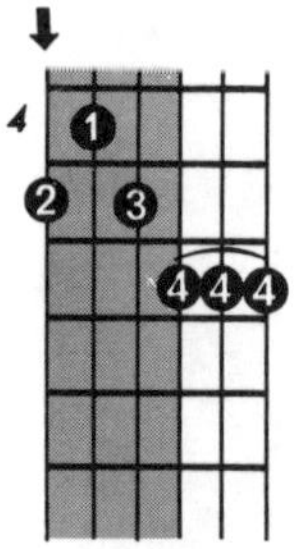

A C♯G C♯F B♭

$A_{6 \cdot 9}$

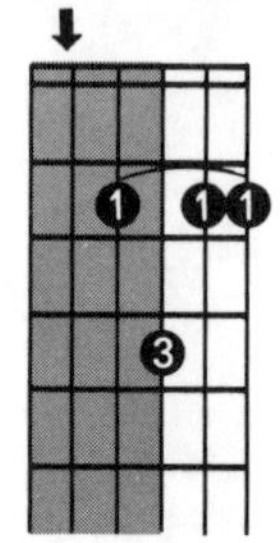

E A E B C♯F♯

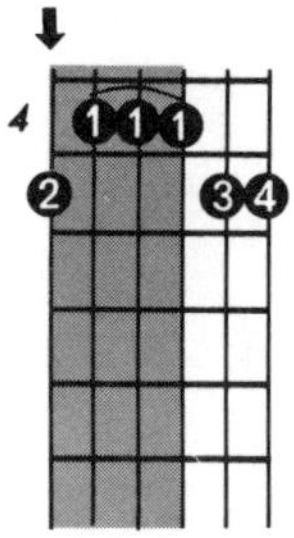

A C♯F♯B E A

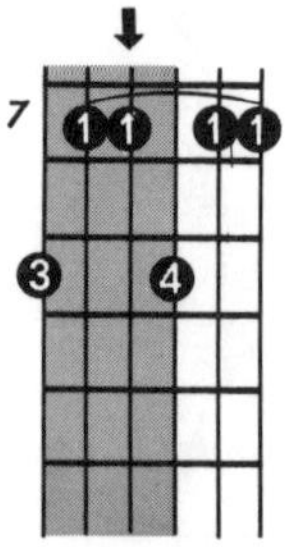

C♯E A E F♯B

A_{dim}

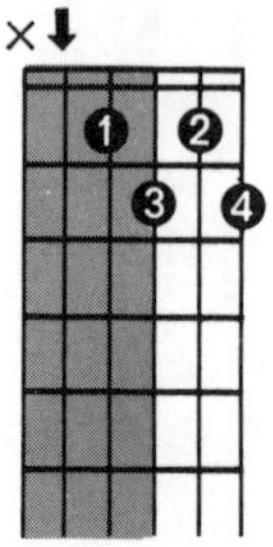

A E♭A C F♯

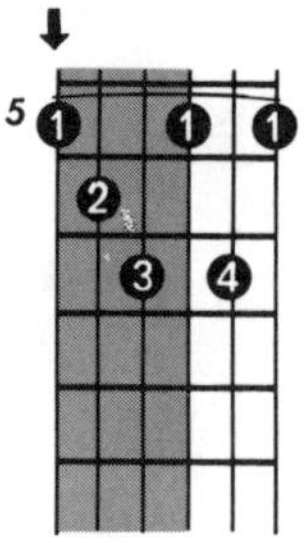

A E♭A C F♯A

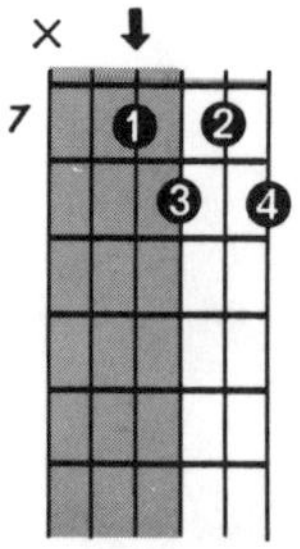

A A E♭F♯C

A_{+5}

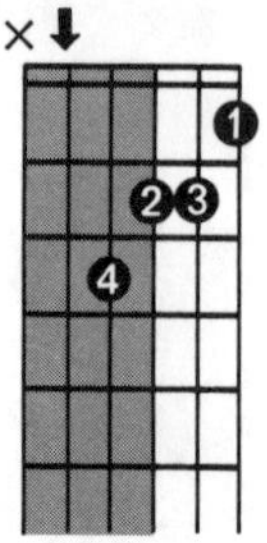

A F A C♯F

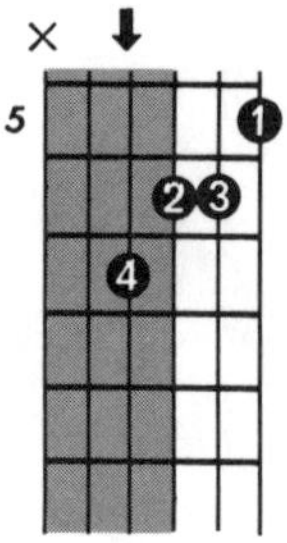

A A C♯F A

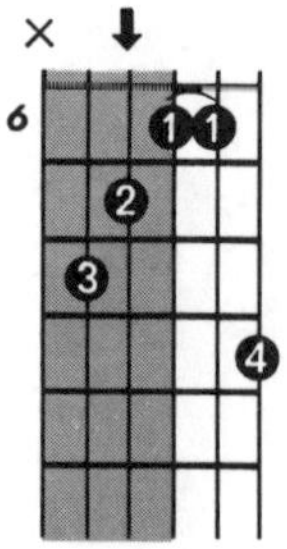

F A C♯F C♯

A

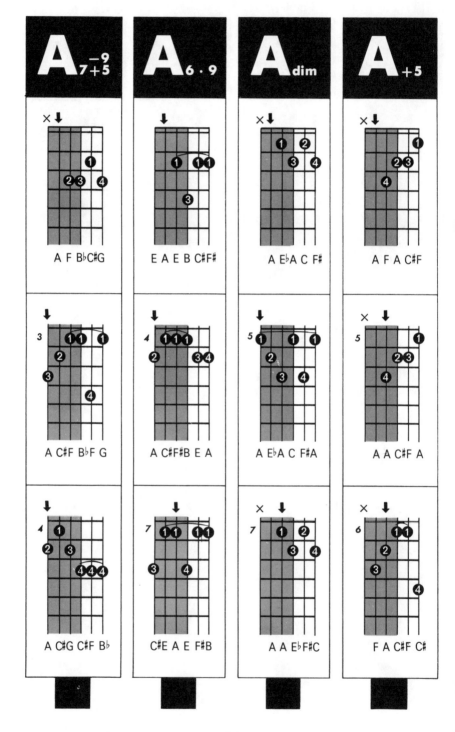

Asus4

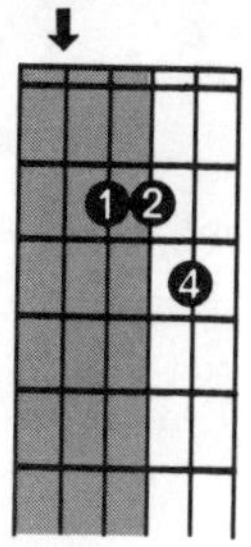

E A E A D E

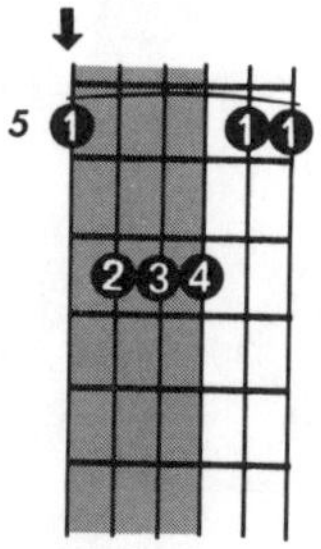

A E A D E A

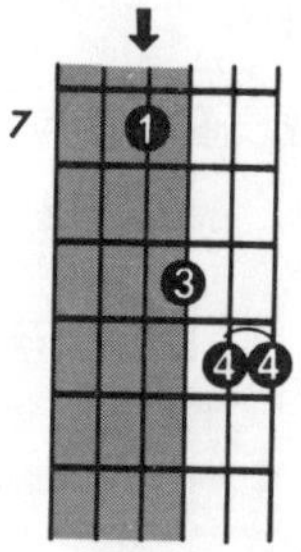

E A A E A D

A7sus4

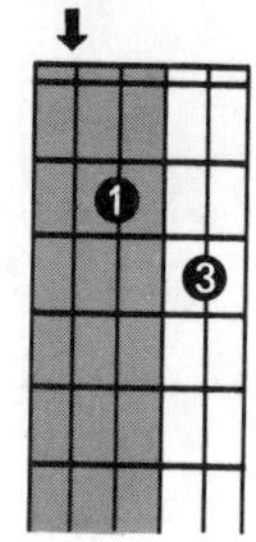

E A E G D E

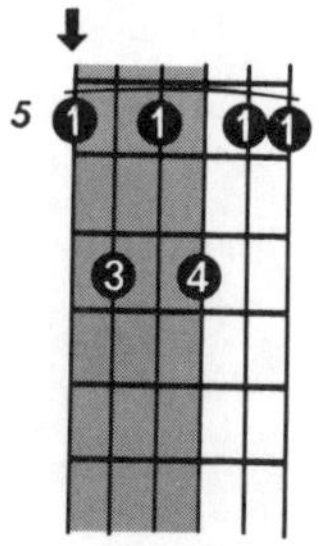

A E G D E A

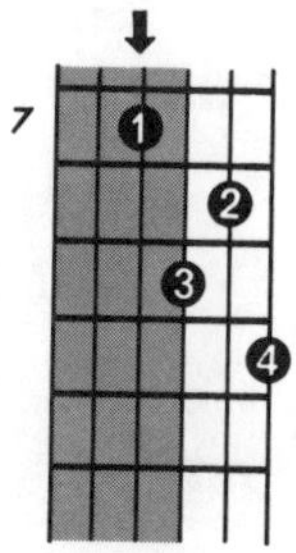

E A A E G D

Am

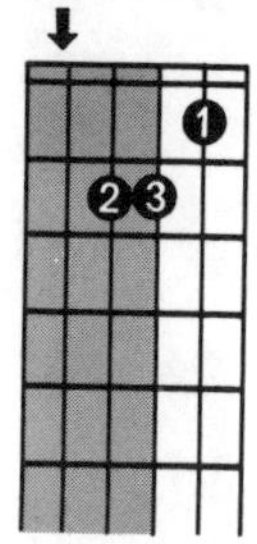

E A E A C E

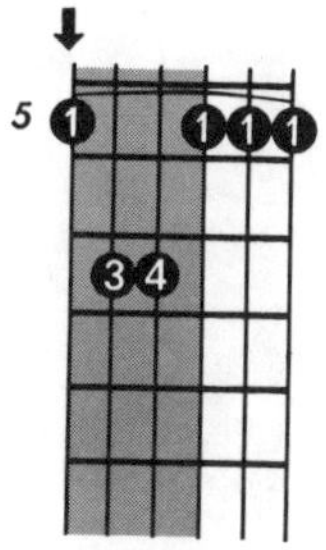

A E A C E A

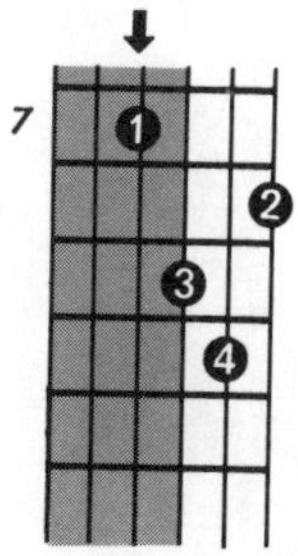

E A A E A C

Am6

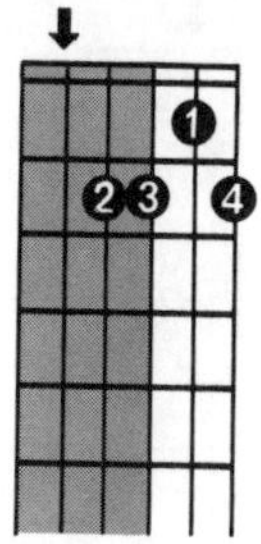

E A E A C F#

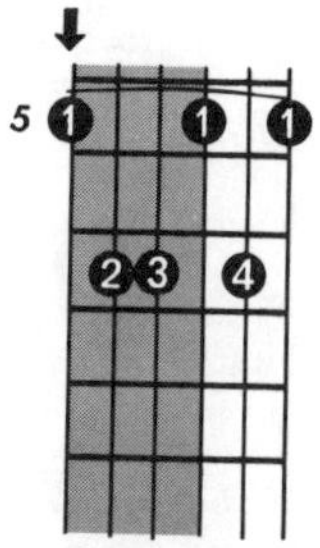

A E A C F# A

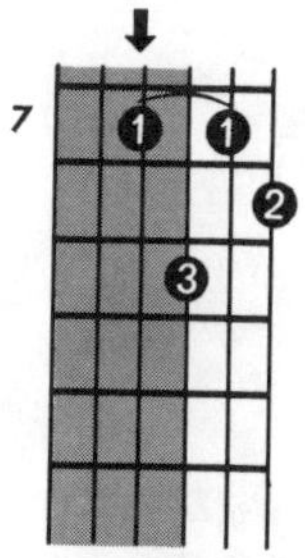

E A A E F# C

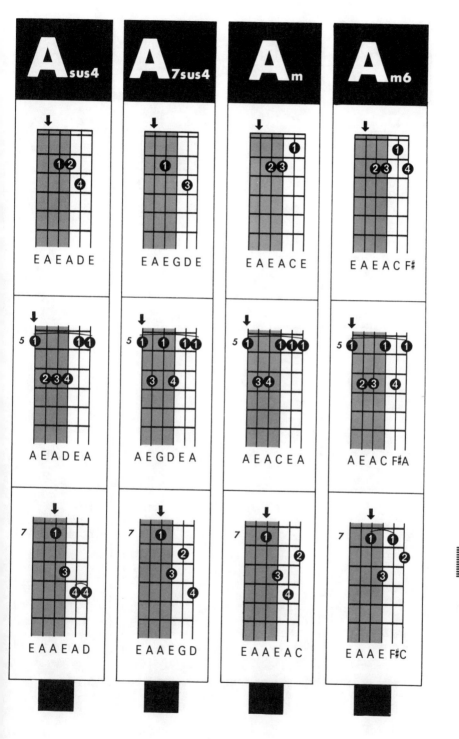

Am7

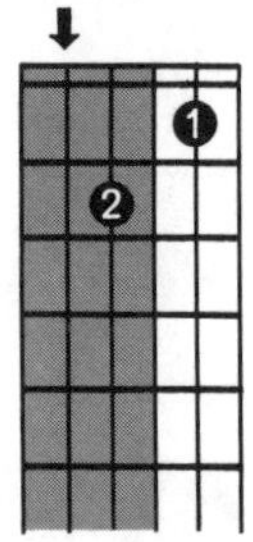

E A E G C E

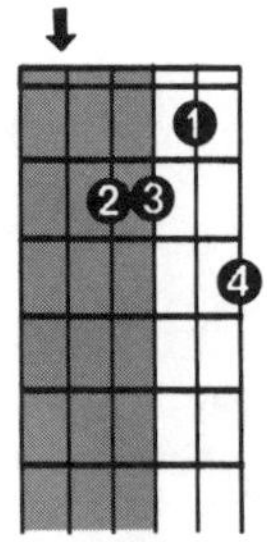

E A E A C G

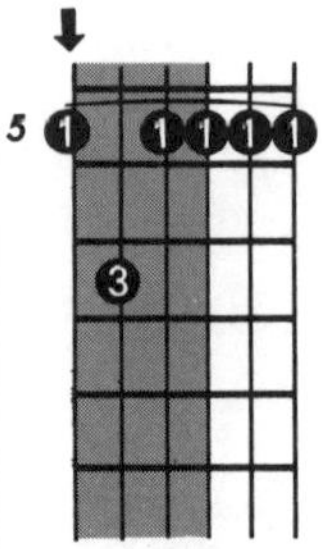

A E G C E A

Am9

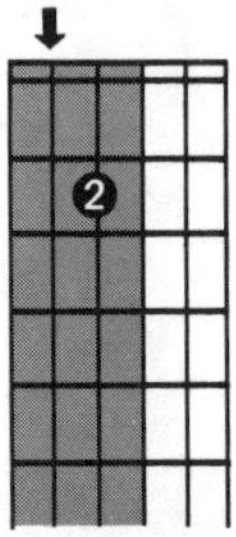

E A E G B E

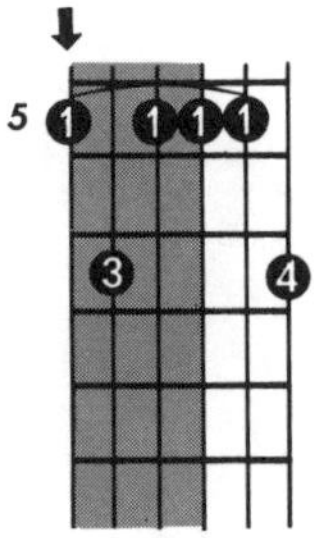

A E G C E B

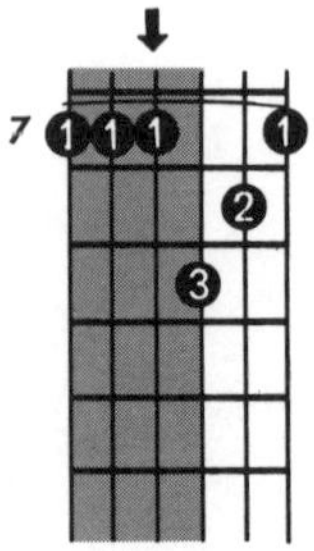

B E A E G B

Am7–5

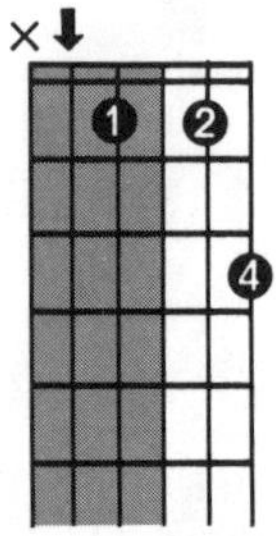

A E♭G C G

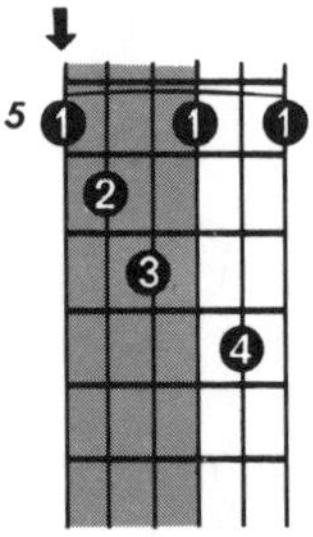

A E♭A C G A

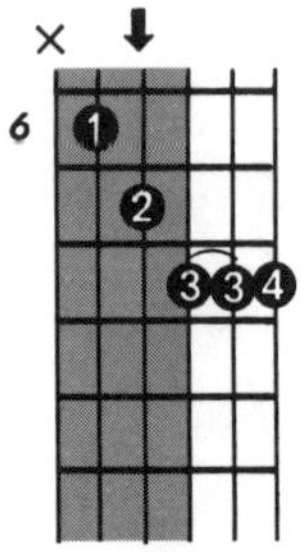

E♭A E♭G C

Am7–9

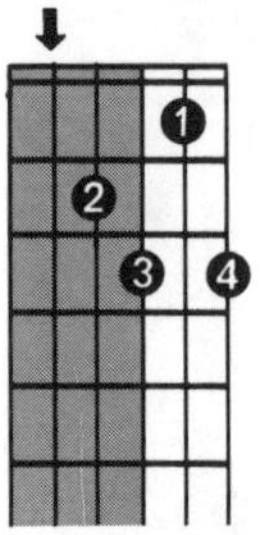

E A E B♭C G

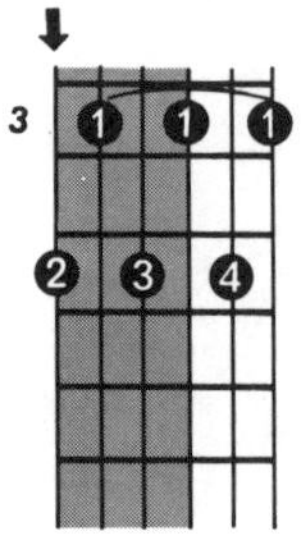

A C G B♭E G

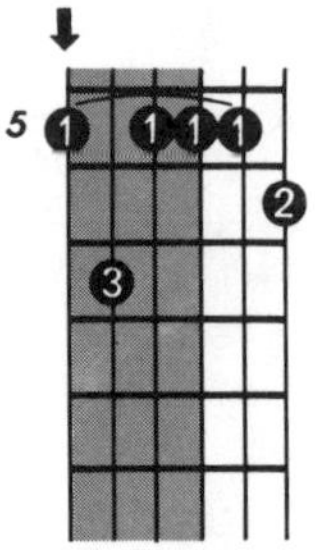

A E G C E B♭

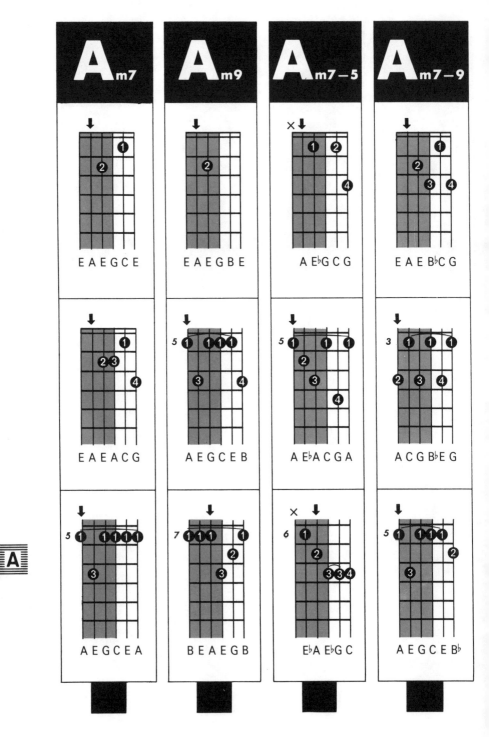

Am+7

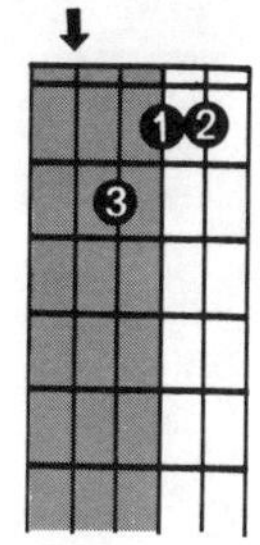

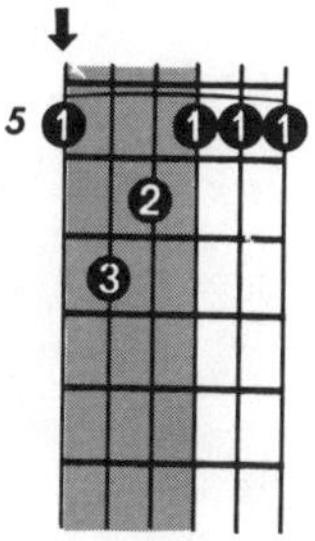

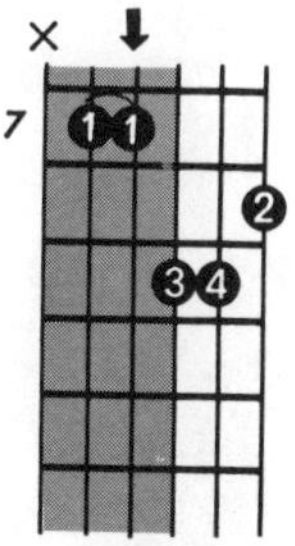

Am9+7

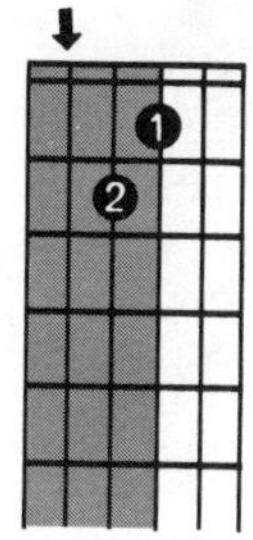

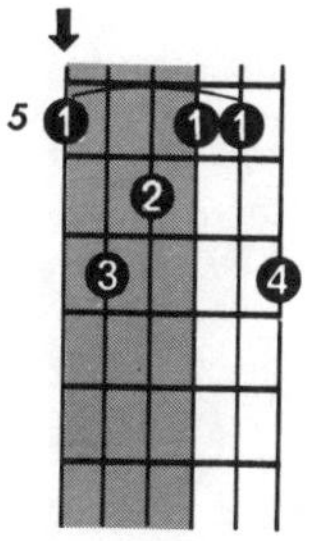

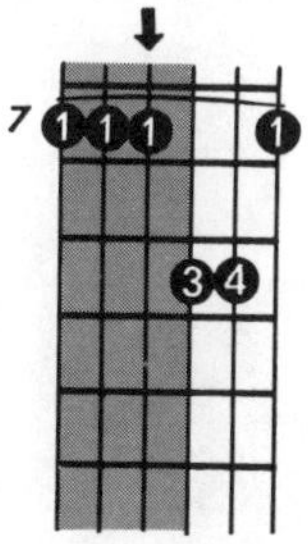

Am+5

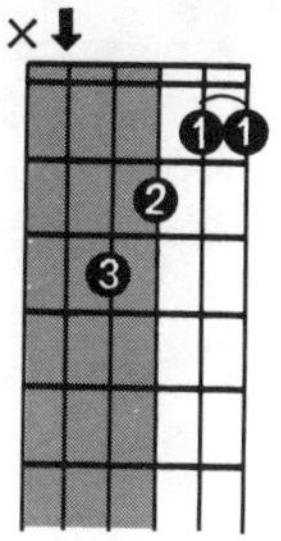

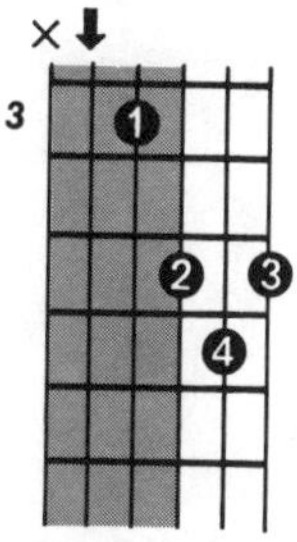

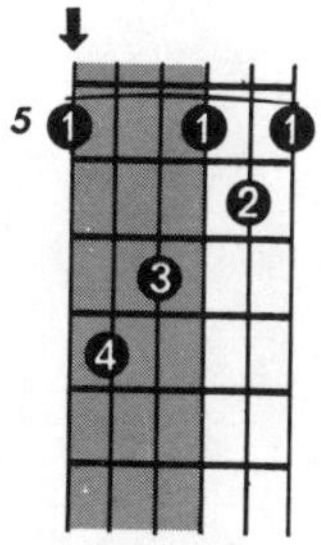

Am6·9

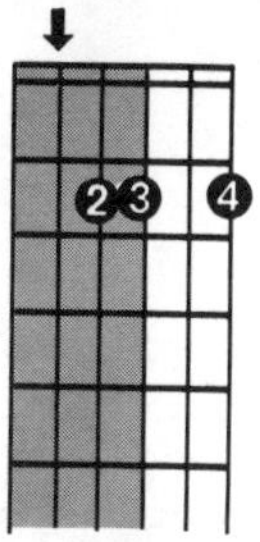

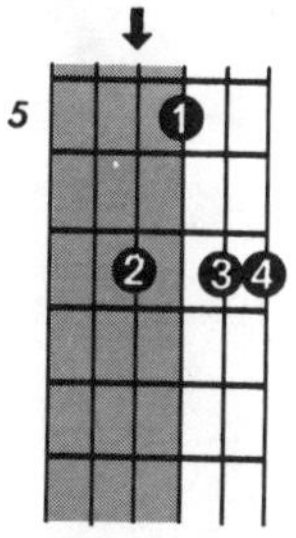

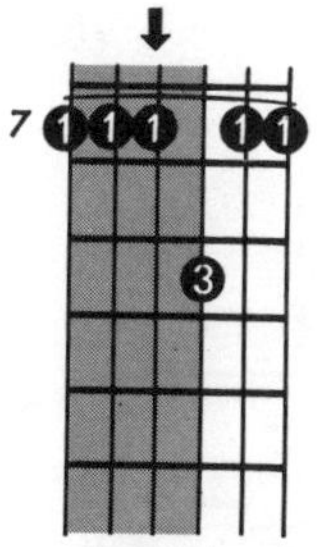

A

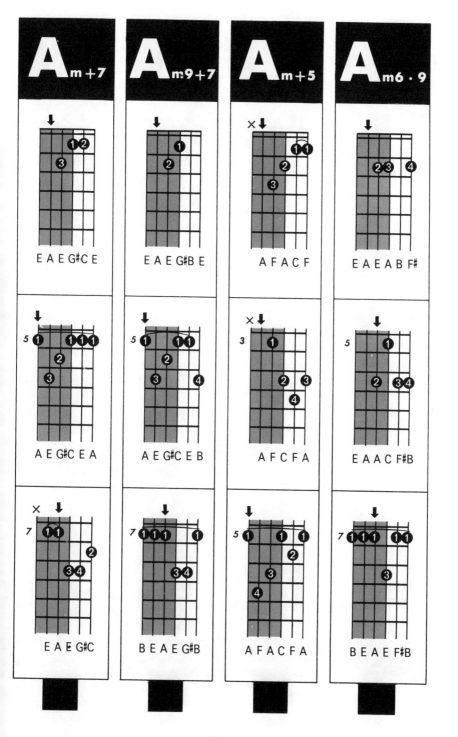

B♭

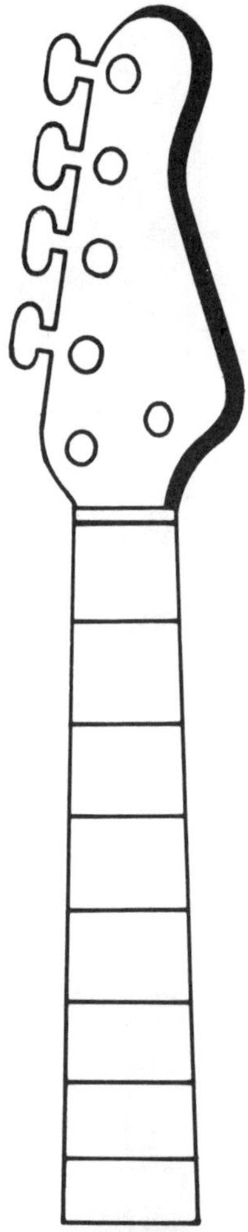

A♯

B♭

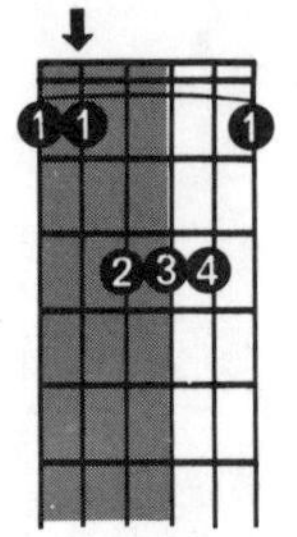

F B♭F B♭D F

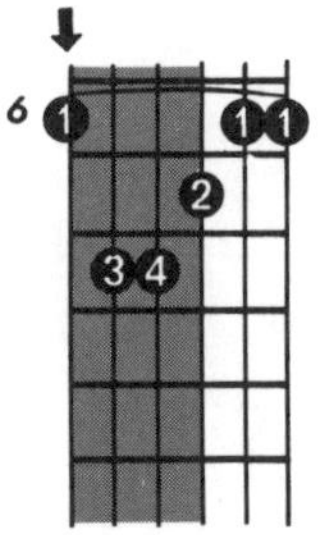

B♭F B♭D F B♭

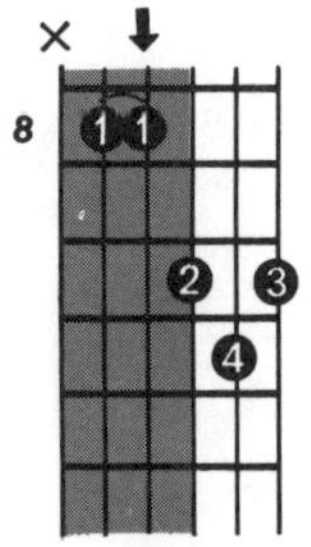

F B♭F B♭D

A♯

$B^{\flat}_{6}$

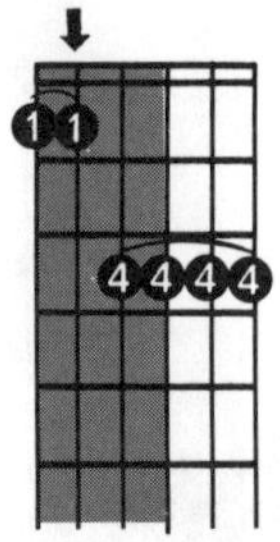

F B♭F B♭D G

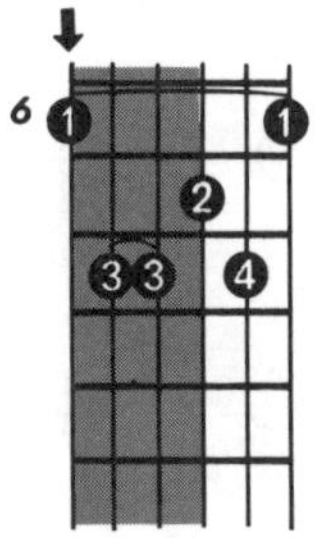

B♭F B♭D G B♭

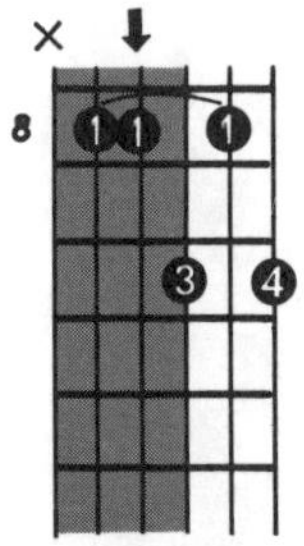

F B♭F G D

$A^{\sharp}_{6}$

$B^{\flat}_{7}$

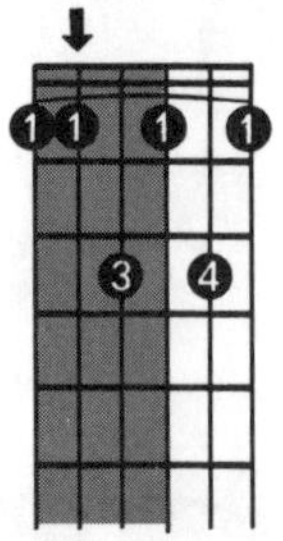

F B♭F A♭D F

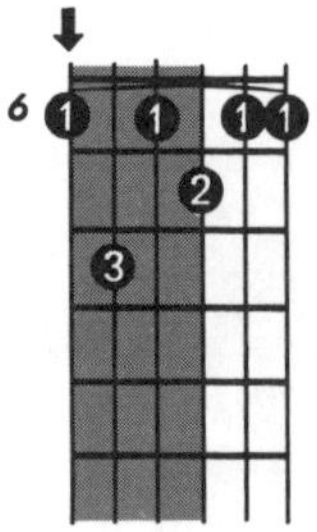

B♭F A♭D F B♭

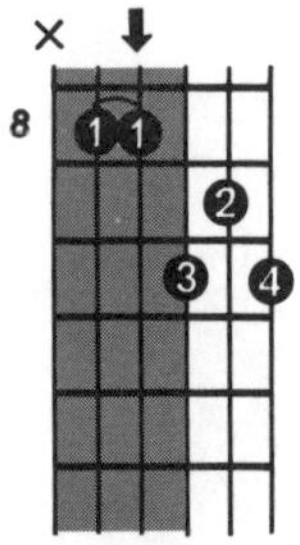

F B♭F A♭D

$A^{\sharp}_{7}$

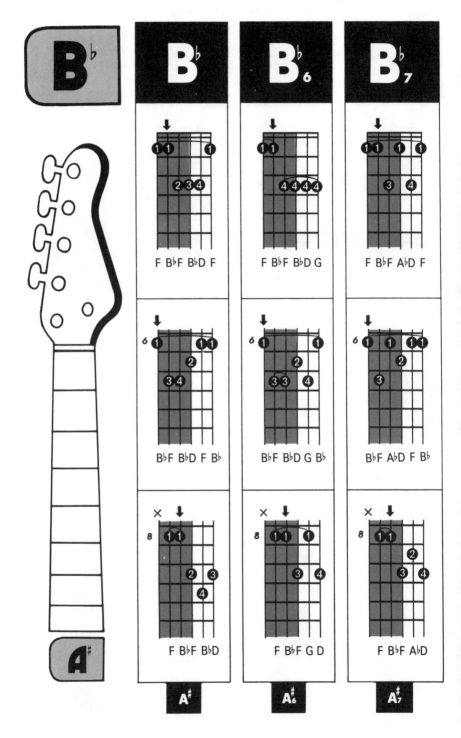

B♭9

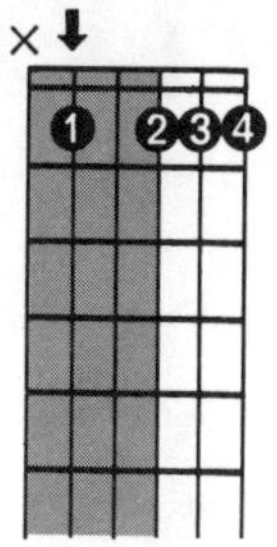

B♭D A♭C F

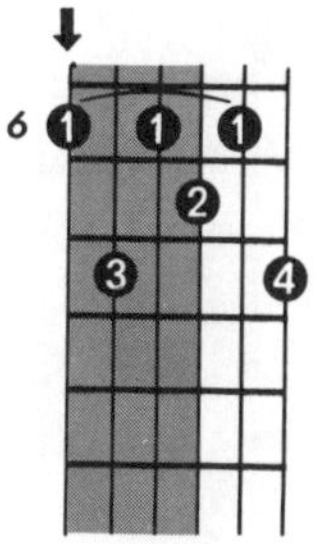

B♭F A♭D F C

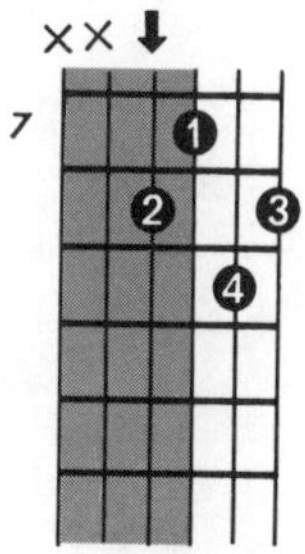

B♭D A♭C

A♯9

B♭11

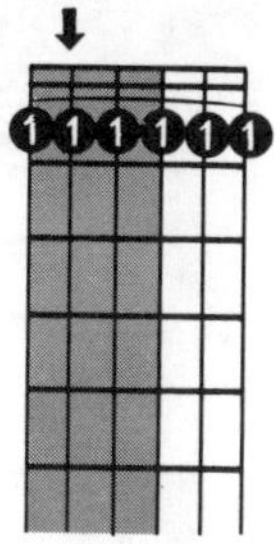

F B♭E♭A♭C F

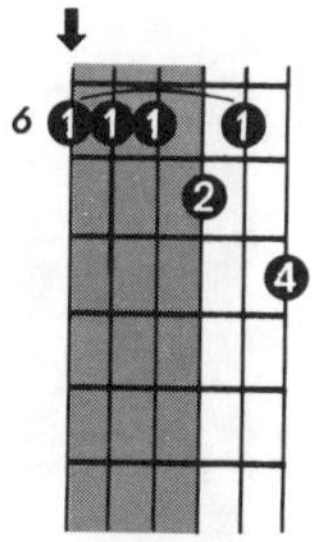

B♭E♭A♭D F C

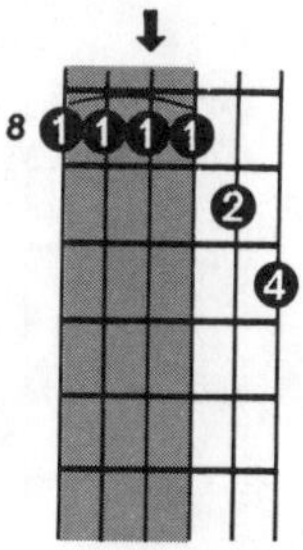

C F B♭E♭A♭D

A♯11

B♭11+

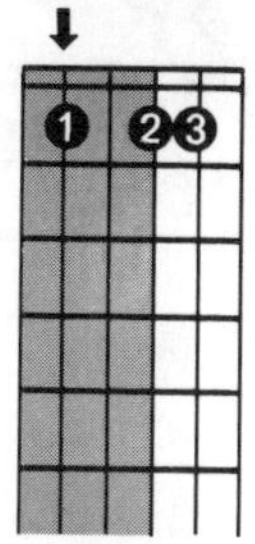

E B♭D A♭C E

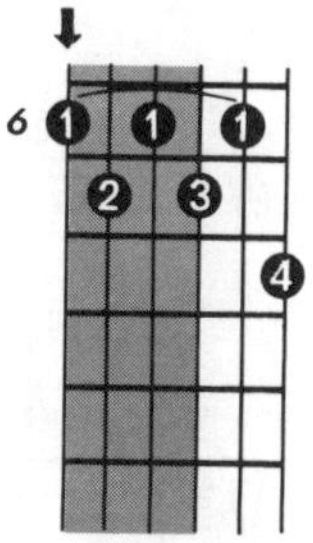

B♭E A♭D F C

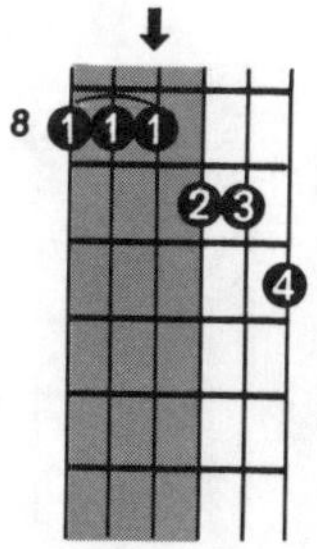

C F B♭E A♭D

A♯11+

B♭13

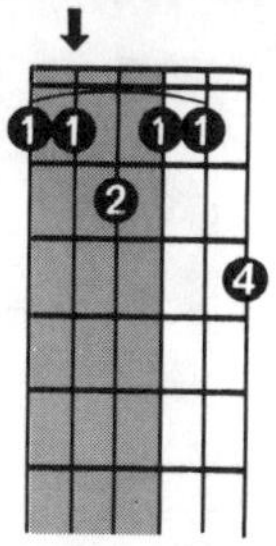

F B♭E A♭C G

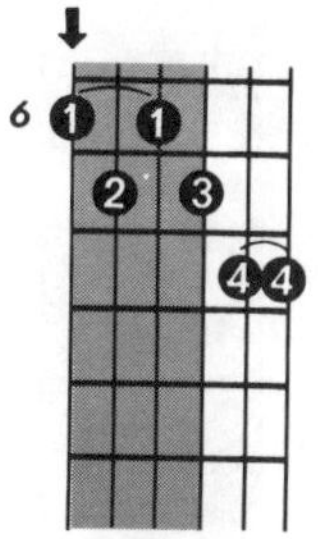

B♭E A♭D G C

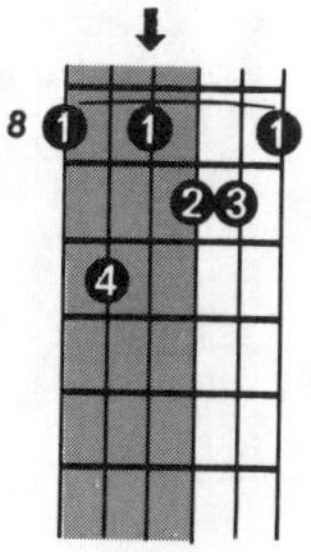

C G B♭E A♭C

A♯13

B♭

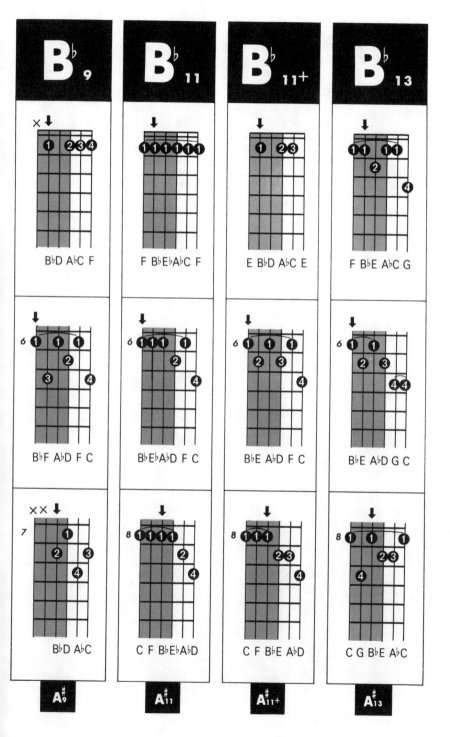

A♯

B♭maj7

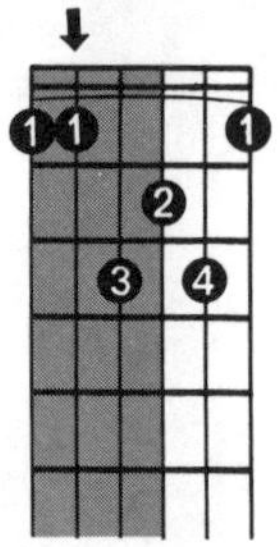

F B♭ F A D F

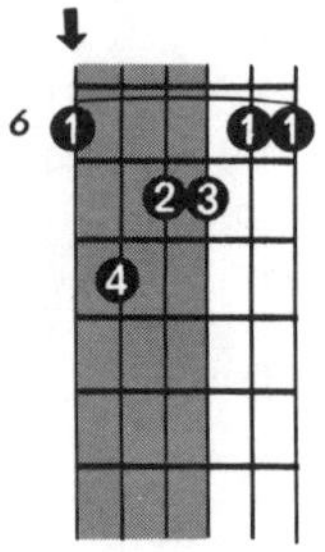

B♭ F A D F B♭

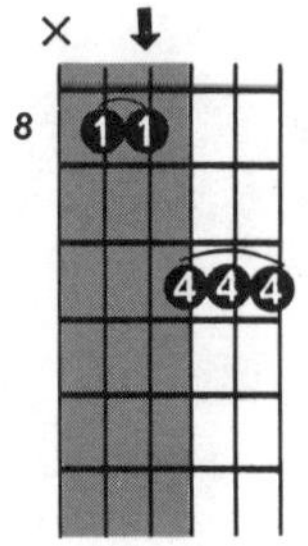

F B♭ F A D

A♯maj7

B♭maj9

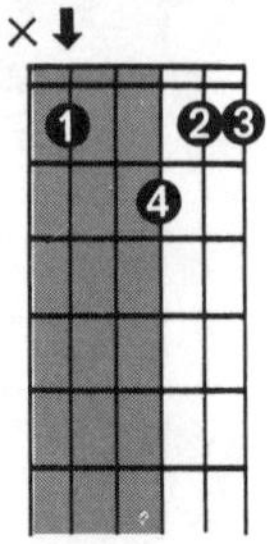

B♭ D A C F

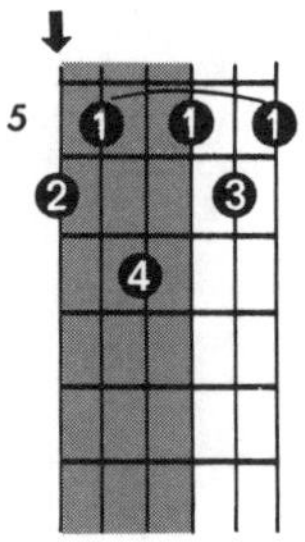

B♭ D A C F A

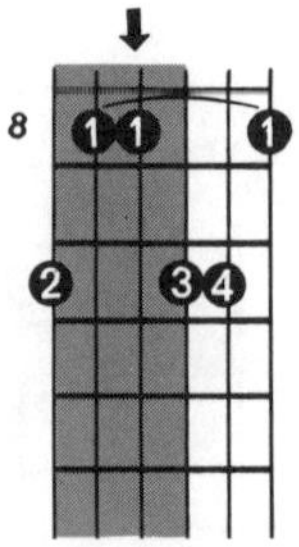

D F B♭ F A C

A♯maj9

B♭maj11

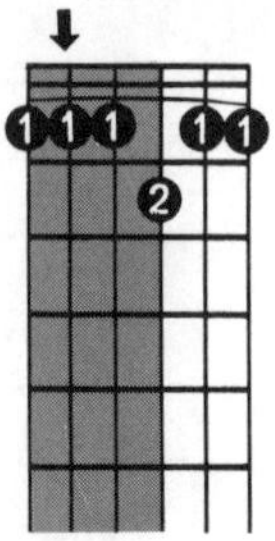

F B♭ E♭ A C F

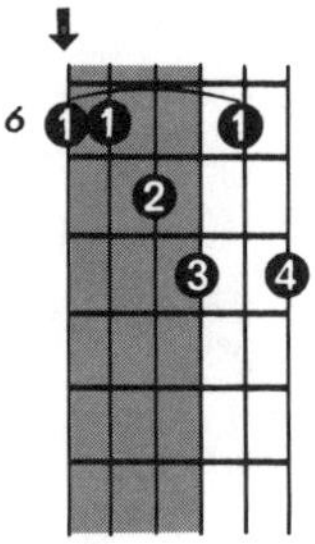

B♭ E♭ A E♭ F C

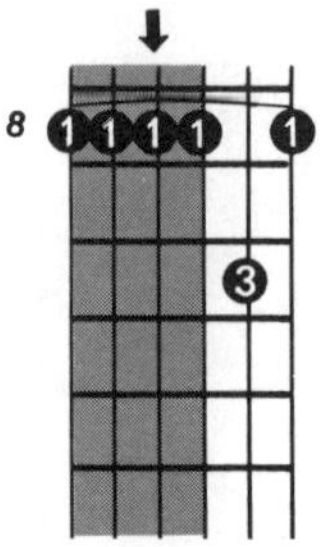

C F B♭ E♭ A C

A♯maj11

B♭7−5

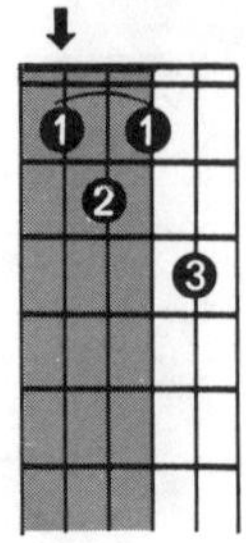

E B♭ E A♭ D E

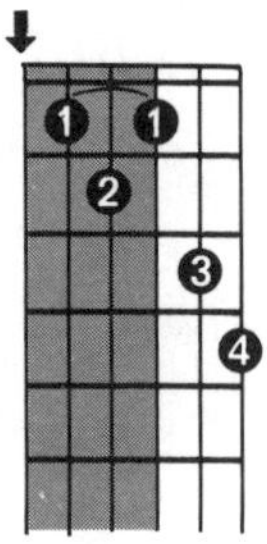

E B♭ E A♭ D A♭

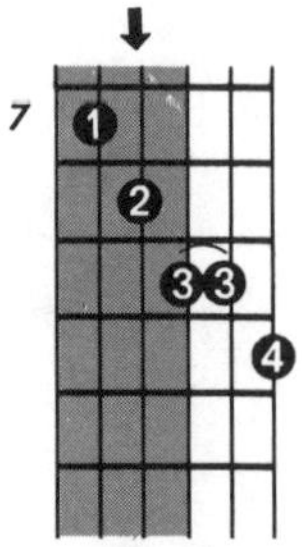

E E B♭ E A♭ D

A♯7−5

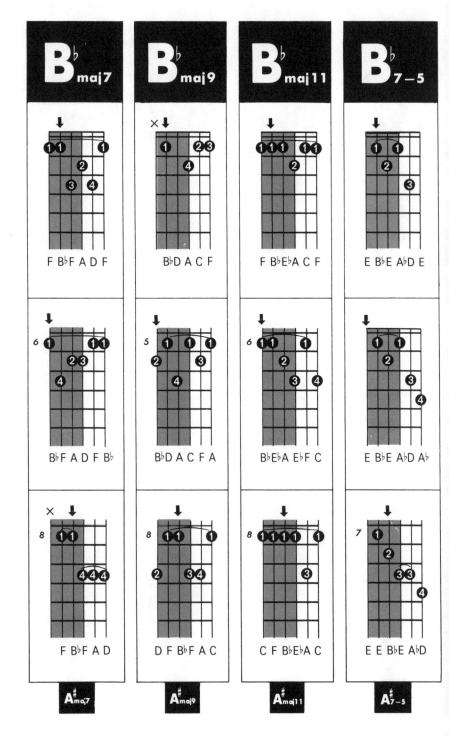

B♭7−9

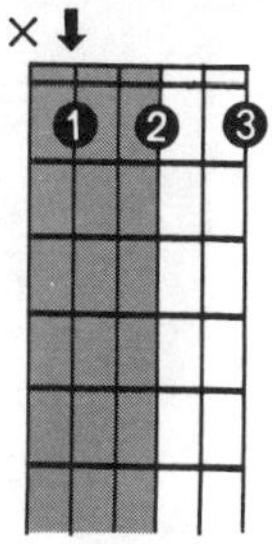

B♭D A♭B F

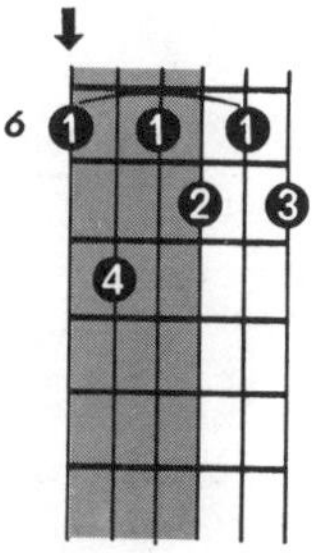

B♭F A♭D F B

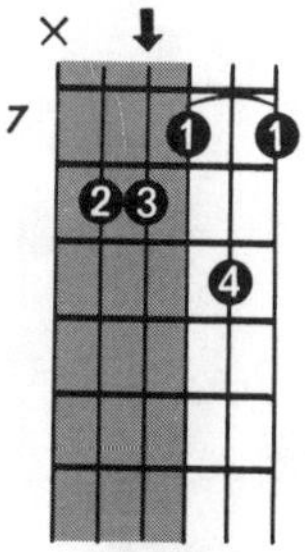

F B♭D A♭B

A♯7−9

B♭7−10

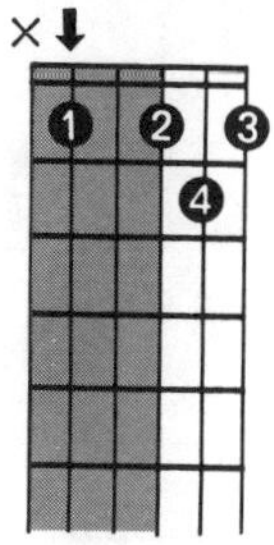

B♭D A♭D♭F

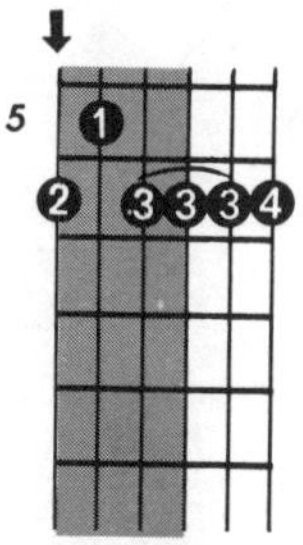

B♭D A♭D♭F B♭

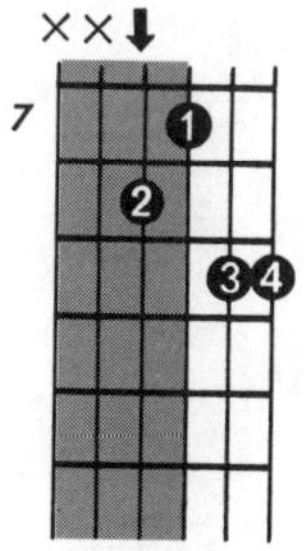

B♭D A♭D♭

A♯7−10

B♭7+5

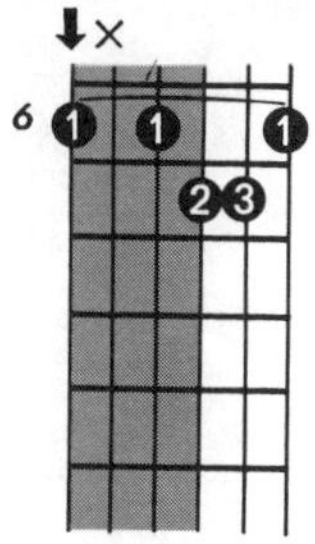

B♭ A♭D F♯B♭

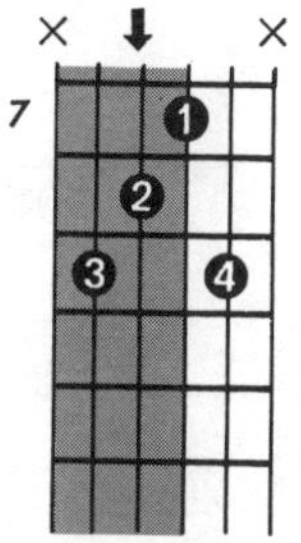

F♯B♭D A♭

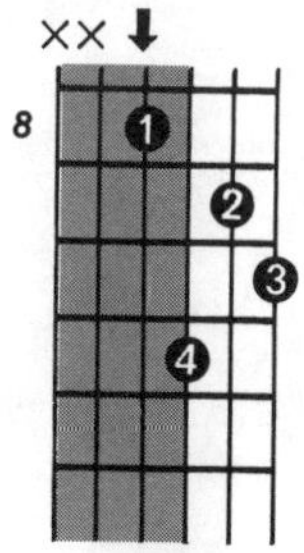

B♭F♯A♭D

A♯7+5

B♭9+5

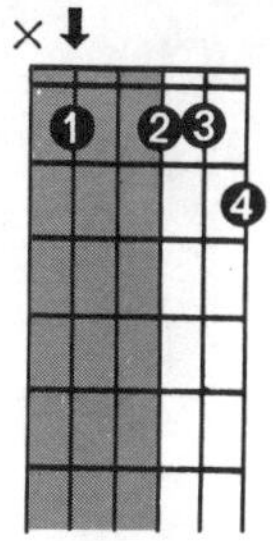

B♭D A♭C F♯

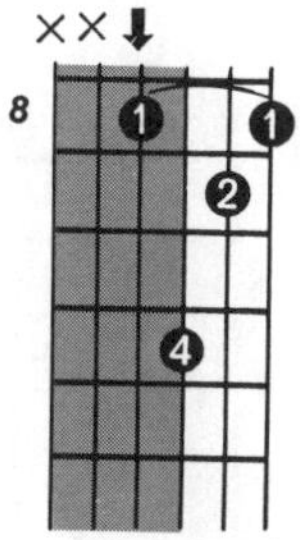

B♭F♯A♭C

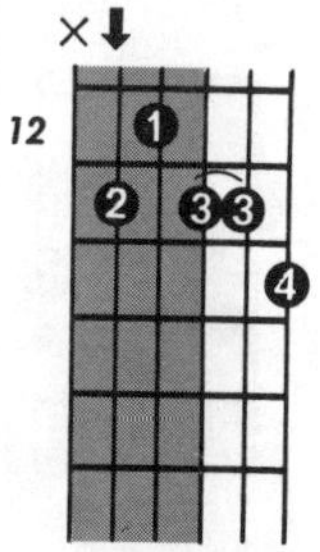

B♭D A♭C F♯

A♯9+5

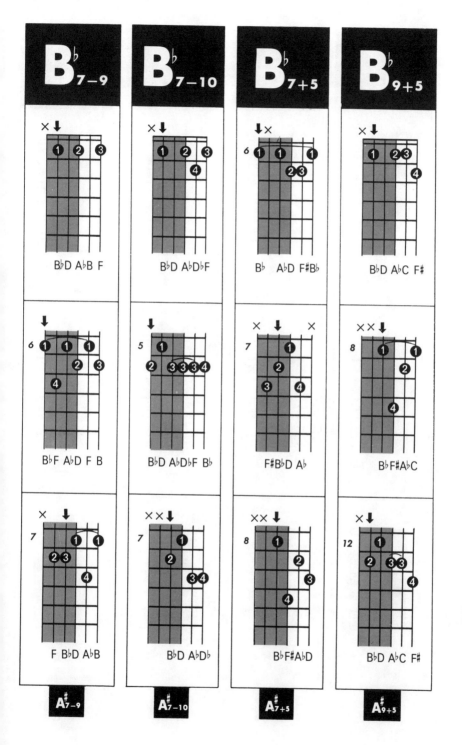

$B^{\flat}{}^{-9}_{7+5}$

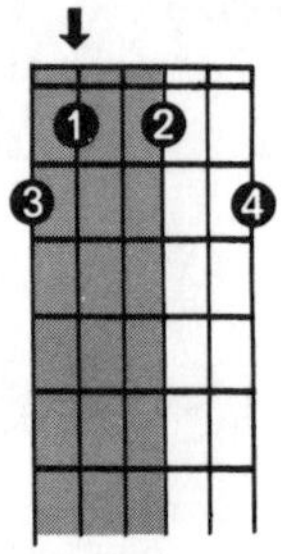

F♯B♭D A♭B F♯

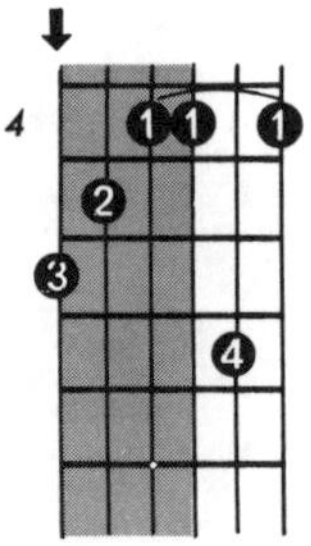

B♭D F♯B F♯A♭

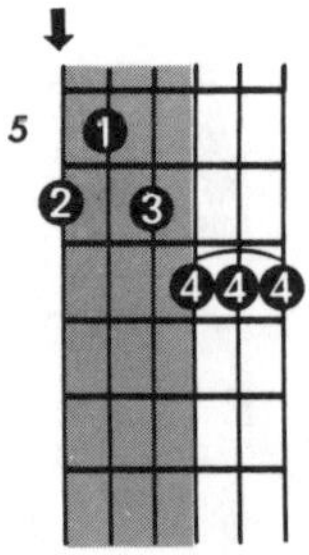

B♭D A♭D F♯B

$A^{\sharp}{}^{-9}_{7+5}$

$B^{\flat}_{6\cdot 9}$

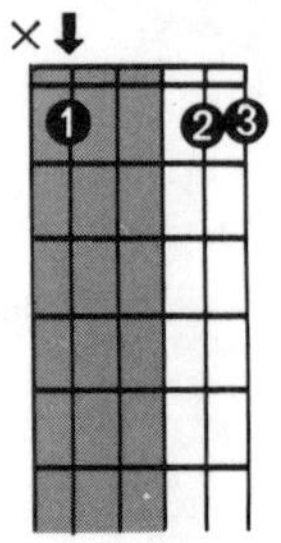

B♭D G C F

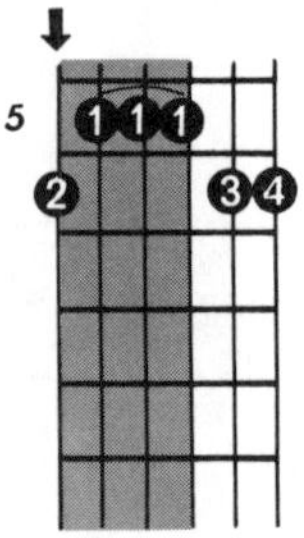

B♭D G C F B♭

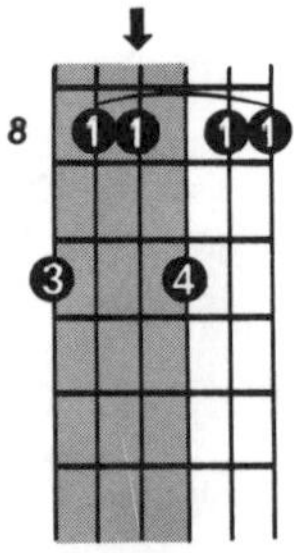

D F B♭F G C

$A^{\sharp}_{6\cdot 9}$

$B^{\flat}_{dim}$

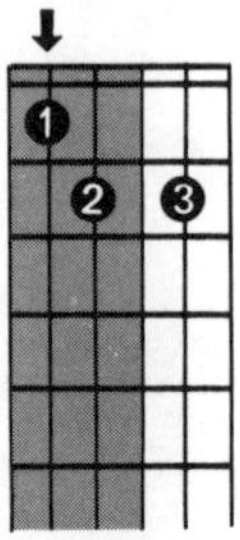

E B♭E G D♭E

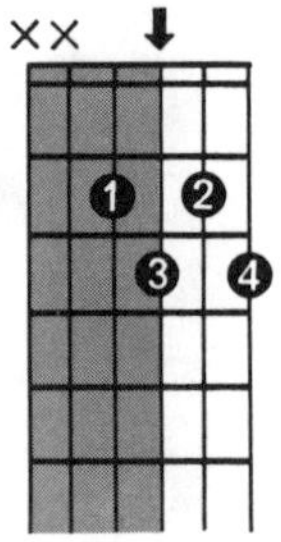

E B♭D♭G

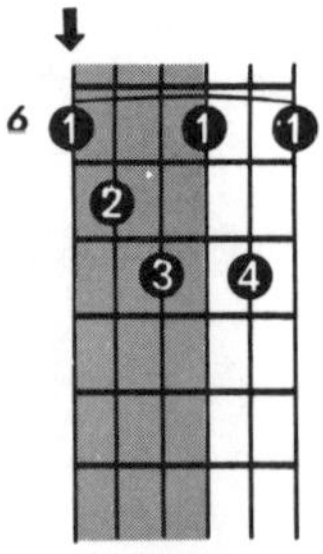

B♭E B♭D♭G B♭

$A^{\sharp}_{dim}$

$B^{\flat}_{+5}$

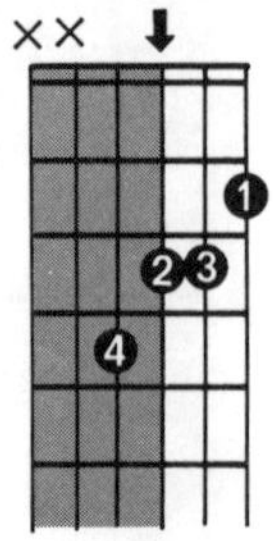

F♯B♭D F♯

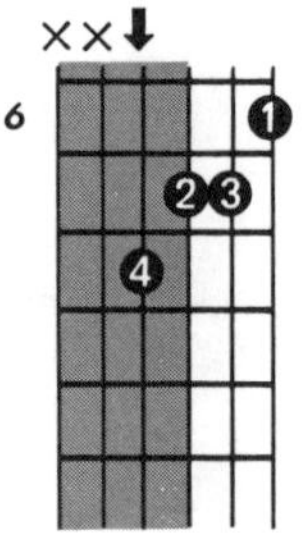

B♭D F♯B♭

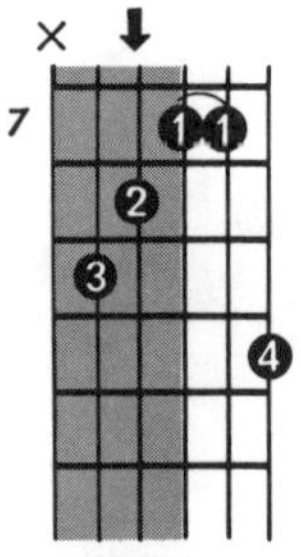

F♯B♭D F♯D

$A^{\sharp}_{+5}$

A♯

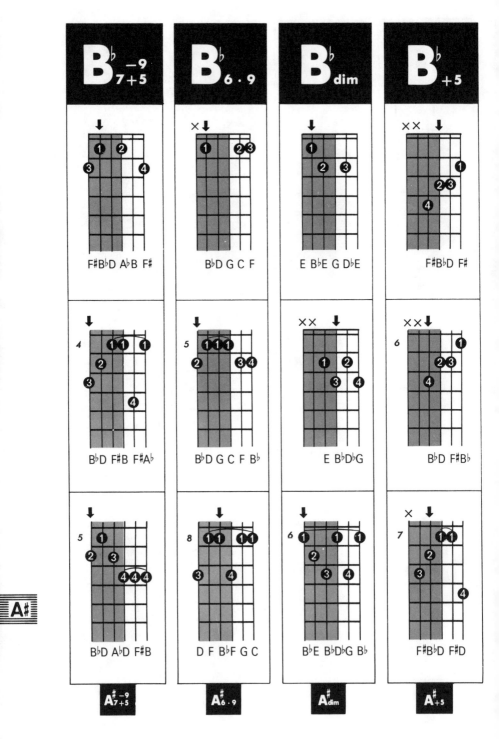

B♭sus4

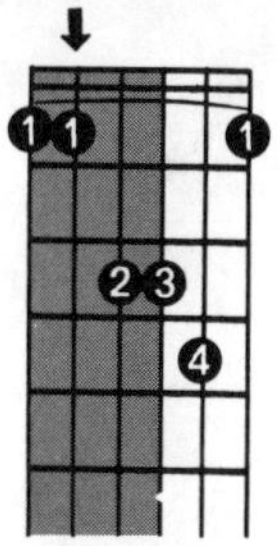

F B♭F B♭E♭F

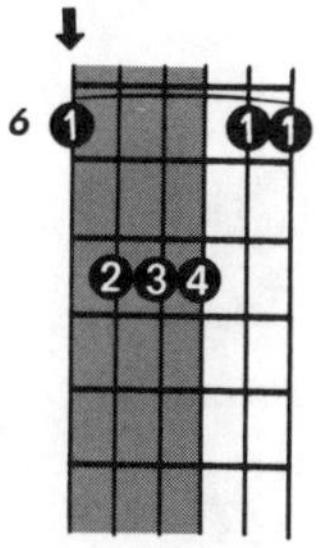

B♭F B♭E♭F B♭

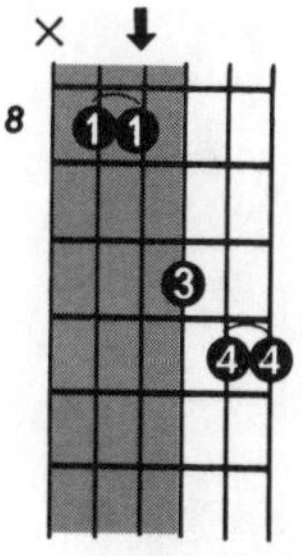

F B♭F B♭E♭

A♯sus4

B♭7sus4

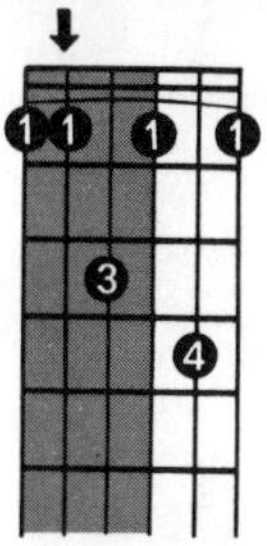

F B♭F A♭E♭F

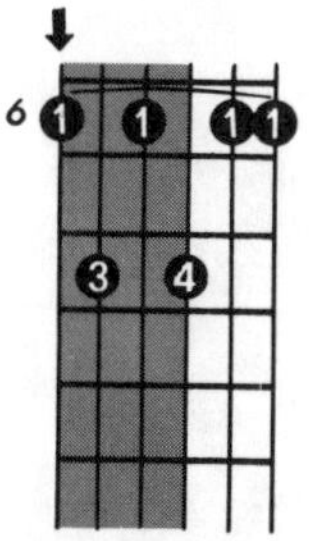

B♭F A♭E♭F B♭

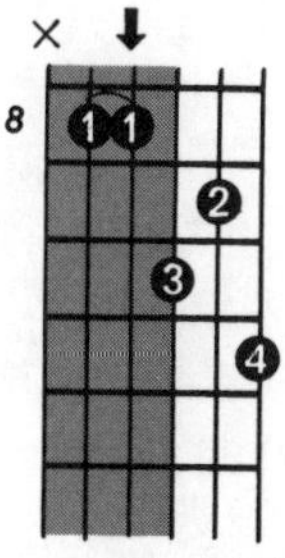

F B♭F A♭E♭

A♯7sus4

B♭m

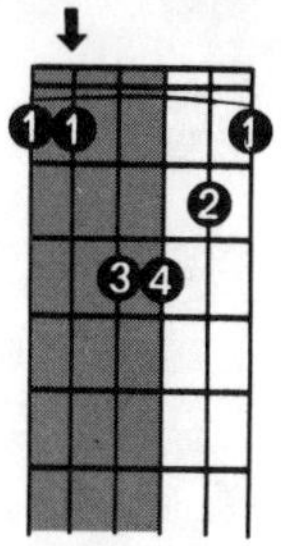

F B♭F B♭D♭F

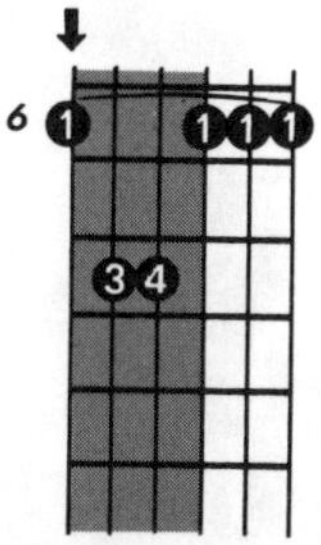

B♭F B♭D♭F B♭

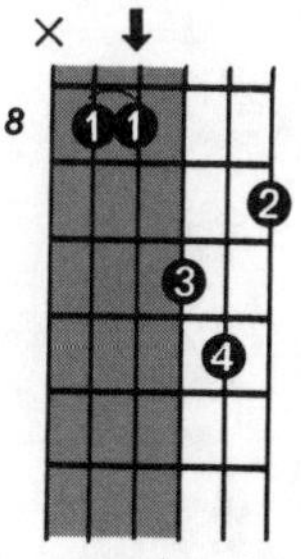

F B♭F B♭D♭

A♯m

B♭m6

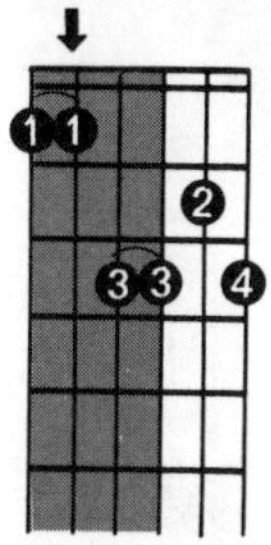

F B♭F B♭D♭G

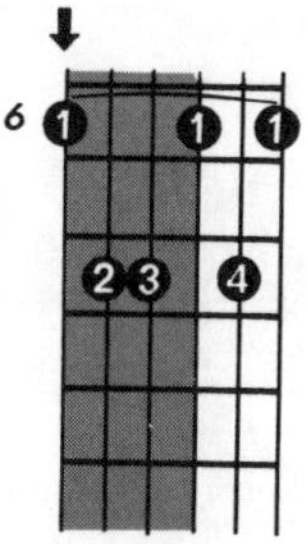

B♭F B♭D♭G B♭

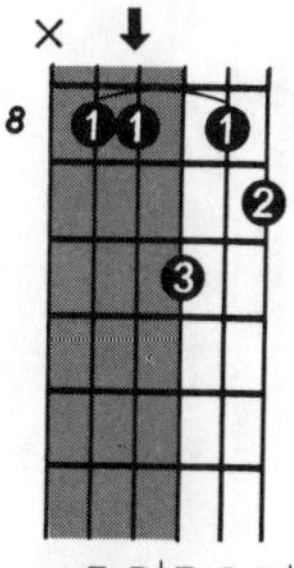

F B♭F G D♭

A♯m6

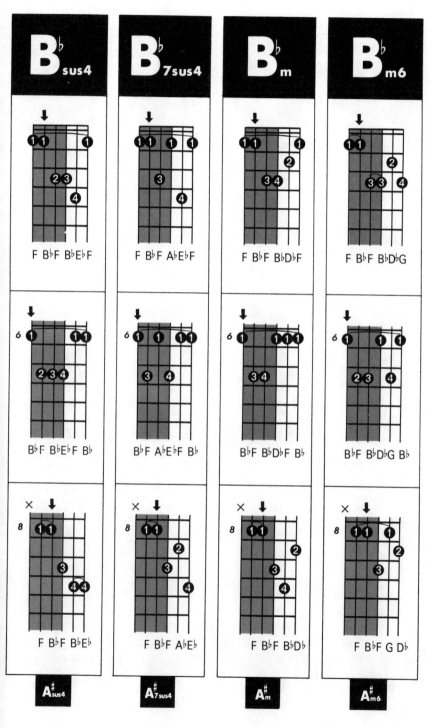

B♭m7

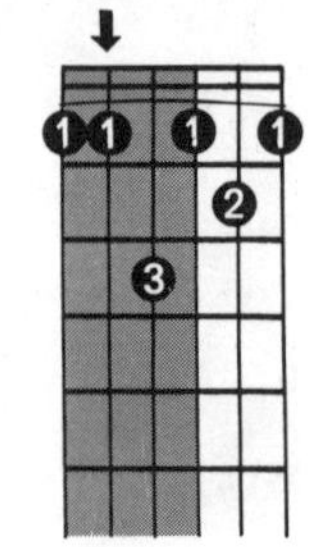

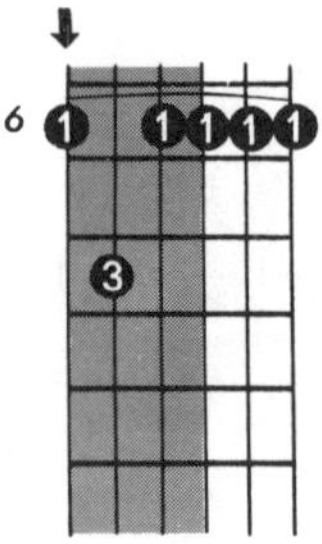

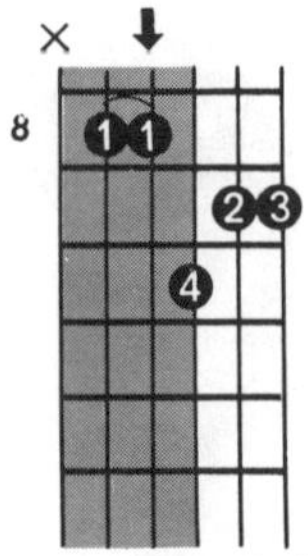

A♯m7

B♭m9

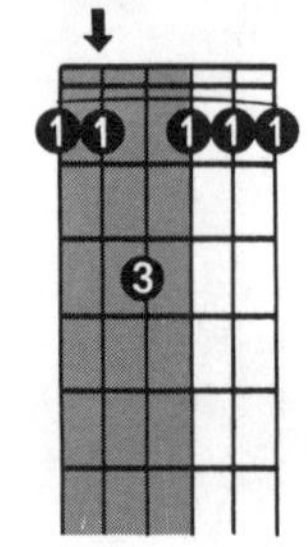

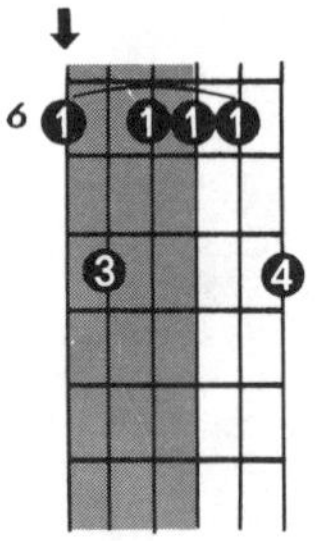

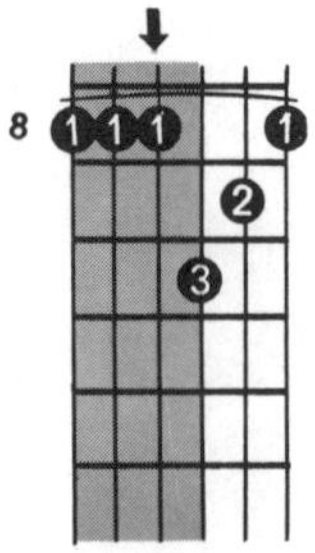

A♯m9

B♭m7–5

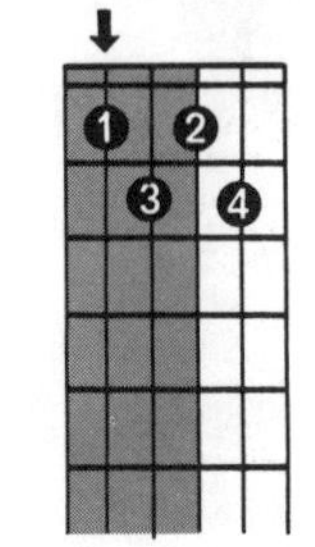

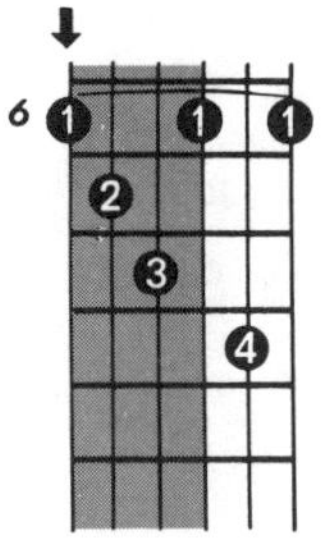

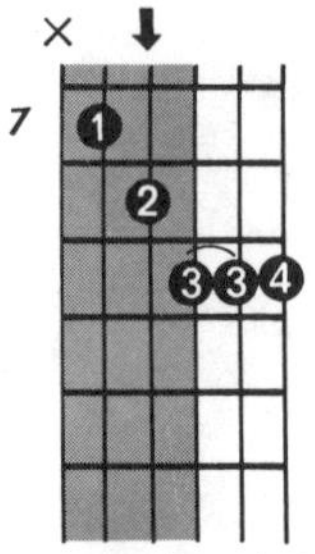

A♯m7–5

B♭m7–9

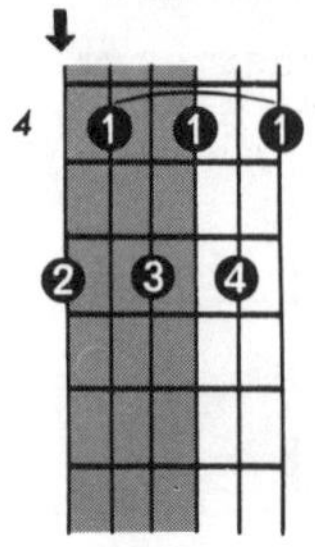

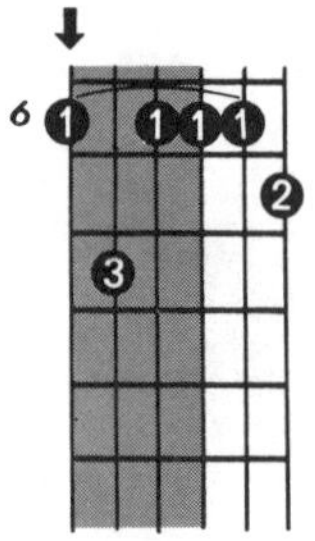

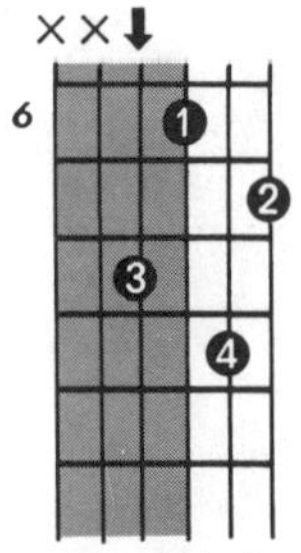

A♯m7–9

A♯

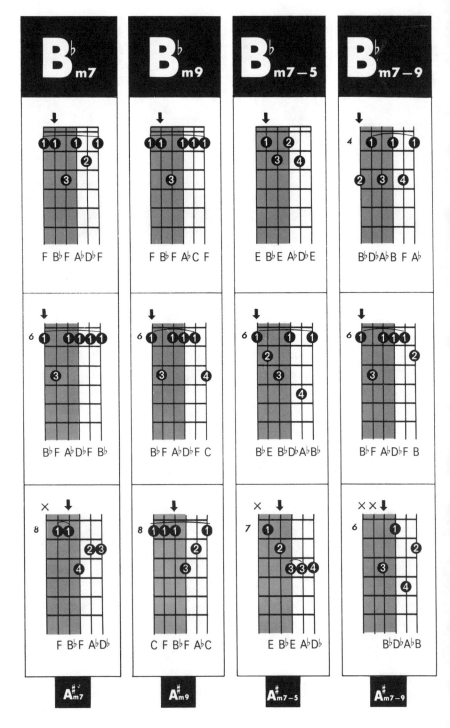

B♭m+7

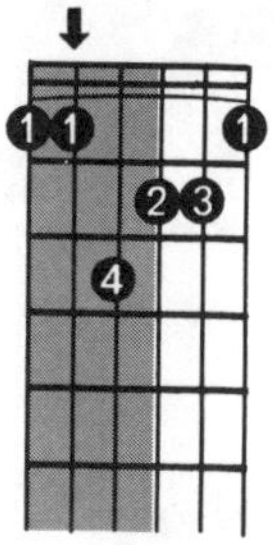

F B♭F A D♭F

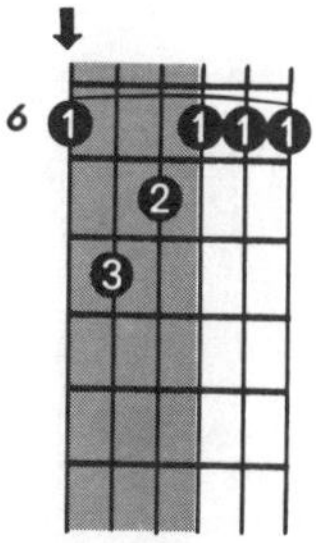

B♭F A D♭F B♭

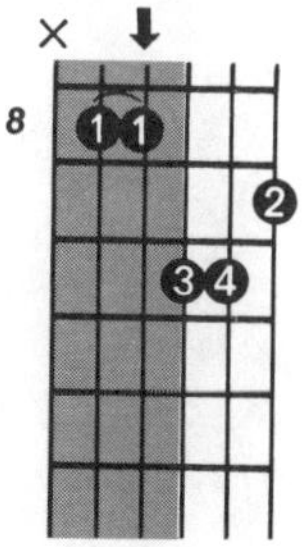

F B♭F A D♭

A♯m+7

B♭m9+7

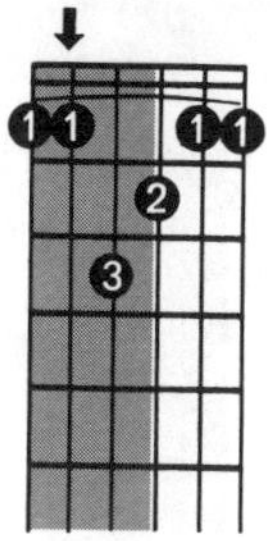

F B♭F A C F

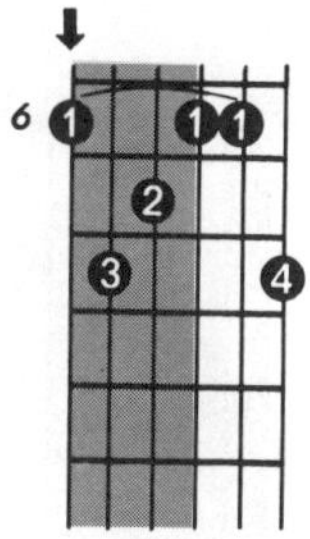

B♭F A D♭F C

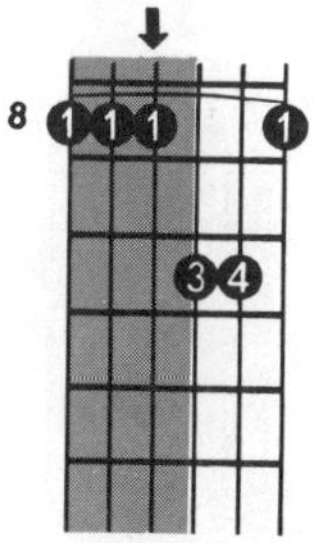

C F B♭F A C

A♯m9+7

B♭m+5

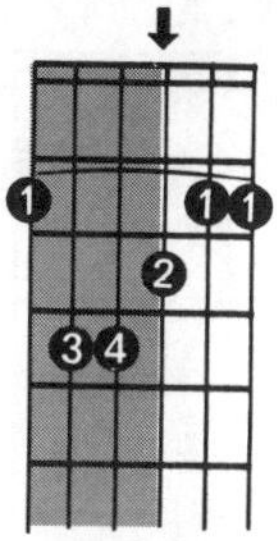

F♯D♭F♯B♭D♭F♯

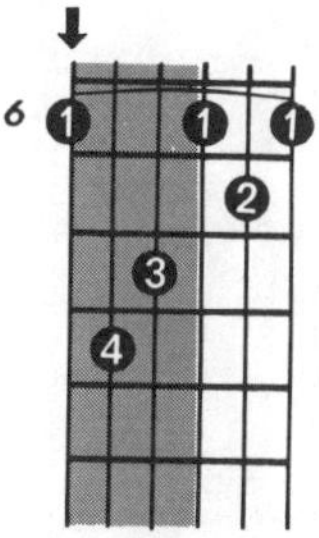

B♭F♯B♭D♭F♯B♭

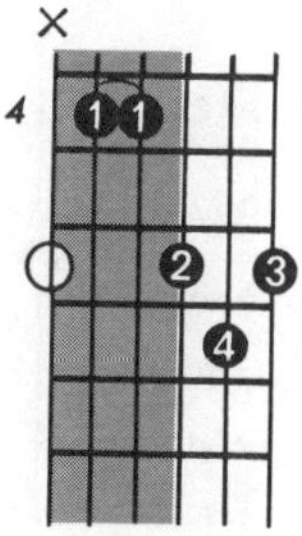

D♭F♯D♭F♯B♭

A♯m+5

B♭m6 · 9

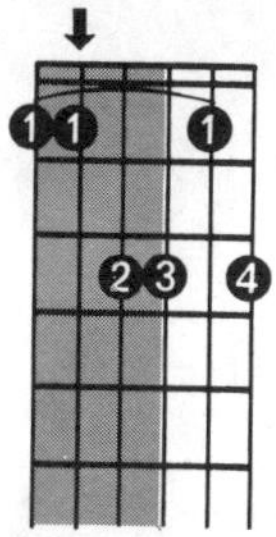

F B♭F B♭C G

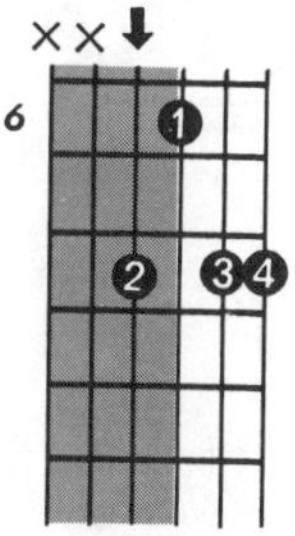

B♭D♭G C

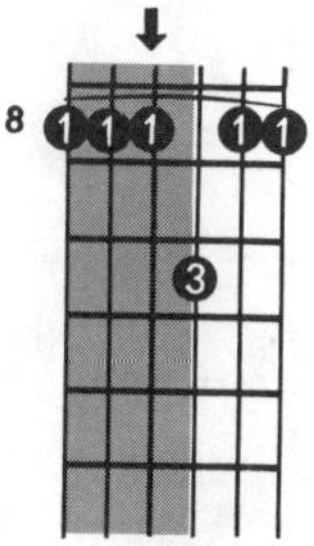

C F B♭F G C

A♯m6 · 9

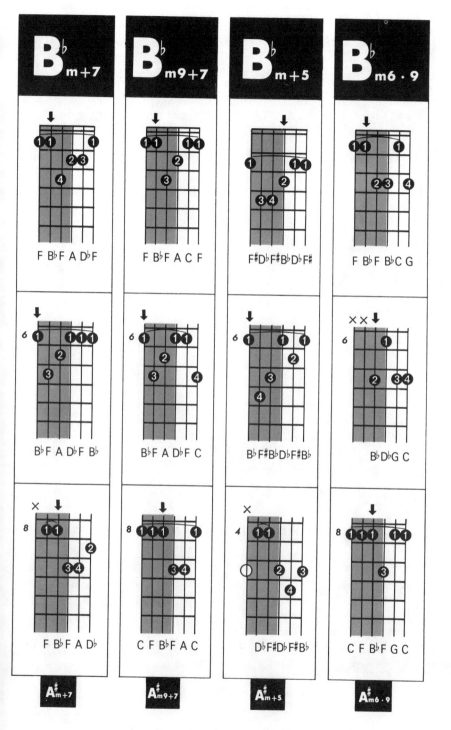

B

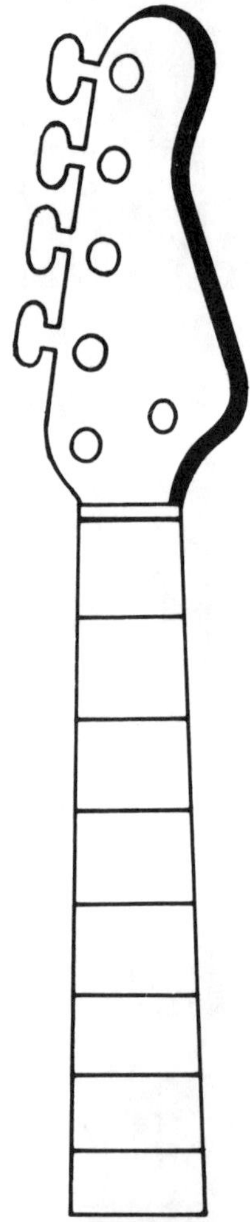

B

B

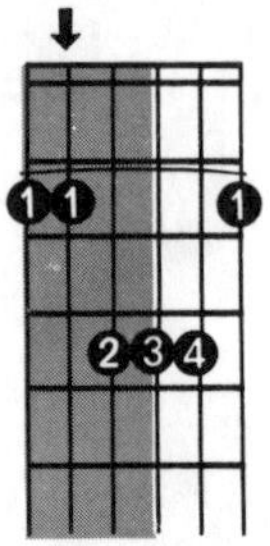

F#B F#B D#F#

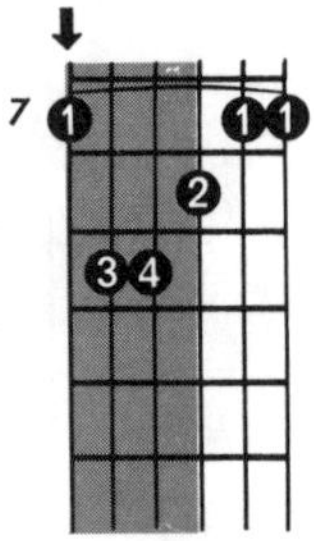

B F#B D#F#B

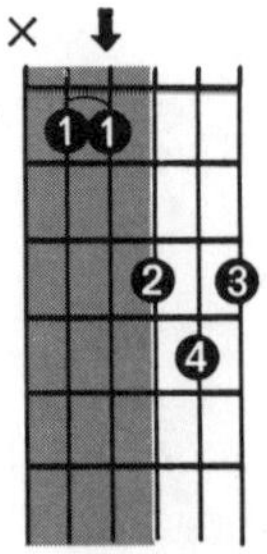

F#B F#B D#

B_6

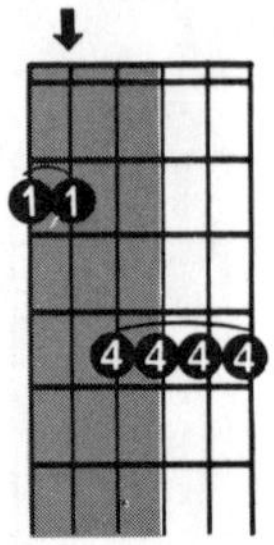

F#B F#B D#G#

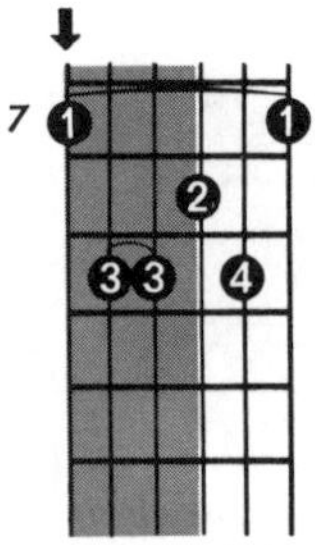

B F#B D#G#B

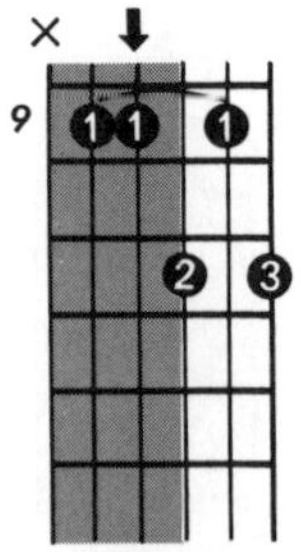

F#B F#G#D#

B_7

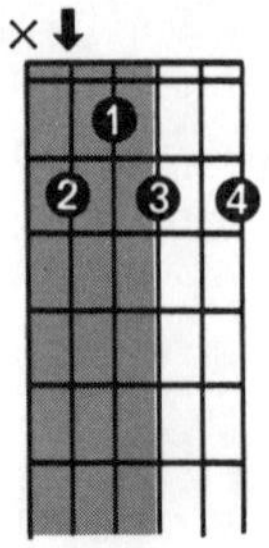

B D#A B F#

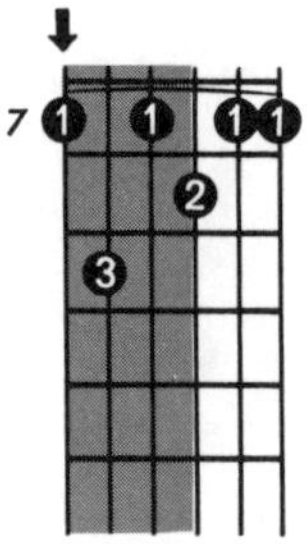

B F#A D#F#B

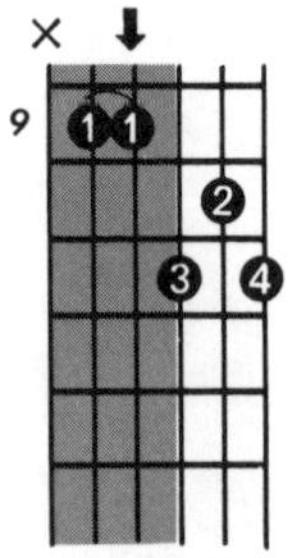

F#B F#A D#

B9

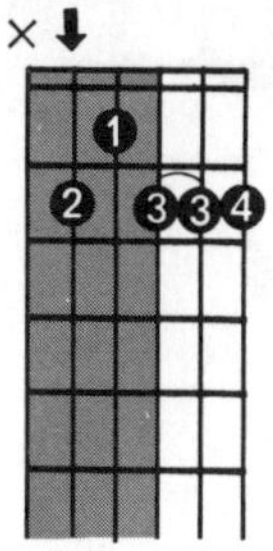

B D♯A C♯F♯

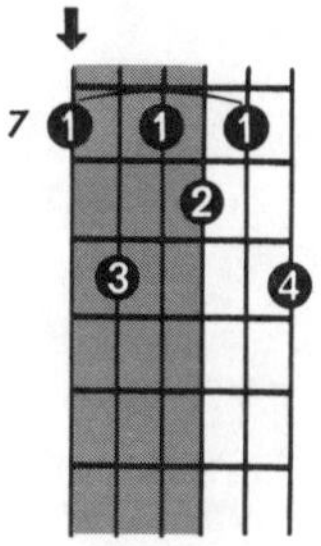

B F♯A D♯F♯C♯

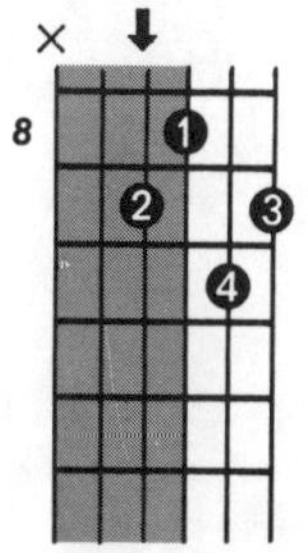

A B D♯A C♯

B11

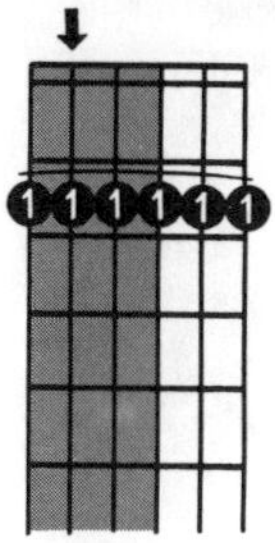

F♯B E A C♯F♯

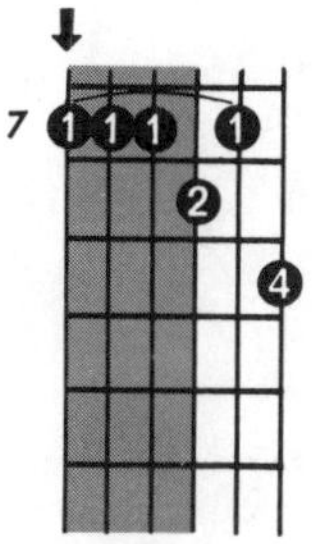

B E A D♯F♯C♯

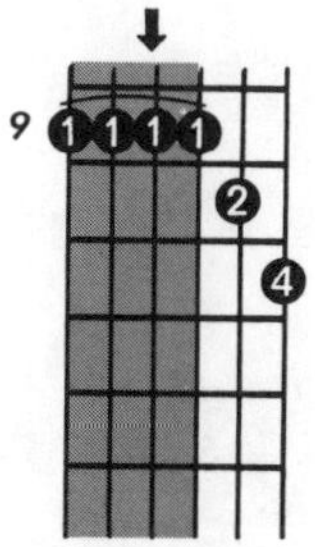

C♯F♯B E A D♯

B11+

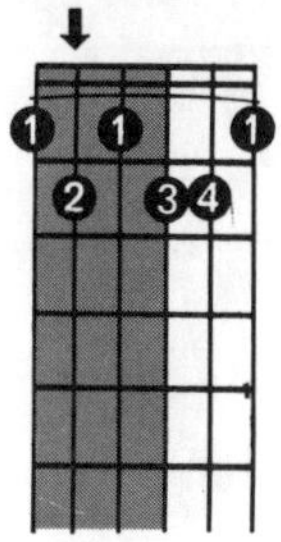

F B D♯A C♯F

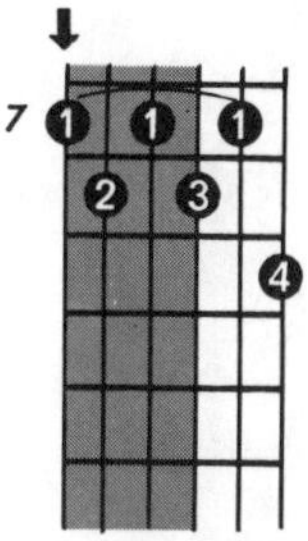

B F A D♯F♯C♯

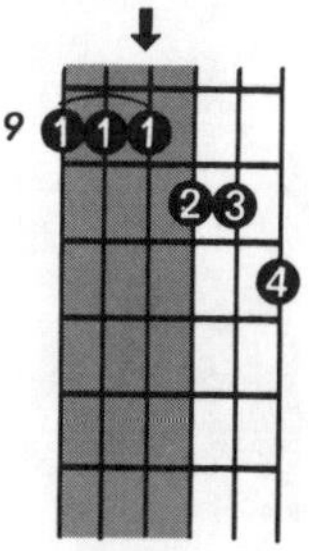

C♯F♯B F A D♯

B13

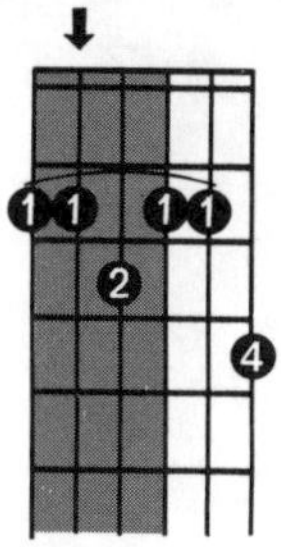

F♯B F A C♯G♯

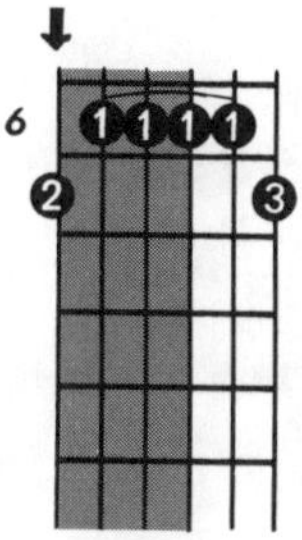

B D♯G♯C♯F B

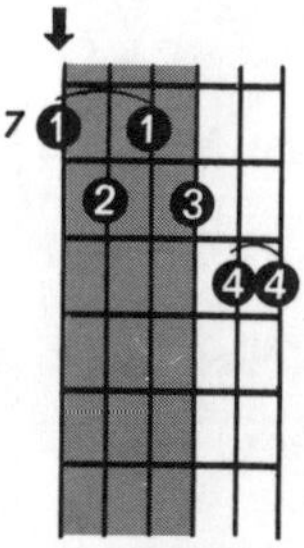

B F A D♯G♯C♯

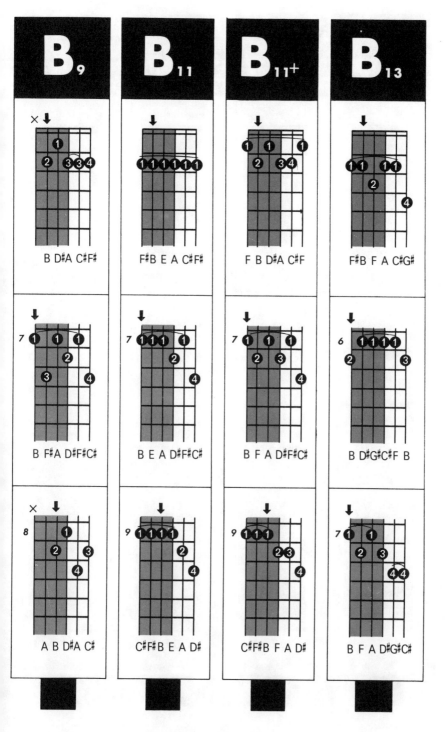

B maj7

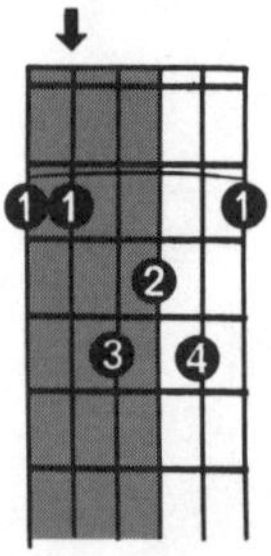

F♯B F♯A♯D♯F♯

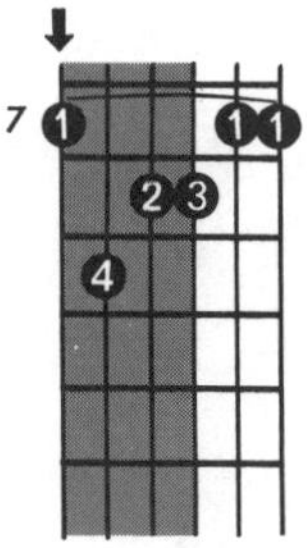

B F♯A♯D♯F♯B

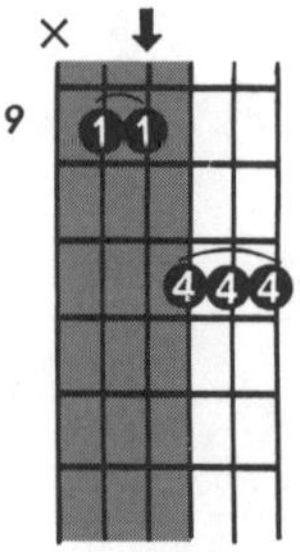

F♯B F♯A♯D♯

B maj9

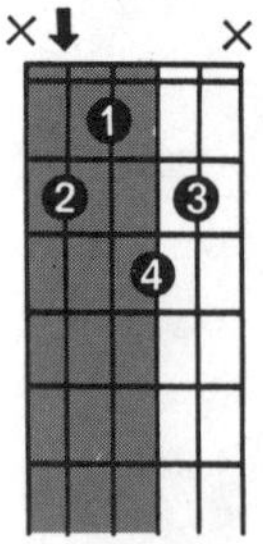

B D♯A♯C♯

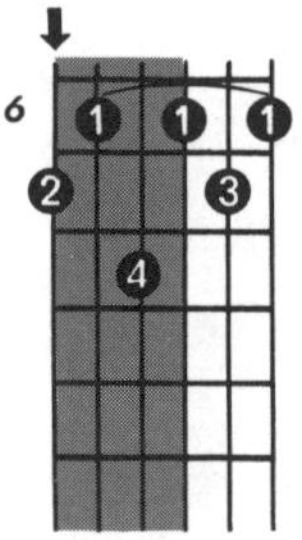

B D♯A♯C♯F♯A♯

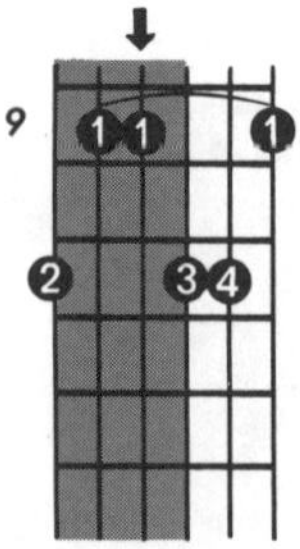

D♯F♯B F♯A♯C♯

B maj11

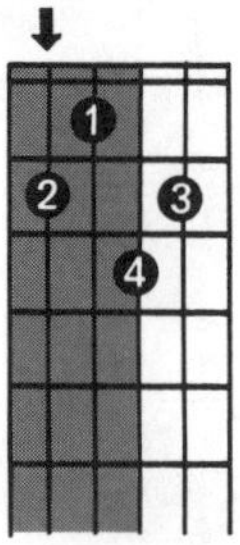

E B D♯A♯C♯E

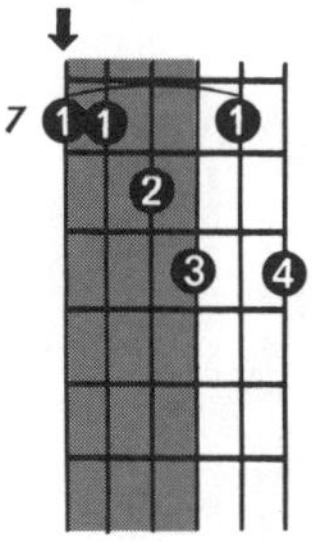

B E A♯E F♯C♯

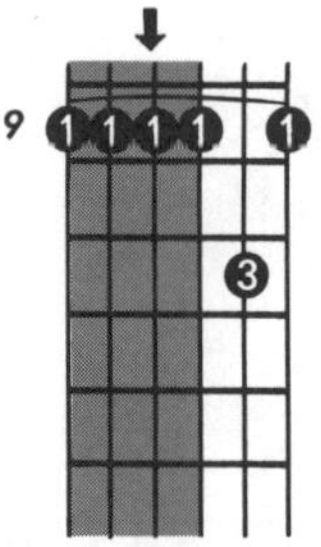

C♯F♯B E A♯C♯

B 7−5

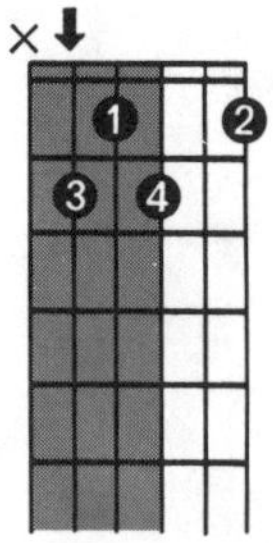

B D♯A B F

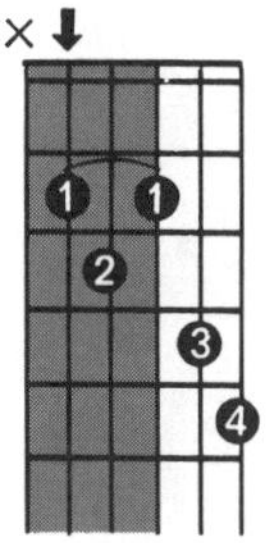

B F A D♯A

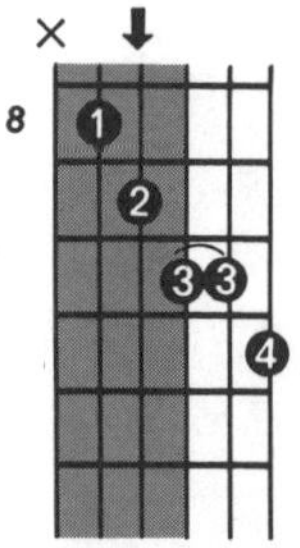

F B F A D♯

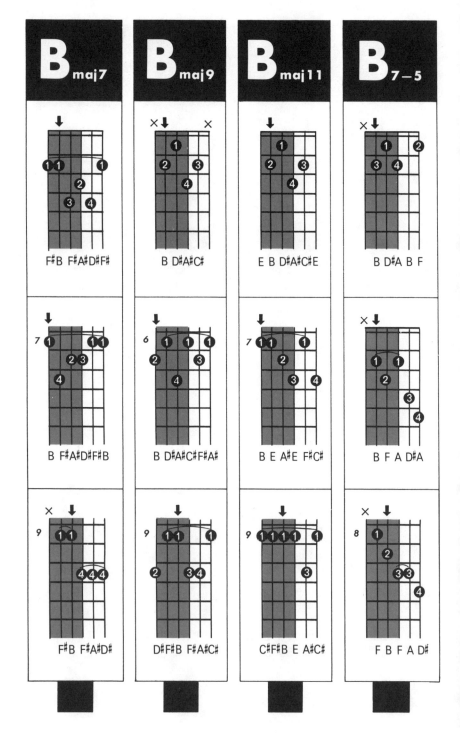

B_{7-9}

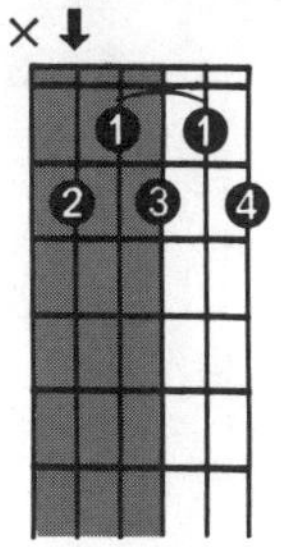

B D#A C F#

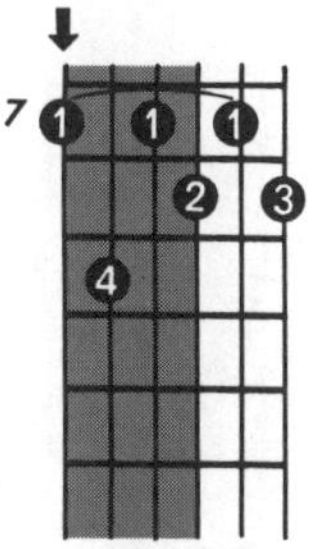

B F#A D#F#C

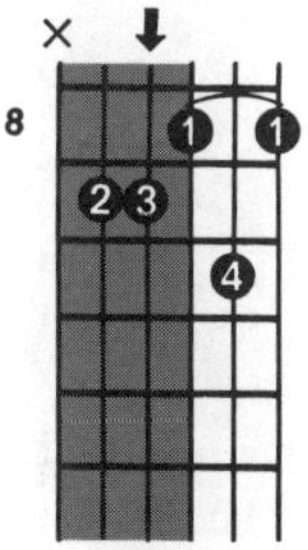

F#B D#A C

B_{7-10}

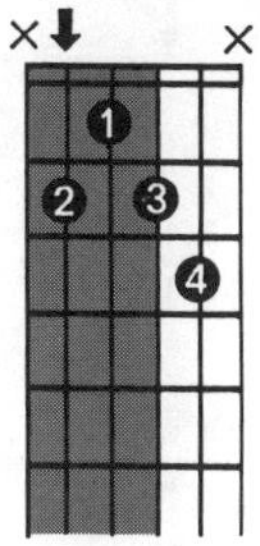

B D#A D

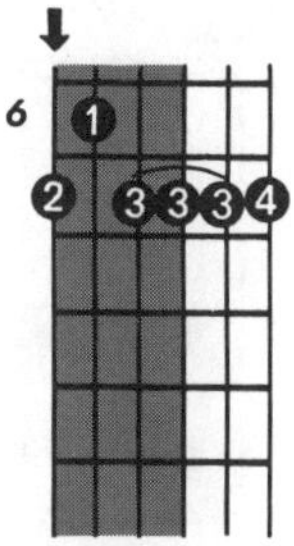

B D#A D F#B

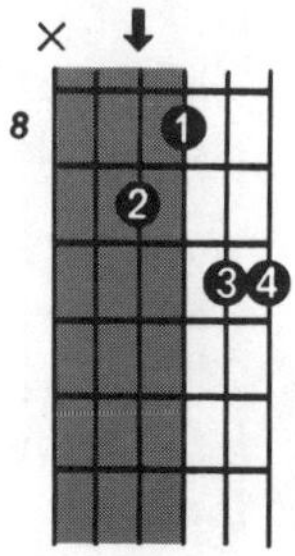

A B D#A D

B_{7+5}

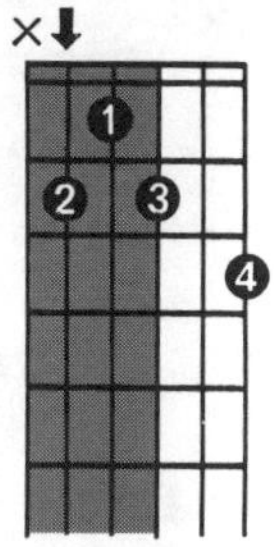

B D#A B G

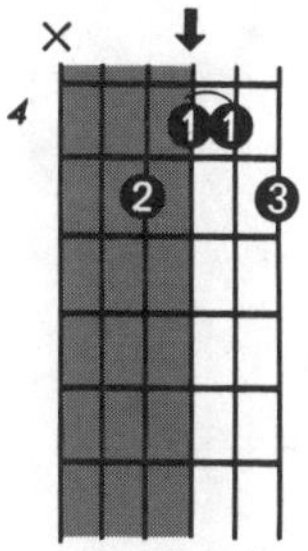

A G B D#A

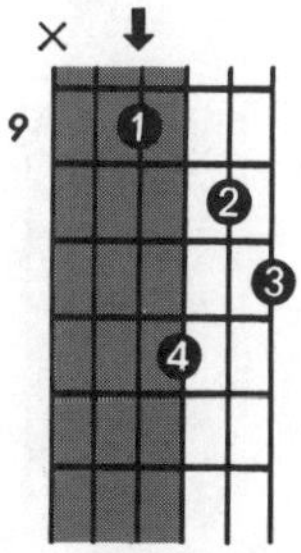

A B G A D#

B_{9+5}

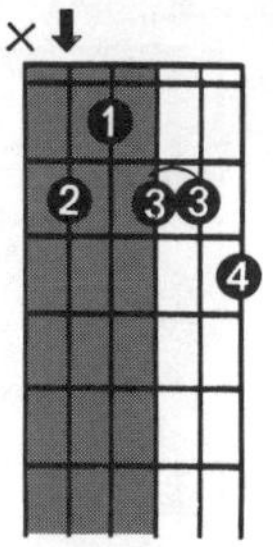

B D#A C#G

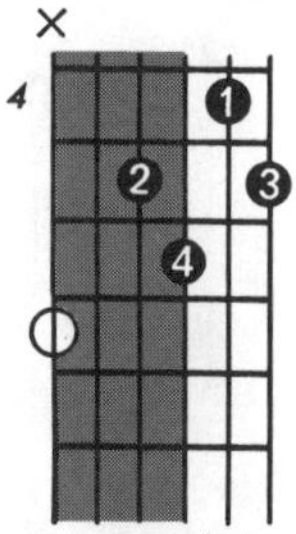

A G C#D#A

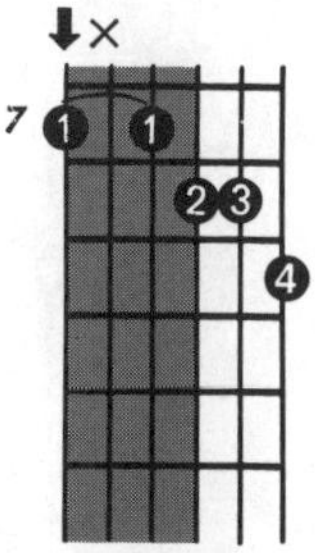

B A D#G C#

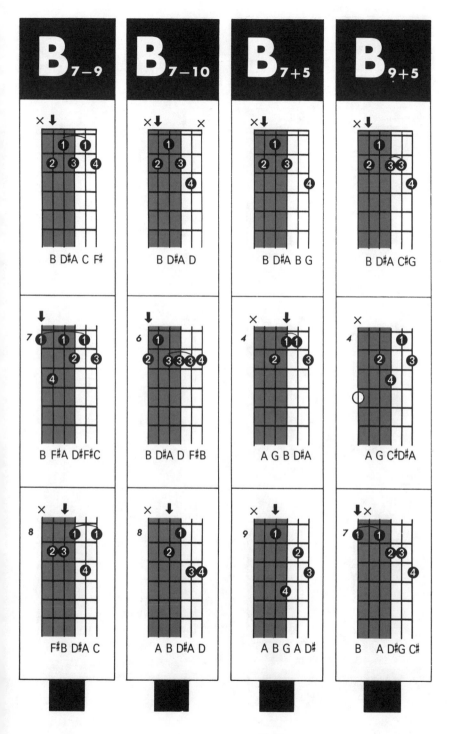

B_{7+5}^{-9}

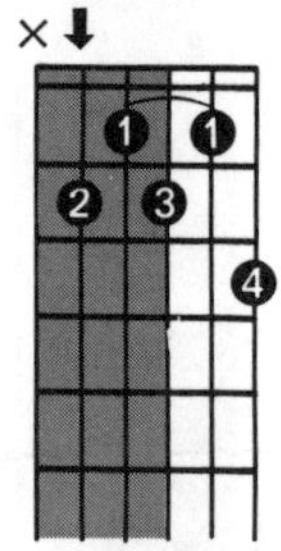

B D♯A C G

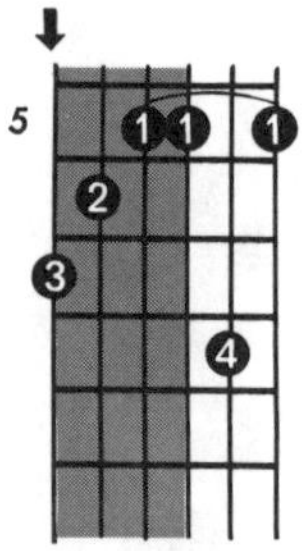

B D♯G C G A

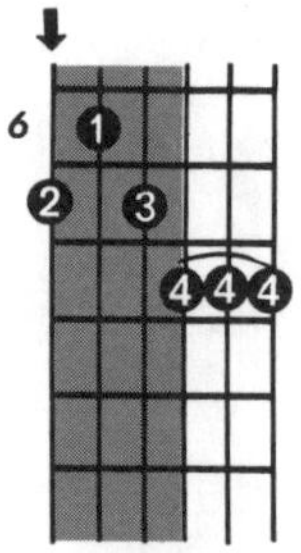

B D♯A D♯G C

B6·9

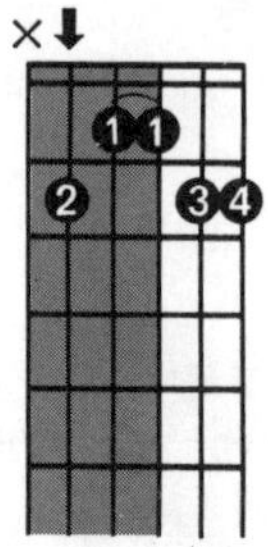

B D♯G♯C♯F♯

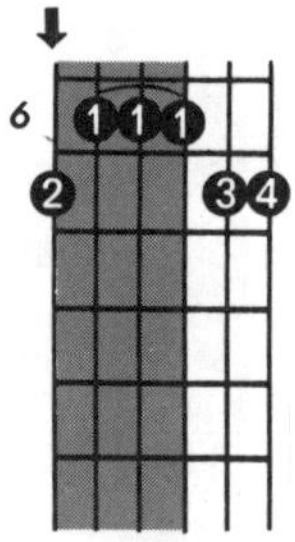

B D♯G♯C♯F♯B

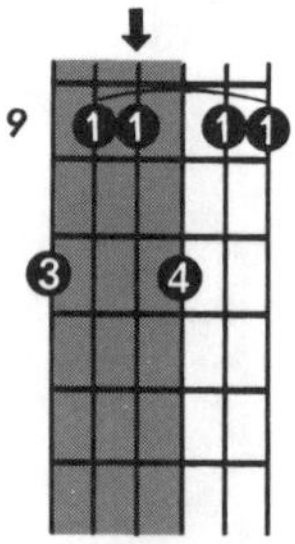

D♯F♯B F♯G♯C♯

Bdim

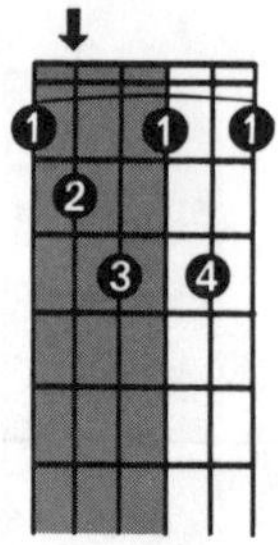

F B F G♯D F

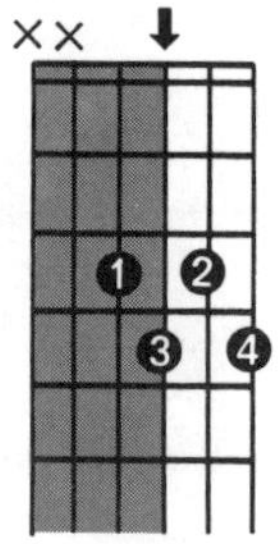

F B D G♯

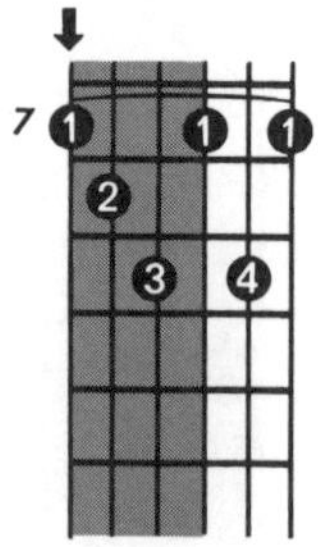

B F B D G♯B

B+5

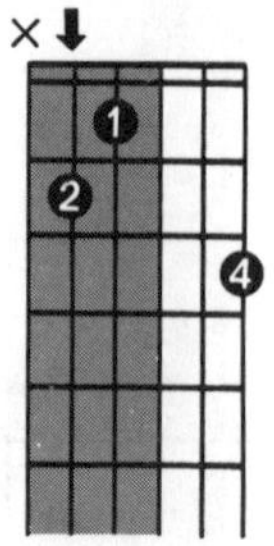

B D♯G B G

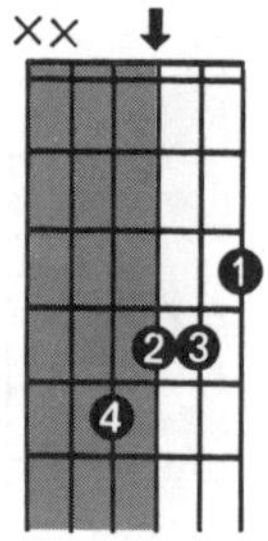

G B D♯G

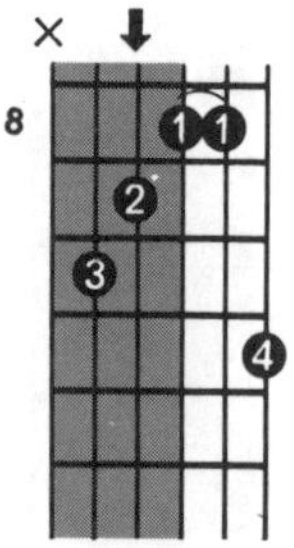

G B D♯G D♯

B

Bsus4

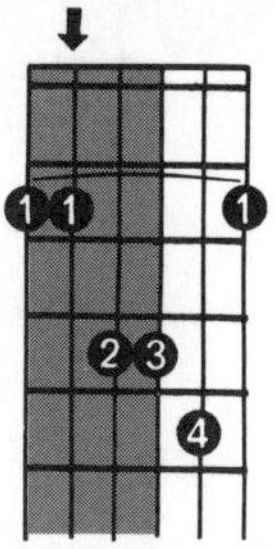

F♯B F♯B E F♯

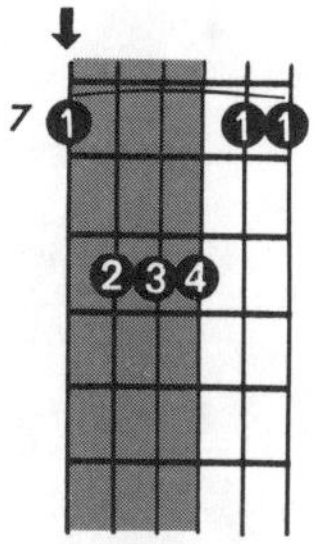

B F♯B E F♯B

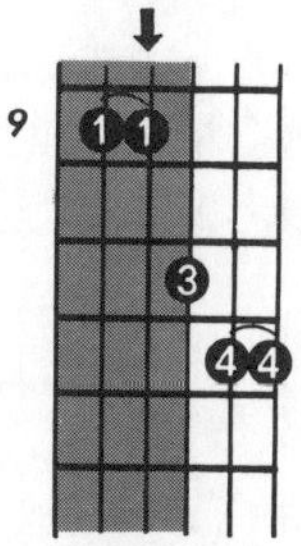

E F♯B F♯B E

B7sus4

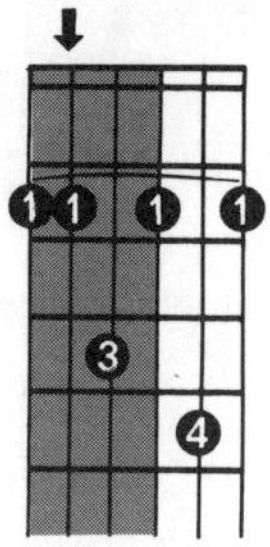

F♯B F♯A E F♯

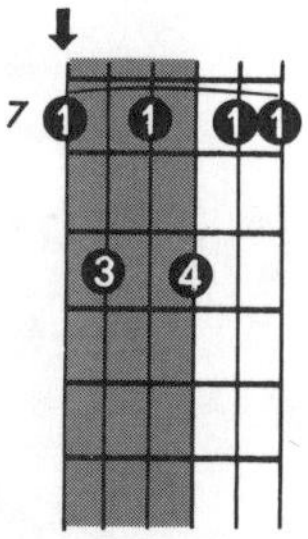

B F♯A E F♯B

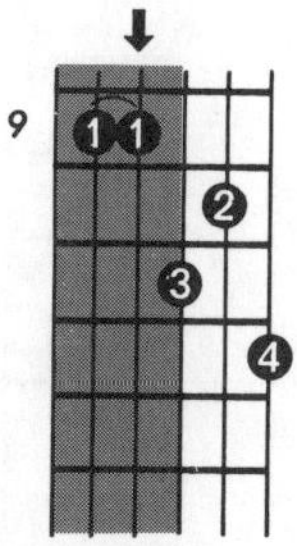

E F♯B F♯A E

Bm

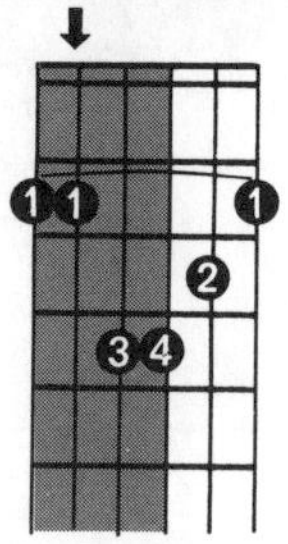

F♯B F♯B D F♯

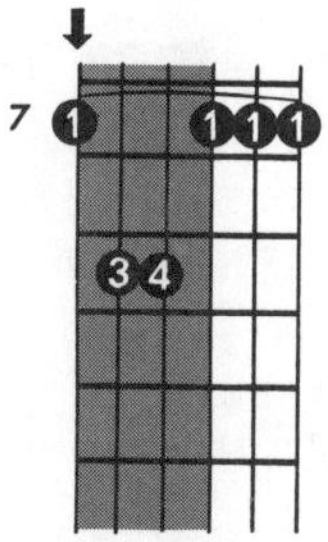

B F♯B D F♯B

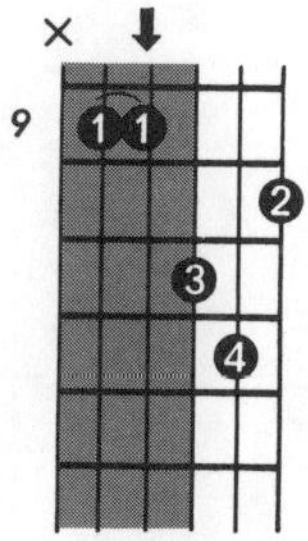

F♯B F♯B D

Bm6

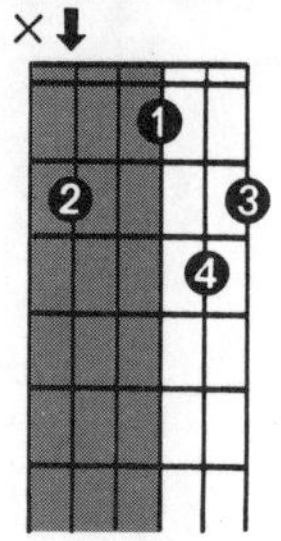

B D G♯D F♯

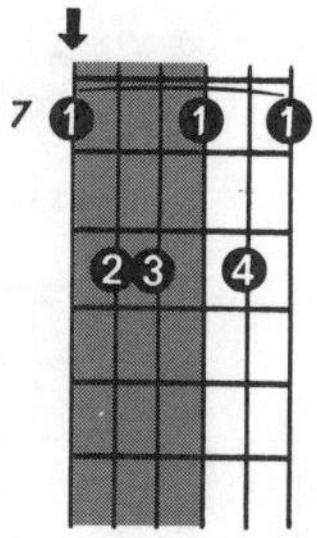

B F♯B D G♯B

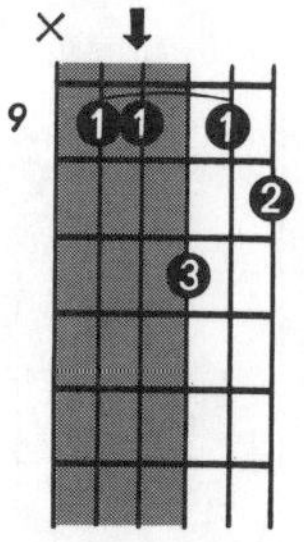

F♯B F♯G♯D

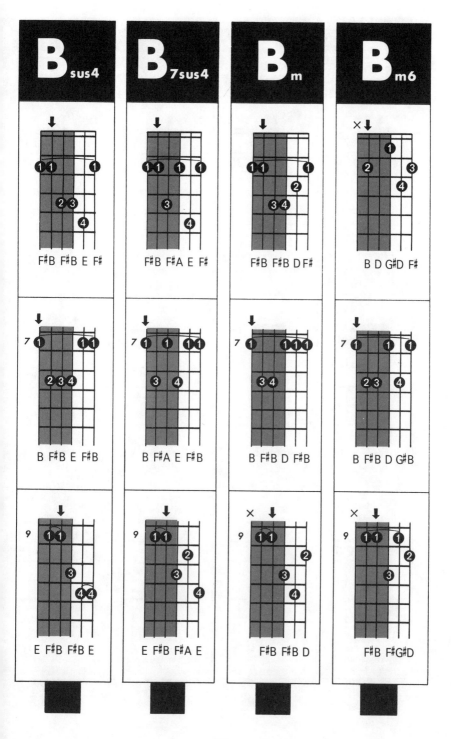

Bm7

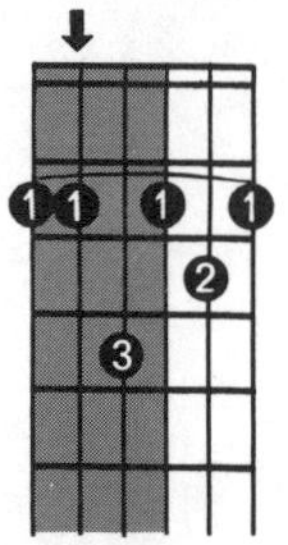

F#B F#A D F#

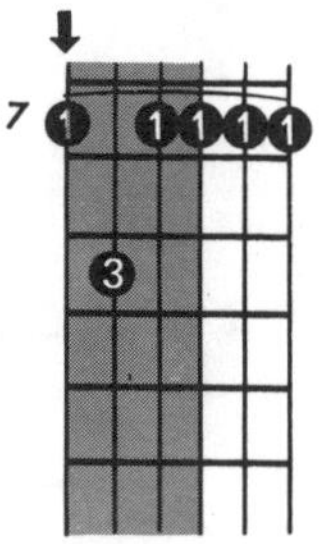

B F#A D F#B

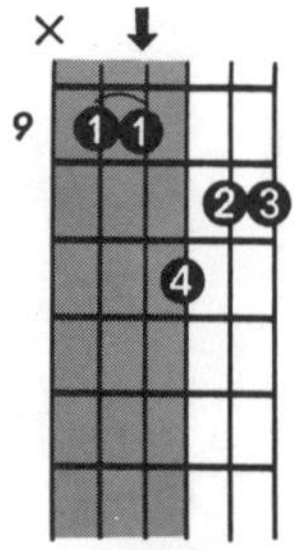

F#B F#A D

Bm9

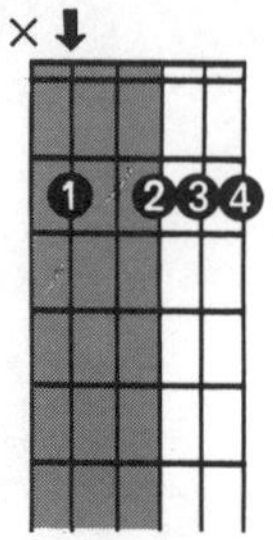

B D A C#F#

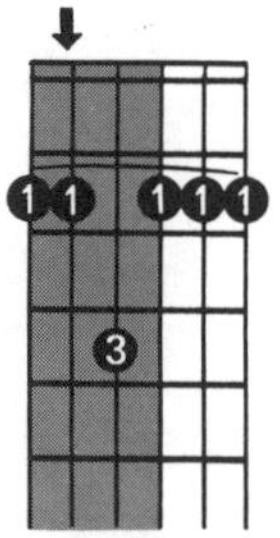

F#B F#A C#F#

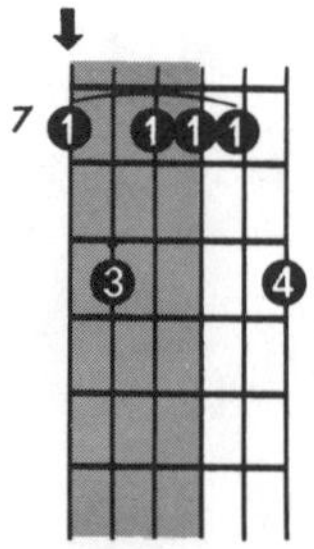

B F#A D F#C#

Bm7−5

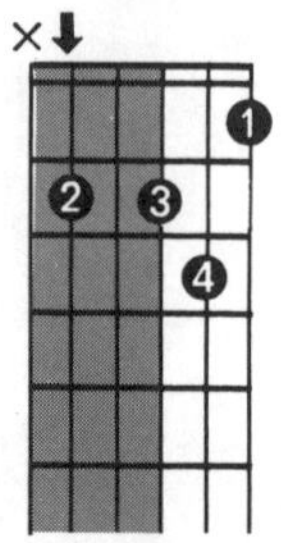

B D A D F

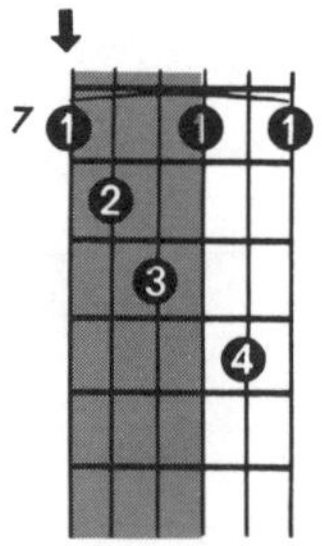

B F B D A B

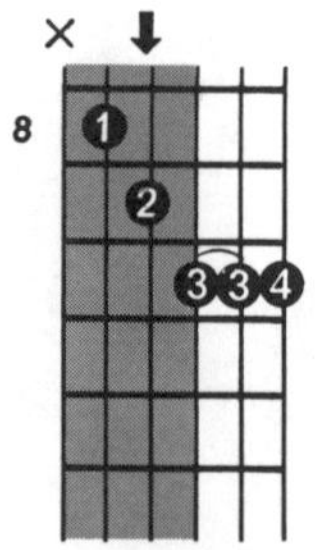

F B F A D

Bm7−9

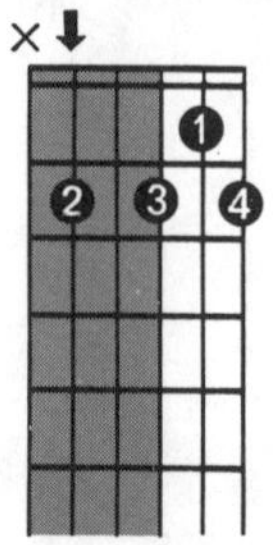

B D A C F#

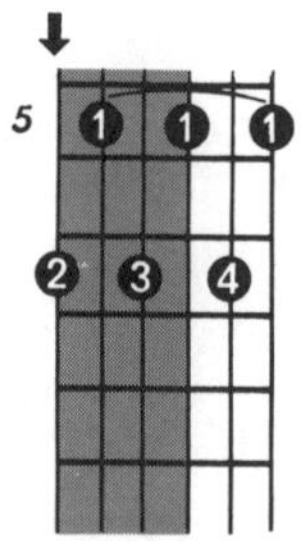

B D A C F#A

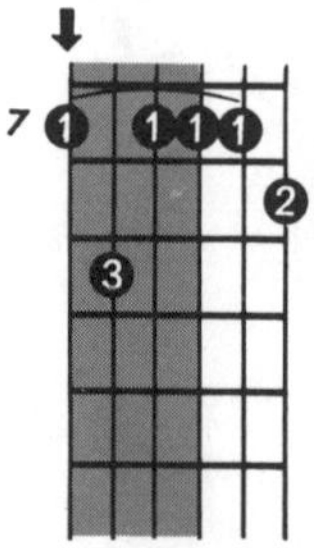

B F#A D F#C

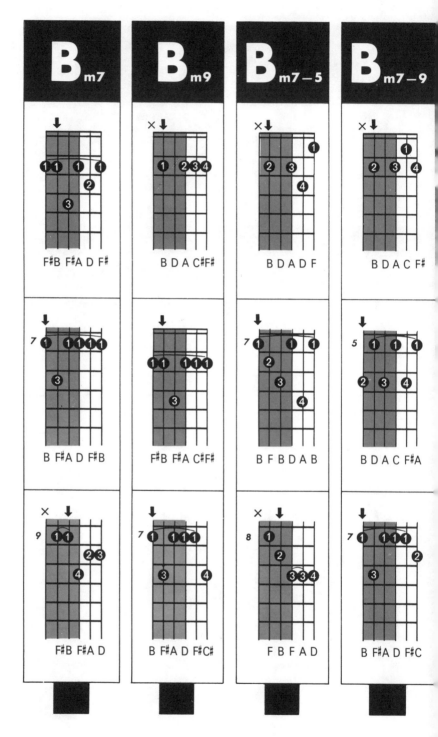

B m+7

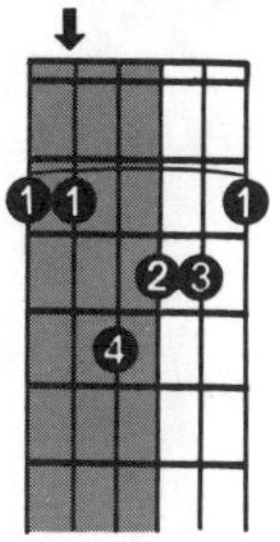

F#B F#A#D F#

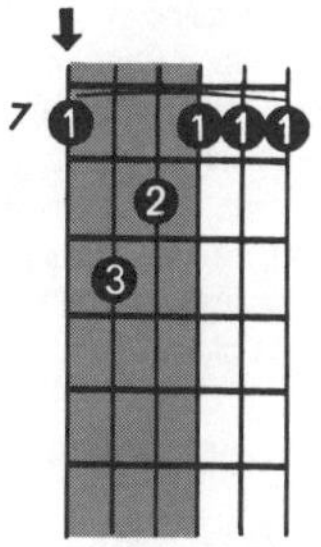

B F#A#D F#B

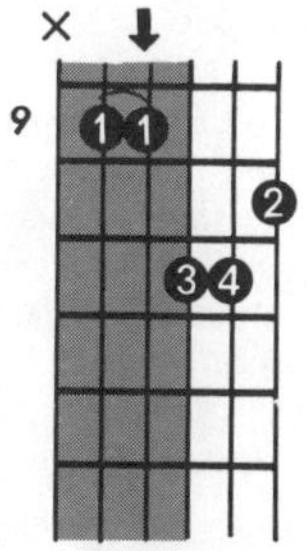

F#B F#A#D

B m9+7

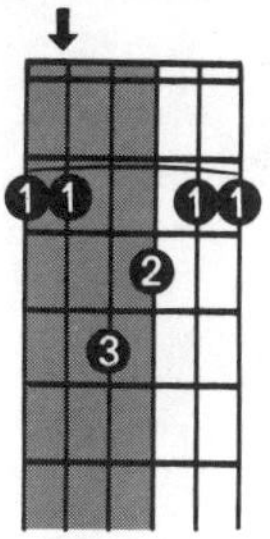

F#B F#A#C#F#

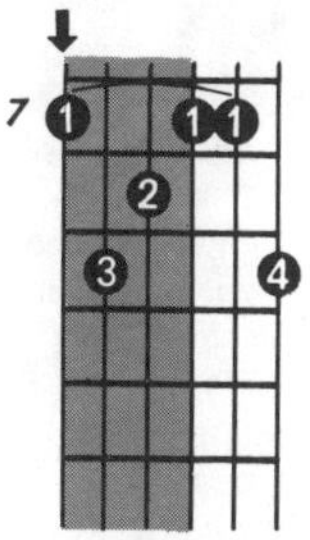

B F#A#D F#C#

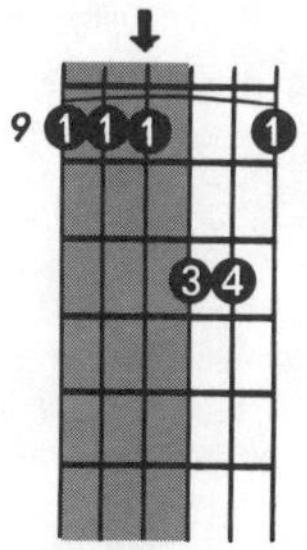

C#F#B F#A#C#

B m+5

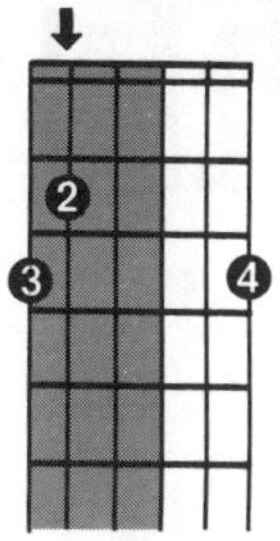

G B D G B G

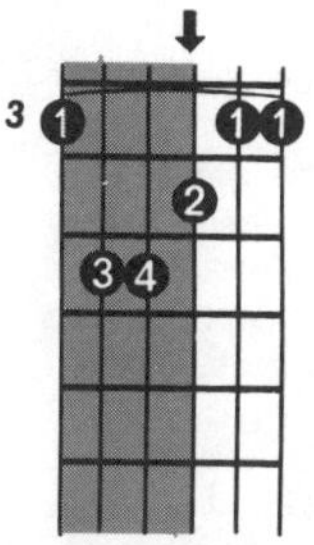

G D G B D G

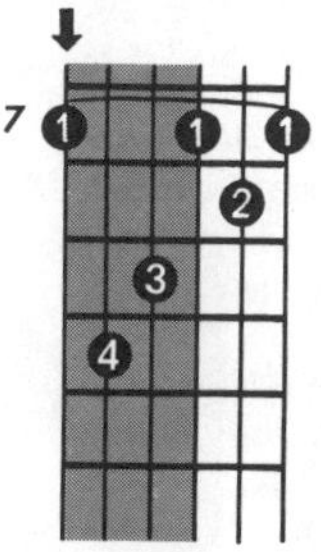

B G B D G B

B m6 · 9

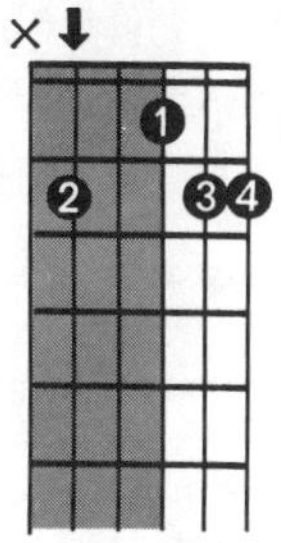

B D G#C#F#

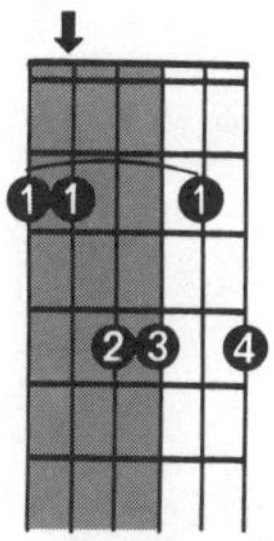

F#B F#B C#G#

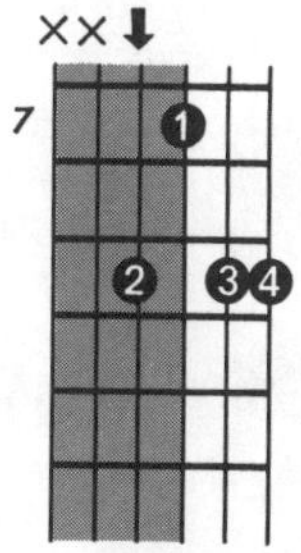

B D G#C#

B

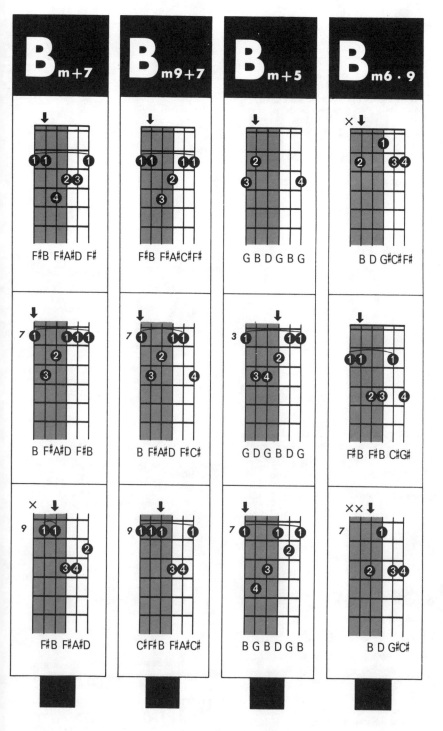